Guitar Gods

The 25 Players Who Made Rock History

BOB GULLA

GREENWOOD PRESS
Westport, Connecticut · London

Library of Congress Cataloging-in-Publication Data

Gulla, Bob.
    Guitar gods : the 25 players who made rock history / Bob Gulla.
        p. cm.
    Includes bibliographical references and index.
    ISBN 978–0–313–35806–7 (alk. paper)
1. Guitarists—Biography. 2. Rock musicians—Biography. I. Title.
ML399.G92   2009
787.87'1660922—dc22   2008034765
[B]

British Library Cataloguing in Publication Data is available.

Library of Congress Catalog Card Number: 2008034765
ISBN: 978–0–313–35806–7

First published in 2009

Greenwood Press, 88 Post Road West, Westport, CT 06881
An imprint of Greenwood Publishing Group, Inc.
www.greenwood.com

Printed in the United States of America

The paper used in this book complies with the
Permanent Paper Standard issued by the National
Information Standards Organization (Z39.48–1984).

10 9 8 7 6 5 4 3 2 1

Contents

Contents

Introduction

For almost 20 years now, I've made it my business to follow the comings and goings of rock and blues guitar players for major guitar magazines. I've anticipated their new releases, contemplated the arc of their career, and deliberated on their importance to my readership.

I've battled other editors for the rights to feature particularly hot artists on our magazine covers, hoping to maximize newsstand success, and I've spent many a day and night pulling my hair out wondering who the next guitar hero will be.

Over the years, I've picked some hits and missed some picks. As an observer of the rock music world for that time, I've learned that navigating the waters of rock, especially in the turbulent 1990s, was a lot like trying to stand up in a canoe on a fast-flowing river. Helping to run a monthly magazine meant predicting trends, staying two steps ahead, and keeping an ear to the ground when the locomotive still could have been weeks away.

On the other hand, putting guitar magazines together helped me maintain proper perspective on the instrument and its best players, most of which are considered so unanimously, at least by the journalists who cover the beat. Sure, I'm as guilty about overstating the ability of some promising players as the next optimistic journalist. Some of the players I've fingered as the Next Big Thing have long since drifted agonizingly into the sunset, victims of bad work habits and/or the vagaries of the industry. Generally speaking, though, the old adage holds: the chaff sifts through, and there's nothing left but the finest wheat.

The Players

In assembling this book, I selected only the most important guitar players in rock music. But before you nitpick through the table of contents dismissing certain players, please understand that I did not judge them by the typical conventions: technical dexterity, songwriting prowess, or sonic innovation. Rather, I chose the guitar players whose playing made the biggest impact on rock music. All the players profiled in this book threw rock 'n' roll for a loop; their advancements in music left the genre in a different place than when they arrived.

In a sense, these guitarists are party crashers. They came into an established framework, rearranged the furniture, tipped over a few chairs, and ditched, leaving the stragglers to pick up the pieces. Chuck Berry, for example, the first guitar player to jumpstart rock 'n' roll, left audience eyeballs in spirals when he blasted them with his patented Chuck Berry intro, a clarion call that served as rock 'n' roll's reveille. (For those of you feeling argumentative, Elvis Presley may have established the imagery for rock 'n' roll, but it was Chuck Berry who provided it with its engine.)

A few years later, Jimi Hendrix, inspired in part by Chuck, made a lasting impression on rock 'n' roll in so many ways, leaving us all in a purple haze and sending guitar players scurrying to take a new look at their instruments. The ripple-like effect of Hendrix continues to this day. Likewise for Jeff Beck, who did so a little further under the radar than Hendrix. But his radical changes over the years with the Yardbirds and later with the Jeff Beck Group and 1970s solo recordings were mind-expanding advancements on electric guitar playing. And then, certainly, there is the obvious instance of Eric Clapton, who single-handedly escorted the stinging classic blues style of Chicago into rock music.

Stevie Ray Vaughan did the same thing for the State of Texas and then the world, in the way that he dowsed blues with gasoline and lit a match. Vaughan's fiery playing injected the blues with commercial adrenaline, and his work has kept the genre alive, to this day, nearly 20 years after he himself saw his own fire extinguished in a helicopter crash.

In metal, the dynamic duo of Kirk Hammett and James Hetfield of Metallica shaped the galloping riffage of bands like Iron Maiden and Judas Priest into molten, speeding torpedos, upping the torque and velocity of heavy metal in the process. The same went for Darrell Abbott of Pantera, who twisted thrash and metal into steely idioms few could have predicted. In the beginning, of course, there was Sabbath's Tony Iommi, whose funereal licks and downtuned riffs frightened and exhilarated millions, often at the same time.

On the more wholesome side, consider the work of Duane Allman, Randy Rhoads, and Kurt Cobain, three guitar players, along with Dime, Vaughan, and Hendrix, who left this mortal coil before they even hit their stride. Yet even then they were able to pass through this life, and stamp rock 'n' roll with their life-size imprint. They left us work that will never diminish: *Nevermind, Layla,* and *Are You Experienced?,* to name just a few of the stunning albums they left us before departing.

Also, I've contemplated at length the impact and careers of players like David Gilmour, Carlos Santana, and Jerry Garcia, guitarists who sent their own ripples through the electric guitar community and altered rock music permanently on albums like *Santana, Dark Side of the Moon,* and, in Garcia's case, thousands of gigs across four decades. The same can be said about the incredibly versatile, leftfield playing of Frank Zappa, the hair-raising shred of Yngwie Malmsteen, or the incendiary pyrotechnics of Eddie Van Halen.

At the peak of their talent, all of these guitar players left behind a massive impression of their work. Considering all of the people throughout the years who've made it their job to pick up the guitar and play it, astonishingly few of them have created these kinds of wholesale disruptions in style, let alone ripples in the rock pool. That's why we call them "Guitar Gods," and that's why they're included in this book.

ASSEMBLING THE LIST

Rest assured, this list was assembled and reassembled, checked and triple-checked. I consulted with my elite, guitar-playing friends, who were also editors of such magazines as *Guitar One, Guitar World,* and *Guitar Player* and authors of many books—technical or otherwise—on the art of playing guitar. They in turn consulted others and reported back. We shuffled and reshuffled our subjects and signed off on them together. Given only 25 slots, each entry had to be accepted without reservation. Hence, it is certainly not just one man's opinion.

Here are a few other points:

Women don't exist in the upper echelon (Top 25) of guitarists. Of course, there are exceptional women who play the instrument, but none fit the definition of the book's subtitle about "making rock history." Please understand that I do not mean to be argumentative or sexist here. And I certainly don't have any sociocultural explanation for women's absence in the top tier of players. But I did not want to include a woman because someone somewhere along the line said to me, "You've got to put a woman on the list," which was often the case in editorial meetings at the magazines I worked for. There is too much research, too much sweat involved in this book to include a "token gesture."

Also, understand that all of the players I included didn't have to be technically gifted. "Feel" players like Neil Young, U2's the Edge, and Nirvana's Kurt Cobain rendered revolutionary work as much or more from the heart than through the fingers. The fingers sure helped though.

Another way to gauge the impact of players is to look at what came after them on the rock 'n' roll time line. Did they, like Slash or Cobain or Hammett/Hetfield, yield a stampede of imitators? Do they, like Iommi, Zappa, Garcia, Rhoads, and Malmsteen, still get name checked by other players in interviews as major influences and inspirations? If so, they made an enduring impact on their instrument and are included in this work.

As you can tell, I am well aware of the debates and controversies surrounding issues like this. In fact, in a piece I did for a Web site called "Rock's 100 Most Important Guitarists," a full-length list of 100 players, I still receive inboxes of seething hate mail about my inclusions, exclusions, and ranking order. This is indeed a very personal topic for many people, and so many fantastic guitarists have intensely loyal fan bases.

In another cover story I did for *Guitar One,* my colleague and I put together a "March Madness" bracket for the very best 64 guitar players in all genres, pitting one player against another in hypothetical "battles," then choosing a victor based on a variety of factors like technical facility, innovation, creativity, and emotional elements like "feel." After a victory, each advanced to face the winner of another "battle." Yes, it was a little complicated and a little indulgent, but that's the way we are in this business of guitar journalism. We scrutinize talent and argue constantly about the merits and demerits of players, songs, albums, riffs, and solos. Oh, and if you're wondering who won the bracket, no, it wasn't Jimi Hendrix. Jazz great Wes Montgomery placed first.

Essentially, that's what you've got in your hands now, a book-length argument—in my opinion a pretty persuasive one—on the players who made the greatest impact on rock 'n' roll's long and winding history. And if you want to argue about it, you may or may not know where to find me.

Darrell Abbott

Immune to trends, oblivious to prevailing wisdom, Darrell "Dimebag" Abbott stood up to the caprice and unpredictability of music in the 1990s like a stone breakwater in a hurricane. With his band Pantera, Abbott battled through the trendiness of the alt-rock juggernaut to do nothing less than keep heavy metal alive. Where many of the 1990s hard rock guitar players—including Alice in Chain's Jerry Cantrell, Nirvana's Kurt Cobain, Smashing Pumpkins' Billy Corgan, and Rage Against the Machine's Tom Morello—were employing their six-string skills to "serve the song," Dimebag thumbed his nose at the "alt-rock songwriter" archetype and protected the legacy of high-decibel shred guitar. Many metal guitarists, including Kirk Hammett and James Hetfield of Metallica, compromised their metal roots in an attempt to change with the times. Dimebag and Pantera did no such thing, and their loyalty to metal earned them the respect of all the hardcore heavy metal fans, at least the ones remaining.

In the early 1990s, heavy metal hit a low point. Shred, hair, and glam, the popular metal styles of the mid to late 1980s, lost metal fans with its combination of glitz and over-indulgence. The excesses in both sound and style eventually turned off loud music fans, yielding instead to the much more down-to-earth approach of genres like grunge, electronica, and other alternative styles. Metal had a hard time keeping up with the changes. Shred and glam virtually disappeared and the rest of metal—thrash, speed, prog, metalcore, and other hyphenated types—all retreated underground.

But Pantera did no such thing. There was no room underground for their boisterous, larger-than-Texas personality and their grisly, in-your-face metal attack. They soldiered on, releasing albums on a major label, anchoring massive national and international metal package tours as a headliner and trumpeting the cause.

If alternative rock resonated with college-educated anxieties, Pantera offered a focused, sympathetic outlet to another side of disaffected youth. "Nirvana spun things off in one direction and hipsters jumped on that train," recalls writer Anthony DeCurtis. "Pantera, on the other hand, continued in the metal mode. While they got big and had a number one record they never really became hip" (Helmore, Edward, "Just a Good Old Boy," *The Guardian,* December 17, 2004, London, UK).

Their album titles pretty much tell it all: *Cowboys from Hell, Vulgar Display of Power, The Great Southern Trendkill.* They read like a description not only of the band but of their mission as well. Not only did they keep metal alive, they helped stomp out the lingering spandex and teased hair image of their metallic predecessors, in effect, redefining metal at a time when it needed definition most.

As its spiritual leader, Dimebag, who died unexpectedly in a freakish murder rampage at an Ohio club gig, embodied the monstrous heart and soul of Pantera. His personality dominated the stage, and his technical mastery of shred and thrash guitar idioms shaped the band's sound. Dime's riffs were central to the devastating power and soaring triumph of Pantera, and he was worshipped as heavy metal's reigning guitar hero.

Thanks to those riffs, by the time Pantera unleashed their 1994 album, *Far Beyond Driven,* they were the most popular metal band in the land. The new album debuted at the top spot on the *Billboard* album list and its first single, "I'm Broken," enjoyed a generous reception from FM rock radio.

Just as the band ascended the charts, just as they were hitting their peak, they were also beginning to self-destruct. Though they had a well-known reputation as a hard partying, heavy drinking bunch, lead singer Phil Anselmo took that label one step further and got hooked on heroin. Because of his drug use, he became less accountable to Pantera; he grew distant, and a rift separated him from Dimebag and the band. Anselmo began recording with a couple of side projects, including Superjoint Ritual and Down. Pantera could not hold its act together. Drummer Vinnie Paul, bassist Rex Brown, and Dimebag formed another band Damageplan to keep busy.

It was at a Damageplan show on December 8, 2004 that Darrell Abbott's life was taken, along with three other people, when a mentally ill Nathan Gale jumped on stage and shot Dimebag four times, with two of those shots hitting him point-blank in the head. At the time of his death he was 38 years old. Incidentally, Abbott was shot on the twenty-fourth anniversary of the death of John Lennon, an icon also gunned down by a fan.

Many of those familiar with the intense world of heavy metal would tell you in a heartbeat that Pantera was the only metal band that mattered. Throughout the 1990s, the band and its legendary guitar master ruled the metal scene, both in the underground and on the charts. Dimebag Darrell was the guitar virtuoso at the center of the band's high-decibel maelstrom. Shortly after his death, he was listed by *Guitar World* magazine as one of "The 10 Most Important Guitarists Ever." High praise, considering Dime's career was cut dramatically short.

"Pantera were initially a nice combination of hardcore aggression and catchy rock riffs," says Brad Tolinski, editor-in-chief of *Guitar World.* "Darrell played it straight up and Pantera were the bridge between the thrash music of bands in the late 1980s like Metallica and Megadeth and the nu-metal of today, whether you're talking about Linkin Park or Disturbed" (Helmore, 2004).

EARLY YEARS

On August 20, 1966 in Arlington, Texas, Darrell Lance Abbott was born into a musical family. His father, Jerry Abbott, was a country and western songwriter and producer. Young Darrell used to go to recording sessions and rehearsals with his father and he soaked up all the music he could.

Early on, Darrell listened to the music of his dad's clientele, which ranged from blues and roots music to country. As a child, he'd watch his father record Texas blues players like Bugs Henderson and Jimmy Wallace. He listened to Merle Haggard and country maverick David Allen Coe, and later, ZZ Top and Skynyrd.

With his dad so involved in the music world it was inevitable that the music would rub off of Darrell. But it wasn't country that Darrell became infatuated with initially. It was Kiss. At first, he wanted to play the drums. But he soon discovered that he wasn't as good as his brother Vinnie Paul, so he decided to try the guitar instead.

Kiss had a great, accessible guitar sound and the young Abbott delved into the work of the band, and notably their lead guitarist Ace Frehley. He went to see them play a few times, and immersed himself in the sound of the band. About the same time, in the mid-1970s, Darrell also got exposed to the guitar playing of Eddie Van Halen. Van Halen's electric pyrotechnics sold the young Abbott on the instrument. With so many guitars all around his house and at his father's workspace, Dimebag picked up one and started teaching himself the instrument.

Facility came quickly and he soon began entering local guitar talent competitions and then statewide contests as well. (Word has it that he entered many of these talent shows, and won every one.) The prize for first place was a Dean guitar, specifically a radical-looking ML model, a cross between a Gibson Flying V and a Gibson Explorer. That guitar, and the Dean Company, supplied Abbott with his trademark axe/style throughout his career.

By the age of 16, Abbott customarily scorched the competition. Not surprisingly, he was banned from entering because he had won too often and other contestants began to complain. He often competed against players with much more experience, yet his skills were unique and refined, so much so that he was invited to begin judging the contests rather than competing in them. It was through the cash and equipment prizes he won that he was able to start Pantera.

In 1981, Darrell, now going by his nickname "Diamond" Darrell, and his brother Vinnie, both talented young musicians, pulled a band together. They called it Pantera. It also featured bassist Rex Brown (aka "Rex Rocker") and singer Terry Glaze.

Early on, the band reflected its influences: Kiss, Def Leppard, Judas Priest, and Mötley Crüe. Their sound, which they've since disowned, actually sounded more of its time, with lite-metal pop hooks, a flashy style, and glitzy stage shows. They issued a trio of albums with this configuration and this approach, beginning in 1983 with *Metal Magic*, 1984's *Projects in the Jungle*, and 1985's *I Am the Night*.

Looking back, the band was never proud of this work, and they even used it as motivation to obliterate the

Courtesy of Neil Zlozower

memory of it with pure metallic noise. That road began when singer Glaze left the lineup and Phil Anselmo joined on.

Shortly before Anselmo joined, Diamond Darrell had an opportunity present itself in 1985. He was invited to become a member of Megadeth. The thrash act's front man Dave Mustaine asked him to enter the fray after he had been dumped unceremoniously from his original star vehicle, Metallica. According to the accounts of both Darrell and Mustaine, Darrell was willing to sign on, but insisted that Megadeth also bring on his brother Vinnie. The problem was, Mustaine had already hired a new drummer, Nick Menza. The sticking point was a deal breaker and Darrell turned down the offer. Mustaine hired shredder Marty Friedman instead. Had Darrell accepted the position, the future of metal would have been altered from that point on.

MUSIC

Dimebag made his principal contribution to heavy rock in Pantera "Mach II," when Glaze exited and Anselmo entered. Their first attempt at a less commercial sound, *Power Metal,* doubled the band's primal approach with its release in 1988, but still didn't turn many heads. Their fan base, however, thanks to constant regional and some national touring, remained loyal and growing.

Record companies began to notice the band's work. Legend has it that an Atco Records A&R rep named Mark Ross discovered the band by chance. Ross was stranded in Texas during Hurricane Hugo and so he decided to take a night out and catch the band. Impressed by Pantera's performance and star quality, he signed them to the Atco label. At the same time, they changed management companies, choosing to sign with Walter O'Brien at Concrete Inc. in New York. These administrative changes breathed new life into the band's hopes, and when they emerged in 1988 after a two-year hiatus, those who knew them from the early "Metal Magic" days would barely recognize them.

First, they altered their physical appearance. Phil Anselmo sported a close haircut and a patchwork of tattoos, and the band's conventional metal "look," with long hair and showy attire, had disappeared in favor of a more down-to-earth style. *Power Metal,* while amped up and aggressive, was only a precursor to the more outrageous and uncompromising *Cowboys from Hell,* Pantera fans' unanimous choice for the album that announced the band's true arrival on the heavy metal scene.

Recorded at the band's own Pantego Sound Studios outside of Dallas and delivered in July 1990, *Cowboys* offered bludgeoning hardcore riffs, the solid intensity of their new songs burying any comparisons to their more melodic predecessors. Word had it that Diamond and company spent some time listening to Slayer's epic thrash/punk album *Reign in Blood* and Metallica's equally landmark recording, *Master of Puppets.*

Pantera's breakthrough album, *Cowboys from Hell,* is largely driven by the band's powerful rhythm section and guitarist Diamond Darrell's unbelievably forceful riffing, which skittered around the downbeats to produce unexpected rhythmic phrases and accents, as well as his inventive soloing. Phil Anselmo displayed a vocal range that could switch from a growling shout to a high falsetto—listen to him match Darrell's harmonic squeals at the end of "Cemetery Gates." The album gradually becomes more same-sounding as it goes on, but the first half, featuring such brutal slices of thrash as "Psycho Holiday," "Primal Concrete Sledge," and the title track, pretty much carries its momentum all the way through. (Huey, Steve, *All Music Guide,* www.allmusic.com)

The Cowboys from Hell tour opened in North America with Pantera sharing the stage with thrash legends Suicidal Tendencies and Exodus. Additional road work, topped by an appearance at the Tushino Air Field in Moscow on September 28, 1991, featured Pantera on a bill alongside legendary acts like AC/DC, Metallica, and the Black Crowes playing to a crowd of over half a million people. In fact, the band spent two and a half years on the road touring the material on *Cowboys* and their success inspired them to take their formula to the extremes. In 1992, they released *Vulgar Display of Power,* an early crystallization of that excessive approach.

One of the most influential heavy metal albums of the 1990s, *Vulgar Display of Power* is as advertised, "a raw, pulverizing, insanely intense depiction of naked rage and hostility that drains its listeners and pounds them into submission" (Huey, Steve, *All Music Guide,* www.allmusic.com).

The album silenced critics—those who cursed the band's lack of nuance and droning decibels—with its high chart debut in both the United Kingdom and the United States where it nearly cracked the Top 40 on the *Billboard* album chart. Curiously, Pantera never managed to make significant impressions on the *Billboard* charts, though their records sold steadily year in and year out.

When it met with such surprising success, *Vulgar Display of Power* also served to cement the band's modus operandi. They also began collectively putting their mouth where their mission was, talking up their new approach, their resolve to save metal, whenever they could. It became a self-fulfilling prophecy.

*   *   *

Fans lapped up the Pantera MO, grateful to have a metal savior in their midst. Their post-hardcore metal, full of testosterone and teeth-gnashing ire, opened doors for the band as well as dozens and dozens of metal-savior wannabes. It also paved the way for alternative metal, which was just around the corner—Tool, Korn, Limp Bizkit, and Slipknot—to name the most apparent opportunists.

Vulgar Display of Power is considered by hardcore fans to be Pantera's definitive album with memorable tracks like "Walk" and "F**king Hostile." Their success reached Asia, and they played Japan for the first time in 1992. They also headlined the Monsters of Rock Festival in Italy in the fall of that year with their heroes Iron Maiden and Black Sabbath. It certainly set the stage for the band's most impressive feat: their next album, *Far Beyond Driven,* debuted at No. 1 on the *Billboard* album chart, a first for a heavy metal band since the charts were originated. It is also, without a doubt, the most extreme music to ever land in the top spot.

Many diehard metal fans believed that Pantera lost the essence of songwriting in their quest for ever-louder expression. But many more and newer converts bought into it quite willingly. A succession of singles like "Walk," "This Love," and "Mouth for War" dominated radio and music television.

Two years later the band released *The Great Southern Trendkill,* a direct reference to the fact that they'd so far defied the musical shifts and finicky audiences of the 1990s.

Despite their wild successes, the band's relationships began to break down. Anselmo began to abuse heroin in order to numb his increasing back pain. He became erratic and distanced himself from the band, especially the Abbott brothers. He even recorded his vocals for *The Great Southern Trendkill* in a separate studio. A wedge had split the band, and despite the release of another successful album in 2000, *Reinventing the Steel,* Pantera officially disbanded in 2003, even though they had reached a new height in popularity.

SIDE PROJECTS

While Phil Anselmo's side projects Down and Superjoint Ritual pulled him away from the band, Vinnie, Darrell, and Pantera bassist Brown would pursue their own side activities as well. They had an ongoing affiliation with country and western outlaw songwriter David Allen Coe. Between 1996 and the onset of Damageplan, Pantera, sans Anselmo, partnered with Coe on a country rock project called Rebel Meets Rebel. In fact, Vinnie Paul's favorite recorded Dime solo came during this partnership, part of a track called "Get Out of My Life." These same musicians also pushed toward a southern rock project called Gasoline, but it never came to fruition.

New Found Power was unveiled in January 2003 by Dimebag and brother Vinnie with Patrick Lachman (Halford, Diesel Machine), and Sean Matthews on bass (Jerry Cantrell). But this didn't go as planned and it morphed into something called Damageplan, without Matthews. Damageplan's debut, *New Found Power,* released at the end of 2003, sold nearly 45,000 copies in its first week of U.S. sales and reached #37 on the *Billboard* album chart.

Throughout 2004, Anselmo with his Superjoint Ritual project and the Damageplan members played out a very public feud. In August of that year, Pantera reached a posthumous milestone when the Recording Industry Association of America certified *Vulgar Display of Power* as double platinum, marking two million U.S. sales 12 years after its release.

FIRST PERSON

Dime certainly lit up a room. Personally speaking, during an interview I had with him following the release of *Reinventing the Steel* (2000), a clutch of us were waiting for him in a hotel room, having lunch, when, two hours late, the guitarist stormed the room. He roared, barreled through the door and stomped over to our table with combat boots. Then he proceeded to climb on *top* of the table, all over our lunches, perhaps a little indignant that we had been eating without him.

During our interview, Dime laid down on a couch in front of me, in a sort of patient/therapist posture. Every once in a while he'd get up and train the site of his video camera on me, perhaps to keep me in check, and at least to let me know how it felt to be on the other side of the spotlight.

Though he gave the impression of being casual and good-timey, though he often appeared to be lost amid a growling, larger than life persona, Dime was also super savvy. He demonstrated real awareness of what was going on around, how he was being represented by the media, and the various misconceptions on the rock scene about his band.

This could perhaps have been the key to Pantera's career. They understood how to manipulate the climate and how to work the media to its advantage. They were often depicted as being disorganized, untimely, and sloppy by the press, who were always waiting for the band to make its next move. Yet, in fact, all they were doing was building anticipation and creating the kind of excitement they knew they could deliver when the time came.

Damageplan continued to play until the death of Dimebag in late 2004. Their manager confirmed that the band was working on a second album when Dimebag died.

After his death, it was discovered that Darrell had been in discussions with erstwhile Alice in Chains guitarist Jerry Cantrell, Nickelback songwriter/singer Chad Kroeger, and former Default front man Dallas Smith regarding another proposed project. In December 2007, the month he died, a collaboration with Kid Rock and Kroeger surfaced, a rollicking rendition of Elton John's "Saturday Night's Alright (for Fighting)."

Throughout his career, Dimebag played guest guitar solos on several Anthrax tracks, "Riding Shotgun" from *Stomp 442,* "Inside Out" from *Volume 8: The Threat Is Real,* and "Strap It On" and "Cadillac Rock Box" from *We've Come for You All.*

Shortly before Dime's death, he went into the studio with a band named Premenishen to do a guest solo on a track entitled "Eyes of the South." The band consists of two of Dime's cousins (bassist Heather Manly and guitarist April Adkisson). There was speculation that Dimebag and close friend Zakk Wylde would collaborate with Eddie Van Halen, however nothing was confirmed. Chad Kroeger of Nickelback received permission from Vinnie to use a sample of a Dime guitar solo for the Nickelback tribute track "Side of a Bullet."

After his brother's death, Vinnie Paul went on to form his own record label called Big Vin. He's said that he possesses copious amounts of unreleased music and that in time he will compile it and release a portion of it to the public.

DEATH

On December 8, 2004, Dimebag was performing on stage with Damageplan at the Alrosa Villa in Ohio when a man named Nathan Gale stormed the stage. He shot Abbott and three others, a concertgoer, Nathan Bray, Alrosa Villa employee Erin Halk, and Jeff Thompson, a Damageplan security guard. A nurse in the audience attempted to resuscitate Darrell with CPR but it was too late. Tour manager Chris Paluska and drum technician John Brooks were also injured. Police reports state that Gale fired about 15 shots and stopped to reload once. Thompson and other members of the audience tried to prevent Gale from reaching the stage to no avail. Gale took the band's drum technician John Brooks hostage in order to get away, but when Brooks moved quickly a policeman shot Gale and killed him.

Witnesses say they overheard Gale blaming Darrell for the breakup of Pantera. Gale, they said, was a loner who lived with his mother and wanted to become a tattoo artist. "Nathan was infatuated with a certain lifestyle that he thinks tattoo artists live," recalled Lucas Bender, the owner of Bear's Den Tattoo Studio in Columbus. "You know, a wild lifestyle. But that's not true, so I had to run him out of here" (Helmore, guardian.co.uk).

Abbott was buried in the Moore Memorial Gardens Cemetery in Arlington, Texas. In a touching display, Darrell had his boyhood dreams granted when he was buried in a Kiss coffin with Eddie Van Halen's guitar wrapped in his arms. The funeral, at the Arlington Convention Center, was attended by hundreds of Dime's musician friends. Members of scores of bands Pantera either toured with, influenced, or both, paid their last respects in a tribute, poignant and celebratory, most fitting to the life of such an icon.

Family, friends, and fans have sought a motive for the killing but have found little to go on. Some point to an interview with Phil Anselmo, the former lead singer of Pantera, published in a British magazine called *Metal Hammer* that ran in November of 2004. On the cover, Anselmo, who split acrimoniously with his former band in 2002, is shown holding two knives, one with a reflection of Darrell's face on it. In the interview, he told the magazine that Darrell "deserves to be beaten severely." Gale seems to have been obsessed with Pantera. It's been suggested that he may have thought he was doing Anselmo a favor.

Reportedly, Anselmo was devastated by his former bandmate's death, though he was not in attendance at, nor did he receive an invitation to, Dime's funeral.

The Abbott family has decided to sue the arena where Darrell was killed, stating that poor security facilitated their son's death. Also in the wake of Dime's murder, many tribute songs have been written, perhaps most famously "In This River" by Zakk Wylde, one of Darrell's best friends, and Kroeger's "Side of a Bullet."

TECHNIQUE/STYLE

Though his dad was a country music songwriter and had many clients, Darrell's musical influences came mainly from metal bands such as Judas Priest, Iron Maiden, Eddie Van Halen, and of course the reason why he began to play the guitar, Ace Frehley of Kiss. Darrell was such an admirer of the band Kiss that he actually has a tattoo of Ace on his chest. Ace heard about the tattoo and gladly signed his name over the tattoo, and Darrell had the tattoo artist ink in the autograph.

Darrell gave acknowledgment to Kerry King of the heavy metal band Slayer, Zakk Wylde of Black Label Society, and Metallica's James Hetfield. Dimebag over the course of many interviews gives credit to Tony Iommi of Black Sabbath for influencing his guitar riffs. In some of Dimebag's solo spots, you can hear the influence and dynamic of Iommi.

Abbott was well-versed with the tremolo, which was one of his strengths as a player. He had a remarkable legato skill and often utilized the harmonic minor scale in tracks like "Primal Concrete Sledge," or the Phrygian major mode in the "Domination" solo. Darrell also implemented a battery of alternate guitar tunings, and he was one of the first players to down tune, or tune every string down a quarter step, something that became part of his signature tone. From their landmark album, *Cowboys*, to *Vulgar*—the band's peak years— Abbott tuned down a quarter, a half step, or sometimes an entire step. He also used drop-d (DADGBE) tuning. From the *Vulgar* record on, Darrell's tunings descended to the lower depths, and the ploy gave his sound more of an edge. This downward tuning followed him to his work in Damageplan as well, which had a murkier and heavier feel. Some Damageplan cuts saw Dime tuning a whole step and a half lower.

When Dimebag played he often used the scales and slide of the guitar for his leads and in his rhythms. Dimebag also used a blues scale in his playing and a start and stop dynamic with good pedal tones. Dimebag influenced a whole generation of young metal guitar players with his Eddie Van Halen hybrid scale runs, large interval bends, screaming harmonics with his whammy bar, and roaring approach.

EQUIPMENT/GEAR

In his early career as a musician, Dimebag used Dean Guitars ML guitars, most notably the "Dean from Hell," a customized guitar with an exclusive paint job and a lightning bolt design. He also used Bill Lawrence L500XL pickups, which he would install in a reversed position to have the "hot" blade facing the neck. Following the demise of Dean, Dimebag opted for Washburn guitars up until a few months before his death. Seymour Duncan also manufactures a signature pickup called the Dimebucker (codesigned by Dimebag).

Just before he died, Darrell returned to the resurrected Dean company to endorse their new line of guitars. Following his death, Dean Guitars president Dean Zelinksy produced a line of axes called the Dime Tribute. These guitars, in the company's ML line, come in various models. Lower end models have a stop tail piece, a bolt-on neck, Basswood Body, and a decent quality pickup. High end instruments in the line come with Dimebuckers, a Floyd Rose bridge, and set neck construction. Dean has also produced an updated version of a Dime signature-design guitar called the "Razorback," which recalled the company's prototypical ML design from Dime's early Dean years.

Dimebag also collaborated extensively with MXR and Dunlop to produce the MXR Dime Distortion and the Dimebag Crybaby from Hell wah wah. Dimebag's rig also featured Randall Century 200 heads and cabinets with Celestion and Jaguar speakers, Furman parametric equalizers, MXR flanger/doublers, Lexicon effect modules, Korg tuners, Rocktron silencers, and Digitech Whammy pedals. At the same time Dime departed Washburn, he also left Randall Amps. He chose to invest in a brand new amplifier company called Krank. Before he died, he endorsed these amps heavily. He had intended this new amp company to help him redefine his guitar sound, specifically with a signature amp called the "Krankenstein." Unfortunately, his sonic ambition was cut short. He never had the opportunity to undergo this change.

ESSENTIAL READING

Abbott, Darrell, and Zac Crain. *Black Tooth Grin: The High Life, Good Times, and Tragic End of "Dimebag" Darrell Abbott.* New York: Da Capo Press, 2009.
Armold, Chris. *A Vulgar Display of Power: Courage and Carnage at The Alrosa Villa.* New York: MJS Music Publications, 2007.
Helmore, Edward. "Just a Good Old Boy." *The Guardian,* London, UK, December 17, 2004.
Huey, Steve. *All Music Guide,* www.allmusic.com.

ESSENTIAL WORK

"Cemetery Gates" (1990)
"Cowboys from Hell" (1990)
"I'm Broken" (1994)
"This Love" (1992)
"Walk" (1992)

ESSENTIAL LISTENING

Cowboys from Hell (Atlantic, 1990)
Reinventing the Steel (East West, 2000)
Vulgar Display of Power (East West, 1992)

Duane Allman

Duane Allman essentially designed the blueprint for playing electric bottleneck (slide) guitar. If you prefer lists to outright boasts, Allman is ranked Number 2 on *Rolling Stone*'s list of the Greatest Guitarists of All Time, right behind Jimi Hendrix and above, well, everybody else. For a player who began his recording career in 1966 and ended it tragically just five years later in 1971, that is no small feat. In his short life, he died at 24, he was one of the most emotionally charged and viscerally talented players to ever plug in.

In his star-making gig, Duane headed up the Allman Brothers along with his brother Gregg and guitarist Dickey Betts. The Allmans had a legendary, powerhouse combination of tight ensemble arrangements, soulful vocals, and explosive improvisations for two guitars. This sound was immortalized on four classic albums—*The Allman Brothers Band, Idlewild South, Live at Fillmore East,* and *Eat a Peach.*

Duane Allman's trip to stardom was characterized by tireless work and inspiration. He fiercely dedicated himself to his guitar craft from a young age, scrutinizing and studying the work of his musical influences by delving into their recordings. Allman's influences were many, including but not limited to many blues players: Albert King, T-Bone Walker, Slim Harpo, Robert Johnson, and Blind Willie Johnson. There were also a handful of country and rock players, like Hank Garland and Chet Atkins on the country side, and Chuck Berry, Hendrix, and Clapton on the rock side. Duane even studied the jazz idiom and plunged into the work of players such as Kenny Burrell, Miles Davis, and John Coltrane. His diverse taste in music was equaled only by his ambition to achieve greatness on the guitar.

Mike Johnston, Duane's bunkmate at the military academy they attended, recalls Duane playing along with a B.B. King album barefooted, stopping and holding the record with his toe while he learned a lick, letting the record go until he got to the next lick, then going through both sides of the record and repeating the entire process for hours at a time. He was a tremendously quick learner, capable of absorbing licks and reconstituting them in his own style, in minutes rather than days. Like other tactile, intuitive players—John Lee Hooker, Bo Diddley, Jimi Hendrix—Allman became an integral and identifiable part of every song he played on.

Duane also became the first rock 'n' roll player to master the slide guitar. His strengths as a slide player, outlined in further detail below, were his impeccable notes choices and his ability to make his slide ring out like the voice of a soul singer. Beyond his slide playing, he also regularly tore the roof off a blues jam on conventional electric guitar. This dual mastery enabled Allman to become one of the first American rock players to reach such sublime, creative heights.

His dexterity on early Allman Brothers discs and onstage turned heads in the late 1960s, and he was invited to guest on numerous high-profile recording sessions, most notably alongside Eric Clapton on Derek and the Dominos' *Layla and Other Assorted Love Songs* (see sidebar). But he also cut material with, among others, Wilson Pickett, King Curtis, John Hammond, Johnny Jenkins, Boz Scaggs, and Aretha Franklin.

To many guitar players today, Allman's legend doesn't loom as large as it should. He's been gone a long time, and his music doesn't resonate the way, say Hendrix does. But to his legions of fans, however, Duane is a revered messianic figure who's playing sounds as beautiful today as it must have sounded for those five brief years beginning in 1966.

EARLY YEARS

Howard Duane Allman was born on November 20, 1946 in Nashville, Tennessee. When he was three years old and his family was living near Norfolk, Virginia, his father, Willis, a sergeant in the Army, was murdered in a robbery by a veteran he had befriended that day. Geraldine "Mama A" Allman and the boys moved back to Nashville. In 1957, they moved to Florida, near Daytona Beach.

One Christmas in the late 1950s, it's unclear which, Duane received a Harley as a gift and his younger brother, Gregg, received a guitar. Duane, while loving his motorcycle and tirelessly running it into the ground, also became infatuated with his brother's guitar, which happened to be a Silvertone acoustic. The two often squabbled about who would play it; it was evident, even from Gregg's point of view, that Duane had an affinity for the instrument, and he learned quickly. Not so with Gregg. The younger Allman did, however, know enough to teach Duane the rudiments of playing, only to see his older brother zoom past him.

In 1959, the boys visited their family in Nashville. While there, they went to see B.B. King perform, and both Duane and Gregg fell in love with the music. Gregg recalls Duane turning to him in the middle of the show and saying, "We got to get into this" (Gregg Allman Anthology, liner notes, n.p.).

Back home, Duane wrecked his bike and, enterprisingly, dissembled it and sold the pieces. He used the money from those parts to buy a guitar of his own. Soon enough, Duane graduated to electric guitar and began taking pointers from a guy named Jim Shepley, who introduced him to the music of Jimmy Reed, B.B. King, and others. He gorged on the work of blues players and spent hours every day listening and practicing. His intense dedication bred a fiery, individualistic style and eventually led to the formation of their brothers' first band, the Escorts. Duane quit high school and focused his efforts on a career in music.

Incidentally, Duane's nickname was "Skydog," which was a merger of two nicknames he'd already had: "Skyman" was a name given to him by soul singer Wilson Pickett, and "Dog" was a name given to him by his friends for his shaggy, canine appearance.

MUSIC

The Escorts didn't last long. Its members were all playing with other bands while keeping the Escorts going. Duane and Gregg wanted to name the band the Allman Joys, but the other members of the band bristled at feeling left out. Early on, Duane did most of the singing. The band made a demo to get bigger and better club shows, but their success was too slow for the Allmans, who thought they deserved more notoriety.

DEREK AND THE DOMINOS

Always willing to help out a friend in need, Allman's musical collaborations often extended far beyond the call of duty.

"When Eric Clapton was stuck for an intro during the historic *Layla* sessions that marked a high point in Duane's career, Allman adjourned to another room and returned shortly thereafter with a gift for his friend—the title song's signature opening riff. Those seven notes would help secure Allman a permanent place in rock history. (His epic slide part on the song didn't hurt either!)" (Gress, Jesse, "10 Things You Gotta Do to Play Like Duane Allman," *Guitar Player,* www.guitarplayer.com, April 2007).

Tom Dowd, the album's producer, is responsible for introducing Duane Allman and Eric Clapton. In 1970, Dowd was in the middle of recording the Allman Brother's second album, *Idlewild South,* when he received a call from the Clapton camp saying that Clapton's band, Derek and the Dominos, were coming to Florida to record. Duane found out that Clapton was in line for a visit to record with Dowd, and he asked the producer if he could tag along. Clapton's band arrived in late August. They jammed out some ideas in the first week, awaiting inspiration and new songs.

At the end of the week, Allman rang up Dowd to invite him to a benefit show Duane's band was doing. Clapton himself found out about the show and was eager to attend.

Tom and Eric snuck into the show after it had begun. Eric later said, "I just remember driving down to this park and while we were parking the car about one-half mile from this open-air gig. I just heard this wailing guitar coming through the air louder than anything else. You could just hear the band and then this really high-in-the-air sound like a siren. It was just amazing. We walked down to the gig, sat down in front of the bandstand, and there were The Allman Brothers" (Schumacher, Michael, *Crossroads: The Life and Music of Eric Clapton,* Citadel, New York, 2003).

Formal introductions were made after the show. Eric invited the entire band to Criteria Studios for a jam and that they did, for nearly 18 hours, talking shop, trading licks, swapping instruments, and anything else eager players do.

Originally, Duane hoped merely to sit in the studio as an observer while the Dominos recorded *Layla,* but Clapton did him one better. "Get your guitar," he said. Duane was invited into Criteria Studios to lend his talents to "Tell the Truth," and by all counts he elevated the recording to a higher level. Impressed, Clapton also invited Duane to join the band permanently, a flattering request indeed. But Allman declined, adding his work with the Allman Brothers was his first priority. Duane did, though, take him up on the invitation to join the Dominos in concert that December at a gig in Tampa.

Later that month, an Atlanta DJ interviewed Duane about his work with Clapton. Duane said, "Eric is a real fine cat. I considered it a privilege and honor to play on his Derek and the Dominos album. He's a true professional in the studio. It's his style and his technique—is what really amazes me. He has a lot to say too, but the way he says it just knocks me out" (Derek and the Dominos: *The Layla Sessions 20th Anniversary Edition,* liner notes, n.p.).

Michael Ochs Archives/Getty Images

One of his Escort bandmates, Van Harrison, described Duane at this early point in his career:

> Duane had what I would call a conflicting personality. He had this highly responsible attitude towards how good we had to be and how hard we had to practice. He and Gregg practiced all the time together since they were brothers, and when we got together we'd practice hard—we did it over and over again 'til we got stuff right and it sounded good. But on the other hand, he had this lack of conviction. He would disappear. He would go off when we were supposed to do something or be somewhere, and we wouldn't know where he was.

For the Escorts second demo, they started calling themselves the Allman Joys. They had discovered another band with the Escorts name and took that opportunity to satisfy their original desire. Harrison was gone, replaced by bassist Bob Keller. On that demo, which featured a dozen songs all recorded in one day, Duane demonstrated his guitar chops on a couple of instrumentals, including Lonnie Mack's "Memphis." It was Gregg who foreshadowed things to come, though, with early versions of Bobby "Blue" Bland's tune "Turn On Your Love Light," a song that would become an Allman Brothers staple.

The Allman Joys added drummer Butch Trucks to the lineup. The year was 1965, and the Allman Brothers were still three years away. The Allman Joys toured the southeastern states constantly, motoring around the circuit affectionately known as "east of the Mississippi." They recorded a single, "Spoonful," a fuzzed out cover of the Willie Dixon tune, but they were still searching for a sound. They filtered their blues through a prism of rock, pop, and garagey sounds, which made them hard to pin down and appear slightly, sonically unfocused.

They also enjoyed partying. Their producer/manager John Loudermilk recalls the craziness of the band in those early days. "These kids were doing some drugs, you know, and I didn't want to get involved with that. And they brought little girls that were way underage out to the house—scared the hell out of me" (Skydog, pp. 32–33).

In the later part of the decade, Duane and Gregg moved to Los Angeles to become part of a group called the Hour Glass. But the record company the Hour Glass signed on with gave the band virtually no artistic control; they found themselves recording songs that they had neither written nor appreciated.

Live, however, the Hour Glass came alive. They tore it up regularly on the Strip in Hollywood, especially at the Whisky a Go Go, where Duane began developing a reputation as a guitarist extraordinaire. Their performances transcended the banal material they were handed and the real Allman Brothers began to surface. They opened for the biggest acts of the time, including Jefferson Airplane, Janis Joplin's Big Brother and the Holding Company, and Buffalo Springfield.

Duane's dedication to the instrument increased in Los Angeles. He'd keep his guitar around his neck day and night, falling asleep on the couch with it at three or four in the morning. Then waking up a few hours later, the guitar still slung around his neck. A roommate, Johnny Townsend, even recalls seeing Duane go to the bathroom with the guitar around his neck " . . . careful not to pee on the strap. [He'd] make his coffee and he'd still be playing. I'd never seen anybody that dedicated."

The band released two albums. The second contained more "southern-inspired" material, and fit the band more comfortably. But still, Duane was at constant odds with the producer. Duane was in control of the band, but the producer wanted to control the recording session. The two locked horns regularly and the experience was dismal. Duane left the band every other day only to return. One day, after two years in Los Angeles, he finally returned home to Florida.

* * *

Along the way, Duane's playing had pricked the ears of Rick Hall, owner of FAME (studio in Muscle Shoals, Alabama). Hall hired him to play on recording sessions for Wilson Pickett; those sessions resulted in the hit album *Hey Jude* in 1968. Duane was then invited to join FAME's house band, which he did. In the few months he worked at FAME, he would play on sessions for Aretha Franklin, Clarence Carter, Otis Rush, Boz Scaggs, and King Curtis.

One of Allman's brightest moments came when he played on Pickett's cover of "Hey Jude." The lead break at the end of the song, in particular, caught the attention of many, including Eric Clapton. Allman's performance on "Hey Jude" also blew away Atlantic Records producer and executive Jerry Wexler. Hall, working in conjunction with Atlantic on the Pickett album, played it over the phone for him. Wexler immediately bought Allman's recording contract from Hall and wanted to use him on sessions with all sorts of Atlantic R&B artists.

* * *

But the limitations of playing in a full-time session band frustrated Duane Allman. As a result, he often returned to Florida to be with friends. Butch Trucks, Dickey Betts, Berry Oakley, and Jaimoe were among them. His stint at FAME served Allman well. He met and played with many well-known artists and rubbed elbows with industry magnates, who often sent their artists to FAME to record. He also spent hours upon hours continuing to refine his playing style. While employed at FAME, Allman rented a secluded cabin on a nearby lake and after hours were spent in solitude, doing what he liked best: playing his guitar.

Shortly after he recorded his lead break in "Hey Jude," he recorded the lead guitar in Boz Scaggs' "Loan Me a Dime." His soloing in the song is noted as some of the best he ever put on record. For his first Aretha sessions, Allman traveled to New York, where in

January of 1969 he attended a show at the Fillmore East to see Johnny Winter. He told Shoals guitarist Jimmy Johnson, who was with him that night, in a year he'd be on the same stage. Indeed, the Allman Brothers Band played the Fillmore that very December.

By the spring of 1969, Duane assembled a new band in Jacksonville, also including jazz drummer Jaimoe from FAME and Jaimoe's friend Berry Oakley. Oakley recruited his friend Dickey Betts to join them. With the pieces in place, Duane petitioned his brother Gregg, still working in Los Angeles, to come home. Within months, they had a manager, Phil Walden (Otis Redding's manager) who encouraged them to relocate from Jacksonville, Florida to Macon, Georgia. After a bit of rehearsing and gigging, the sextet heeded Walden's advice. It was in Georgia, at Macon's Capricorn Sound Studios, that they recorded their first album, *The Allman Brothers Band.*

*   *   *

Reviewers loved it. "This might be the best debut album ever delivered by an American blues band, a bold, powerful, hard-edged, soulful essay in electric blues with a native Southern ambience. Some lingering elements of the psychedelic era then drawing to a close can be found in 'Dreams,' along with the template for the group's on-stage workouts with 'Whipping Post,' and a solid cover of Muddy Waters' 'Trouble No More' " (Eder, Bruce, All Music Guide, *allmusic.com*).

Their next album, *Idlewild South,* fared just as well. Many, in fact, call it the best studio album in the group's history. It combines electric blues rock with acoustic richness, a soul feel, and, of course, Duane's virtuosic guitar work on songs like "Midnight Rider," "Revival," "Don't Keep Me Wonderin'," and "In Memory of Elizabeth Reed." The latter, an Allmans classic, is here in its early studio version, at just around six minutes. It would later evolve into a much longer and more intricate jam, and come to represent the Allman Brothers generous, jam-oriented sound.

In the time following the release of the album, the Allmans' live shows had become epic, thanks in part to the complex interplay between Duane and Dickey Betts, and they were soon one of the rock scene's most sought after tickets. Occasionally, their jams would run on for over 30 minutes, and their improvisational seasoning bordered on the sublime.

To mark this milestone in their development, they released the immortal live album *At Fillmore East.* Recorded during the spring of 1971 and released in July of that year, it depicts the Allmans as a versatile, talented, jazzy rock band, presenting its songs in a flexible and stimulating exhibition of musicianship and expert dynamics. It is here that the Allmans came to be known as one of rock's greatest bands, and it is here that their reputation as such became cemented. "Whipping Post," for example, one of the gig's highlights, is a rock song that fuses elements of the blues, hard rock, jazz, gospel, country, and soul into a fiery mélange of passionate rage.

The record became an instant classic and the band, though they never cracked the Top 10 on *Billboard*'s album chart, proved they could also sell records. It was certified gold in the middle of October 1971. Two weeks later, Duane was dead.

DEATH

Duane Allman was killed riding his motorcycle while in Macon on October 29, 1971. He was enjoying a little downtime from the band after releasing and touring in support of *At Fillmore East,* when he swerved to avoid an oncoming truck. The truck, turning well in front of him, stopped in mid-intersection and Duane, attempting to veer off to the left, lost control of his bike, crashing into the back of the truck or its crane ball. He flew off his motorcycle, which landed on him and skidded with him. He died a few hours later, after three hours of emergency surgery, less than one month away from turning just 25. (In a strange turn of events, the Allmans' bassist Berry Oakley would also die in a motorcycle accident less than 13 months later and just three blocks away from the site of Duane's fatal wreck.)

Services were held the following Monday in Macon's Memorial Chapel. Nearly 300 friends, relatives, and admirers attended. Duane's guitar case stood in the front of the floral-wreathed casket, and the band's equipment was set up in the rear. After the official memorial service, the band played. They began with the familiar pattern of an introduction to a slow blues, and then from behind his dark glasses, Gregg sang: "The sky is crying, look at the tears roll down my cheeks."

They also played "Keys to the Highway" which Duane had recorded with Eric Clapton on *Layla,* then did "Stormy Monday" and "Elizabeth Reed." They played through the music with Dickey Betts playing for Duane in the places where Duane would normally have been heard and with the fans and friends who really knew Duane's music supplying from memory the missing lines to the fondly remembered harmonies Duane and the band were famous for. When the band was finished, Betts placed the Gibson Les Paul he had been playing—Duane's own guitar—next to Duane's casket, then walked off.

A few weeks after the funeral, the five surviving members carried on, resuming touring and finishing the recording work already underway when Duane died. They called the next album *Eat a Peach,* after a line Duane used in an interview. In response to the question, "How are you helping the revolution?" Duane said, "There ain't no revolution, only evolution, but every time I'm in Georgia I eat a peach for peace."

The quote is emblematic of the kind of attitude Duane had toward life. Whether on stage, in the studio, or fishing in his favorite hole, the guitarist was a happy guy who truly enjoyed life. His epitaph betrays his lifelong ideals: "I love being alive and I will be the best man I possibly can. I will take love wherever I find it, and offer it to everyone who will take it, seek knowledge from those wiser and teach those who wish to learn from me."

"Ol' Duane was married to his music, the truth be known," a close friend reflected after the funeral rites.

> I guess him dyin' so young, though, was almost inevitable. He had a wild and reckless streak in him, and apart from pickin' his git-tar, he'd get bored. I guess you could call it. On that account, he ran through a lotta chicks and a lotta mean dope in his green time, and he purely loved to smoke up the highways on bikes that was too fast for him. You don't live long if you live impulsive like that. Duane was basically just a good ol' country boy, but he could jump salty, too, now and again. Hell, I'll miss him, myself. I'm just sorry he had to up and leave America so early. He had a fat lot left in him to do. (Landau, Jon, "Band Leader Duane Allman Dies in Bike Crash," *Rollingstone.com*)

TECHNIQUE/STYLE

Duane educated himself by listening. He'd listen to and absorb nearly everything he heard, from the blues icons like Muddy Waters, Robert Johnson, and Blind Lemon Jefferson to his contemporaries like Eric Clapton, Jeff Beck, and Jimi Hendrix.

His brother Gregg often told a story about Duane relative to his slide guitar playing. In 1968 Duane came down with a serious cold and was taking a medication called Coricidin. Gregg brought him a copy of Taj Mahal's self-titled first album to perk him up. Mahal, incidentally, also arranged "Statesboro Blues," the old Jefferson classic, and that arrangement served as the blueprint for the Allman Brothers' own version.

When Gregg saw Duane a few days later, he was playing slide guitar and using a small glass bottle, the one that held the Coricidin medication, on one finger. From then on, the Coricidin bottle became Duane's trademark tool for slide playing.

Duane's tone on the slide is unique for a few reasons. Primarily, that glass medication bottle he used was not actually long enough to cover the whole neck of a Les Paul, so he could never play full chords with it, only triads, or three-string chords. Using such a small slide also meant that he had to position the slide differently as he moved across the neck. The second knuckle of his ring finger sat on the rim of the medicine bottle, and he positioned the tip of that finger to slide over the frets.

In order to position the slide correctly, he held the guitar high and pointed it up a little bit higher than most players. He also placed his middle finger across the strings behind the slide to mute possible overtones and to have better control of his tone in general. As a slide player, and as a regular fretting player, Allman had fantastic phrasing and impeccable note choices. He also, very significantly, used alternate open tunings, including Open E ("Statesboro Blues," "Done Somebody Wrong," "One Way Out," and "Trouble No More (Live)," etc.).

Duane's fretted technique also had some quirkiness. He picked in a circular style, which means the pick doesn't move perpendicular to the strings, but in a circular motion. Not only did this soften what would otherwise be an aggressive picking attack, it also enabled him to jump strings in a controlled way. Duane held his pick between his thumb and forefinger, keeping his three other fingers on his picking hand still, making his right hand appear motionless.

Oddly enough, Duane was left-handed, though he played guitar right-handed. Because of this, his fretting hand was particularly strong and gave him greater control when bending notes or adding vibrato. On the same hand, his picking technique, done with his weaker hand, made it sound like he had a lighter touch. Duane used a pick when playing his leads, but picked with his thumb when playing slide. He used his thumb, index, and middle fingers to pluck the strings.

Duane employed a variety of pickup positions, depending on how trebly he intended to get with his leads. When his notes extended beyond the frets, as they did in "Layla" and "Mountain Jam," among others, he used the Bridge or Treble pickup. On much of his other work, he used the Neck or Rhythm pickup, or both. "When he played extended, fretted leads, he used both pickups, and he often manipulated the tone controls. He would also end the solo for example, in 'Whipping Post' by getting gradually quieter—this let him reset the volume controls gradually lower to the required rhythm volume for the next verse—this was necessary since he had used both pickups at full whack" (Fothergill, Julian, www.hotguitarist.com).

Amazingly, throughout his career, Allman managed to conjure up a slide vibe with only a pick and bare fingers as well, meaning that he simply heard this sound in his head and that's how he interpreted it as a guitarist. Or, as Duane once said, "Just rock on, and have you a good time!"

EQUIPMENT/GEAR

Duane's first electric was a cherry-red 1959 Gibson Les Paul Junior, but he soon moved on to a variety of other instruments, from a Fender Telecaster with a Stratocaster neck, to a

1957 Gibson Les Paul Goldtop, a 1961 Gibson Les Paul/SG (for slide), a sunburst Gibson ES-335 (1958–1962), and, most famously, a tobacco sunburst Gibson Les Paul he picked up in June of 1971. As a session player, he used a sunburst, three-tone 1961 Strat. His favorite acoustic was an old Gibson L-00.

Amp-wise, Allman started out with a Vox Super Beatle, with six 10-inch speakers and two horns. He then switched to a Fender Twin Reverb. But for his work in the Allman Brothers, Duane utilized a pair of Marshall 50-watt heads driving two Marshall 4x12 cabs loaded with JBL D-120F speakers. For sessions, Allman preferred a Twin Reverb with JBLs.

In the studio, Duane continued to use Fender amps occasionally. As far as Marshall amps are concerned he tried 100-watt heads, but switched to 50 watts soon after as he could push them to heavier distortion at quieter volumes. There is extant photo evidence that Duane used a Bass top cab, which let him achieve a smoother, bass-heavy tone that he preferred.

The development in Duane's technique and sound was in part a result of his move from a Fender guitar/amp combination to Gibson/Marshall. He started off using a Fender Tele-caster with a Stratocaster neck, so in order to thicken out that sound a little he used a Fuzz Face distortion box, used in conjunction with nearly flat 9-volt batteries. His justification was that the sound takes on a softer richness when the batteries are almost flat, so the amp can then be used to provide the main power and overdrive.

He moved to Gibson/Marshall shortly after the formation of the Allman Brothers Band in 1969. During the recording of their debut album he used a Gibson ES-345, while Betts used a variety of Gibsons, in particular an ES-345 and a 1968 SG. The tiger-striped sun-burst Les Paul is the guitar he played primarily in the Fillmore concerts, and it's also the guitar he used to complete the recording of the *Layla* album. The axe had been owned by singer Christopher Cross, and was found for Duane by Billy Gibbons of ZZ Top.

ESSENTIAL READING

Derek and the Dominos: *The Layla Sessions 20th Anniversary Edition,* liner notes.

Eder, Bruce. All Music Guide, *allmusic.com.*

Fothergill, Julian, www.hotguitarist.com.

Gibbons, Billy F., and Randy Poe. *Skydog: The Duane Allman Story.* San Francisco: Backbeat Books, 2006.

Gregg Allman Anthology, liner notes.

Gress, Jesse. "10 Things You Gotta Do to Play Like Duane Allman." *Guitar Player,* www .guitarplayer.com, April 2007.

Landau, Jon. "Band Leader Duane Allman Dies in Bike Crash." *Rollingstone.com.*

Perkins, Willie. *No Saints, No Saviors: My Years with the Allman Brothers Band.* Mercer University Press, 2005.

Schumacher, Michael. *Crossroads: The Life and Music of Eric Clapton,* New York: Citadel, 2003.

Skydog. pp. 32–33.

ESSENTIAL WORK

"Dreams" (The Allman Brothers, 1969)
"Hey Jude" (Wilson Pickett, 1969)
"Layla" (Derek and the Dominos, 1970)
"Livin' on the Open Road" (Duane Allman, 1971)

ESSENTIAL LISTENING

The Allman Brothers Band (Polydor, 1969)
At the Fillmore East (Polydor, 1971)
The Fillmore Concerts (Polydor, 1971/1992)
Idlewild South (Polydor, 1970)

Jeff Beck

As one of the instrument's most skilled rock stylists, Jeff Beck has burned a template for guitarists second in importance and critical weight only to Jimi Hendrix. He is a guitarist's guitar player, one who enjoys immense respect from his peers, if not from the general public, which remains at arm's length largely because Beck's material has never been targeted to or focused on the commercial marketplace.

In 1966, Jeff Beck was voted the #1 lead guitarist in the influential British music magazine *Beat Instrumental*—an honor bestowed on Beck in spite of all the obvious competition. His work during this period was monumental; Beck influenced all the major players at the time, including Eric Clapton and Jimi Hendrix who himself was paying close attention to the rock scene at the time, as well as amateur musicians in garages and on stages all over the world. During this time, albeit a relatively short tenure of perhaps somewhere less than two years, Beck stood alone atop rock's guitar mountain.

His stint with the Yardbirds vaulted him to a place of prominence, and initial work with his own Jeff Beck Group immediately followed, securing his place in rock history and permanently altering the course of high-decibel rock 'n' roll guitar.

Since then, Jeff Beck has done it all, and impressively. He's been universally lauded for his work across all styles, first in blues and blue rock—which was a revolutionary movement of the British music scene—then in rock, psychedelia, and early metal, and later in his groundbreaking 1970's work in fusion and pop.

Jeff had his greatest commercial, and some say artistic, successes during this period in the 1970s, with landmark guitar albums *Blow by Blow* (1975) and *Wired* (1976). Taken together, these works are largely considered to be the most respected and acclaimed instrumental guitar albums in the history of the genre, and without them, without Beck's abundant originality laying the groundwork, future icons like Joe Satriani, Steve Vai, and Eddie Van Halen might never have come to be.

Despite all the overwhelming creative successes and artistic innovations, Beck's career has also been plagued by long gaps of inactivity, erratic behavior, and under-the-radar releases that tended to subordinate his landmark experimentation. Since breaking up the Jeff Beck Group with lead singer Rod Stewart, Beck never again found the kind of singer he cared enough about to work with. He once said that apart from Stewart, Robert Plant would have been his only other choice, but Plant was busy, as we know, with former bandmate Jimmy Page's new band, Led Zeppelin (then called the New Yardbirds).

Beck's reluctance to hire a new vocalist that could serve as his front man and the voice of his group proved the sticking point that ultimately prevented Beck from earning the same commercial prominence as his peers, namely Clapton and Page, both of whom are often mentioned ahead of him on lists of rock's greatest players largely because these players spent an exponentially longer and more commercially rewarding time in the limelight.

While Beck ranks far behind his former comrades in those terms and those terms only, Beck, arguably, eclipsed them in terms of sheer technical mastery, creative audacity, and sonic innovation. He just never had the opportunity to exercise his guitar playing genius in front of massive audiences.

EARLY YEARS

Born on June 24, 1944, just before the end of World War II, Beck grew up in Wallington, England, the younger of two children. His older sister Annetta, four years Jeff's senior, was the apple of her dad's eye and a lovely pianist. Still, Jeff had the advantage of parents who recognized opportunities, and they made sure their children took advantage of the educational opportunities available to them.

Jeff's mother also played piano and the family radio was always buzzing in the house, so young Jeff remembers constantly being surrounded by music. The presence of that music helped ease the tension of the war and served as a source of comfort for the Becks. As a boy, he recalled the advent of jazz in the United Kingdom and the excitement it created in his house. Not that his parents condoned the genre. Jeff used to sneak off to his bedroom to listen to it on the radio.

At the insistence of his mother, Beck sang in the church choir and took piano lessons as well. He tolerated the instrument the best he could, but ultimately he had his own ideas. One day, following a particularly distasteful piano lesson, he ripped off one of the family piano's black keys and hurled it. From then on, he retreated to his favorite instrument: the drums.

He first heard the guitar when Les Paul's hit "How High the Moon" dominated radio in the early 1950s. The young Beck was transfixed by the eerie slapback effects he'd heard on Paul's guitar. An uncle taught him the rudiments of upright bass and violin as well. But the young boy's future was sealed when, at 14, he went to a Buddy Holly concert. He was so inspired by what he witnessed, he built his own guitar and started strumming. His father soon replaced his homespun model with the real thing.

His progress on the guitar came quickly, and before long he was playing in and around London. Early on, he attended Wimbledon's Art College, but his studies interfered with his music and he left school to devote himself full time to music. At the outset of the 1960s, Beck played in a few bands, including the Nightshift and the Del-Tones, with whom he stayed for a year. The latter band habitually took the stage wearing pink sports jackets when performing.

As a well-respected musician amongst his peers, Jeff was asked to join many bands. But he first worked as a session player around 1963 and 1964 with, among others, Screaming Lord Sutch and the Savages, a popular, eccentric blues rock act that hired some of the best talent in London. It was during this time that Beck met Jimmy Page.

In a *Hit Parader* magazine interview, Jeff was asked, "What were you doing when Eric (Clapton) was in the Yardbirds?" Beck replied, "Apart from being a tramp, I was playing on records whenever I could. I was lucky enough to be known. Whenever they needed a rock and roll guitar break, I'd play it. But work was limited because there weren't very many rock and roll records being made at the time. I met Jimmy Page at these sessions and he recommended me to the Yardbirds when Eric left" (www.ainian.com).

Beck played with bands such as the Tridents and the Crescents at this time in addition to his studio cameos. Interestingly, John Mayall's Bluesbreakers wanted Jeff to replace Clapton, but Beck demurred. "John Mayall phoned me up and it was so long ago I was still living with my mum. My mother said, 'This John Mayall sounds a very nice chap!' I would have loved to play with him but I didn't think I was good enough to take over from Eric."

Peter Green was eventually the guitarist to replace Clapton; Clapton was eager to expand his horizons, and so he joined the Yardbirds. In 1965, the restless Clapton left that band, too, and Beck stepped in. Beck's stint in the Yardbirds lasted only 18 months, but it was the band's most successful and pioneering period. It was at this time that the Yardbirds began moving away from their blues-based sound—the reason why Clapton departed—and toward a more eclectic and psychedelic noise. Beck's adventurousness played beautifully into this reinvention. Not that he couldn't play blues and R&B. On tracks like "The Train Kept A-Rollin'" and "I'm Not Talking," Beck mastered an evil sort of sustain from his instrument by bending the notes and using fuzz and other

Courtesy of Neil Zlozower

types of distorted amplification. There was also a striking Middle Eastern influence, most audaciously on his first single with the band, "Heart Full of Soul."

The innovations of Clapton, Beck, and Page redefined the role of the guitar in rock music, breaking immense ground in the use of feedback, distortion, and amplification with finesse and breathtaking virtuosity. Thanks to these players, especially Beck, and their eclectic, risk-taking approach, the Yardbirds laid the groundwork for much of the hard rock and progressive rock from the late 1960s to the present.

While most expected the Yardbirds to take a significant setback following the departure of Clapton, Beck actually moved the group forward into positive and even more progressive artistic territory. In fact, many early blues and rock experts define his work during this time as revolutionary, not to mention more commercially viable than the Clapton-era Yardbirds. Certainly, in terms of their influence and prominence in the U.K. music scene, Beck's Yardbirds had more of an impact than the band's original incarnation. The Yardbirds embarked on their first U.S. tour late in the summer of 1965 and returned for three other U.S. jaunts during Beck's tenure with the group. These stateside appearances cemented his reputation as the most devastating and forward-thinking guitarist on the world's rock scene.

The Beck-era Yardbirds produced a handful of classic recordings, including hit singles like "Heart Full of Soul," an explosive cover of Bo Diddley's "I'm a Man," and the epic "Shapes of Things." The Yardbirds album popularly referred to as *Roger the Engineer,* a recording first issued in the United States as *Over Under Sideways Down,* sent repercussions throughout Europe and the States and established Beck as one of the most electric of artists.

After Jeff Beck finished up his 18-month tenure with the Yardbirds in 1967, producer Mickie Most signed him to a management deal, thinking that Beck, the best looking and most intriguing member of the band, would have a career as a pop artist. How wrong he was! Not only did the introverted Beck have no desire to be a pop star, he also had much grander musical ambitions, most of which had to do with wreaking utter havoc with his Les Paul.

Beck quickly formed the Jeff Beck Group, which featured his favorite musicians: Rod Stewart on vocals, Nicky Hopkins on keys, Aynsley Dunbar on drums (replaced by Mickey Waller), and Ron Wood on bass. The band released two albums—*Truth* (1968) and *Beck-Ola* (1969)—that became musical touchstones for hard rockers in the years to come.

During a "Rod Stewart Special" on MTV sometime in June 1984, Martha Quinn asked Rod Stewart how he met Jeff Beck: "It's about I would say 1967, 66, Jeff had left the Yardbirds he well, actually I think he got fired for non-appearances a few times with the Yardbirds as so many people don't know. I'd been fired from the group I was in and the group Woody was in, the Birds, they formed the Part Seems so basically we were all unemployed."

Jeff Beck: "I was lurking in this club one night and uh I think we were the last two people (laughs) in there."

Stewart: "I came up to you and said are you a taxi driver and you said 'No, I play the guitar.' You said are you a bouncer and I said 'No, I'm a singer.'"

Jeff Beck: "It was a London Club, where all sorts of things go on at three o'clock in the morning."

Stewart: "Yeah like Ron Wood was there for instance."

With their brazen and deafening reworkings of blues songs and vocal and guitar interplay, Beck and the boys established the blueprint for heavy metal. But neither of the band's records was particularly successful, and the band tended to fight regularly, especially on their frequent tours of the United States. The behavior signaled doom for the band.

In 1970, Rod Stewart and Wood left to join the Faces with the Small Faces' Steve Marriott. Beck disbanded the group; he suffered a serious car accident in 1970. And in 1971, he formed a new version of the Jeff Beck Band, which then recorded two albums, *Rough and Ready* (1971) and *The Jeff Beck Group* (1972). Beck again dissolved the group and formed a power trio with bassist Tim Bogert and drummer Carmine Appice, which released *Beck, Bogert and Appice* (1973).

In the meantime, Jeff spent much of his time building and tinkering with his hot rod collection and working occasionally on other people's musical projects. His playing on the Honeydrippers' *Rockin' at Midnight* gave Beck the chance to emulate some of his earliest musical influences, Cliff Gallup of Gene Vincent's band and Paul Burlison of the Rock 'N' Roll Trio.

On September 20, 1983, at London's Royal Albert Hall, Beck reunited with the two other former Yardbirds' guitarists, Clapton and Page, in a benefit show for ARMS (Action and Research into Multiple Sclerosis). Pleased with the results, he continued on to play 10 dates on the ARMS tour of 1984.

Beck also teamed with his former lead singer, Rod Stewart, on two separate occasions in 1984 and 1985. *Flash* featured Stewart's stirring vocals on "People Get Ready" as Beck furthered his distance from jazz and began to turn up some hard rock heat on his wildest, wang bar-infected solo yet on "Ambitious." "A guitar can take you wherever you want it to go," Beck told me in *Guitar for the Practicing Musician*. "I could do a country and western album if I wanted to, heaven forbid" (Gulla, Bob, "He's Beck," *Guitar for the Practicing Musician,* April 1999, p. 78).

SOLO WORK

His power trio work faltered, and so Beck, tired of being panned by critics and unfulfilled as an artist, left his rock/pop roots in the dust and began working up a stylistic redefinition. Working with former Beatles producer George Martin, Beck reemerged in 1975 with the epic *Blow by Blow.* He followed that up the very next year with *Wired,* a collaboration with fusion specialist Jan Hammer, former keyboardist for the Mahavishnu Orchestra.

Both all-instrumental albums were critical and popular successes and remain two of the top-selling guitar instrumental albums of all time. A live album, *Jeff Beck with the Jan Hammer Group Live,* followed in 1977.

After the Hammer tour, Beck retired for three years, working on his hobby, car racing and hot rods in his estate outside of London. He returned in 1980 with another Hammer work, *There and Back,* and again five years after that with Nile Rodgers of Chic on the slick *Flash.* The latter is notable largely because it's a pop/rock album recorded with a variety of vocalists, including his former mate Rod Stewart on a cover of Curtis Mayfield's "People Get Ready," and the instrumental "Escape," which actually won a Grammy for Best Rock Instrumental. He won another Grammy for Best Rock Instrumental thanks to his album *Jeff Beck's Guitar Shop* with Terry Bozzio and Tony Hymas. He toured with Stevie Ray Vaughan in 1989 and retired, sort of, once again.

Obviously, Beck possesses a love/hate relationship with rock 'n' roll and touring. He returned to the studio in 1993 backed by the Big Town Playboys to record *Crazy Legs,* a tribute to seminal rockabilly artist Gene Vincent and his guitarist Cliff Gallup. The recording took just six weeks to record and mix, but Beck totally immersed himself in the work of Gene Vincent for that time. Beck played his latter day bebop to the nines and he thoroughly captured the detailed technique of Gallup's archetypal leads.

Six years later he released *Who Else!* But that album, released to a great deal of publicity and acclaim, seemed to rejuvenate Beck standards. Two years later, the finicky creator released *You Had It Coming* (2001), which earned Beck his third Grammy for Best Rock Instrumental for the song "Dirty Mind."

In 2003, he released *Jeff* and hit the road on a coast-to-coast tour with blues legend B.B. King on the Twelfth Annual B.B. King Music Festival. The next summer he toured the United Kingdom for the first time in nearly 20 years, based in part on securing his fourth Grammy for Best Instrumental for the track "Plan B."

Beck's resurgence continued through the rest of the decade, with a new band, a tour of Japan, and a new album, entitled, *Official Bootleg.* In 2007, he appeared on the popular television show "American Idol" in a duet with Kelly Clarkson. Jeff also had another very high profile appearance, this one with Guns N' Roses on a Paris stage. He showed up for a rehearsal with the band, but an excruciating case of tinnitus, an ear affliction Jeff has had for decades, prevented him from following through on the guest spot.

TECHNIQUE/STYLE

Jeff Beck's electric rock style is as unique as any player in the genre, second perhaps only to Hendrix in his impact on exposing rock's vast tonal and stylistic spectrum. In his earliest work, he's credited with bringing to prominence, and popularizing something no less seminal than feedback and distortion.

At the time, in the early 1960s, guitars sounded clean, bright, and jangly—at least in the bands of the British Invasion. Or they sounded bluesy, ala Muddy Waters and Bo Diddley and their landmark electric work of the previous decade. In his work with seminal blues-rock act the Yardbirds, a post he kept for a very short time as Eric Clapton's replacement, he demonstrated a penchant for experimentation and pushed the band into directions that would open the door to psychedelic rock. Beck's guitar experiments with fuzz tone, feedback, and distortion jolted British rock forward with a bold dropkick, punching a psychedelic time-clock, and evincing world-music influences. In addition, the Yardbirds began serious experiments with things like adapting Gregorian chant and world-music influences ("Still I'm Sad," "Turn into Earth," "Hot House of Omagarashid," "Farewell," "Ever Since the World Began") and various European folk styles into their blues and rock rooted music, and this gained them a new reputation among the hipster underground even as their commercial appeal had begun already to wane.

One of Beck's signatures as a player is his canny sense of pitch. Whammy bars and Stratocasters don't typically go very well together; the whammy often throws the guitar out of tune. Yet, Beck exercises his whammy vigorously, creating everything from nose-diving bombs to subtle, perfectly pitched harmonic melodies.

Another key trait to his style is his dynamic sense of timing. He regularly plays either slightly behind the beat or slightly ahead of it, and the irregularity gives his rhythms and licks a distinctive flair. He also exercises a sweeping legato style phrasing, especially in his ballads, which creates intensity and melody.

Other Beck quirks, and there are many, include a tendency to pre-bent notes, or bends when they're least expected. He possesses an immense kind of courage and an impeccable

HOT ROD GOD

Music may have been one of Beck's earliest passions but it has always shared space with a love of hot rods that began as soon as he could see over the dashboard. The majority of Beck's cars are 1932 Fords, though over the years there have been Model Ts and a hammered 1934 coupe. He houses the majority of them at his manor house in England, and has had most of them shipped from California. He loves tinkering with them himself, customizing and refurbishing them, and he can often be seen in England at the bigger rod runs held in the United Kingdom.

After the success of *Blow by Blow* and *Wired,* Beck began devoting more time to his fleet of hot rods. "I like the studio because it's delicate; you're working for sound. I like the garage because chopping up lumps of steel is the exact opposite of delicate," explains Beck. "The garage is a more dangerous place though. I've never almost been crushed by a guitar, but I can't say the same about one of my Corvettes."

instinct when it comes to playing notes. He chooses notes quite unexpectedly and makes them work in nearly any situation, regardless of the key. He is quite creative when it comes to creating tonal variety by switching pickups and manipulating his tone and volume controls as well.

Although Jeff is known as a solo artist, throughout his career he has worked with top producers and musicians who have helped to bring out the best in him. "Working on the *Blow by Blow* album, George Martin brought a certain Beatles-like lightheartedness which made it easier to play in the studio. I would be trying to do these really difficult bits and he would say, 'Jeff, you played like an angel this morning but now you suck. Just take a break!' I love that 'cause I hate to be patronized about my playing. I like to have input from Joe Public or from someone I respect if they can explain what they don't like about what I'm doing. What's lacking in a lot of people is that they live in their own little world in a vacuum and eventually the door slams shut and they freeze to death" (www .djnoble.demon.co.uk).

EQUIPMENT/GEAR

Beck admits he owns nearly 50 guitars, many of which are prototypes that didn't work out, experiments designed for Beck and others that fell short of the mark. He possesses a few vintage instruments as well, including a 1953 Stratocaster once owned by the late Steve Marriott.

The first time Jeff Beck saw a Strat, still his instrument of choice, it was hanging in the window of a music shop on Charing Cross Road. He was with a bandmate from the Del-Tones on a day they'd skipped school. They hopped a bus and went looking around guitar shops. From the upper deck of the bus he saw the Strat in the shop, went barreling down the stairs, knocked the conductor out of the way and jumped off the bus. It was a sunburst Strat and a blond Tele with an ebony fingerboard. Of course, at 14, Beck didn't have any money to speak of, but the clerk let him play to his heart's content.

During his career, Jeff has played both Strats and Les Pauls, generally going with whichever style suits the music best. With his louder, lower end, three-piece power rock sound, he opted for the Les Paul. He was pleased with the fat midrange and the richness of the higher notes and planned to form a three-piece so it made sense. He also enjoyed the thick neck of the Les Paul. He credits that initial impression the Les Paul made on him to watching Eric Clapton, though he opted for his own setup in terms of amplification.

The Jeff Beck Signature Strat is well known for the thickness and weight of the neck. He was finding that the necks of most Strats were too thin and his hand ached soon after starting to play. After he played the weightier Les Paul, he proposed the idea of a thicker neck to the people at Fender. They nearly doubled the size of the traditional Strat neck for the Beck Signature model. This surf green warhorse is named "Little Richard;" the rock 'n' roll legend signed his name on the body in mile-high letters.

By the Yardbirds era, Beck had abandoned the Strat he started on. He experimented with a few Telecasters before settling on a 1954 Fender Esquire as his main guitar. He played his Esquire through two Vox AC30 combo amps. Beck befriended Jimi Hendrix during the Jeff Beck Group period around 1968 and Hendrix gave Beck several pieces of advice. Jimi told him he was playing on strings that were too thin. At the time, Beck's strings were as thin as he could get. But since that encounter with Jimi, his string gauges have been rising ever since. Now he's starting at .011s and getting ever heavier. Hendrix also told him he should consider returning to the Strat after playing the Les Paul with the Jeff Beck Group. It was also Hendrix who rekindled Beck's interest in the Strat.

For much of the early 1970s, he fluctuated between Strats, Teles, and Les Pauls. Beck's right-hand technique is highly idiosyncratic. He's one of the only true rock guitarists who picks with his bare fingers rather than use a pick.

"When the tailpiece of the Strat is properly set up, for me, I can feel the spring balance," he says. "There's a balance between the tension of the strings and the counter-tension of the springs on the back. I have it set so there's just enough tension to bend the arm up a whole step. That's about it. If the bridge is leaning forward too much because of string tension, then you're not going to get the downward press you need. So it's about 75% down, 25% up. That will do it for me" (Di Perna Alan Fender Player's Club, www.fenderplayersclub.com, 2003).

To accommodate Beck's vigorous string bending, a double roller nut was devised to stop the extraneous ringing noise and help the intonation. And, over the years, he has also used a variety of amps, often with a wall of cabinets.

For his now legendary "The Fire and the Fury" tour with the late Stevie Ray Vaughan in 1989, he went a different direction. "I had a couple of Fender Twins and that was it," Beck says. "Stevie couldn't believe it. He had a huge stack with about 15 different amps, all gaffer-taped to a rolling platform. At the end of each night's gig, we'd alternate between him coming on to play with me and my band, and me going on with his band. The volume coming out of those amps was so unbelievable. And every night he'd say, 'You know man, I'm talking to my guys about getting your setup.' And I said, 'I'm talking to my guys about getting yours.' He sounded amazing" (Di Perna, 2003).

"I don't understand why some people will only accept a guitar if it has an instantly recognizable guitar sound," says Beck. "Finding ways to use the same guitar people have been using for 50 years to make sounds that no one has heard before is truly what gets me off. I love it when people hear my music but can't figure out what instrument I'm playing. What a cool compliment" (uncredited biography, www.jeffbeck.com).

"I've just got one head. One JCM 2000 (DSL50) head. As long as I spend time dialing in sound through the side fills on the stage, and give the front of the house guy plenty of time to dial out the nasty fizz, it's been fine. Although I am going to change up and go back to all four cabinets and two tops (after the B.B. King tour), 'cause that's not for B.B. They went berserk on me 'cause it was too loud on stage at one point. And I just went, 'OK, if I turn it down, I don't get the fatness and the importance of the sound. It just disappears into a country sound,' (laughs) which is fine if you're playing country. But if you want powerful attack to replace a 20-piece band, you need to be louder. Have the capacity to be loud" (St. James, Adam, "Jeff Beck," guitar.com, 2003).

Beck also uses a Snarling Dog wah-wah pedal. "That's a radical pedal. I mean it's one or two steps further than any wah pedal ever known. It's got an active circuit, as opposed to just a battery-powered toggle pot. So it kicks in a lot more dB and a lot more sweep and a lot more depth variable in the wah wah itself. You can preset it so it won't take your head off, which is good" (St. James, 2003).

ESSENTIAL READING

Carson, Annette. *Jeff Beck: Crazy Fingers.* San Francisco: Backbeat Books, 2001.
Di Perna, Alan. Fender Player's Club. www.fenderplayersclub.com, 2003.

Gulla, Bob. "He's Beck." *Guitar for the Practicing Musician,* April 1999, 78.
St. James, Adam. "Jeff Beck." guitar.com, 2003.

Essential Work

"Beck's Bolero" (1968)
"Cause We've Ended as Lovers" (1975)
"Freeway Jam" (1975)
"Goodbye Pork Pie Hat" (1976)
"Led Boots" (1976)
"Shapes of Things" (1968)

Essential Listening

Beck-Ola (Epic, 1969)
Blow by Blow (Epic, 1975)
Jeff (Epic, 2003)
Truth (Epic, 1968)
Wired (Epic, 1976)

Chuck Berry

Chuck Berry's music transcends generations and helped to define the experience of American youth. Known as "The Father" or "The Architect" of rock 'n' roll, Berry wrote tunes like "Johnny B. Goode," "Maybellene," and "Memphis" that have become anthems to music fans and cornerstones of American popular culture. He established rock 'n' roll as a musical form and united the worlds of black and white through his music.

He is also, arguably, the most important guitarist in rock 'n' roll history. His style, a souped-up hybrid of country, jump blues, Delta blues, and boogie-woogie piano, has inspired and influenced generations of rock musicians from the moment they first heard it, from Elvis, the Beatles, and the Rolling Stones in the late 1950s, to second-generation rockers like the Who and the Beach Boys, and on up to the White Stripes in the 2000s. Not bad for a convicted car thief and former cosmetician.

He electrified popular music, literally and figuratively, and his primal chords formed the transition from rhythm and blues to rock 'n' roll. He was also the first to define the classic subjects of rock 'n' roll in songwriting, including girls, school, and cars. Oddly enough, this happened when Berry was in his thirties.

Berry gave rock 'n' roll an archetypal character in "Johnny B. Goode" and was responsible for several inimitable stage antics, including his patented "duck walk" and playing the guitar behind his head and between his legs.

All the while, his repertoires—not only the hits, but lesser-known songs like "Little Queenie" and "Let It Rock"—were being absorbed by eager apprentices on the other side of the ocean. Keith Richards, John Lennon, Eric Clapton, Jeff Beck, and many other soon-to-be legends flocked to Chuck Berry and learned their trade at his hands.

"He was the first great poet laureate of rock and roll. He tapped into the teenage years especially," said Andy McKaie, producer of Berry's *Johnny B. Goode: His Complete '50s Chess Recordings.* "He made the format for rock and roll from the lyric content to the guitar riffs to the rhythms. He was the architect" (WGBH Radio, "Fresh Air: Chuck Berry, Father of Rock and Roll," produced by Farai Chideya, March 28, 2008).

Berry was awarded the "Grammy Lifetime Achievement Award" in 1984, and in 1986 he was among the inaugural inductees to the newly christened Rock 'n' Roll Hall of Fame. In 2003, *Rolling Stone* named him #6 on its list of the "100 Greatest Guitarists of All Time." The next year, a half dozen of his songs were counted in that same magazine's list of "The 500 Greatest Songs of All Time," including "Johnny B. Goode," "Maybellene," "Roll Over Beethoven," "Rock and Roll Music," "Sweet Little Sixteen," and "Brown Eyed Handsome Man." Also in 2004, Berry was given the #5 spot in *Rolling Stone*'s "100 Greatest Artists of All Time."

These are heady accolades indeed, awarded only to the most significant and influential artists of the popular era. In fact, it is hard to imagine how rock 'n' roll would have evolved had Chuck decided to stay at one of his odd jobs, as a carpenter, a painter, or a hairdresser, rather than pick up, and stay with, his beloved Gibson guitar.

Early Years

Chuck Berry was born in St. Louis on October 18, 1926 in a middle-class neighborhood of the city known as "The Ville." He was the third child in a family of six. His father was a contractor and a deacon of the Antioch Baptist Church and his mother served as a school principal.

Because he enjoyed a relatively comfortable upbringing, he pursued music with confidence from an early point in his life. He sang from a young age, emulating the smooth vocals of his first idol, Nat King Cole. At age 14, he appeared at Sumner High School's All Men Review at which he sang Jay McShann's "Confessin' the Blues," a risque blues tune, accompanied by a friend on guitar. He listened heavily to the blues, namely Muddy Waters, but it was still objectionable to perform the blues in front of a middle-class audience. At the time, blues was considered unsavory, as it clearly divided white and black audiences. But the young Berry's performance received hearty applause for taking the risk, and his success emboldened him, encouraging him to pursue performing.

Unfortunately, the law interfered with his plans. In 1944, at 18, before he could graduate, he was arrested and convicted of armed robbery after taking a joy ride with his friends to Kansas City, Missouri. As he tells it, Berry's automobile broke down and he flagged a passing car for assistance, using a "non-functional pistol." The car-jacking victim phoned the police and soon Berry was in prison for the first time, serving a three-year sentence. While there, Berry joined a gospel group and boxed briefly before being released on his twenty-first birthday in 1947.

Berry took up the guitar more seriously after that, in 1947; he learned the critical rhythm changes and blues chords that would enable him to play most of the popular songs on the radio at the time. A friend of his, a local jazz guitarist named Ira Harris, showed him techniques on the instrument that would become the foundation of Berry's original sound. He set out playing on a four-string tenor guitar, but switched to a six-string around 1950.

A year after his release from prison, Berry married Themetta Suggs and began a series of miscellaneous jobs: as a janitor at the Fisher Body auto assembly plant, trained to be a hairdresser at the Poro School, freelanced as a photographer, assisted his father as a carpenter, and began his career as a musician. During this time, he continued playing the guitar and developing a reputation around St. Louis.

In 1952, he performed in a house band at a local club, whose songs ranged from blues to ballads and from calypso to country. The next year he joined a second, more legitimate touring band called the Sir John's Trio, after their sax player called in sick for an important New Year's Eve gig at a popular East St. Louis venue. Berry jumped at the chance and made the most of his break. That night, he tore it up with a country, hillbilly number in a bluesy style that knocked the audience out.

At the time, country and western music and the sounds of Hank Williams were all over the radio, especially in the Midwest, so Berry, eager to capitalize, delved into the sound of hillbilly guitar. His band's black fans thought it inscrutable for a young black guitar player to be strumming out hillbilly chords, but they started dancing to it. At the same time,

Courtesy of Photofest

Berry's white audience loved the country genre, so they started grooving as well. From that point, at 26, he began to attract the first multiracial audience in pop.

Berry, an ebullient, often silly showman, began stepping up his stage antics as well, as did other members of the Sir John's Trio band. This included pianist Johnnie Johnson, whose own style on the ivories was almost as influential to pianists like Jerry Lee Lewis as Berry was to guitar players. Johnson and Berry traded licks back and forth and performed gymnastic stage maneuvers. Crowds ate it up. In retrospect, critics have made the case that Berry and the Sir John's Trio served as a prototype of the first rock 'n' roll band. Chuck Berry took the band over as front man and it soon became known as the Chuck Berry Combo.

MUSIC

In 1955, Berry migrated north to Chicago to sniff around at opportunities. Chicago was home to Chess Records, the soon-to-be legendary blues label owned by Leonard Chess that also released records by Bo Diddley, Howlin' Wolf, and Etta James. On a fortuitous night at a West Side club, Berry met one of his idols, Muddy Waters, then a recording artist for

Chess. Waters heard Berry's sound, and despite being a very competitive performer, referred Berry to the Chess offices on forty-seventh and Cottage. Perhaps Waters, after hearing Berry's postblues pop sound, didn't feel threatened by this particular competitor.

Leonard Chess asked Berry for music that day, which, of course, Berry didn't have. So Chess sent Berry back to St. Louis to make a demo and return when it was done. Berry went home and recorded some originals, including a hillbilly song called "Ida Mae," and he ventured back to Chicago later in the week. Chess dug the bucolic vibe of "Ida Mae," though he suggested Berry change the name to "Maybellene." Berry agreed, signed with Chess in the summer of 1955, and rock history was made.

"Maybellene" reached #5 on the Pop Charts and #1 on the R&B Charts. That record, and many other Chess sides that Berry performed, were made with Chess studio musicians that played with their blues artists: pianist Johnnie Johnson, bassist Will Dixon, and drummer Eddie Hardy. Through his quick-witted lyrics, words full of winking insinuations and minor puns about cars and girls, Berry laid the groundwork for rock 'n' roll attitude. The song included a brief but scorching guitar solo built around his trademark double-string licks. A template, and a star, was born. Through Chuck Berry, Chess Records moved from the R&B genre into the mainstream and Berry himself rocketed to stardom.

He had hits throughout the rest of the 1950s. On April 16, 1956, he entered the Chess studio with some new tunes he wanted to cut. "By that time, the writer/artist had his formula down: a guitar riff, a beat, a girl, a car, raging hormones, a ringing high school bell, an unfolding story line—and he ran through the new tunes for the other musicians on the session: drummer Fred Belew, Chess power hitter Willie Dixon on stand-up bass, and Johnnie Johnson, Berry's secret weapon, on the ivories" (Scoppa, Bud, *Chuck Berry: The Definitive Collection,* liner notes, Chess, p. 4).

On that one day, Berry ran through recordings like "Too Much Monkey Business," "Roll Over Beethoven," and "Brown Eyed Handsome Man." These three songs serve now as the cornerstones of rock 'n' roll. He even established the lineup: guitar, bass, drums, and piano. During a two-day stint after Christmas in 1957, Berry topped that achievement with three other tunes: "Reelin' and Rockin'," "Sweet Little Sixteen," and "Johnny B. Goode."

"One can plausibly assert, then, that Berry claimed his piece of rock 'n' roll turf in May 1955, drew up the blueprint in April 1956, and completed construction in December of 1957" (Scoppa, *Chuck Berry,* p. 5). Appearances in films like *Rock Rock Rock* and *Mister Rock & Roll* and numerous cross-country tours with package shows made Berry a major star.

In May of 1957, Berry released his debut album, *After School Session,* and the second album issued by the Chess label, which had been releasing singles at the time. In fact, both rock 'n' blues album were mainly collections of singles. But in a sign of respect that the Chess label had for Chuck's rising significance and popularity, they included every master completed during Chuck's 18-month tenure (four sessions) with the label that weren't included on the movie *Rock Rock Rock.* The song list also included two tunes from his fifth session, "School Day" and "Deep Feeling."

As a result, the album is a mix of styles and contexts that would continue throughout his career, with anthems, story lines, blues, and tasty instrumentals. Even at 30 years old, Chuck continued his dialogue with his teenaged audience and he managed to communicate skillfully with this demographic. Many artists—Buddy Holly, the Everly Brothers, and later the Beatles—would address this audience effectively, but none did it quite as convincingly as Berry.

By the end of the 1950s, Berry's incredible string of hits began to slow, though he continued to make great music. But in 1961, he stalled completely. He found himself back in jail again, this time for violating the Mann Act, accused of transporting an underage girl over a state line. As the story goes, Berry met a 14-year-old waitress in El Paso, Texas after a gig there in December of 1959. He invited her to work as a hat-check girl in his nightclub. Later that night, the girl was arrested on a prostitution charge in a St. Louis hotel room, and Berry was arrested for transporting her across state lines for the purpose of prostitution. An appeal on Berry's behalf was denied and he was sentenced to serve 20 months in prison.

Looking at the bright side of his imprisonment, this was about the same time that Berry's music began to take root in the United Kingdom, so his career stayed viable. The Beatles covered "Roll Over Beethoven" and the Rolling Stones made his song "Come On" their first single. By the time he earned release from prison at age 37, his tune "Memphis, Tennessee" had hit the Top 5 on the U.K. chart.

Back in the United States, the Beach Boys had co-opted his song "Sweet Little Sixteen" and turned it rather transparently into "Surfin' U.S.A." a larceny that eventually went into litigation. Berry won that particular lawsuit and the Beach Boys forked over a percentage of their publishing royalties—the song was a massive hit—to Berry.

A couple of songs Chuck had written in prison, "No Particular Place to Go" and "Nadine (Is It You?)" surged up the charts in 1964 and Berry enjoyed his first real chart success since the late 1950s.

In 1966, Berry left Chess and signed to the Mercury label. But none of the five albums he released for his new label, which included one live set backed by the Steve Miller Band, ever sparked commercial interest. In 1970, he returned to Chess and released a handful of albums that demonstrated he'd regain something of his original magic. Still, at the time, he joined the oldies circuit.

In 1972, he released his only #1 hit. "My Ding-a-Ling" was a lewd gig staple that Chuck used to get a cheap laugh from his audiences. A version of it, recorded live at a gig in Manchester in the United Kingdom, found its way into the hands of a local disc jockey. The song earned a tremendous reception and Chess decided to rush-release it as a single. A dubious feather in his cap, the song nonetheless added years to his career and lined his pocket.

By this time, his music had grown so entrenched that he didn't even tour with a band, preferring to recruit pickup musicians in each new town. In those days, if you knew how to play rock 'n' roll, it was a given that you'd cut your teeth on the songs of Chuck Berry.

TECHNIQUE/STYLE

If ever there was a legitimate challenger to the throne of Elvis as the "King of Rock and Roll," it would be Chuck Berry. By putting boogie-woogie piano patterns on his electric guitar, Berry invented a highly distinctive style that has become synonymous with the genre. Like other pioneering performers—Little Richard and Fats Domino—Berry began his career in R&B after hearing the guitar sounds of Charlie Christian, T-Bone Walker, and Carl Hogan, the guitarist in R&B legend Louis Jordan's band. He also worshipped the rustic work of Muddy Waters and Howlin' Wolf's guitar player Hubert Sumlin. Chuck's pure, bright tenor voice contrasted significantly with the rough baritones of blues artists like Waters or Howlin' Wolf and he played a poppier version of the blues early on.

THE ROLLING STONES AND CHUCK BERRY

Of the hundreds and thousands of guitar players and music makers that took their inspiration from Chuck Berry, perhaps no one is more legendary, and legendary for his pilfering, than the Rolling Stones' guitarist Keith Richards.

"Chuck was my man," he said in an uncredited interview. "He was the one that made me say, 'I want to play guitar, Jesus Christ!' And I'd listened to guitar players before that. I was about 15, and I'd think, 'He's very interesting, nice, ah, but . . . With the difference between what I'd heard before 1956 or '57 and right after that with Little Richard and Elvis and Chuck Berry, suddenly I knew what it was I wanted to do" ("The Salt of the Earth, 1955–1960, R&B-derived Rock & Roll," www.timeisonourside.com).

When Keith Richards inducted Berry into the Hall of Fame he famously copped to stealing Chuck's act, hook, line, and sinker. "It's hard for me to induct Chuck Berry, because I lifted every lick he ever played!" (Richards, Keith, www.rockhall.com).

Keith and Chuck's paths have crossed a number of times throughout the years, occasionally producing hilarious results. The Stones met Chuck Berry for the first time in June 1964, on the Stones' first American tour, when they stopped in to record at Chess Studios in Chicago, the very same place Chuck had recorded most of his hits. Later, the Stones, in a gesture of gratitude, invited Chuck to open for them on some of their shows during their blockbuster 1969 American tour.

One of two embarrassing moments for Keith and Chuck occurred in January of 1972, in Los Angeles, when Keith joined Chuck onstage at a club. Chuck didn't immediately recognize Keith and he stopped playing and threw the uninvited performer off the stage after a few numbers for playing too loudly.

Years later, in the summer of 1981, a similarly humiliating occasion went down when Keith took in one of Chuck's club gigs, this time in New York City. After the show, Keith went backstage to congratulate him and say hello. When Keith tapped Chuck on the shoulder, Chuck turned around quickly and took a big swing, landing his punch and giving Keith a black eye. Berry would assert later that he hadn't recognized Keith and thought he was just somebody giving Chuck the business.

On January 1986, however, Keith was the one selected to induct Chuck at the inaugural Rock 'n' Roll Hall of Fame ceremonies in New York. The induction also involved a jam with Chuck afterwards. This musical collaboration led to Keith serving as musical director to celebrate Berry's sixtieth birthday in October of 1986, with two concerts performed in Chuck's hometown of St. Louis.

At those shows, Keith played guitar, sang backup, and was the musical director of the project. Still, despite the history and friendship between Richards and Berry, the Rolling Stone had considerable trouble dealing with Berry's ego and personality antics during the rehearsals and concerts. These were filmed for a concert biography called *Hail! Hail! Rock and Roll.*

As a player and as a songwriter, he mixed melodic hooks and distinctive rhythm patterns with socially significant lyrics and wrapped it all up in his own poetic way.

Guitar-wise, the so-called "Chuck Berry intro" or "Wandering intro" is the building block for any traditional rock 'n' roll tune. These were the intros he played in "Johnny B. Goode" or "No Particular Place to Go." Perhaps one of the first serious leads a new guitarist tries his hand at is the introduction to "Johnny B. Goode." In this particular tune, there are more rock leads than in most other traditional rock songs. The intro itself is a case study, albeit a rather difficult one for new players, in bending, sliding, and hammering notes.

Berry is also famous for his two-note chords (also often called "double stops"). He used this technique in his intros and solo play. He also often used a blues-shuffle rhythm for his verses. His repeating riffs and bends are still incorporated by guitar players today.

The fusion of country and the blues can be found at the crux of Berry's technique. The country-influence in his songs can be heard in the beat, the vocals, and the guitar. The drums play a swing beat in songs like "Sweet Little Sixteen" and "Roll Over Beethoven." This beat, one that Chuck loved, is derived from the country-swing of artists like Hank Williams or Bob Wills.

* * *

"It's not so much what he played—it's what he didn't play," says Joe Perry of Aerosmith in his entry on Berry (#5) in *Rolling Stone* magazine's "Immortals" issue. "His music is very economical. His guitar leads drove the rhythm, as opposed to laying over the top. The economy of his licks and his leads—they pushed the song along. And he would build his solos so there was a nice little statement taking the song to a new place, so you're ready for the next verse" (Perry, Joe, "The Immortals," *Rolling Stone,* www.rollingstone.com).

Berry was also a talented slide player, though not known for it at all. On a song called "Deep Feeling," the b-side to "School Day," one of Chuck's biggest hits, he actually plays the Hawaiian steel guitar with much success. In fact, Berry recorded quite a few rock, blues, and diverse instrumentals, many of which remained unreleased until 2008. These recordings were very conservative, frequently urban blues, as if he needed a safety net if the whole teenage rock 'n' roll phenomenon didn't come through for him. It did, which is why these songs remain relatively unacknowledged.

Finally, as a songwriter, Chuck Berry is magically concise; Aerosmith's Perry called him,

> The Ernest Hemingway of Rock and Roll. He gets right to the point. He tells a story in short sentences. You get a great picture in your mind of what's going on, in a very short amount of time, in well-picked words. He was also very smart: He knew that if he was going to break into the mainstream, he had to appeal to white teenagers. Which he did. Everything in those songs is about teenagers. I think he knew he could have had his own success on the R&B charts, but he wanted to get out of there and go big time. (Perry, www.rollingstone.com)

EQUIPMENT/GEAR

Few guitar players of Berry's majestic stature boast a gear description as downright simple as his. In his early days, on his earliest recordings, Chuck used a 1955 blonde Gibson 350ET with two P90 single-coil pickups through a small Fender amp. He changed his pickups in 1957 to Humbuckers and, later, began playing Gibson ES330s and Gibson ES355 guitars, instruments with which he is more commonly associated. It is a thinner, double cutaway, introduced in 1958. The 355 is essentially a fancier version of the 335, both of which are similar, perhaps not coincidentally, to one of his heroes' axes: B.B. King's "Lucille."

His first amp was an Epiphone, until he switched to Fender in the mid-1950s. Less frequently, Chuck would plug into Orange Top amps. All his amps were tube based. On tour, he'd use two Fender Dual Showman amplifiers for his ES355.

ESSENTIAL READING

Berry, Chuck. *Chuck Berry: The Autobiography.* New York: Random House, 1989.

Pegg, Bruce. *Brown Eyed Handsome Man: The Life and Hard Times of Chuck Berry.* London: Routledge, 2002.

Perry, Joe. "The Immortals." *Rolling Stone,* www.rollingstone.com.

Richards, Keith. www.rockhall.com.

Scoppa, Bud. *Chuck Berry: The Definitive Collection.* Liner notes, Chess, 4.

"The Salt of the Earth, 1955–1960, R&B-derived Rock & Roll," www.timeisonourside.com.

WGBH Radio. "Fresh Air: Chuck Berry, Father of Rock and Roll." Produced by Farai Chideya, March 28, 2008.

ESSENTIAL LISTENING

The Chess Box (Chess/MCA, 1988)

Chuck Berry: Johnny B. Goode: His Complete '50s Chess Recordings (Chess/MCA, 2008)

The Great Twenty-Eight (Chess, 1984)

ESSENTIAL VIEWING

Chuck Berry: Hail! Hail! Rock 'n' Roll (Taylor Hackford, Director, Delilah Studios, 1987)

Go, Johnny, Go! (Paul Landres, Director, Hal Roach Studios, 1959)

Rock Rock Rock (Will Price, Director, Vanguard Studios, 1956)

Eric Clapton

One fact more than any other is perhaps most revealing about guitarist Eric Clapton: he has been inducted into the Rock 'n' Roll Hall of Fame not once, not twice, but three times, and the case could be made that the legendary English guitarist deserves a fourth, and even a fifth.

Clapton's first induction came as a member of the Yardbirds in 1992, then with Cream in 1993, and finally as a solo artist in 2000. But it doesn't end there. His stays with the Yardbirds and Cream were both under two years, as were his epic performances with Derek and the Dominos and the purported supergroup Blind Faith with Steve Winwood, Ginger Baker, and bassist Rick Grech. Could it be that one or both of *those* vehicles will also be honored with induction? No other artist has enjoyed a triple induction, while a few (Paul McCartney, John Lennon, Michael Jackson, Neil Young, etc.) have enjoyed two.

Clapton has, throughout his career, been festooned with accolades. He has either shared in or outright won 18 Grammy awards as a songwriter, singer, and guitarist, making him one of the most respected artists of the rock era, as well as one of the most influential instrumentalists. His guitar playing in the 1960s laid the groundwork for blues, psychedelia, and hard rock, and his rock-pop songwriting over the last three decades has maintained a consistently high level of quality.

A great portion of Clapton's entire body of work is unassailable, in terms of composition, in terms of his singing, and in terms of his guitar playing. In the 1960s, Eric Clapton was an absolute wiz-kid. He earned the nickname "Slowhand" while playing guitar for the Yardbirds, John Mayall and the Bluesbreakers, Cream, Blind Faith, and Derek and the Dominos. While with Derek and the Dominos, he recorded the rock classic "Layla" with its stunning lead guitar work and moving piano outro. During the 1970s, Clapton played as a guest with some of the greatest performers of the era, and had solo hits with "Cocaine," "Lay Down Sally," "After Midnight," "Wonderful Tonight," and a cover of Bob Marley's "I Shot the Sheriff." In the 1980s and 1990s, Clapton met with even more critical and popular success and had a string of hits, including the top single "Tears in Heaven," about the tragic death of his young son.

Eric has also graced the work of many other artists as a guest player. His best-known session occurred in September 1968, when he added his distinctive guitar voice to George Harrison's evocative composition "While My Guitar Gently Weeps" on the Beatles "White" album. Clapton also strummed on high-profile recordings by artists as distinguished as Aretha Franklin, John Lennon, Bob Dylan, Elton John, Sting, and Roger Waters.

As Clapton progressed through his career, he stepped up his emphasis on pop-rock and de-emphasized his role as guitar hero. This dismayed many fans of his guitar-oriented music, which, according to many, was the best blues-based guitar rock of all time. In fact, many credit Clapton with keeping the flame of the blues alive worldwide by making it commercially viable. So, by stepping away from his Stratocaster he let his loyal legions down.

But the argument can be made that Eric Clapton is actually a better guitar player now than he was 30 years ago, both on electric and on acoustic. His sound has changed through the years. Now, playing exclusively Strats, he sounds more elegant, more like the 60-plus-year-old guitarist he is. In the 1970s and prior, he played with a stinging, ringing, classic Chicago blues-derived tone, more like a traditional Chicago electric player like Buddy Guy. Now he has added subtlety and elegance to his playing, and, at retirement age, is more multidimensional than he's ever been.

EARLY YEARS

Eric Patrick Clapton was born in March of 1945 in Surrey, England. He was the son of 16-year-old Patricia Molly Clapton and Edward Walter Fryer, a 24-year-old Canadian soldier stationed in England during World War II. Fryer returned to Canada before Eric was born, leaving his mother to raise a child on her own.

Eric's grandparents stepped in as surrogate parents and raised Eric as their own and he grew up believing his mother, Patricia, was actually his sister. His grandparents never

Courtesy of Photofest

legally adopted him, but remained his legal guardians until 1963.

Eric grew up in a house suffused with music. His grandmother played piano and his family enjoyed listening to the sounds of the big bands popular in the 1940s and early 1950s and, the story goes, his birth father was also a gifted musician. He learned of his natural father at the age of nine, and the news affected him deeply.

Introspective and polite, he was characterized as an above-average student with an aptitude for art. But after he discovered the truth about his parents, he became moody and distant. The truth scarred him emotionally and his grades dropped and he began studying art almost exclusively.

By 1958, Elvis, Little Richard, and Fats Domino introduced rock 'n' roll to the world. The young Clapton also vividly recalled seeing an electrifying performance of Jerry Lee Lewis singing "Great Balls of Fire" on his television. Eric, then 13 and excited to try his hand at music, asked for a guitar for his birthday. But the inexpensive

German-made, steel-stringed Hoyer was difficult to play and he lost interest in it. But he picked it up again two years later and started playing more consistently. His artwork suffered and he was expelled from art school for not producing enough work.

When that happened, he began listening exclusively to American blues. The rock explosion piqued his curiosity. But the blues, the foundation of that rock 'n' roll music, really excited him. Let everyone else dig rock 'n' roll, he thought. I can make the blues my own. His quiet, outsider personality pushed him to the fringes of popular music. And there resided other outsider artists like Howlin' Wolf, Muddy Waters, and the three Kings: Freddie, B.B., and Albert.

Sometime in 1962, he asked for his grandparents' help in purchasing a double cutaway Kay (a Gibson ES-335 clone) electric, similar to the ones he saw his new blues heroes playing. During this time, Eric supported himself working alongside his grandfather, a master bricklayer and plasterer.

MUSIC

Eric spent his early days in music busking around London's West End, Richmond and Kingston. In early 1963, at the age of 17, he joined his first band, the Roosters. It only lasted nine or so months, a longer tenure than his next band, the pop-oriented Casey Jones and the Engineers, which lasted only a single month. Still, the exposure these bands brought him gave Clapton an excellent reputation on the city's pub scene.

In October of 1963, Clapton got the attention of Keith Relf, an art-college classmate of Clapton's, and Paul Samwell-Smith of an up-and-coming band called the Yardbirds. At the time, the Yardbirds had been taking American blues and electrifying it, adding a British rock flavor, but still staying loyal to the Delta tradition, Clapton's singular musical love.

At first, the Yardbirds were a dream come true for Clapton. He earned his nickname, "Slowhand," (see sidebar), and recorded his first albums with the band, one of which featured a blues hero of his, *Sonny Boy Williamson and The Yardbirds,* in which the Yardbirds essentially backed Williamson.

The Yardbirds assumed the Rolling Stones' residency at the legendary Crawdaddy club and began overshadowing Jagger and Richards as the best R&B band in town. For the first few years, Giorgio Gomelsky, a bizarre character who also mentored the Stones, managed the activities of the Yardbirds.

But the band didn't discover their true sound until 1964 or so, when they stretched their R&B/blues grooves into extended jam passages they referred to as "raveups." The band simply expanded on the blues, exerting a fiercer, more heavily amplified electric base and improvising ala jazz by expanding solos and heightening tension. The dynamic worked. They became deft at bringing their din to a crescendo live, and just as it seemed about to implode, they'd take it back down again. This innovation remains as a performing device to this day.

Eric delved into the blues throughout his 18 months with the band and he solidified his reputation as one of the best young blues guitarists in London's fast-growing R&B circuit. But when the Yardbirds decided to move toward a more commercial sound with their first hit single, "For Your Love," he ditched the band, insisting he still cared deeply for the blues.

And the blues came calling. In the spring of 1965, John Mayall called Eric to invite him to play in his band called the Bluesbreakers. As a young blues enthusiast like Clapton, Mayall formed the Bluesbreakers as a vehicle for the blues, a collective of sorts, rather than

ERIC'S NICKNAMES

"God"

The phrase "Clapton is God" originated during Eric's tenure with John Mayall's Bluesbreakers. Eric was a member of the Bluesbreakers from April to late August 1965 and again from November 1965 to July 1966. It was during this time that Eric first rose to prominence in the burgeoning British Blues scene. The phrase "Clapton is God" was spray painted on a wall in the underground station in Islington, one of the boroughs in the greater London area, in the mid-1960s by an admirer. Strangely enough, it caught on and began to appear in other boroughs of London. The distinctive graffiti was captured in a photograph and spread virally around the world. A hero was made and the legend grew.

"Slowhand"

The Yardbirds' manager, Giorgio Gomelsky, christened Eric "Slowhand" early in 1964. Yardbirds rhythm guitarist Chris Dreja recalled that whenever Eric broke a guitar string during a concert, Eric would stay on stage and replace it. English audiences would wait out the delay by doing what is called a "slow handclap." Giorgio kept referring to Eric as a fast guitar player, so he put together the "slow handclap" phrase, making "Slowhand" a play on words. In a June 1999 online chat, Eric gave a slightly different version of how his nickname came about: In England, in sport, if the crowd is getting anxious, there's something called a slow handclap, which indicates boredom or frustration. Either way, it is now seen or interpreted as an ironic reference.

a firm band with a cemented lineup. Dozens of musicians passed through for various lengths of time. At least 15 different editions of the Bluesbreakers were in existence from January 1963 through mid-1970. And so it was under these rather loose terms that Clapton accepted Mayall's invite and stepped into the Bluesbreakers' lead guitar slot.

By the time he did so, Mayall had been recording for a year and gigging for much longer than that. Not surprisingly, the experience proved turbulent. Eric left once early on, choosing to tour Greece with friends. But when he returned to London, he settled in for a while, long enough to record the classic blues album, *Blues Breakers with Eric Clapton*. It was about this time that a fan spray-painted the phrase, "Clapton is God," on an Islington tube station terminal. That phrase also stuck (see sidebar). While with the Bluesbreakers, Eric also recorded a one-off, four-track session with a band called the Powerhouse. This studio band included John Paul Jones, Steve Winwood, and Jack Bruce, a precursor to Clapton's next band.

In July of 1966, Clapton left the Bluesbreakers for a second and final time and headed to join Jack Bruce and Ginger Baker in Cream, a power trio. On the precipice of psychedelic music as well as hard rock, Cream crystallized at the perfect time. The San Francisco scene had blossomed, sending paisley vibes throughout the western world. Jimi Hendrix was beginning to emerge as a force on the guitar—a force that Clapton reckoned with in many ways—and rock 'n' roll was undergoing a sea change.

Cream only recorded three albums of studio material: *Fresh Cream, Disraeli Gears, and Wheels of Fire.* But these recordings expanded Clapton's reputation from a traditional blues player to an innovative rocker. The band's sonic experimentation, the way they took blues riffs and blasted them into the future, made Cream one of the most influential rock bands of the modern era. It made all three principal members superstars, a tag that has followed Clapton like a faithful pet for going on four decades.

In hindsight, it is irrelevant to emphasize that Cream disbanded after just two years. They were so explosive and so mercurial together that the power trio format couldn't bear the weight of each one's substantial ego. They broke up after two epic nights at London's Royal Albert Hall in November of 1968.

Following Cream, Eric assembled Blind Faith, another superstar band he formed with Steve Winwood (Traffic), Ginger Baker, and Rick Grech. But a single album and a disastrous tour left the band in shambles, and Eric sought quiet refuge from egos and expectations by serving as a sideman with his friends. He desperately needed shelter from his growing fame. A friend named Delaney Bramlett of Delaney and Bonnie and Friends encouraged him to start singing. He also began writing more.

His self-titled debut was released in 1970. That same year, Eric formed still another band, Derek and the Dominos, with Jim Gordon, Carl Radle, and Bobby Whitlock from Delaney and Bonnie's band. Like Clapton's other band stints, none of which lasted longer than two years, Derek and the Dominos lasted for as long as it took to record a single album. But that album remains a classic in Clapton's canon: *Layla and Other Assorted Love Songs,* a concept album centered around Clapton's unrequited love for George Harrison's wife, Pattie Boyd, is, along with his Blues Breakers and Cream work, enduring testament to Clapton's potency as a composer, player, and performer. The band fell apart following a U.S. tour and an aborted attempt at recording a sequel to *Layla.* Clapton was devastated by the commercial failure of Derek and the Dominos, not to mention his unrequited love for Boyd, and he lapsed into heroin addiction. For three years, he locked himself into his Surrey home and dealt with his pain. He also recorded constantly.

In 1973, he kicked his drug addiction and relaunched his career with two concerts at London's Rainbow Theater organized by his friend Pete Townshend. These gigs, called *The Rainbow Concert,* represented a turning point in Clapton's career and he resurfaced following them as a solo artist. In 1974, he trotted out *461 Ocean Boulevard* and added singer-songwriter to his performance resume.

SOLO WORK

As a solo artist, Clapton de-emphasized his persona as a guitar hero and began functioning as a singer-songwriter with a penchant for ballads. He also became a hitmaker. Throughout the 1970s, Clapton churned out hits, from songs like "Cocaine" and "Lay Down Sally," to "After Midnight," "I Can't Stand It," and "Promises." Through the early 1980s the hits flowed consistently. Albums like *Slowhand* (1977), *No Reason to Cry* (1976), and *E. C. Was Here* (1975) were very successful.

That Clapton's career took a slight downturn in the mid-1980s is not surprising. He had held a very high profile for nearly 10 years, and his star faded. A 1985 performance at Live Aid boosted his sagging profile, as did the fine *Crossroads* box set which came out in 1988, a vivid reminder of his outsized talent. The collection of four CDs includes every essential performance, and because it came out so early in the life of the compact disc format, helped to establish the multidisc box set retrospective as a viable commercial proposition.

In the late 1980s, he began scoring films, and in 1992, he scored another victory of sorts, when he released an album for MTV, *Unplugged*. The recording featured the Grammy winning single "Tears in Heaven," a tribute to his five-year-old son, Conor, who died tragically after falling out of a New York City apartment window.

In 1994, Clapton succumbed to the requests of his many guitar-loving fans and, at long last, returned to his blues roots. *From the Cradle* was the guitarist's tribute to his blues heroes, featuring covers of blues classics like "Hoochie Coochie Man," "Driftin' Blues," and Lowell Fulsom's "Reconsider Baby."

"The album manages to re-create the ambience of postwar electric blues, right down to the bottomless thump of the rhythm section . . . As long as he plays his guitar, he can't fail —his solos are white-hot and evocative, original and captivating" (Erlewine, Stephen Thomas, www.allmusic.com).

After a few experiments—one with electronica (*Retail Therapy*) and one with soul (*Pilgrim*)—he returned to the blues again when he recorded with one of his idols, B.B. King. *Riding with the King*, released in 2000, sold 500,000 units and satisfied the blues craving that his fans have had since the 1960s. In 2004, the guitarist mined more blues inspiration with *Me and Mr. Johnson*, an album-length tribute to his seminal influence, the legendary bluesman Robert Johnson.

In 2005, Clapton revisited another phase of his past when he reunited with Cream for a four-night stand at the Royal Albert Hall in London, the same place they had played their farewell show 37 years previous.

Technique/Style

Eric Clapton developed his reputation in, roughly, his first decade as a recording artist. First with the Yardbirds, then with the Bluesbreakers, and on to Cream and Derek and the Dominos, Clapton asserted himself as one of the all-time masters of the modern electric guitar. He came by this high praise in a number of ways.

First, he is an impeccable architect of solos. He can build a solo up slowly, weaving in groups of well-constructed modal riffs and small triad clusters, and bring it all to a crushing apex, before bringing it back down again. His emotional puissance and precisely executed vibrato and bends exhilarated audiences. For Clapton, his solos are never about excessive speed and soaring pyrotechnics. Rather, they are beautifully executed, emotionally intense, and perfectly pitched.

He disagreed when interviewed by Peter Guralnick. "I am very limited in my technique, really, so what matters in my playing is the simplicity of it and that it gets to the point. Rather than playing around everything . . . It's not what is said but how it's said. Not how much is said, but the way it's said" (unattributed).

Clapton's dexterity in vocalizing a blues-based solo with genuine architecture, pick attack, and flawless execution—both live and in the studio—is the one thing he did perhaps better than any other player of his time, and certainly in the blues rock idiom. It was no accident that Hendrix demanded meeting Clapton as one of the conditions for his extradition to England. As an up-and-coming player himself, Hendrix knew immediately after hearing Clapton that it was something he'd never heard before, both in content and in quality.

Another playing trait that Clapton possesses is tremendous finger vibrato. This technical aspect takes years of practice to master; the frequency and tonality of good vibrato is a skill that often comes with age and experience. It also requires tremendous strength, not to mention intuition. Additionally, he excelled at spontaneous alternate picking, like a good and skillful jazz player. This agility separated him from his peers and enabled him to create some of rock's greatest solos. With Clapton, you could always trace the magic of his sound back to his fingers.

In Cream, Clapton played within a looser framework, especially live. Their songs were not riff based and so when it came time for the band members to embark, they set off for parts unknown. This was the furthest "out" Clapton ventured as a player. Still, his playing was rather conventional in comparison to say, Hendrix, who was prone frequently to flights of fancy and various effects, not to mention a peer that exerted substantial influence on Clapton in the mid-1960s.

EQUIPMENT/GEAR

Clapton's choice of electric guitars has been as notable as the man himself. Just as the players he loved influenced him to buy his guitars, so Clapton has exerted a crucial influence in popularizing particular styles of electric guitars. While in the Yardbirds , Clapton played both a Fender Telecaster and a cherry red Gibson ES-335 from 1964. Beginning in 1965, Clapton turned to Gibsons exclusively after picking up a used Les Paul Sunburst Standard guitar at a London guitar store.

Early on, while with the group Cream, the guitarist had that Standard stolen. He found another comparable one and continued to play Les Pauls in Cream until 1967. It was at this time that he acquired his most famous guitar, at least of this phase in his career, a 1964 Gibson SG. The next year, Clapton picked up another Gibson, this time a Firebird, and he started using the Gibson ES-335 as well. Clapton played this infamous 335 at his last Cream show, which went down in the winter of 1968. He also employed the 335 during his short-lived time with the supergroup Blind Faith, and he used it for his slide work in the 1970s. Not long after this time, Gibson produced a limited run of "Crossroads 335" replicas.

On the Beatles' famous recording of "While My Guitar Gently Weeps," Clapton played a refinished Les Paul, then gave the guitar to his good friend George Harrison. Harrison's friend, Jackie Lomax, came into possession of Clapton's SG, and Lomax eventually sold it to Todd Rundgren for a mere $500 in 1972. Rundgren restored the guitar and called it "Sunny" after Cream's epic rock track, "Sunshine of Your Love." Rundgren later sold "Sunny" at auction for $150,000.

In late 1969, Clapton made the switch to the Fender Stratocaster. First was "Brownie," the Strat used during the recording of the *Eric Clapton* album. "Brownie" took a backseat to the most famous of all Clapton's guitars, "Blackie." The story of "Blackie" goes like this: In November of 1970, Eric bought six Strats at a Nashville guitar shop while on tour with Derek and the Dominos. He gave one each to George Harrison, Steve Winwood, and Pete Townshend, then used the best parts of the other three to create "Blackie." It remained Clapton's favorite guitar until its retirement in 1985. Clapton referred to the famous 1956/57 Strat as a "mongrel."

Clapton has also been honored with a signature-model 000-28EC and 000-42EC Martin acoustic guitars. Clapton plays a custom 000-ECHF Martin these days. In 1988, Fender honored Clapton with the introduction of his own signature Eric Clapton Strat, an honor bestowed on only a very small handful of players. In addition, the Fender Custom Shop has produced a limited run of 275 "Blackie" replicas, precise in every detail right down to the "Duck Brothers" flight case. It's also artificially aged using Fender's "Relic" process to simulate 30 years of wear and tear.

In 1999, Clapton auctioned off 100 of his guitars to help finance and support the Crossroads Centre in Antigua, a treatment base for addictive disorders like drugs and alcohol addiction. He sold "Blackie" as well as his 1939 000-42 Martin that he played on the *Unplugged* album for over a million dollars combined. All told, sales raised over $5 million for the Centre.

AMPS

"With Cream I always had two Marshalls set up to play through but I think it was just so I could have one as spare. I usually used only one 100-watt amp. I'd turn the amp and guitar all the way up" (Eric Clapton interview, *Guitar Player,* June 1970, n.p.).

Two stacks were typically set up on stage, but one was a spare.

When Cream formed in 1966, the stacks were nearly required among power bands. Eric upgraded from his Bluesbreaker combo rig to a Marshall stack: Marshall 1959 100-watt Plexi-panelled Superlead Amplifier (3-switch), one 1960 75-watt 4x12 Angle Front Cabinet, and one 1960B 75-watt 4x12 Flat Front Cabinet (extra tall version). This was set with . . . "full on everything, full treble, full bass and full presence" as this was the way he had set the combo. Volume and tonal variations were handled from the guitar controls.

On his most recent world tour, which ended in 2007, Clapton's setup included: Signature Fender Strats, Martin Acoustics (EC signature models), Fender Custom Shop Tweed Twin Amp (a 1957 Tweed Reissue), Leslie Speaker, Samson wireless pack, Vox Wah-Wah pedal, Boss TR-2 Tremolo pedal, and a box to switch from the amp to the Leslie and back.

During his previous world tour, back in 2004, Clapton used Cornell Amplifiers with Tone Tubby Speakers with hemp cones inside the cabinets for his electric guitars. Built by Dennis Cornell, the Eric Clapton Custom 80 (Single Channel) looks very much like a Fender Twin, but sounds bluer with a lot more middle. Designed to his exact specifications, the Custom 80 is made from birch ply and covered in "Fender tweed" that is treated to look old. In addition to this amp, Eric used a Fender Woody for the Robert Johnson set in the middle of each concert during the same 2004 tour. His effects pedals for the 2004 tour were limited to a tri-stereo chorus (Boss Chorus CE-3), a Leslie pedal, a Jim Dunlop 535 Crybaby Wah-Wah pedal (six way selectable), and a box to switch from the amp to the Leslie or to select both. Eric does not use an overdrive pedal. He gets all of the overdrive from the 25 dB boost in his guitar, a Fender Eric Clapton Signature Stratocaster. He also used a Samson Synthetics wireless system on stage. His Martin 000-28EC goes through an Avalon DI box (www.whereseric.com).

ESSENTIAL READING

Clapton, Eric. *Clapton, the Autobiography.* New York: Broadway, 2007.
Clapton, Eric interview. *Guitar Player,* June 1970, n.p.
Erlewine, Stephen Thomas. www.allmusic.com.
Shapiro, Harry. *Eric Clapton: Lost in the Blues.* New York: Da Capo, 1992.

ESSENTIAL WORK

Blind Faith: "Another Ticket" (1969)
Bluesbreakers: "All Your Love," "Hideaway" (1965)

Cream: "I'm So Glad," "Tale of Brave Ulysses" (1967)
Derek and the Dominos: "Layla," "Bell Bottom Blues," "Why Does Love Got to Be So Sad?" (1970)
Eric Clapton: "Tears in Heaven," "Wonderful Tonight" (1977)

ESSENTIAL LISTENING

Bluesbreakers with Eric Clapton (Deram, 1966)
Disraeli Gears (Polydor, 1967)
461 Ocean Boulevard (Polydor, 1974)
Layla and Other Assorted Love Songs (Polydor, 1970)
Slowhand (Polydor, 1977)
Unplugged (Reprise, 1992)

Kurt Cobain

Among the many controversial artists of the rock generation, Kurt Cobain is one of the most hotly debated. This is the case for a variety of reasons. His work with Nirvana, the "grunge" band he formed in the late 1980s, was never intended to engender a sea change in music, but it did. His unassuming but melodically epic style of singing and songwriting never meant to reach the ears of millions of fans worldwide, but it did. And he never intended his guitar playing, sloppy and imprecise, to set a standard for all rock music—alternative and otherwise—in the 1990s, but, finally, it did.

We, as his audience, were constantly asked to decide whether or not to take him seriously. We would guess and second guess about his ambition and goals. He was a star, but said he didn't want to be one. He was a guitar player of substantial renown, but insisted he was more of a hamfisted dilettante on the instrument. Some agreed with his intentions and assessments. Many disagreed. Today, his place in the canon of rock 'n' roll icons is assured. But his place among the greatest rock guitar players of that same canon is more undetermined.

Cobain's controversial fight with fame contributed to his tragic death in 1994. Throughout his career he was an antihero, an embattled artist that grappled constantly with his notoriety. Cobain purposely knocked the arms off his works of art so that he wouldn't be considered "polished." He struggled with the idea of even having fans. While those who worshipped him, and they were legion, inspired him to write often brilliant music, he despised them at the same time, accusing them of trying to make him something he truly did not want to be: a star.

Grunge music's rise, first in the Pacific Northwest, then throughout the country and Britain, served to illuminate the artistry of many unassuming rockers. Kurt Cobain was at the epicenter of that rise and in many ways became the flannel shirt/ripped jeans genre's poster boy and prototype.

Of course, other grunge-styled bands ascended the ranks of rock music at the same time: Pearl Jam, Soundgarden, Mudhoney, Alice in Chains, to name the best known. Eyes within the music industry began turning toward Seattle as the next hot spot at the onset of the 1990s. The city had become a geyser of talented, independently minded bands.

But when Nirvana issued their second album, *Nevermind,* in September of 1991, that geyser exploded, sending Nirvana and a font of other acts soaring to stardom. Alice in Chains (*Facelift*), Pearl Jam (*Ten*), Soundgarden (*Ultramega OK*) all made an impact on the charts. *Nevermind* and company vaulted grunge, and alternative music in general, to a commercially viable position, breathing the rarified air at the top of the charts.

Because of its popularity, *Nevermind* also changed the way people would hear popular music in the 1990s. Radio and music television had scrapped their pop playlists completely and replaced them with playlists consisting mainly of something now known as "Alternative Rock." Perhaps no other record in the modern era, and inarguably in the alternative era, would have so great an impact. It virtually defined every other rock subgenre that would follow and obliterated the memory of the music it immediately followed; namely, the pop or "hair" metal of the late 1980s.

Nirvana's success not only changed what fans wanted from their rock 'n' roll, it also dictated what they didn't want to hear. The antimusician stance of Kurt Cobain, primarily, and so many of his grunge colleagues—that is, his relative disdain for slick, overproduced material—made those "hair" metal bands and commercial pop groups look like has-beens. Suddenly, thanks to Nirvana and grunge's image and sound any pretense of glamour seemed dated and irrelevant. Grunge and the underground music scene had taken over the mainstream and stripped away everything but the music.

But the more prominent and successful Nirvana became, the less comfortable Kurt Cobain had become. Inadvertently and quite unexpectedly, he became an icon, a spokesperson for a generation. But the limelight made him feel uncomfortable in his own skin. When he committed suicide in 1994, America was saddened, but not shocked.

"Thank you all from the pit of my burning, nauseous stomach for your letters and concern during the past years," he wrote in his suicide note. "I'm too much of an erratic, moody baby! I don't have the passion anymore, and so remember, it's better to burn out than to fade away."

Cobain's death put an emphatic end to the grunge movement in Seattle. Still, Nirvana's success changed the course of rock music in the 1990s. In the process, it provided a dividing line between the earlier Baby Boomer generation and the subsequent, disaffected legion known as Generation X-ers.

Nirvana's deep impression also sent repercussions through Cobain's own musical idols, in Cobain elegies like Neil Young's *Sleeps with Angels* album and Patti Smith's tune "About a Boy." He had touched everyone, at least in the music industry, with his voice and guitar. And that impact is still being felt today.

MUSIC

Kurt Cobain was born on February 20, 1967 in Hoquiam, Washington. He grew up in a broken home in Aberdeen, Washington. He had a dismal adolescence, and, like many others in his situation, looked to music for his escape. He met one of those simpatico spirits, Chris Novoselic, at a rehearsal for a local punk band called Melvins. Together, under the name Ted, Ed, and Fred, among a couple of other names, they started playing small gigs around Seattle and Tacoma, with drummer Dale Crover, later of Melvins, in tow.

Both Cobain and Novoselic had strong feelings of alienation, social and political, so the rebellious nature of punk rock resonated deeply. Early on, they honed their sound at gigs around the Olympia area, particularly at the liberal clearinghouse for independent music, Evergreen State College. As they matured their sound reflected their influences more profoundly, fusing their affinity for Led Zeppelin and Black Sabbath with punk.

They entered the recording studio in January of 1988, calling itself Nirvana, to lay down a few demos. Producer Jack Endino captured the performances in six hours, and gave the tapes to a young label executive, Jonathan Poneman, at Sub Pop Records. Later that year, now with drummer Chad Channing and second guitarist Jason Everman in the lineup, Sub Pop released *Bleach*, rather quietly but to good reviews.

THE SEATTLE SOUND

When Kurt Cobain and Chris Novoselic formed Nirvana in 1987, they, like other musicians in the grunge movement, had brought with them an upbringing in the classic rock and metal of the 1970s. Nirvana was rooted in 1980s indie rock as well, the sound around Seattle and elsewhere. They grew up watching Melvins, a Black Sabbath-inspired metal/noise band that indirectly influenced more area bands than any other with their extreme waves of unpredictable rumbling. Nirvana also dug deeply into the D-I-Y realm of bands in the surrounding area, such as Olympia, and overseas.

The first wave of grunge bands—Green River, Mudhoney, and Soundgarden in particular—was characterized by a sludgy guitar sound with blasts of distortion, fuzz, and feedback. Classic grunge fused hardcore punk with heavy metal; they sported punk attitudes, and the music possessed a raw sound and similar lyrical concerns.

These bands also shared a certain recklessness, a combination of passion and an aversion to conformity. Generally, the musicianship was coarse, even unskilled, yet the energy and urgency of the music gave these works emotional gravity and physical power. They often sang of social alienation, apathy, confinement, and a desire for freedom.

The music scene in Seattle, like the epic scenes in mid-1960s San Francisco and early 1990s London, was also built on humor and sarcasm. The generation of young people that had come of age during the Reagan years had grown disaffected by the overwhelming affluence, some would say greed, of the time, an indulgence they witnessed yet never participated in. Coined "Slackers" or "Generation X-ers" because they (seemingly) couldn't be bothered with politics, social causes, careers, or the general state of humanity, these teens and 20-somethings were jaded and media-savvy. They were ready for the real world, but not inspired to become a part of what they saw. They were disillusioned by politics and pop culture. To them, even punk rock, long a bastion of free and liberal thinking, had become boring and predictable. Worse still was that popular music at the time was thought by many to be abysmal. The synthesizer pop and the spandex and teased hair of 1980's metal did little to satisfy the appetites of serious music fans.

By the late 1980s, all of these styles had expired, run their course. They had worn music fans down with shallow expression and uninspired writing. Slackers were by and large looking for something to quench their sardonic humor and dissatisfaction. Indeed, they were ready for a change, both culturally and musically. They'd soon receive both.

As grunge and the Seattle scene gained momentum, musicians, inspired by the city's Everyman approach to music-making, assembled bands, hundreds of them. In the process, they gave little consideration to the rock star posing of their youth, choosing instead to dress down; most wore flannel shirts and jeans—the same clothes they wore to their day jobs. Their down-to-earth style closed the gap between audience and performer, essentially knocking the rock star image off its pedestal and placing it on the floor next to the ticket-buyer. In the process, rock 'n' roll became infinitely more accessible, more immediate, and music fans responded.

Cobain and the band toured with greater frequency and began building a buzz based on their dynamic live shows. But it did not take long for the road to take its toll on Kurt. Performing wore him down. He also had a sensitive stomach and was prone to ulcers. He began leaning on drugs to alleviate the pain.

AP photo

In April of 1990, the trio, now with new drummer Dave Grohl, went in to a Madison, Wisconsin studio with producer Butch Vig to lay down more music. They returned to the studio in May and June of the next year to finish. They released *Nevermind* in September of 1991 and hit the road. Though the band had little idea of the chart impact *Nevermind* would soon make, they did know something was up. Shows were selling out. Bigger venues were being booked, and the buzz grew ever louder. The record's first single, "Smells Like Teen Spirit," reached #1 on the charts, and was followed by a handful of other hits. The album itself knocked Michael Jackson out of the top spot, putting the awkward guys from the Washington backwoods in a very unfamiliar, and uncomfortable, place: in the spotlight.

Magazines featured the band on its covers. Cobain became a spokesperson, if a somewhat reluctant one, for the burgeoning alternative rock scene. Based on the commercial viability Nirvana embodied, grunge bands began popping up and getting signed not just in Seattle, but all over the country. Nirvana opened the door, only to see a deluge of uninvited guests flood the music industry's dance floor.

To cope with all of the attention Cobain began to indulge further in drugs, specifically heroin. He met the outspoken and audacious Courtney Love—a frontperson of her own band Hole—at a concert in 1991, and they were married in Hawaii the following year. A daughter, Frances Bean, was born six months later. The pull of his family combined with the stress of fame weighed heavily on Cobain, whose slight shoulders were not built for all the responsibility.

In early 1993, the band began laying down music for its third album, *In Utero,* with brash producer Steve Albini. The choice of producer was telling: Albini's was considered extreme and uncompromising, a reputation Cobain considered critical at this crossroads in his career. He wanted desperately to retain, or regain, his own credibility after his brethren branded him a "sellout" after the success of *Nevermind.*

Despite its sandpapery edges and excessive bluster, *In Utero* hit #1 when it was released in the fall of 1993. Nirvana's fame escalated, and they toured stadiums and large venues worldwide to close out the year. In January of 1994, they returned to the States to play Seattle. In February, Nirvana flew back to Europe, where they gigged in France, Italy, and Germany. On March 5, Kurt, plagued by stomach problems and addicted to pain killers and heroin, attempted suicide while staying in Rome. He had taken more than 50 pills and briefly lapsed into a coma.

He and wife Courtney returned to the States in late March after his recovery. Courtney organized an intervention, but Kurt resisted. Finally, on March 30, he checked into the Exodus Recovery Center in Los Angeles. But his recovery was short-lived; he fled on April 1, after telling staff members he was going outside for a cigarette.

The ride ended abruptly on April 8, when Kurt was found dead in a room above the garage of the couple's Seattle home. An electrician hired to install an alarm system made the grim discovery. Cobain died as a result of a self-inflicted .20-gauge shotgun wound to the head.

Despite its immense impact on the world of modern rock music, Nirvana's recording career was relatively short-lived and its discography is disappointingly curt. The fact is the band only recorded for five short years. In the beginning, after their unofficial early work, Nirvana released a few singles prior to their debut, *Bleach,* one of which, "Spank Thru," established its post-Zeppelin sound quite well. *Bleach* itself carried that post-Zeppelin theme through, with sound-defining songs like "Negative Creep" and "Floyd the Barber."

Nevermind, of course, is the Nirvana recording that has come to define its sound, with its punky melodicism and archetypal grunge production. *In Utero* finds the pendulum swinging clearly in the opposite direction, with an uncompromising sound, courtesy of punk producer Steve Albini (Big Black, the Pixies) and songs that seemed to come from a more defiant place inside Kurt Cobain. It would be his parry in a duel he had with superstardom. Many refer to it as his suicide note.

Posthumous works continued, including an *MTV Unplugged Live in New York,* on which the band demonstrated its depth and diversity, covering songs like David Bowie's "The Man Who Fell to Earth" and Lead Belly's "Where Did You Sleep Last Night?" It is a naked and soul-bearing recording, made all the more poignant given the circumstances of Cobain's death and the band's tragic dissolution. A live disc called *From the Muddy Banks of the Wishkah,* the second posthumous album, presents the band in much of its roaring glory. It doesn't feature all of its best songs—"All Apologies," "Come as You Are," and "About a Girl" are all missing—but it is a searing performance and an accurate representation of Cobain, Grohl, and Novoselic's onstage potency.

Due to some contentious lawsuits regarding the ownership and executorship of the Nirvana catalog, it took some time for posthumous collections to emerge. The band had legal wrangles with Cobain's widow, Courtney Love, about how Cobain would have wished his legacy to be presented. Finally, in the fall of 2002, *Nirvana* came out, a spotty collection of hits and choice album cuts that also included a new single, "You Know You're Right," which made some impact on radio at the time.

TECHNIQUE/STYLE

The 1990s was a time when the barriers came down and Nirvana helped unhinge them. The decade was a smorgasbord of microgenres, slivers of styles that attracted, repelled, and cross-pollinated each other. The age barrier disappeared as different generations ripped off each other's styles and sounds and mashed them together with their own. New music rubbed shoulders with old styles, and suddenly anything new earned at least 15 minutes of fame.

Grunge was one of those styles. And *Nevermind* was the album that popularized grunge, the so-called "Seattle Sound." No album in modern rock 'n' roll history had such an overwhelming impact on a generation of music fans. *Nevermind*'s slashing riffs, throat-burning vocals and vague, ambiguous songwriting, brought home by the rhythmic bassist Novoselic and muscular drummer Dave Grohl, injected rock 'n' roll with a danger and edginess it hadn't seen since the 1970s.

Kurt Cobain's guitar was pivotal in the mix, raging in distortion, with heavy doses of melody and simple, single-note solos. His genius, though, in songs such as "Lithium," "Breed," and "Smells Like Teen Spirit" was the soft-loud dynamic he created between verse and chorus, restraint and assault. Cobain loved pop music, too, and this assault was tempered by his affection for the Beatles and their melodies. *Nevermind* producer Butch Vig remembers Cobain playing John Lennon's "Julia" repeatedly at those recording sessions. This dichotomy, dividing his passions for punk, hard rock, and pop music, is found at the center of Nirvana's distinctive craft.

The Beatles were an early and important musical influence on Cobain. Cobain expressed a particular fondness for John Lennon, whom he called his "idol" in his journals. Cobain once related that he wrote "About a Girl" after spending three hours listening to *Meet the Beatles*. He was heavily influenced by hardcore and often paid homage to bands like Black Flag and the Sex Pistols for contributing to his style and attitude.

Even with all of Cobain's indie influences, Nirvana's early style was dominated by the major rock bands of the 1970s, including Black Sabbath, Led Zeppelin, Kiss, and Neil Young. In its earliest incarnations, Kurt and his bands would cover Zeppelin tunes like "Whole Lotta Love" and "Heartbreaker." Cobain also reached into earlier eras for inspiration. On their "Unplugged" show on MTV, the band ended the set with "Where Did You Sleep Last Night?" an old folk song popularized by Lead Belly. He loved kitschy bands, too, like the Knack and the Bay City Rollers, pure pop acts otherwise known as guilty pleasures. All of these influences seeped into his songwriting.

Cobain also took advantage of his pedestal by boosting his favorite performers during his period of influence. At the major U.K. concert called the Reading Festival, Cobain invited Eugene Kelly of the Vaselines onstage for a duet of "Molly's Lips," a moment Cobain later proclaimed to be one of the proudest moments of his life. In 1993, when he decided that he wanted a second guitarist to help him on stage, he recruited Pat Smear of the legendary L.A. punk band the Germs. When rehearsals of three Meat Puppets covers for Nirvana's 1993 performance for "MTV Unplugged" had stalled, Cobain recruited the band's Curt and Cris Kirkwood to join them on stage to perform the songs. Cobain's respect and appreciation for these acts bolstered their audiences significantly, and in some cases kept or resurrected their careers.

EQUIPMENT/GEAR

Kurt's guitar sound set the tone for 1990s alternative rock, but its basic elements were simple. For the *Nevermind* sessions in particular, he employed a late 1960s Fender Mustang, (his first real love), a 1966 Fender Jaguar with DiMarzio pickups and several new Stratocasters with humbuckers in the bridge positions. And while he didn't favor Gibsons, early on he did play an Epiphone SG and a redburst Epiphone ET270.

"The '66 Jaguar. That's the guitar I polish and baby—I refuse to let anyone touch it when I jump into the crowd. [laughs] Lately, I've been using a Strat live, because I don't want to ruin my Mustang yet. I like to use Japanese Strats because they're a bit cheaper, and the frets are smaller than the American version's" (Gilbert, Jeff, *Guitar World*, February 1992).

Cobain also worked with the Fender Custom Shop to develop the "Jag-Stang," a very functional combination of Fender's Jaguar and Mustang designs. To combine the two, he took photos of each and literally pieced them together to see how they'd look. He conceived the style and Fender complied, offering the details and contours Kurt had requested.

The guitar featured a Mustang-style short-scale neck on a body that borrows from both designs. There's a DiMarzio humbucking pickup at the bridge, and a Texas Special single coil at the neck, tilted at the same angle as on a Mustang. Cobain was quite satisfied with the guitar, telling the folks at Fender,

> Ever since I started playing, I've always liked certain things about certain guitars but could never find the perfect mix of everything I was looking for. The Jag-Stang is the closest thing I know. And I like the idea of having a quality instrument on the market with no preconceived notions attached. In a way, it's perfect for me to attach my name to the Jag-Stang, in that I'm the anti-guitar hero—I can barely play the things myself.

He also loved effects, and his principal favorites were a Boss DS-1 distortion pedal, a Roland EF-1 distortion pedal, and an Electro-Harmonix Small Clone Chorus. Kurt's go-to amplifier was a Mesa/Boogie Studio .22, but he also used a Fender Bassman and a Vox AC30. Cobain insisted on recording live, with few overdubs. Then he'd go back and double up the rhythm guitars and touch up solos. Live, anything goes. By one fan's unofficial count, he smashed close to 300 guitars on stage. He first smashed a guitar in a concert in the Evergreen State College, Washington, on Halloween night, 1988.

Cobain's nonchalant attitude toward playing is evident in this exchange with *Guitar World*'s Jeff Gilbert.

GW: The acoustic guitar you play on "Polly" sounds flat.

Kurt: That's a $20 junk shop Stella. I didn't bother changing the strings. It barely stays in tune. In fact, I have to use duct tape to hold the tuning keys in place.

GW: Considering how violently you play the guitar. I have to assume you use pretty heavy-duty strings.

Kurt: Yeah. And I keep blowing up amplifiers, so I use whatever I can find at junk shops. Junk is always best. (Gilbert, 1992)

Stylistically, Cobain was a primitive player, who changed music more with his songs than with his technique. In fact, he is one of rock guitar's antiheroes, revered by regular fans, but despised by more technical guitar aficionados. Cobain is often seen as the player who killed guitar playing in rock. When Nirvana stormed the scene, it laid waste to everything that came before it, including the heretofore popular hair metal bands, all of which featured spectacular guitar playing—also known as "shredding."

Following the ascension of Nirvana, guitar playing became accessible again, as if anyone could pick up the guitar and lead a band. Nirvana's popularity prompted thousands of kids to play guitar and start bands; the results of this enthusiasm are still being heard today.

ESSENTIAL READING

Cobain, Kurt. *Kurt Cobain: Journals.* New York: Riverhead Books, 2002.
DeRogatis, Jim. *Milk It!: Collected Musings on the Alternative Music Explosion of the '90s.* New York: Da Capo Press, 2003.
Erlewine, Michael, Vladimir Bogdanov, Chris Woodstra, Stephen Thomas Erlewine, and Richie Unterberger, eds. *All Music Guide to Rock.* San Francisco: Miller Freeman, 1997.
Gilbert, Jeff. *Guitar World,* February 1992.
True, Everett. *Live Through This: American Rock Music in the '90s.* London: Virgin, 2001.

ESSENTIAL WORK

"Been a Son" (1991)
"Come as You Are" (1991)
"Floyd the Barber" (1989)
"Lithium" (1991)
"Love Buzz" (1989)
"Smells Like Teen Spirit" (1991)
"Spank Thru" (1988)

ESSENTIAL LISTENING

Bleach (Sub Pop, 1989)
From the Muddy Banks of the Wishkah (DGC, 1996)
In Utero (DGC, 1993)
Nevermind (DGC, 1991)

The Edge

From the memorable opening notes of "I Will Follow" from U2's 1980 debut masterpiece, *Boy,* to the explosive rock power that informed the band's Grammy-winning *How to Dismantle an Atomic Bomb* in 2002, the guitarist who calls himself the Edge has created a guitar sound unlike any other in the short history of modern rock music.

They roared out of Dublin with a handful of populist, spiritually oriented anthems. Paul Hewson, Dave Evans, Adam Clayton, and Larry Mullen Jr. were barely teens when their sound hit audiences and airwaves. But it came across as astonishingly original. It screamed with urgency, rang out with earnestness, and rocked the house in a deep and meaningful way.

Central to the band's sound was Evan's chiming guitar. It sounded more like the trumpet of an angel than the pummeling power chords of the rock and punk that had immediately preceded it.

The sound resonated and the band quickly gained a commercial foothold. Fans were drawn to the band's credibility, the novelty in Evans' guitar, and the passion of U2's live shows. They approached each album in their first decade with genuine sincerity and passion. Bono and the boys seemed to reach deeper inside themselves with subsequent releases, outdoing themselves in terms of quality and innovation. For albums like *The Unforgettable Fire* and *The Joshua Tree,* response grew exponentially bigger until they were one of the world's most popular acts.

Following in the footsteps of the Beatles, the Band, and the Who, U2 were the fourth band ever to land on the cover of *Time* magazine. The April 29, 1987 cover featured the band's name in flames with the headline, "Rock's Hottest Ticket." *Rolling Stone* magazine named U2 "The Band of the '80s."

In their second decade together, the band added an ironic edge to their sound, beginning with 1992's Zoo TV Tour, a flashy extravaganza that seemed to run against the grain of the band's organic approach. At the very least it heralded a new phase. *Zooropa,* a quirky techno album followed, deepening the band's commitment to change. Yet despite the radical departure, and the hullabaloo created by it among fans, U2 soldiered on, following their own very distinctive muse.

In the process, the band glamorized its image slightly. Bono relented to his superstar status and became a credible spokesman for various causes, social and political. He actually became the first person to be nominated for a Grammy, an Academy Award, and a Noble prize.

Still, if Bono was the voice of the band, Evans, aka the Edge, was its sound. Not only did it become one of the most recognizable guitar sounds in the modern age of rock, it also launched a million imitators, guitarists who refrained from picking up on power chords in favor of the Edge's more progressive and inventive licks.

> I've always liked trying to take the guitar in a different direction. There are a lot of guitarists out there who play in a conventional way and do extremely well, so I don't really feel the need to tread that ground too. I'm always looking for territory that is more unique to me. For me it was liberating to see that sound and texture could really make a big statement in our new songs. I'm still fascinated by melodies, and I'm certainly not leaving that behind, but I think that for some of these songs it was a good twist to not do a conventional guitar hook kind of melody but to try to find some extraordinary sound that could create the same effect. (Gill, Chris, "In Excess," *Guitar World*, September 1997)

EARLY YEARS

David Howell Evans was born on August 8, 1961 in Barking, Essex, in East London, to Gwenda and Garvin Evans. When he was a year old, the family, including little sister Gillian and older brother Richard, moved to Dublin. There, David grew up as a shy, intelligent kid that excelled in school, first at St. Andrew's Primary School and then at Mount Temple High School.

Evans' parents, both of Welsh descent, sang in local choirs and in fact the Evans family enjoyed an active spiritual life. Music was always a part of family life as well. However, it was never the focus until Gwenda bought son Richard a used white acoustic guitar for a pound at a fund-raising sale at a local convent. Soon both brothers were playing a little, jamming on Beatles tunes.

In the fall of 1976, Evans saw a posting on the Mount Temple school bulletin board advertising a band audition. Evans was the first to respond. At the audition, held by classmate Larry Mullen in his family's kitchen, Evans came with his brother Richard, and met a few other school musicians, including Adam Clayton and another aspiring guitarist named Paul Hewson.

> I think between us there was one kit of drums, one bass without amp ("I had a purple Marshall amp with a tatty little speaker that used to blow up every time I wound it up," protested Adam), one borrowed electric guitar and a borrowed amplifier. It was like first day in the army, everyone was knocked into shape and telling everyone else what to do. It was Larry's kitchen so he was sort of in charge, but he was only really interested in playing drums, so eventually it winnowed down from four lead guitarists to three, then two, then Bono started to concentrate fully on vocals, so it developed from there. (Gill, 1997)

Evans, only 15, demonstrated excellent skills and was accepted into the band as one of two guitar players, the other being his brother. His parents still had designs on their sons going to the university to study medicine. But, now that son David had met a group of boys he felt comfortable playing music with, plans changed. When he finished high school, he told his parents he and the band were going to take a year off the career path, to see where their music would take them.

MUSIC

Together, they decided on a band name: "Feedback." The year was 1976 and punk had begun sweeping through Britain. "Feedback," one of the only musical terms they were familiar with, embraced the new punk style and began playing gigs. In March 1977, the band changed their name to "the Hype." Dick Evans, older and at college, was becoming the odd man out. The rest of the band was leaning toward the idea of downsizing to a four-piece and he was "phased out" in March 1978.

During Dick Evans' farewell concert, consisting of covers, he ceremoniously walked offstage. He'd later join the Dublin band called the Virgin Prunes. The remaining four band members completed the set playing original material as "U2," a name suggested by a family friend of Clayton's named Steve Averill.

Hewson, singer and front man, had begun calling himself "Bono Vox." He in turn baptized Evans "The Edge" because of the sharp features of his face, as well as for the sharp way Evans "observed things." Edge learned guitar mainly by playing over records that the rest of the band supplied him with. Rory Gallagher and Tom Verlaine were early influences, although the fledgling U2 covered anything from the Moody Blues to the Sex Pistols.

WHAT'S IN A NICKNAME?

There is considerable speculation as to how the Edge received his nickname. Many credit Bono with originating it. Once he made reference to the name in the commentary track of the movie *The Million Dollar Hotel,* saying that the Edge tends to stand close to the edges of buildings because of his comfort with heights. A second theory states that Edge got his name due to his "edgy" guitar style, while a third posits that Edge rarely got into the middle of anything, and therefore always stood on the edge.

In still another interview, Bono explained that the name came from the unique profile of Evans's face and nose, as well as the affinity the guitar player had for walking on the edges of very high places, like walls, bridges, and tall buildings.

The book *U2 by U2* states that his nickname comes from, as Bono mentions, his angular facial features, which is also supported by the man himself. In an interview with Ireland's Channel 4 program *T4,* Evans was asked how he came by his nickname, and he replied simply, "It's the nose."

After 18 months of rehearsals, the band was ready to get busy. On St. Patrick's Day in 1978, U2 won a talent show in Limerick, Ireland. One of the judges for the show happened to be CBS Records' Jackie Hayden; they won the contest, earning a £500 prize. Hayden was impressed enough with the band that he gave them studio time to record their first demo. They made their demo at Keystone Studios in Dublin, in April 1978. During this nascent time, Edge worked hard at developing a distinctive flair. He couldn't play guitar well technically speaking, so he made up for it with his own innovations. (More on that subject later.)

Their first foray into recording involved releasing a few inconsequential singles. They compiled those singles with a three-song EP, called U2-3, in 1979. It topped the charts in their homeland. While the recording didn't sell particularly well outside of Ireland, they had definitely solidified a reputation around Dublin as a "can't miss" show. In December 1979, U2 performed in London for their first shows outside Ireland, although they failed to get much attention from audiences or critics. Based on this word-of-mouth, Island Record executives came to witness the band, and signed them to a contract in 1980. Paul McGuinness became U2's manager.

Released on October of 1980, U2's debut album, *Boy,* included the minor hit "I Will Follow," the first of many anthems. The track, built around a repetitive, echo drenched guitar riff, would establish an early blueprint for the Edge's guitar style. *Boy,* produced by Steve Lillywhite, also helped to shape the group's unique sound in other ways, with electronic flourishes, deep, resonant vocals, and anthemic song structures.

It was met with critical praise and is considered one of the more auspicious debuts in rock history. That album's release was followed by U2's first tour beyond Ireland and the United Kingdom.

*   *   *

The band's second album, *October,* was released in 1981. Fans and music critics quickly made note of the band's spiritual lyrics. In fact, Bono, Evans, and Mullen were committed Christians and made little effort to hide that fact. The three band members joined a religious group in Dublin called "Shalom," which led all three to question the relationship between their Christian faith and their more decadent rock 'n' roll lifestyle. The crisis nearly dissolved the band. The Edge, in particular, had many doubts, and he nearly left U2 prior to going into the studio again. But Bono advised him to follow his heart and, after a period of soul searching, Evans chose the band as well.

In the end, they all decided it was possible to reconcile the two by continuing to make music without compromising their personal beliefs. *October* reflected on the difficulty of this reconciliation. In the end, they dedicated themselves to putting their collective voice to use by raising public consciousness.

*   *   *

This consciousness-raising manifested itself in a big way on the band's third album, *War.*

The album included the song "Sunday Bloody Sunday," which dealt with the troubles in Northern Ireland. The song starts off by expressing the anger felt in Ireland over the Bloody Sunday incident of 1972, but in successive stanzas moves through different imagery that disown that anger and place the song in a religious context, using imagery from Matthew 10:35 ("mother's children; brothers, sisters torn apart") and a twist on 1 Corinthians 15:32 ("we eat and drink while tomorrow they die") before finishing off with a call for Christians to stop fighting each other and "claim the victory Jesus won, on a Sunday bloody Sunday" (www.u2boy.nl).

War has been described as a powerful fusion of politics and militant rock 'n' roll and even the band called it "a positive protest record." Bono referred to "Sunday Bloody Sunday" as "a song of hope and a song of disgust," and Mullen noted it was "the first time we ever really made a statement" (www.u2boy.nl).

The album's first single, "New Year's Day," was the quartet's first worldwide hit. It climbed to #10 on the British charts and almost broke into the Top 50 on the U.S. list. The folks at MTV put the song's video into heavy rotation, exposure that helped introduce the Irish lads to a wider American audience. For the first time the band began playing sold-out concerts in both mainland Europe and the United States. During this tour, the band recorded the EP *Under a Blood Red Sky* and produced a live video of the same name.

"Sunday Bloody Sunday" gave U2 their first #1 hit in the United Kingdom, and the album entered the charts there at #1, appropriately enough, on St. Patrick's Day. *War* reached #12 in the United States and was their first album to achieve platinum status.

Working with producers Brian Eno and Daniel Lanois on 1984's *The Unforgettable Fire,* U2 learned to use technology as a creative tool and it became their most experimental and adventurous effort to date. The recording, named after a series of paintings made by survivors of the atomic bombs at Hiroshima and Nagasaki, featured the tribute to civil rights leader Martin Luther King, Jr., "Pride (In the Name of Love)." The song became the first radio hit from the album, entering the U.K. Top 5 and the U.S. Top 50. The centerpiece of the album is a tune called "Bad," a cathartic exploration on the theme of heroin dependency, a critical problem in Dublin at the time, that provided one of the album's defining moments.

The Unforgettable Fire signified a milestone in U2's career, with its complex lyrics the Edge's experimental guitar, and the band's laid-back rhythm section. Bono continued to address political issues in a big way though, and so the band's sound, after four albums, started to settle in. They began drawing comparisons to other salient acts of the day, including Springsteen and the Clash, both of whom had done topical albums around this time.

* * *

More than a billion people worldwide watched the Live Aid concert for Ethiopian famine relief in July 1985. U2 were not expected to be one of the main draws for the event, but the band provided the show with one of its most memorable moments, a 13-minute version of "Bad" in which Bono left the stage and danced with the Wembley Stadium crowd. Unfortunately, this interfered with the band's time to play (and promote) "Pride (In the Name of Love)," and the ploy enraged the band and its crew.

Courtesy of Neil Zlozower

Mullen admitted he and the band considered leaving the stage as he was performing, and after the gig the band reprimanded Bono, asking him to quit the band. Instead, Bono took a few weeks off and was welcomed back. Ironically, with the benefit of hindsight, the "Bad" performance has earned legendry status in rock circles. It also brought attention to the personal connection Bono was capable of making with audiences.

Following Bono's break and Live Aid, U2 embarked on a headlining, six-show tour to benefit Amnesty International. This tour helped Amnesty International triple its membership. It was at this time that *Rolling Stone* magazine called U2 the "Band of the '80s." "For a growing number of rock-and-roll fans, U2 has become the band that matters most, maybe even the only band that matters" (Unattributed, *Rolling Stone*, www.rollingstone.com, November 1985).

* * *

The band made good on that promise in 1987 with *The Joshua Tree,* a chart-topping effort on both sides of the Atlantic that went on to win the Grammy award for Album of the Year. Its singles, "With or Without You" and "I Still Haven't Found What I'm Looking For," also quickly went to #1 in the United States. *Time* magazine ballyhooed that they were the hottest ticket in rock 'n' roll.

The band sold out stadiums the world over, the first time they had played venues of that size consistently. The band filmed and recorded various shows from the tour for a 1988 documentary and album called *Rattle and Hum.* At that point in time, U2 tipped its hat to elements of American music. They recorded *Rattle and Hum* at the legendary Sun Studios in Memphis, shared the stage with Bob Dylan and B.B. King, and sang about blues great Billie Holiday. The band also returned to its roots by covering the Beatles' "Helter Skelter."After taking some time off, the band reconvened in 1990 in East Berlin to begin work on their next studio album. Brian Eno and Daniel Lanois were again tapped to produce. The original sessions did not go well, but following the inspirational completion of the hit song "One," the band eventually emerged from the studio with renewed energy and a new album under its belt. *Achtung Baby* received stellar reviews and gave those who resisted U2 till this point a reason to jump in the pool. To take advantage of all the enthusiasm, the group set out in 1992 on its first American tour in more than four years.

The multimedia event known as "The Zoo TV Tour" confused audiences with hundreds of video screens, upside-down flying Trabant cars, mock transmission towers, satellite TV links, subliminal text messages, and over-the-top stage characters such as "The Fly," "Mirror-ball Man," and "Mister MacPhisto." Many enjoyed the irony of all this excess. In fact, the tour was, among other things, U2's attempt at mocking the excesses of rock 'n' roll by appearing to embrace greed and decadence. But many missed the point of the tour and thought that U2 had begun losing its bearings.

The band intended to record the tour for an additional live EP, something to accompany and expand on the *Achtung Baby* canon, but creativity reigned within this context and the band proved to be more prolific than originally planned. *Zooropa,* an even greater departure than they had made previously, with more electronics and technology, grew into a full-fledged LP, released in July of 1993. Surprisingly, while this departure dismayed the band's longtime fans, it too helped to widen the group's overall fan base, attracting more enthusiastic followers. It helped that the band did a duet with Johnny Cash called "The Wanderer," a savvy marketing ploy that appealed to fans that may have been furthest from caring for the band.

After some time off from the exhausting *Zooropa* tour and a few side projects, including the *Batman Forever* and *Mission: Impossible* soundtracks, the band returned with Brian Eno under the moniker "Passengers," an under-the-radar project in 1995. They also released an experimental album called *Original Soundtracks No. 1,* which featured another surprising collaboration, "Miss Sarajevo," with none other than Italian tenor Luciano Pavarotti.

In 1996, the band hurried through the recording process of *Pop,* a sonic experiment involving heavy postproduction, tape loops, programming, and sampling. But the band's sense of chameleonic entitlement—they seemed intent on changing their spots every time out—began to wear on their fans. *Pop* fared poorly, and U2 felt like they had been sent a message.

Still, the Popmart tour, with its sold-out crowds worldwide, demonstrated the band could continue to draw impressive crowds. Both the Popmart Tour and Zoo TV Tour were intended to send a sarcastic message to all those accusing U2 of commercialism.

Their point was well taken. It was the second-highest grossing tour of 1997 (behind the Rolling Stones' "Bridges to Babylon" tour) with revenues of just under $80 million. Of course, it cost U2 more than $100 million to produce, so the numbers didn't quite add up.

All That You Can't Leave Behind, released in late October of 1999 and advanced as the band's return to form, debuted at #1 in 22 countries and spawned a worldwide smash, "Beautiful Day," which also earned three Grammy Awards. U2 followed that release with a major tour in the spring of 2001.

The subsequent Elevation tour was the top live draw in all of North America. U2 played 80 shows and grossed $110 million. The tour culminated in 2002 with a performance during halftime of Super Bowl XXXVI in New Orleans. The highlight of the three-song set was a passionate rendition of "Where the Streets Have No Name," in which the names of the victims of the recent 9/11 attacks were projected onto backdrops and scrolled up toward the sky. At the end of the set, Bono opened his jacket, which he had worn throughout the Elevation Tour, to reveal the American flag printed on the lining. A few months later, *All That You Can't Leave Behind* picked up four more Grammy Awards.

The band's next album, *How to Dismantle an Atomic Bomb,* was released on November 22 in much of the world and November 23 in the United States. The album debuted at #1 in 32 countries, including the United States, Canada, the United Kingdom, and the band's native Ireland. Bono continued his campaigns for debt and HIV/AIDS relief and world poverty throughout the first decade of the new millennium. In April 2004, *Rolling Stone* magazine placed U2 at #22 on its list of the "100 Greatest Artists of All Time." Chris Martin of Coldplay wrote the tribute:

> What I love most about U2 is that the band is more important than any of their songs or albums. I love that they're best mates and have an integral role in one another's lives as friends. I love the way that they're not interchangeable—if Larry Mullen Jr. wants to go scuba diving for a week, the rest of the band can't do a thing. U2—like Coldplay—maintain that all songs that appear on their albums are credited to the band. And they are the only band that's been around for twenty years with no member changes and no big splits. (Martin, Chris, "100 Greatest Artists of All Time," *Rolling Stone,* April 15, 2004)

On March 14, 2005, U2 was inducted into the Rock 'n' Roll Hall of Fame in their first year of eligibility. Here is an excerpt of the U2 summary on the Rock Hall's Web site:

> From the beginning, U2 has been a band on a mission. With each album and concert, the Irish quartet has endeavored to create music of lasting worth and substance. At various points in their career U2 have been not only the most popular band in the world but also arguably the most important—although success in their own minds is purely conditional on the caliber of their work. (www.rockhall.com/inductee/u2)

TECHNIQUE/STYLE

Through extensive exploration of delay and overdubs, the Edge's ethereal and subtle work on guitar became a key signature of U2's sound and, in the bigger picture, helped to redefine guitar playing in the new millennium.

> We always try to do things differently, we never accept the normal, so it was mainly trial and error. I like a nice ringing sound on guitar, and most of my chords I find two strings and make

them ring the same note, so it's almost like a 12-string sound. So for E I might play a B, E, E and B and make it ring. It works very well with the Gibson Explorer. It's funny because the bass end of the Explorer was so awful that I used to stay away from the low strings, and a lot of the chords I played were very trebly, on the first four, or even three strings. I discovered that through using this one area of the fretboard I was developing a very stylized way of doing something that someone else would play in a normal way. (Gill, 1997)

A lead guitarist without the compulsion for fretboard pyrotechnics, the Edge's explorations of sound and technology helped U2 reach new creative heights on *Achtung Baby* and *All That You Can't Leave Behind*. These of course, came well after his groundbreaking efforts in the early 1980s like *Boy* and *War*. Throughout it all, the Edge has remained an enigmatic original.

The Edge is widely recognized as having a trademark sound characterized by understatement, a chiming, shimmering sound (thanks in part to the signature sound of classic VOX AC-30s amps) achieved with extensive use of digital delay effects, reverb, and a focus on texture and melody.

The Joshua Tree (1987) is probably the best example of the Edge's sound, especially on tracks like "With or Without You" and "Where the Streets Have No Name." The album was recorded at the height of the 1980s indulgent glam and shred guitar era, with an emphasis on speed and dexterity. But the Edge's guitar playing served in opposition to that. Rather than pushing his guitar to the front of the mix and make his contributions obvious, The Edge focused on serving the song and the mood, often contributing just a few simple lines, adding depth and richness with his use of digital delay.

Delays make up a big part of Edge's sound. He uses modulated delays that add a vibrato/chorus effect to the delay repeats. To achieve an "Edge-like" sound, the digital delay's delay is set to a dotted eight note (3/16 of a measure), and its "feedback" adjusted until the number of repeats is about 2 or 3 (Darling, Tim, "A Study of the Edge's Guitar Delay," www.amnesta.net/edge_delay, 2006).

For example, the introduction to "Where the Streets Have No Name" is simply a repeated six-note arpeggio broadened by a modulated delay effect. The Edge has said that he views musical notes as "expensive," in that he prefers to play as few notes as possible. The Edge has stated that many of his guitar parts are based around guitar effects. This is especially true from the *Achtung Baby* era onwards, although much of the band's 1980s material made heavy use of echo. His influence as a guitarist can be seen on many popular rock bands. "I don't think a lot of people realize the musical benefit harmonics can give to a song. I just developed that a bit and brought the harmonics more to the foreground. Some of our songs use harmonics as the main guitar part" (Gill, 1997).

* * *

Edge's guitar picks also contain a critical element of his chiming sound. His Herdim guitar picks have a dimpled half and a flat half. The dimpled half is designed to be where a player holds the pick for a better grip. But Edge holds the pick either backwards or sideways so that the dimpled part of the pick grates the strings to sharpen the sound and give it a punch or chime (Darling, 2006).

Edge also uses the open strings—often the low A and D strings—as droning notes. This technique is often used in traditional Irish music. Incidentally, it is probably why many of the songs are in the key of D and many of the riffs are around a D chord, the D and A strings drone best in that key. The song "Bad" is an example.

64

Palm muting is also a needed technique if you use a lot of delay. The Edge would rest his palm just behind the bridge so that part of his palm slightly touched the strings. You get a more staccato feel and almost a harmonic quality to the notes too. This technique was used by many of the punk bands that were early influences on Edge, although they would use it with distortion instead of delay. (Darling, 2006)

EQUIPMENT/GEAR

The Edge's main guitar, of course, is his Gibson Explorer.

I think it's the most distinctive of my guitars. It seems that the body shape affects the sound somehow. It's a very vibrant guitar with lots of treble. I had a Strat what I wasn't that pleased with in those days, and when I was in New York with my parents, I went to some stores to look around. I picked up this secondhand Explorer and played around on it for a while. It was just so naturally good, and it felt right, so I bought it. It was quite cheap as well, about 450 dollars. A lot of people look at it and think it's one of the originals (under 100 of these were made in 1958 and they are very rare) but it's one of the '76 limited edition reissue models. (Gill, 1997)

The Edge's other guitars include many that are dedicated to specific pitch and string gauge needs. There's the 1967 Fireglo Rickenbacker, a 1966 Cream Telecaster, a 1966 Lake Placid Blue Telecaster, a 1962 Epiphone Sunburst Casino, a 1963 Gretsch 6122 Walnut Country Gentleman, a 1965 Gibson Pelham Blue SG, a 1962 Sunburst Strat, a 1961 Gibson Sunburst ES-335TD, and a Gibson Blonde Pete Townshend J-200 Acoustic. Though he doesn't collect any vintage guitars, he does have a lap steel, circa 1940, by Epiphone.

His setup is basically solid guitar into a small case of effects and from there to two Vox AC30s. But he uses a few additional amps as well, including a 1956 Fender Deluxe Tweed with Vox speakers, a 1958 Fender Deluxe Tweed with original Jensen Alnico speakers, and a customized Fender Blues Jr.

For the delays, he has always used a Korg SDD-3000 or the Electro-Harmonix Memory Man Deluxe. The Korg is a digital delay that allows the user to dial in the exact delay length. The Edge splits his signal at the end of his other effects chains and runs it into two SDD-3000s. Those feed directly into his Vox AC30s. Since *The Joshua Tree,* he has also used two TC Electronic 2290 delay racks.

On the floor, his effects include a volume controller, an original Digitech Whammy, a Dunlop wah wah, a Boss Tu-2 tuner, and a Skrydstrup SC-1 system foot controller.

For rack effects, the Edge also uses an Eventide Ultra-Harmonizer, two Lexicon PCM Processors, two Line 6 Pod Prop rackmounts, and a Rocktron DVC dynamic volume controller.

For strings, the Edge isn't particular. Depending on the guitar, he uses Ernie Ball, D'Addario, or Fender strings (.010s to .046s, or .011s to .052s).

ESSENTIAL READING

Bono, The Edge, Adam Clayton, and Larry Mullen, Jr. *U2 by U2.* New York: HarperCollins, 2006.
Darling, Tim. "A Study of the Edge's Guitar Delay," www.amnesta.net/edge_delay, 2006.
Flanagan, Bill. *U2 at the End of the World.* New York: Delta, 1996.
Gardner, Elysa, ed. *U2: The Rolling Stone Files.* London: Sidgwick & Jackson, 1994.
Gill, Chris. "In Excess." *Guitar World,* September 1997.

Martin, Chris. "100 Greatest Artists of All Time." *Rolling Stone,* April 15, 2004.
Rolling Stone. www.rollingstone.com, unattributed, November 1985.

ESSENTIAL WORK

"Beautiful Day" (2000)
"I Still Haven't Found What I'm Looking For" (1987)
"I Will Follow" (1980)
"New Year's Day" (1983)
"Pride (In the Name of Love)" (1984)
"Sunday Bloody Sunday" (1983)
"With or Without You" (1987)

ESSENTIAL LISTENING

Achtung Baby (Island, 1991)
All That You Can't Leave Behind (Interscope, 2000)
Boy (Island, 1980)
The Joshua Tree (Island, 1987)
War (Island, 1983)

ESSENTIAL VIEWING

Rattle and Hum (Paramount, 1999)
U2 Go Home: Live from Slane Castle (Interscope, 2003)
Vertigo 2005: Live from Chicago (Island, 2004)

John Frusciante

In many ways, John Frusciante was born to be a guitar player and he plays as if that trite adage were true. His parents were both musicians and he had started listening to punk rock at the ripe old age of 9. Quite simply, Frusciante was a prodigy, eventually joining the Red Hot Chili Peppers, his favorite band, at the age of 18. Not only did he join the band to play guitar, not only had he *never* been in a band before the Chilis, he shaped the band's funky, hard edged sound.

Instilled with a deep sense of musicality and a stunning, near encyclopedic knowledge of riffs, licks, and other technical skills, he derived inspiration from a vast spectrum of guitar players, from Zappa and Robert Fripp to Greg Ginn of Black Flag and Parliament-Funkadelic. With this sort of insight and a fertile imagination, Frusciante single-handedly created his own style that ranged from funk to psychedelic to avant-garde.

In interviews, Frusciante is strikingly forthright and often downright ethereal. There's something in his voice that sounds like a child, a candor that taps gently at your heart. He is constantly enveloped in thought, attempting to resolve psychic problems, problems that once threatened to swallow him whole. Now he counts (among those problems) things like songwriting and other aspects of music that he considers challenges. "I've been spending a lot of time furthering my understanding of chords on the guitar, so it got to the point where I felt that in order to truly see chords clearly, I was going to have to learn them on piano" (Parker, Lyndsey, "Two Sides to Every Story," *Guitar One,* January 2003, p. 98).

When he emerged from his drug stupor in 1998 and rejoined the band, he did so with a sense of renewed vitality. Having resolved those drug dependencies, he revealed the vibrant artist that had to that point been shrouded inside of him.

"I don't need to take drugs," he notes emphatically. "I feel so much more high all the time right now because of the type of momentum that a person can get going when you really dedicate yourself to something that you really love" (Cleveland, Barry, "John Frusciante Puts His Stamp on Stadium Arcadium," *Guitar Player,* September 2006).

Frusciante proved to have a voracious musical appetite. He teeters between the mesmerizing shred of Steve Vai and Frank Zappa one moment and the vintage blues sound of John Lee Hooker, not to mention the fringe jazz of Cecil Taylor. He's repeatedly professed an admiration for the New Wave guitarists of the early 1980s, who never called attention to themselves at the time because they realized they were overshadowed by the shred and metal players of the day. Joy Division, Heaven 17, and the Human League, all provided him not necessarily with guitar licks to learn from, but with great vocal melodies to translate to his guitar. Such was one of the major sources of his melodic inspiration. And this doesn't even touch on the expected influences behind his playing: Sabbath, Clapton, Page, and Hendrix.

Complementing Frusciante's passion for music are his love of recording and his fascination with pure sound. "As a person whose job it is to make sounds, it's important for me not to overlook any of the various properties that sound possesses," he explains. "Studying modular synthesis has taught me how to approach music in a completely different way, and now I think in terms of giving sound width and dimension, rather than just in terms of what my fingers are doing. You don't have a chance to think that way when you're caught up in the actual playing. It's only in the studio that you can really explore that" (Cleveland, 2006).

Throughout his career, Frusciante has been an intrepid discoverer, a guitar player unafraid to break new ground, despite what the fallout or consequences might be. He often has traveled against the grain in hopes of finding fresh territory on which to tread. And after finding a fertile path to go down, he'll never stay long enough to become predictable. In fact, that's one of the reasons why he left the Chili Peppers originally in the early 1990s. "When I was 21 I thought the whole thing was to throw away your technique," he told *Guitar One* (Parker, 2003).

How rare is it when a guitar player can knowingly toss out his technique and still find a means of expression? Very. Only one exists and his name is John Frusciante.

EARLY YEARS

Born on March 5, 1970 in Queens, New York, John Frusciante came into this world as a member of a very musical family. His father was a Juilliard-trained concert pianist, his mother a singer, his grandfather proficient on guitar and fiddle, and his great-grandfather a renowned mandolin player. His parents, John and Gail Frusciante, provided a good life for their family. John Sr. became a lawyer and later a judge. Gail, too, was a promising musician, who remained a homemaker because her husband ruled out the possibility of a musical career. The family grew up in Queens, relocated to Tucson, Arizona, and then moved to Florida for a year, during which time John's parents separated.

He picked up an acoustic guitar at the age of seven. But he soon became disillusioned with the fact that he couldn't emulate the sounds he heard on his Zeppelin and Van Halen records. It seemed too far away, so he put the guitar down and moved on.

A couple of years later, though, he rekindled his interest thanks to the burgeoning sounds of punk and New Wave. Bands like Devo and the Germs, the Clash and the Sex Pistols piqued his curiosity and he figured that playing good guitar was something you had to work at.

He discovered: "As long as you put the right kind of energy and feeling into your playing, that was what mattered. Then one day I was feeling a lot of rage—I was angry at two kids that I didn't like and didn't like me—so I went home and wrote thirty short punk songs in a row on my acoustic guitar. That was the first day that I really started playing" (Fortnam, Ian, "John Frusciante," *Kerrang!*, March 2001).

John utterly immersed himself in rock 'n' roll, devouring music and slavishly practicing guitar licks in his bedroom. By age 10, he'd figured out a bunch of Germs songs in his own tuning that allowed him to play everything with a single-finger barre. It was a habit he'd have to break as he started lessons a year later while living in nearby Mar Vista with his mom and new stepdad, an avid philosophy reader and black belt who listened to Beethoven and 1950s R&B but understood where punk rock was coming from. He also had valuable support from his stepfather.

In the late 1970s, John moved with his mother to Santa Monica, California and, like a million other California kids, he added skateboarding to his short list of obsessions. He left

Kiss and the classic rock of the decade behind in favor of punk and prog and New Wave. Then, at 17, he moved to Hollywood, began playing with a like-minded bass player, and finally rejected technique-based rock for something more visceral.

From punk, Frusciante graduated to Jimmy Page, Jeff Beck, and Jimi Hendrix and tackled the almighty barre chord and blues scale. He also began pursuing increasingly compli-cated rock like King Crimson, Yes, early Genesis, and Zappa, whose work he'd study for hours, learning solos and syncopations in detail.

He dropped out of high school and moved to Los Angeles, where to appease his parents he and a friend registered for classes at G.I.T., the Gui-tar Institute of Technology, where they said they'd learn technical classes on guitar playing. They never actually attended class though, choosing instead to roam around the city at their leisure and audition for bands. He even showed up at a Frank Zappa audition, only to leave the rehearsal

Courtesy of Neil Zlozower

room before stepping into the spotlight. "I realized that I wanted to be a rock star, do drugs and get girls, and that I wouldn't be able to do that if I was in Zappa's band" (Rotondi, James, "Till I Reach the Higher Ground," *Guitar Player,* November 1997).

Frusciante jammed throughout his teenage years, searching for direction and a group he could get along with. He'd soon find one he was waiting for. In a single, unexpected jam session experience, he'd encountered his future.

In the summer of 1986, Frusciante witnessed the Red Hot Chili Peppers play at the Variety Arts Center in Los Angeles for the first time, and the attraction was instant. From that day on he became the band's biggest fan, following them wherever they went. Frus-ciante became mesmerized by the proto-funk and extraordinary talent of the band's Hillel Slovak, and became his biggest idol.

MUSIC

It didn't take long for Frusciante to meet the members of the band. In 1986 and 1987, they became rather close. And in 1988, Frusciante was invited to jam with Michael Balzary, aka Flea, the bass player of the band. It happened indirectly: Frusciante had met and begun jamming with former Dead Kennedys drummer D. H. Peligro, who would soon tempo-rarily replace Jack Irons in the Peppers. Peligro invited Frusciante when Peligro learned of the young guitarist's obsession with the band. The jam happened at Flea's house on Fairfax Avenue.

Less than a year later, tragedy struck the Pepper camp when guitarist and founding member Slovak suffered a fatal heroin overdose and died. The band at the time had begun to ascend the Los Angeles scene and attract a much wider audience and had recently released their most popular album, *The Uplift Mofo Party Plan.* Slovak served as an architect of the band's pioneering rap/rock/funk sound and his death was a massive blow.

The death of Slovak altered the Peppers permanently. They had already been in upheaval before his death. In fact, Slovak himself had left the band briefly, grappling with demons. After his death, the upheaval followed. Singer Anthony Kiedis, himself a junkie, took an extended break to quit his own narcotic habit. Drummer Irons, a founding member with Slovak, had trouble coping with the loss of his best friend. He suffered a nervous breakdown and was hospitalized. When he recovered, he later joined Pearl Jam. On the outside of the Peppers camp, Frusciante took the news of his idol Slovak's death very hard. The influence Slovak had on his guitar playing was enormous.

* * *

For a year, the Peppers—just Flea and Kiedis at this point—lay suspended in time, their future uncertain. At the point in which they were ready to start up again, Flea and Kiedis invited the old Dead Kennedys' drummer Peligro and Frusciante in for a jam. The two Peppers were amazed by his guitar skill. At 18, he demonstrated an outstanding ability, and especially the kind of style that Slovak had established within the framework of the band. "I tried to play everything exactly like him, people said I had found my own style but all I did was to follow him" (www.slovakopedia.com). Even though there were eight years between John and the members of the band they developed a very close friendship.

They asked him to join the band on the spot. Peligro joined briefly on the drums but was replaced by Chad Smith. The new lineup was set, much to the jubilation of Frusciante.

"Their music meant everything to me. Joining the band was like the most fantastic thing on earth" (www.slovakopedia.com).

Frusciante joined the Chili Peppers at the perfect time. They were beginning to attract a wider audience, and with *Mother's Milk* the band exploded onto the scene. Exposure on MTV with their songs "Knock Me Down" (a song written about Slovak) and "Higher Ground" (a cover of a Stevie Wonder tune) finally pushed them into the spotlight.

Mother's Milk also secured the band a deal with Warner Brothers and put a little distance between the Slovak tragedy and their bright future together. Soon enough, they would join the ranks of rock 'n' roll superstars.

Sensing something significant afoot, the group recruited a major music guru in Rick Rubin to control the production effort of the next album. They moved into a mansion-turned-recording studio in 1990 to work on what would become their biggest release yet, the stripped-down *Blood Sugar Sex Magik,* their first for the Warner Bros. label.

But things were not particularly rosy when the Red Hot Chili Peppers retreated to the mansion. Kiedis and Frusciante struggled with drugs and their musical output had sagged somewhat, devolving into a tiresome formula of sex-obsessed camp and gratuitous riffage. Rubin would change all that. He insisted on airborne melodies and he filtered the band's rhythmic rumble to its primal essence. Songs like "Give It Away" and the incendiary "Suck My Kiss" established a pummeling template for rock punctuated by the relentlessness of hip-hop that would be appropriated by everyone from Limp Bizkit to Dr. Dre.

Beyond the funk, though, the band—thanks to the input of Rubin—started serving up more introverted material like "Breaking the Girl" and "Under the Bridge." These more fragile tunes showcased a new dimension of the band, adding to its appeal and broadening their audience. The rhythm section displayed a growing curiosity about studio texture and nuances, and it proved to be a side of the band that would expand over the next decade on future projects.

A monster hit upon its September 1991 release, *Blood Sugar Sex Magik* eventually sold a staggering seven million copies in the United States alone, 12 million worldwide. Three years after he expressed an interest in the world of rock 'n' roll, girls, parties, and massive gigs, Frusciante got his wish; he was thrust into the limelight with the Chili Peppers, one of the biggest bands in the United States.

Accolades and awards poured in. The band won a Grammy for Best Hard Performance with Vocal for "Give It Away," and it became the band's first #1 single on the Modern Rock chart. "Under the Bridge," the album's second single, peaked at #2 on the Hot 100 chart and became the band's signature song. Other singles followed. The album itself crested on the *Billboard* album chart at #3. History has also been kind to the recording. *Rolling Stone* magazine slotted it at #310 on its list of the "500 Greatest Albums of All Time."

One of the reasons for the band's immense success was their good nature: "We really like to have fun—that's probably why people like our band," says Smith. "People have this image in their minds of what the Chili Peppers are like, but Jimi Hendrix was the mellowest, most soulful, soft-spoken, coolest guy, and then you'd get him onstage, and he'd go wild. You'll find that, too, with Flea and Anthony—they're articulate, smart people who are cultured, not just knuckleheaded funk guys with funny hair jumping around" (Foege, Alec, "Red Hot Chili Peppers," *Rolling Stone,* October 1995).

But even after *Blood Sugar*'s triumph, the band's future remained precarious. In 1992, while on their world tour in support of the new album, Frusciante broke down. Just 22, he had obvious trouble coping with the demands and rigors of fame and his drug abuse took its toll. One half hour before going onstage at a gig in Japan, he quit the band.

Stunned, the band canceled the rest of its tour. They scrambled to find a new guitar player. Anthony Kiedis, lead singer for the Chili Peppers, told David Fricke of *Rolling Stone,* "He's one of the most deeply soulful guitar players that we've ever been connected with. Also, he's a good friend, and we had something going that was cosmic and special. And we're going to have to find that elsewhere" (Fricke, David, *Rolling Stone,* June 1992).

A headlining slot on that summer's Lollapalooza tour lay ahead. They first sought the services of guitarist Dave Navarro, who had recently become available with the dissolution of his band, Jane's Addiction. At the time, though, Navarro had committed to Deconstruction, a project begun with former Jane's bassist Eric Avery. They contracted wiz kid Arik Marshall and, later, Jesse Tobias to fill in for Frusciante, but neither lasted very long, each one suffering from a lack of chemistry.

For a band haunted by the specter of death, selecting Dave Navarro, 28, as its newest member seemed appropriate. When Navarro was 15, his mother and aunt were brutally murdered by his mother's ex-boyfriend.

"After my mother was killed, everything was about escape," Navarro says. "I tried to escape school, I tried to escape by using drugs, but the No. 1 thing that I was already into intensely was music." Only after Jane's Addiction broke up was Navarro able to conquer the drugs and concentrate on the music. By the time he met with the Chili Peppers, his mental state was surprisingly compatible with theirs. "We all had really personal, major issues to deal with while we were making this record," he says (Foege, 1995).

That recording, made with Navarro, was *One Hot Minute,* released in 1995, four years after *Blood Sugar Sex Magik.* Navarro, a guitar player unlike any of the players that had come before him in the band, changed the Chili Peppers sound radically. He'd come from a rock background, not funk, and grew up idolizing Jimi Hendrix, not James Brown. Still, he soldiered on, bonded by emotional trauma and the willingness to hold on to a group of talented musicians with whom he felt tremendous camaraderie.

* * *

After leaving the band, Frusciante descended into a serious drug addiction. He battled it for more than three years, suffering financial and physical ruin.

Frusciante: "I had so many years of terrible, terrible ... " He breaks down. "I'm sorry," he says, turning the tape recorder off and drying his eyes. "Sometimes I get into situations of just being so overwhelmed by what I've been through, so many years of regretting everything, all the things I could have done when I was 22 years old ... " The tape is back on. "But I was totally incapable of it; I had just so many mental problems. It wasn't until I was 28 that my brain actually felt like a spacious place. When I was 18, 19, 22, my brain was just clogged all the time—non-stop voices. I couldn't figure out what was going on. There was a lot of confusion inside me, this flood of voices, often contradicting each other, often telling me stuff that would happen in the future, and then it would happen, voices insulting me, telling me what to do" (Fortnam, 2001).

He worked sporadically. He engaged in different projects, including playing with Bob Forrest of the L.A. band Thelonius Monster, Trulio Disgracias and the Three Amoebas, a trio including Flea and Jane's Addiction drummer Stephen Perkins. He also recorded a black and white movie called "Stuff" with his friend Johnny Depp in his house in Hollywood.

Frusciante also became intermittently productive. He released two solo recordings, *Niandra LaDes and Usually Just a T-Shirt* and *Smile from the Streets You Hold.* Both held strange and haunting sounds, the kind of sounds created by a brilliant musician and instrumentalist who'd lost his way in a foggy haze. Few, perhaps besides other addicts, could truly understand what he meant, and the albums, poorly reviewed, didn't succeed commercially at all.

Between solo efforts, he spent a lot of time painting, doing yoga, and soul-searching, trying to break free of drugs and make peace with himself.

> I might have made things a bit more balanced if my head had been a little clearer, but it wasn't, with the amount of pot I smoked—24 hours a day by the time I was 20. I had this feeling that there was something else I needed to do for myself on the inside that had nothing to do with my outward presentation to the world, so playing live in the Chili Peppers was making me severely depressed. If I had quit at the end of *Blood Sugar Sex Magik,* I think I could have gone through this stuff easier, without becoming a drug addict. But by the time I did leave, hard drugs were the only way I could be happy enough to live and not just be the most hopeless person who can't even listen to music and is about to die. I made a clear-cut decision that I was going to be a drug addict. (Fortnam, 2001)

He assembled various and sundry tracks he had laying around and packaged it as his 1997 solo outing, *Smile from the Streets You Hold.* He put little time into it and needed to release it almost solely for getting his hands on drug money. His addiction nearly

SOLO PEPPER

Beginning in 2004 and concluding in early 2005, Frusciante embarked on a coura-geous project to release six recordings in six months. While artwork delays held up the process and prevented him from getting all six out in the designated time, Frus-ciante *was* incredibly prolific.

The set, taken as a whole, exhibits an artist in the process of a creative rebirth. In terms of sheer productivity, Frusciante came back to life, working in an incredible spec-trum of styles and voices. The series is also a well collected, amazingly orchestrated amalgamation of songs that outline Frusciante's growth experienced after his heroin addiction. Recordings include *Shadows Collide with People* for Warner Brothers and *The Will to Death, Inside of Emptiness, A Sphere in the Heart of Silence,* and *Curtains,* all on the Record Collection imprint.

The five albums of Frusciante's fruitful period represent an array of rock music that often incorporates instruments, tempo changes, and electronic sounds uncom-mon to traditional western rock. People may question Frusciante's decision to release all these songs on separate albums instead of producing some sort of ''best of'' work for this series, but when the series was listened to, it becomes clear that all the sounds are grouped together in terms of style. It did not make any sense for Frus-ciante to, for example, put a song from *Curtains* and a song from *A Sphere in the Heart of Silence* on the same record because they are too different in style, theme, and genre.

He also teamed up with Joe Lally of Fugazi and Josh Klinghoffer in a band called Ataxia. All the while, Frusciante maintained his creative and touring obligations with the Chili Peppers.

proved fatal when an overdose in 1997 almost killed him. He had finally hit bottom. An article in a *Los Angeles Weekly* caught up with him and explained the story to its readers. It portrayed him as a gray-skinned and toothless junkie, with ravaged veins and burns all over his body. Concerned friends found him and staged an intervention. Five years after Frusciante left the Chili Peppers, five years of sheer hell in the vise of addiction, the guita-rist checked into rehab.

Things were also in upheaval with the Chili Peppers. Citing musical and personal dif-ferences, Dave Navarro abruptly exited the band. Kiedis and Navarro didn't work well together in the studio. Historically, the Peppers took a spontaneous approach to songwrit-ing and arranging, while Navarro liked to record several guitar tracks and work more thoughtfully. To make matters worse, after cleaning himself up following the death of Slo-vak, singer Kiedis rekindled his addiction to hard drugs.

Now a threesome without a guitar player, the remaining band members began to doubt that they would even continue. Instead of dissolving, though, the band discovered that Frusciante had cleaned himself up successfully in rehab. So they did the obvious thing and invited him back. Shortly after Navarro's departure, Flea negotiated Frusciante's return, where he was literally welcomed with open arms by Kiedis.

In describing their first rehearsal together, Kiedis told Gavin Edwards of *Rolling Stone,* "When he hit that first chord, it was so perfect—this blend of sounds from these people who I hadn't heard play together in so long" (Edwards, Gavin, *Rolling Stone,* April 29, 1999, p. 38).

The resulting recording project following this reunion, 1999's *Californication,* turned out to be a colossal triumph and one of the Chili Peppers greatest works. With Rubin as producer, the quartet put together a work that sold well and received some of the best reviews the band ever had. While familiar sexy funk and tender ballads filled the album, the songwriting displayed mature and thematic unity.

While they retained their musical flair, the band appeared to have grown up considerably. They had been through an unreasonable amount of strain and trauma, so the band that emerged on the other side seemed more reserved, more deliberate, and all the more wise. Their sense of humor remained, but their frenzied stage shtick ebbed somewhat. The first single and hit off *Californication* was "Scar Tissue," a meditation on the past by Kiedis. While many insiders doubted that the band would remain together long enough to achieve anything more, the success of *Californication* demonstrated their strength, endurance, and resilience.

* * *

As if to show their appreciation for all that strength and resilience, fans of the Chili Peppers turned out in vast numbers to buy their *next* album, *Stadium Arcadium,* in 2006, enough to shoot it to #1 in its very first week of release.

The album earned the band seven Grammy nominations in 2007, the most nominations that the band had garnered in their 25-year career. Kiedis attributed the album's success to less abrasive dynamics within the band, saying that the band's "chemistry when it comes to writing is better than ever. There was always a struggle to dominate lyrically. But we are now confident enough in who we are, so everybody feels more comfortable contributing more and more valuable, quality stuff" (Cohen, Jonathan, "Peppers Double the Pleasure with *Stadium Arcadium,*" www.billboard.com, January 2006).

TECHNIQUE/STYLE

Even when Frusciante is talking about something as concrete as guitar technique, his language possesses a distinctly spiritual bent.

> Playing is a collaboration with an instrument. You have to work within the limitations of that instrument, and those limitations define the music as much as any part of your personality, if not more so. When I'm playing guitar, I'm listening to what's coming out of the amp, and that's what's inspiring me. "Okay, this guitar is making this sound, so let's see what I can do with it." You have to respect the instrument as its own entity rather than trying to force yourself on it. That said, however, if you are really listening to what's coming out of the amp, and letting that guide you, then you should be able to play any guitar and still have it sound like you. (Cleveland, Barry, "Exclusive Outtakes from *GP*'s Interview with John Frusciante," *Guitar Player,* September 2006)

Frusciante's guitar playing centers on rhythm and melody and feel rather than virtuosity. Yet, though he is often referred to as a "feel" player, he understands the technical and theoretical side well. He also doesn't like it when guitar players excuse themselves from learning theory by saying they are exclusively "feel" players.

I have more in common with that way of thinking than with people who normally get associated with theory. The people who inspire me when they talk about theory are Jazz musicians like Miles Davis, Charles Mingus, Eric Dolphy and Charlie Parker. These people didn't play by feel and were thinking completely in terms of theory. We are all playing by feel, but not in the definition of these ignorant guitar players who don't want to spend time learning theory. People pretend there's an advantage to not learning theory, but I think they're just lazy. (Cleveland, 2006)

Certainly, in Frusciante's later years laziness was not a factor. He's grown successively more productive as his years have progressed, and he's developed his technique significantly along the way in both "feel" and theoretical aspects. Throughout his career, he attempted to combine these two polarities. As a teenager, he delved into technical players like Hendrix, Frank Zappa, and Steve Vai. "When I was a kid I would figure out Jimi Hendrix solos but I was learning a skeleton or I would learn it and there would be some little detail that I wasn't picking up. In the first few months that I was meditating, I made the first progress that I ever made. I felt like, "Jesus Christ! I'm learning exactly what he's doing" and not only learning it but I'm learning to feel it in the same way that he was feeling it and I'm learning to hit the string in the same way and to put the same vibrato on it. It's not enough to make a mental observation what kind of vibrato you think he was using, you've got to feel it the way he was feeling it" (Unattributed, *Total Guitar,* July 2006).

When he was growing up in the 1980s, many mainstream guitarists chose to focus on speed. Because of this, he feels that the skills of many defiant New Wave and punk guitarists were largely overlooked. He struggled to establish his own identity. Around the time the band started in on *Blood Sugar Sex Magik,* he finally put aside those guitarists' styles and began concentrating on simpler, more emotional styles.

In addition to his rhythmic and melodic playing, Frusciante is also a superb lead player in the classic rock tradition. He chooses beautiful notes and creates gorgeous melodies in his solos, whether it's a single note or arpeggios. Every time that he begins a phrase he does it with a chord note (of the backing track) and he ends it also with a chord note. This means that most of the time he is playing arpeggios (chord notes) when he is soloing.

I'm a person that likes to contradict himself and go against what he was doing before, and on *By The Way* I was completely against soloing. I didn't enjoy listening to solos and I didn't enjoy soloing. My guitar playing at the time was influenced by John McGeoch from Siouxsie and the Banshees and Magazine, Johnny Marr from the Smiths, and Bernard Sumner of New Order and Joy Division. If I was going to play lead guitar I wanted it to be something you could sing. But as one would expect I got sick of that at a certain point and by the time we were going to start writing this record I was really into soloing. I started getting particularly excited about anybody who was doing off-time stuff. A lot of musicians play within a 16th note grid: on any one of those 16th notes. That was the last thing I wanted to do. At first It wasn't so much that I was listening to Jimi Hendrix or Cream, I was listening to singers like Beyonce, Alliyah and Brandy and rappers like Wu-Tang Clan, Eminem and Eric B and Ramkin. I would translate the rhythmic phrasing and bluesy kind of things that they do to the guitar and it would come out sounding like Jimi Hendrix. I was playing a Strat through a Marshall with a wah-wah pedal and Fuzz Tone, and it quickly became apparent that the result of trying to do this off-time stuff led to an unexpected parallel to what a lot of blues influenced people were doing back in the 1960s. (*Total Guitar,* July 2006)

Considering most of the Chili Pepper's songs stem from jam sessions, Frusciante has managed to come up with some solid and memorable melodies. In fact, Flea, Smith, and Frusciante rarely need to verbally communicate with each other to delineate the direction of a song. Their language is musical rather than spoken. "Everything just constantly falls into place every time we play together . . . See, there's a thing about hearing spaces in music, which is kind of what you don't have when you're playing with someone you've never played with before . . . With Chad and Flea, if I play something that has a lot of space in it, they will always come in with the perfect accents" (Parker, 2003).

EQUIPMENT/GEAR

Frusciante splits his time between Fenders and Gibsons, though he's been partial to the former throughout his 20-year professional career. He loves his Strats and Teles. He's got a 1962 Stratocaster, a 1957 Stratocaster with a maple neck, an Olympic white 1961 Strat, a 1962 fiesta red Strat, and many other Fender models, including a 1962 Jaguar and a 1969 Mustang. On the Gibson side he plays a 1969 Les Paul Custom Black Beauty with dual pickups, a 1956 sunburst Gibson ES-335, and a 1956 SG Custom. He also plays a Gretsch White Falcon occasionally and an Epiphone Joe Pass Emperor II.

As for amps, he uses Marshall Major 200-watt head with KT88 Tubes for a clean powerful sound, and three Marshall Silver Jubilee 2550 heads for crunch, one for White Falcon, one for other electric guitars, and one backup on the side of the stage. He also employs a Fender Dual Showman Silverface head. For effects, Frusciante goes pretty wild. A partial list of this ever-changing facet of his playing includes the following: Boss CE-1 Chorus Ensemble, DS-1 Distortion, DS-2 Turbo Distortion, Electro-Harmonix English Muff'n fuzz, Holy Grail Reverb, Big Muff Pi fuzz, POG Polyphonic Octave Generator, Electric Mistress Flanger, DOD 680 Analog Delay, Moog MF-105 MuRF, MF-105B Bass MuRF, MF-101 Low-Pass Filter, MF-103 Phaser, Ibanez WH-10 Wah, and a Dunlop DB-02 Dime Custom CryBaby. For strings, it's D'Addario XLs (.010s–.046s) and picks he uses Orange Jim Dunlop Tortex 0.60 mm picks.

ESSENTIAL READING

Cleveland, Barry. "Exclusive Outtakes from *GP*'s Interview with John Frusciante." *Guitar Player*, September 2006.

Cleveland, Barry. "John Frusciante Puts His Stamp on Stadium Arcadium." *Guitar Player*, September 2006.

Cohen, Jonathan. "Peppers Double the Pleasure with *Stadium Arcadium*," www.billboard.com, January 2006.

Edwards, Gavin. *Rolling Stone*, April 29, 1999, 38.

Foege, Alec. "Red Hot Chili Peppers." *Rolling Stone*, October 1995.

Fortnam, Ian. "John Frusciante." *Kerrang!*, March 2001.

Fricke, David. *Rolling Stone*, June 1992.

Parker, Lyndsey. "Two Sides to Every Story." *Guitar One*, January 2003, 98.

Rotondi, James. "Till I Reach the Higher Ground." *Guitar Player*, November 1997.

Sloman, Larry, and Anthony Kiedis. *Scar Tissue*. New York: Hyperion, 2005.

Unattributed. *Total Guitar*, July 2006.

ESSENTIAL WORK

"Californication" (1999)
"Give It Away" (1991)
"Scar Tissue" (1999)
"Under the Bridge" (1991)

ESSENTIAL LISTENING

Blood Sugar Sex Magik (Warner Bros., 1991)
By the Way (WEA, 2002)
Californication (Warner Bros., 1999)
Live in Hyde Park (WEA, 2004)
Mother's Milk (EMI, 1989)
What Hits?! (EMI, 1992)

SOLO

Curtains (Record Collection, 2004)
Shadows Collide with People (Warner Bros., 2004)
Smile from the Streets That You Hold (Birdman, 1997)

ESSENTIAL VIEWING

Live at Slane Castle (Warner Bros., 2003)

Jerry Garcia

He was an unlikely hero, this paunchy, bearded man. But he was worshipped by millions for his talent and admired for his pioneering spirit with the Grateful Dead, his star-making vehicle. Those millions came to see him play constantly, often traveling with the band from gig to gig, learning and loving and lapping up all Jerry and the boys had to offer.

And they toured constantly, from their origins in 1965 until Garcia's death in 1995. During this three-decade span, the Grateful Dead played 2,314 shows. During that time, Garcia became the most recorded guitarist in history. Combining the Dead shows with about 1,000 Jerry Garcia Band concerts captured on tape—as well as numerous studio sessions—there are about 15,000 hours of his guitar work preserved for the ages.

What those hours show is that Garcia was an eclectic genius, a player with an instantly identifiable tone and touch. His work explored everything from reggae and folk to bluegrass, rock 'n' roll, blues, jazz, country, and R&B, with streaks of experimental and world music. In his heart a melodic player, Garcia excelled among rock players, choosing colorful notes and subtlety hued ornamentation for his songs. He was also a team player who always chose to serve the music in the context of the moment overemphasizing his own licks.

Binding Garcia's prodigious talents together was an air of authenticity that surrounded his work. Part of it came from his roots as a banjo player and his love for bluegrass. But much of it came from Garcia himself. As a person, Garcia was blessed with "soul." This soul is the reason why he can dig into a bluegrass jam one minute and a psychedelic freak-out the next. These polarities are connected by Garcia's generous soul, a passion that suffuses his playing.

Of course, his greatest gift was his ability to improvise. Aside from being the most sought-after skill among serious musicians, his improvisational technique lifted the music of his band to rarefied heights. He mixed this deftness with an understanding of music theory. While most rock players simply chose a blues or pentatonic scale and let it rip over all of a song's chord changes, playing the same notes, just in different patterns, Garcia considered each chord or series of chords in a certain progression as a separate and distinct entity, using a combination of different scales and arpeggios to outline the changes in the same way that a jazz musician would approach the instrument.

And unlike many other rock players, Garcia never gave up learning. He never drifted into irrelevance as a player, never became the kind of dinosaur many of his colleagues became. His continued progress is remarkable, especially considering that he had to essentially relearn the instrument following a diabetic coma that almost killed him in 1986.

Still, musicians and music lovers alike wonder aloud about his apotheosis as a guitarist. His playing was never flashy, speedy, loud, or otherwise emphatic. He often dismissed the use of distortion, a rock staple for guitar players since the 1960s, and his untrained voice did not possess the qualities typically associated with a rock star strutting his stuff in front of thousands. Nevertheless, he became one of the most legendary figures in all of rock 'n' roll and an eternal goodwill ambassador.

EARLY YEARS

Jerome John Garcia was born in Children's Hospital in San Francisco on August 1, 1942. His grandfather, Manuel Garcia, was an electrician who had immigrated from La Coruña, Spain, to San Francisco after World War I and his father, Jose "Joe" Garcia, was a bandleader and clarinetist. Garcia's mother, Ruth Marie Clifford, was a pianist. Jerome, or "Jerry," the second of two boys, was named after his father's favorite bandleader, Jerome Kern. His father made a decent living as the owner of a saloon and boarding house near the San Francisco waterfront.

But a family tragedy disrupted their happiness. While on a fishing trip, Jerry's father drowned. This left his mother to operate the business and the kids without supervision. Jerry and his brother Clifford were shuttled between the family home and the home of their grandparents. One day, while helping his grandfather chop wood, Jerry lost the top two joints of the middle finger on his right hand. Jerry also suffered from asthma, which often forced him to remain in bed, where he watched TV and read comic books like *Tales from the Crypt*.

When his family moved to Menlo Park, 25 miles from San Francisco, Garcia started listening to KWBR, a rhythm and blues station, and developed a love of music. He'd been taking piano lessons and learning the banjo, his first stringed instrument, and was exposed to bluegrass by his grandparents.

In the mid-1950s, Garcia was introduced to rock 'n' roll. He enjoyed listening to Hank Ballard, Chuck Berry, Ray Charles, and the blues greats. His brother Clifford often memorized vocals of his favorite tunes and Jerry would create the harmony parts.

At 15, his mother gave him an accordion for his birthday. But Jerry, slightly disappointed, convinced her to trade it for a Danelectro guitar he had seen at a pawnshop. While in high school, Jerry practiced guitar and worked at the family saloon. On the weekends, he took classes at a local art school. There his teacher exposed him to the city's budding bohemian scene and he soon became familiar with San Fran's beatnik hangouts.

His exposure to the bohemian life turned him on to *On the Road,* Jack Kerouac's influential book, as well as to marijuana, which he started smoking in high school. In 1959 he joined his first band, called the Chords, and the combination of drugs and music hampered his academic performance. His mother, hoping to improve her son's schoolwork, decided to move the family to a small town called Cazadero outside of San Francisco. But it didn't help. Garcia ended up stealing a car, and law officials forced him to choose between a jail sentence and joining the Army. He chose the latter, enlisting in basic training at Fort Winfield Scott in the Presidio of San Francisco. While there, his basic training squad leader, an acoustic guitar player, turned Jerry on to folk music. At the time, rock 'n' roll had ebbed. Chuck Berry, whose "Maybellene" was one of Jerry's early favorites, had gotten thrown in jail, and Little Richard turned to the church. So the folk and blues boom displaced rock in the short time before the British Invasion. Jerry began playing acoustic music and listened extensively to bluegrass and roots music. But his time in the Army

Larry Hulst/Michael Ochs Archives/Getty Images

didn't last all that long. He was dishonorably discharged after accruing two court martials and eight AWOLs in less than a year.

Upon his discharge Jerry moved to Palo Alto to explore the alternative scene surrounding Stanford University. He began playing guitar in earnest, giving up his love for painting in the process. He dedicated himself to his pursuit of music further when he lived through a car accident in late 1960, a wreck that killed his best friend Paul Speegle. He felt that surviving the accident gave him a second chance to get his life in gear.

He met Robert Hunter while hanging around Stanford. Hunter would go on to be the full-time lyricist for Garcia's band the Grateful Dead. About this time, Garcia also met Phil Lesh, the eventual bass player of that band. Through a mutual friend, Garcia then met Bob Weir in the beginning of 1963. Around this time, Garcia taught guitar lessons and played in bluegrass and other acoustic bands. Inspired by a musician named Jim Kweskin, Garcia formed a jug band he called Mother McCree's Uptown Jug Champions, whose membership included Ron "Pigpen" McKernan.

Garcia began experimenting with LSD in 1964. Jann Wenner of *Rolling Stone* asked Garcia how it changed his behavior: "The effect **was that** it freed me because I suddenly realized that my little attempt at having a straight life and doing that was really a fiction and just wasn't going to work out. Luckily, I wasn't far enough into it for it to be shattering or anything; it was like a realization that just made me feel immensely relieved" (Wenner, Jann, *Rolling Stone,* April 1972, n.p.).

In 1965, the jug band evolved into the Warlocks, after bringing in Phil Lesh on bass and Bill Kreutzmann on percussion. But another band had the same name, and Garcia renamed his group the Grateful Dead after finding the term in a dictionary. No one, incidentally, in the band at the time agreed to the name, but word of it traveled fast and it became accepted.

MUSIC

The Grateful Dead made a name for itself quickly in the Bay Area. But they were a scruffy bunch.

The lead guitarist, Jerry Garcia, was homely, acne-scarred, and frizzy-haired. The bass player, Phil Lesh, looked as though he should be designing computer circuits. Bob Weir, the rhythm guitarist, appeared to be about 14 years old, and the drummer, Bill Kreutzmann, didn't seem much older. And then there was the lead singer and keyboard player, Ron "Pigpen" McKernan, who looked like a close relative of Attila the Hun, huge and gross and hairy and mean, as though he'd just crawled out of a cave ready to plunder and pillage. (McNally, Dennis, liner notes, *Grateful Dead: The Golden Road*. Rhino, 2002, p. 10)

They didn't sound right either. They excelled at playing extended versions of classic blues tunes, improvisational numbers that would get close to being considered for radio. But they attracted fans, legions of them; strange, similarly hairy, beatnik fans. These were the first Deadheads, or the group of enthusiasts that caught every Grateful Dead show, some even going so far as to quit their jobs and follow the band faithfully.

The scene in 1965 and 1966 featured the initial sprouts of drug-fueled psychedelia, and the Grateful Dead were front and center in that movement. The Dead represented the bohemian movement as well as any band. They preached faith in freedom. They believed in peace. They were the latest in a long line of cultural and social idealists that believed in the goodness of the human spirit. They reflected that vibe in their shows, and soon the hippie/beatnik movement expanded from the Bay Area across America.

Ken Kesey, a local author, and his gang, called the Merry Pranksters, began holding parties, called Acid Tests, not just for amusement but for social and intellectual expansion. The acid fit comfortably into the Grateful Dead scheme, given their penchant for exploration and improvisation. They became accustomed to altering their mental states for gigs, and so, not coincidentally, did their audiences.

Madness ensued in the Bay Area around 1966 and 1967, even though new laws prohibiting LSD cropped up on the books. Venues such as the Fillmore Auditorium and the Avalon Ballroom opened and began serving as the main stages for all major San Francisco live music events. In early 1967, they journeyed south to Los Angeles to make their first recording. They had signed a contract with the young Warner Brothers label, a record company that had no rock 'n' roll bands on their roster prior to signing the Dead.

The *Grateful Dead* came out on St. Patrick's Day in 1967, and it received lukewarm reviews. Many critics insisted that listening to the album wasn't as good as seeing the band perform live. That criticism dogged the Grateful Dead for 30 long years. It had no single on it, which became an important issue about this time, when music radio was transitioning from AM pop to FM rock 'n' roll.

Toward the end of 1967 the Dead needed to recruit some help, so they stepped up the contributions of lyricist Robert Hunter. Garcia, assigned to write lyrics, didn't feel all that comfortable in the role and Hunter was a natural poet. Kreutzmann also invited a drummer to sit in with the band. Mickey Hart, a Brooklyn-born son of two professional drummers, became a great find and a mainstay with the band.

Garcia and Hunter collaborated effectively on tunes like "Cosmic Charlie" and "Doin' That Rag." The Dead began to record regularly, issuing albums like *Anthems of the Sun* and *Aoxomoxoa*. The band improved consistently and began coming up with anthems of their own, like "Dark Star," "Uncle John's Band," and "St. Stephen." They mined different genres beautifully, from psychedelia and space rock to blues, R&B, and rock 'n' roll.

At the turn of the decade, Garcia became infatuated with another instrument, the pedal steel guitar. This intense interest led him to delve into country music and join up with a friend, John "Marmaduke" Dawson, a country singer working at a coffeehouse in Menlo Park. Jerry sat in with Dawson, a partnership that led directly to the side project, New Riders of the Purple Sage. That band joined the Dead on tour beginning in 1970.

Bob Weir came up with a couple of Dead melodies, "Sugar Magnolia" and "Truckin'," for which Hunter wrote the lyrics. That same year, 1970, the band released their first great album, *Workingman's Dead,* and then the next year they released another, *American Beauty.* They also made a live album and toured Europe for the first time in 1971. In 1973, they abandoned their Warner Brothers' contract, admitting that they gave the label a harder time than the other way around. For as long as they'd been together, the band had been skeptical of corporate involvement, and their suspicion led to strained relationships.

*   *   *

Five years of endless touring lent the band a certain inadvertent business savvy that many outside the band interpreted as "maturity." They had a solid nationwide audience and had locked into an impressive musical groove as well. But all this touring had helped the band develop into more than merely a group, but a business entity as well. This sophistication would serve the band for its entire career.

At the same time they were pursuing greater musical intricacy, their financial intuition led them to form a record label of their own, a scheme that would ensure they'd be firmly in control of their fate from this point on. They pushed their limits not only as a band, but as a group of independently minded record company executives who wanted autonomy.

But this business end of things didn't end with Grateful Dead Records. Their road manager had set up Out of Town Tours, a booking agency, and another member of the Dead family set up Fly By Night, their own travel agency. When they released *Wake of the Flood,* the first album on their own label, they had many pieces in place to facilitate that autonomy.

They were also playing bigger and bigger gigs. In 1973, they played the massive "Summer Jam" at Watkins Glen, otherwise known as the biggest concert of all time. These venues posed significant challenges for the Dead; they wanted to be sure their sound translated to the big crowds they played to. This led to innovations in concert sound. In 1974, the Dead came to the end of a fruitful search for the ultimate sound system.

It contained 641 separate speakers, powered by 26,400 watts from 55,600-watt preamps. The speakers were set up in a "wall of sound" about 30 feet high. They blasted, of course, but the clarity was so good audience members directly in front of that wall could leave the venue with their hearing intact.

"Playing in front of it was like piloting a flying saucer," said Lesh, "or riding your own sound wave" (McNally, liner notes, p. 12).

It was also incredibly expensive to run and difficult to transport, and a huge undertaking to set up. They couldn't possibly maintain that kind of expense and still be profitable. Or could they? They went into the studio to record their next album, *From the Mars Hotel,* to see if they could reap enough profits to keep their sonic spectacle on the road.

They didn't. The album sold as well as other Dead albums and yielded some classics, like the Garcia/Hunter chestnut, "Scarlet Begonias," and the Lesh masterpiece "Unbroken Chain," not to mention Deadhead favorites like "U.S. Blues" and "Ship of Fools."

Finally, the road often traveled got to the band, and in 1975 they went on what their fans refer to as "The Hiatus." They kicked back and made a casual recording, which sold reasonably well. Weir formed Kingfish, a side project, and Jerry pursued his own solo career for a time. But in the end, the time apart, about a year and a half, left the band members, especially Garcia, rather unfulfilled. He told a reporter,

> I feel like I've had both trips (Grateful Dead and individual) and, really, I'm not that taken with my own ideas. I don't really have that much to say, and I'm more interested in being involved in something that's larger than me . . . As a life problem, the Grateful Dead is an anarchy. It doesn't have any . . . stuff. It doesn't have any goals. It doesn't have any plans. It doesn't have any leaders. Or real organization. And it works. (McNally, liner notes, p. 12)

That last part—about not having any real organization—came back to bite Garcia and the band. The Grateful Dead Record Company had big problems, largely due to the inattention and disorder of the band members themselves. They eventually let their record company die a tragic death, and signed on with Clive Davis's new label, Arista. They released *Terrapin Station* in 1977, *Shakedown Street* in 1978, and *Go to Heaven* in 1980, all with a handful of stellar songs. But again, the curse of the Dead struck again and again. They had no trouble selling concert tickets, but moving records seemed virtually impossible.

Exasperated, they left the studio, some thought for good. They released a couple of live albums and went on tour with Bob Dylan in 1985 and 1986. Two days following the last day of that tour, a sticky date in District of Columbia, Garcia fell into a diabetic coma that lasted several days. The future of the Dead imperiled, Garcia came out of the coma and went into an informal therapy with guitarist Merl Saunders. Saunders nursed Garcia back to full health, a process that included Garcia relearning how to play the guitar. In the fall of that year, Garcia reformed his band and then a few months later reconvened with the Dead.

*   *   *

The next year, 1987, the Dead entered the studio again for *In the Dark,* an album that ironically thrust the band back into the spotlight on the strength of the band's lone Top 40 single, "Touch of Grey." Fans had long mused that the Dead's studio albums lacked the easygoing energy and natural flow of their live performances, and *In the Dark* does come close to capturing that elusive live ability.

After over 20 years together, "Touch of Grey" and *In the Dark* helped the Dead achieve unprecedented reward. They had finally put a song on the radio and their shows became open forums for new fans, not just Deadheads. Interestingly, this is the beginning of the end of the Dead's story. While they played to larger audiences, these fans had little interest in the band's music. They came to "make the scene," and the music was incidental. Massive overpopulation of these gigs was eerily reminiscent of the overpopulation that afflicted and led to the demise of Haight-Ashbury, that section of San Francisco that had served as the epicenter of the hippie counterculture.

The overexpansion of the Dead's shows foreshadowed the 1990s, the Dead's bleakest decade. The era started poorly with the death of keyboardist Brent Mydland in the summer of 1990. Garcia, mourning the death of his bandmate, slipped back into some of his old habits, including drugs, tobacco, and overeating. He also suffered from sleep apnea.

During the beginning of 1995, Garcia's health, both physically and mentally, declined drastically. His ability to play the guitar deteriorated to the point where the crew would turn down the volume of his guitar, and he often had to be reminded of what song he was performing. He checked himself into rehab in July of 1995. On August 9, they found him dead in his room at the Serenity Knolls treatment center. The cause of death was deemed a heart attack.

Twenty-five thousand people attended a public memorial service held at San Francisco's Golden Gate Park.

SIDE PROJECTS/SESSIONS

A peripatetic guitarist, Jerry Garcia engaged in a bunch of side projects throughout his 30 years with the Grateful Dead. He formed the Jerry Garcia Band in 1975, and it became the most important of his projects while not on the road with the Dead. The band played rock music, mainly, infused with folk, blues, roots, R&B, and reggae tones. John Kahn and Melvin Seals were his two loyal bandmates through most of this time, and Seals took over the band, renaming it JGB, in 1995 after Garcia died. The band released one studio album, *Cats Under the Stars,* and one live album while Garcia was alive.

Garcia also formed Old and in the Way, an all-star bluegrass project with mandolinist David Grisman, an intimate friend of Garcia's for many years. They performed traditional tunes and bluegrass versions of more famous rock and pop tunes. Old and in the Way's debut, released in 1975, ended up being the top-selling bluegrass album for decades.

He also lent his services to New Riders of the Purple Sage, a band he helped cofound. In fact, he appeared on their debut album and was listed as a member, but increased commitment to the Dead at the time forced him to leave the fold.

Garcia also loaned his playing talents to upwards of 50 albums by many of his friends and associates—from Jefferson Airplane and Crosby, Stills, Nash and Young, to Ken Nordine and Ornette Coleman—adding guitar licks, vocals, pedal steel, banjo, and even production assistance. Styles included rock, blues, jazz, electronic, gospel, funk, and reggae, among many others. As a solo act, Garcia covered Motown and Dylan generously as well.

TECHNIQUE/STYLE

Garcia's ability to extend his guitar into soulful improvisations has been well-documented and oft-witnessed. His skill in this area, along with the support of his band, gave birth to the so-called "Jam Scene," a fertile breeding ground for talented, post-Dead, improvisational pop, rock and jazz musicians.

Signatures of Garcia's supreme improvisational ability include frequent interplay with his band members. He'd often trade licks or take his jam cues from Bob Weir, who as a rhythm player would often set up Garcia's solo embarkations. His style of playing incorporated all the styles he had absorbed growing up, including roots and acoustic styles like folk, country, jugband, and bluegrass, as well as more electric styles like blues, early rock, soul, and R&B. It all came together during the very turbulent stylistic period of the mid-1960s, which of course featured the budding psychedelic period, Hendrix's acid rock, and even the nascent strains of heavy metal.

Garcia also filtered in more unpredictable influences. He hinted at Celtic music, a close relative of bluegrass, in both traditional terms and in the British finger-picking vein as well. The work of guitarists like Bert Jansch and John Renbourne affected him deeply. He delved into the avant-garde work of jazz players like John Coltrane and Ornette Coleman, whose ideas he snatched for his extended improvisations.

THE DEAD AND THE JAM SCENE

In the waning years of his life, Jerry Garcia and the Grateful Dead helped give way to what became known as the Jam Scene. The many bands influenced by the Dead, especially by their often transcendent improvisational passages, became loosely grouped together and referred to as "jam bands." These bands patterned their performances after the improvisational aspects of the Dead, depending on their own spontaneous improvisational style to come up with their own unique performances. These groups didn't limit themselves to a single, Dead-type roots and rock genre. Rather, they were spread across many, from country, bluegrass, and blues to electronic, folk music, and international styles. What bound them together was the band's willingness to explore unscripted territory and to dazzle audiences with unique and dexterous instrumentation.

In the wake of Jerry Garcia's death, the jam band scene thrived, with hundreds of bands popping up to fill the void left by the Dead. At first, a band called Phish, a Vermont group descending directly from the tie-dyed and exploratory music of the Dead, adopted the mantle of the new Grateful Dead. Led by the group's adventurous guitar player Trey Anastasio, Phish commanded huge audiences and played outrageous, eclectic shows, propelled by the band's instrumental brilliance and a need to surprise their fans with showmanship and improvisation. The immense popularity of Phish in the early 1990s led to many bands forming in their wake. The Jam Band scene became something of a cultural phenomenon, with great acts like .moe, Gov't Mule, Leftover Salmon, and the String Cheese Incident popping up. Since the Grateful Dead departed, second- and third-generation jam bands have arisen to follow in their footsteps.

The surviving members of the Grateful Dead first went on to form a band called the Other Ones, and then simply renamed themselves the Dead. They helped anchor the burgeoning jam scene and are still looked upon as the style's elders. But there's no denying the fertility of the current scene. There seems to be no apparent thread, at least speaking in terms of genres, that binds these bands together. Perhaps, then, it is the enthusiasm of the scene's fans, their passion for live music, that is its common denominator.

Many of those jam bands get together at numerous festivals across the country. But the biggest one is called Bonnaroo Music Festival held each June in Tennessee since 2002. Held on a 700-acre farm, Bonnaroo, French for "Good Street," features many of the biggest acts in both the jam scene and the popular rock scene, and holds nearly 150,000 fans. It is a testament to the diversity and open-mindedness of the jam scene, not to mention to the overwhelming power of live music.

Garcia explained his approach to soloing back in 1985. "It keeps on changing. I still basically revolve around the melody and the way it's broken up into phrases as I perceive them. With most solos, I tend to play something that phrases the way the melody does; my phrases may be more dense or have different value, but they'll occur in the same places in the song" (Guitar.com, April 1985).

Descended from this mosaic of genres, Garcia's playing also had a number of so-called signatures in his work through the years with the Grateful Dead. One of these was playing lead lines, making use of rhythmic triplets, as he did on "Good Morning Little School Girl," "U.S. Blues," and "Brokedown Palace" among many others. He also possessed a very distinctive vibrato technique. Because he used heavier strings on his guitar, he drew his vibrato from his whole hand and wrist, not just his finger. He likened his vibrato method to a violin player, who used his entire wrist to create the modulating sound.

He also constantly adjusted his use of a pick, depending on what he was playing.

I always strike the string with the pointy end. A lot of guys use the rounded shoulder of the pick because it makes it seem like you can play faster. But what you pick up in speed, you sacrifice in point. I like to have a lot of control over the attack of the note. By relaxing or tightening up your grip on the pick, you can get a lot of change in touch, coloration, and harmonic content. With acoustic guitar, that's one of the ways you can really color your playing. I use a real thick pick, one with absolute zero flexibility. (Guitar.com, April 1985)

EQUIPMENT/GEAR

Jerry Garcia was loyal to many guitars, for many different reasons, from Gibson SGs and Les Pauls to Fender Strats. In the beginning, with the early incarnation of the Dead called the Warlocks, he played a Guild Starfire, which he also played on their debut, *The Grateful Dead*. In 1967, he picked up the Gibsons for a few years. He also played a Martin D-18 acoustic and a 1939 Gibson Super 400.

He entered into a pedal steel phase in late 1969 for about five years. His pedal steel guitars were a Fender Pedal Steel and later a ZB Custom D-10. After this flirtation with pedal steel, he jumped to a Fender Stratocaster, which he nicknamed "Alligator" for a sticker on the pickguard. Given to him by Graham Nash, he played it for a year or so before switching to his first custom-made guitar from Alembic. He nicknamed the Alembic "Wolf," and it was a beauty with an ebony fingerboard and other lovely ornamentation. Luthier Doug Irwin worked with Garcia in producing the guitars.

Garcia beat on Wolf, and after a few years onstage it required repair. While in the shop, Garcia took to playing a Travis Bean guitar, made in San Francisco, with an aluminum neck. Meanwhile, Irwin had built him his second Alembic instrument, nicknamed "Tiger," an axe for which the luthier pulled out all the stops. It had gorgeous wood—cocobolo, maple stripe, vermillion, and flame maple—along with a single coil DiMarzio SDS-1 and two humbucker DiMarzio Super IIs. These were removable, in keeping with Garcia's desire to replace his pickups every couple of years. With all its electronics and extra features, Tiger tipped the scales at a very heavy 13 pounds. But that didn't prevent Garcia from playing it exclusively for the next decade.

Irwin built Garcia Rosebud next, which happened in 1990. In many ways it possessed similarities with Tiger. But it also featured different inlays, this with a dancing skeleton, and electronics, tone and volume controls. Rosebud boasted three humbuckers, the neck and bridge pickup shared a tone control, while the middle humbucker had its own tone knob. It was lighter, too, with some sections hollowed out.

A Florida yacht-maker and an upstart luthier named Stephen Cripe built a custom guitar for Garcia based entirely on speculation, doing research from photographs and film to determine what Garcia might prefer. He built it using Brazilian rosewood for the fingerboard and East Indian rosewood for the body which, he said, was taken from a nineteenth-century bed used by opium smokers. Garcia loved it when presented with it in 1993 and called it "Lightning Bolt." It was the first guitar Cripe ever built, and Garcia played it until his death.

For most of his earlier years, Garcia used a silverface Fender Twin amp. He continued to use the preamp from the Fender amp through 1993. From the late 1970s to about

1993 he didn't use the power amp and speakers of the Fender, replacing it with three JBL D120/E120 speakers in a vertical box powered by a McIntosh solid state amp. It was miked with a Sennheiser 421 mic. With the Jerry Garcia Band he used a Mesa Boogie Mark II with the JBL speakers.

As for effects, during the early 1970s Garcia was limited mostly to the Vox Wah-Wah pedal. By the late 1970s, he used the Mutron envelope filter, which he utilized till his death. Also, Garcia used a Mutron Octave Divider, MXR Distortion Phase 100, and Analog Delay. By the late 1980s, he switched to mainly Boss effects, including an Octave Divider, Turbo Overdrive, Super Overdrive, and EQs in two separate effects loops. In the studio, he used Lexicons, a PCM-42 or PCM-60, with a PCM-70, reverb/delay units.

ESSENTIAL READING

Guitar.com, April 1985.
McNally, Dennis. *Grateful Dead: The Golden Road.* Liner notes, Rhino, 2002, 10.
Wenner, Jann. *Rolling Stone,* April 1972, n.p.

ESSENTIAL WORK

"Dark Star" (1969)
"Hobo Song" (Old and in the Way, 1973)
"Off to Sea Once More" (with David Grisman, 1990)
"Panama Red" (Old and in the Way/Jerry Garcia Band, 1973)
"Positively 4th Street" (1973)
"Sugaree" (1972)

ESSENTIAL LISTENING

More so than most bands, the Grateful Dead frequently released live albums in place of studio albums. They recorded their shows constantly, and these live releases, many of which were issued after Garcia died in 1995, filled the role of conventional studio albums. They were recent in nature and often contained newly written material not found on any studio album. Many of the band's studio albums paled in comparison to their live work, which is why so many Deadheads preferred listening (and watching) their heroes live or on bootlegged tapings of their live recordings.

Almost Acoustic (Warner Bros., 1988)
Anthem of the Sun (Warner Bros., 1969)
Europe '72 (Warner Bros., 1972)
Fillmore East: April 1971 (Grateful Dead, 2000)
Hundred Year Hall 4-26-72 (Grateful Dead, 1995)
Live at the Cow Palace: New Year's Eve 1976 (Rhino, 2007)
Live/Dead (Warner Bros., 1969/2003)
Rockin' the Rhein with the Grateful Dead, 1972 (Rhino, 2004)
Steppin' Out with the Grateful Dead: England 1972 (GDM/Arista, 2002)
The Very Best of Jerry Garcia (Rhino, 2006)

David Gilmour

Some guitarists are known for their chops. Some are known for their speed. Some players put on a great show, and others innovated on their instruments. And then there are some, like David Gilmour of Pink Floyd, that are best known for their tone. Sure, he had plenty of gifts. But like other great players before him, including Eric Clapton and B.B. King, Gilmour is a Stratocaster player with impeccable tone. His sublime, bluesy Strat solos established him as one of the finest rock lead men to ever emerge from the 1960s, and his most acclaimed solos rank among rock 'n' roll's finest.

On Digital Dreamdoor's list of the "100 Greatest Rock Guitar Solos," Gilmour's work on "Comfortably Numb," a track off of Pink Floyd's 1979 *The Wall* album, sits at #1, at the very top of the list. Other Gilmour solos, including those found in "Money," "Shine on You Crazy Diamond," and "Atom Heart Mother," are also in the Top 50. Gilmour's classic leads are all over legendary work like *Dark Side of the Moon, Wish You Were Here,* and *Animals.*

Few rock guitarists manipulate sound and space as well as David Gilmour. Through 11 original albums with Pink Floyd and a small handful of solo records, Gilmour has established himself as a master of moody rock. His guitar legacy began officially in 1968, when he stepped in as lead guitarist of the band, replacing founding member Syd Barrett, who'd been dogged by personal problems and drug addiction. Gilmour, along with Roger Waters, Nick Mason, and Rick Wright, went on to establish Pink Floyd as one of the rock era's most spectacular bands.

Of course, it wasn't always easy. From the very start, he maintained a contentious relationship with the difficult Waters, and that relationship debilitated as the band trudged through the 1970s. By the time *The Wall* rolled around, Gilmour had grown tired of waiting for Waters to produce material, and he began making records of his own, essentially bringing the Pink Floyd era to an informal close. In 1983, Waters, Gilmour, and Mason collaborated on *The Final Cut,* though the sleeve notes described it as a piece by Waters "performed by Pink Floyd." The opposite was true with *A Momentary Lapse of Reason* and *The Division Bell,* both considered Gilmour albums "performed by Pink Floyd." In 1985, Gilmour and Waters engaged in a battle over the band name, which spilled over into the media. Gilmour and Mason won the right to use the name and a majority of the band's songs, though Waters did retain the rights to the albums *The Wall* (save for three of the songs that Gilmour co-wrote), *Animals,* and *The Final Cut.*

It was a messy end to a tremendous run for the band, though, a run that vaulted Gilmour from obscurity to one of our greatest guitar heroes. To this day, his guitar lines emanate from his Stratocaster, as he, in our collective mind's eye, stands motionless onstage, relaxed and quiet. His solos penetrate the atmosphere and hang in the air overhead, resonating with richness, depth, and that impeccable tone.

EARLY YEARS

David Jon Gilmour was born on March 6, 1946, in Cambridge, England. He grew up in Grantchester Meadows, an affluent housing estate along the banks of the River Cam. He was raised in a wealthy family. His father, Douglas Gilmour, was a senior lecturer and groundbreaking geneticist in Zoology at the University of Cambridge, and his mother, Sylvia, was a teacher and film editor. Both often found themselves away from home on business, leaving young David, his sister, and two brothers home alone. They often passed the time riding bikes or punting along the river on their boat. But with so much free time on their hands, mischief eventually became the Gilmour boys' chief pastime.

They were often caught in local pubs and taverns checking out the bands and listening to rock 'n' roll, the new sound coming from America in the late 1950s. He had come from a fairly musical family. His parents sang, and his siblings all played instruments. Once, after his parents returned from visiting America, they brought back a stack of blues and folk 1978s, plus Pete Seeger's teach-yourself guitar book and LP.

From there, at 13, David cultivated an interest in the guitar and was ecstatic when a neighborhood friend let him borrow his acoustic. Gilmour loved it so much he ended up buying the guitar from his friend, and he'd go on to spend many hours in his bedroom practicing. He began listening to American rock, especially those by Bill Haley, Chuck Berry, and Elvis Presley, on Radio Luxembourg. He remembers being awestruck the first time he heard Presley's "Heartbreak Hotel." While listening, he'd try to play along to the songs he heard broadcasting from the radio.

He also listened to folk and blues: Sonny Terry, Brownie McGhee, Leadbelly, Pete Seeger, and all those artists his parents had turned him onto. By his mid- to late-teens, Gilmour had picked up on all the contemporary fare he'd heard and then some. And the idea arose to start his own band. His school chum, Syd Barrett, was also interested in rock music, and the two became great friends because of their common interest. Together, they idolized the Beatles and the Stones and tried to play just like them. In David's sixteenth year, he began to join bands, trying to find his niche.

At 18, Gilmour formed a band called the Joker's Wild. They performed mainly covers, and they played all the current dance music, which is what audiences at the time wanted to hear. The band did well on the local pub, village hall, and tearoom circuit. The lure of rock 'n' roll pulled Gilmour away from school and, against his parents' adamant wishes, he dropped out.

Diverging now from his upper-middle-class expectations, Gilmour drove delivery vans and humped sheet metal in order to afford musical equipment, like a PA and microphones, that would allow him to make records and play gigs. On nights off, he'd hitchhike from Cambridge to London, to the Marquee to see acts like Georgie Fame and the Blue Flames, the Who, and the Stones. Then in 1966, he finally made the move to London with the band.

*   *   *

One night, at a Joker's Wild Cambridge gig, the band opened for Paul Simon. Also on the bill was another band, with Syd Barrett on guitar, Roger Waters on bass, and Londoners Rick Wright on keyboards, and Nick Mason on drums. At the time, in 1965, they were wavering over whether to bill themselves as the T-Set or the Pink Floyd.

Soon after that gig, Gilmour met a music manager who wanted him to go to Marbella, Spain to play the tourist crowd there. They changed their name to Bullitt, first, and then Flowers. Eventually, they were booked at a residency in a Paris nightclub called the Bilboquet. The year was 1966.

> We did a lot of soul: Wilson Pickett, the Four Tops and one or two Beach Boys-type-things. We had some mics stolen in France and I had to zoom back to London to buy some new ones. I went to a club called Blaises in South Kensington and saw Hendrix by chance, jamming with the Brian Auger Trinity and it was amazing. So we waited for that first Hendrix record to come out and we started to do those songs as well. We did nearly all of *Are You Experienced?* in our French set. (Sutcliffe, Phil, "And This Is Me," *Mojo,* April 2006, n.p.)

The band struggled to get by in Paris, living off of very little money in cheap hotels on the city's Left Bank. They were in France for about a year before calling it quits. Gilmour returned to London, where he'd run into his old friend Syd Barrett. He noticed that Barrett's band, in the studio recording their first album, *Piper at the Gates of Dawn,* seemed to be doing quite well. In fact, they were the talk of the town. It was 1967, and the Summer of Love had dawned.

MUSIC

Joker's Wild had opened several times for the Pink Floyd, and Barrett was Gilmour's longtime friend, so the two bands knew each other quite well. When Gilmour returned from Paris, the Pink Floyd had been making inroads on London's underground circuit, developing experimental rock sounds with psychedelic light shows, building a cult following, and developing a reputation as the loudest and hippest underground band in town.

During this time, Barrett had begun using drugs as an adjunct to the whole psychedelic experience and, as a result, he began to exhibit erratic behavior. He'd become quite unpredictable, not to mention undependable. He often missed shows or showed up incapacitated, unable to play.

"He'd go catatonic on stage, playing music that had little to do with the material, or not playing at all. An American tour had to be cut short when he was barely able to function, let alone play the pop star game" (Unterberger, Richie, allmusic.com).

Barrett's behavior threatened the band's livelihood, and even though he had been a founding member, Waters, Wright, and Mason decided they needed someone to step in for him.

At first, this didn't mean a total replacement. When the band members asked Gilmour to fill in, they meant they needed someone more reliable in the lineup on lead guitar. Slowly, though, they phased Barrett out of the lineup. Gilmour recalls one afternoon in particular when the four of them piled in the van to drive to a gig, and together they decided not to pick Syd up. That was the beginning of the end of Barrett's involvement with Pink Floyd. He had guided the band through their first album, *The Piper at the Gates of Dawn,* a pyschedelic romp some liken in quality to the Beatles' *Sgt. Pepper's Lonely Hearts Club Band.* But his time with the band had come to a rather ignominious end.

To help Syd maintain his dignity, the band signed on unofficially to manage Barrett's career. Gilmour in particular, perhaps to assuage his guilt for replacing his friend, oversaw Barrett's two solo recordings, *The Madcap Laughs* and *Barrett.*

Jon Sievert/Michael Ochs Archives/Getty Images

For *A Saucerful of Secrets,* the first Pink Floyd album Gilmour played on, the guitarist remembers trying his best to sound like Syd, and also imitating his new hero Jimi Hendrix. The year was 1968 and Hendrix was the guitar player on *everybody's* mind. Barrett assumed guitar responsibilities on three songs, while Gilmour contributed performances on five. *Saucerful* is the only studio album on which all five members of Pink Floyd appear.

Released in the summer of 1968, Gilmour put his guitar prints all over *Saucerful.* His playing, less frolicsome and more rock and blues derived than Barrett's, marked the beginning of the band's transition from psychedelic and space rock to a more progressive sound. They had strayed from the mad energy and whimsy of the Barrett material and ventured into a more futuristic sound.

Saucerful also marked the beginning of the band's struggle to come up with original material. With Barrett more or less on the outs, the band had trouble finding its songwriting voice. Both Waters and Rick Wright struggled to develop songs on their own. They plunged further into space jams and improvisational avant-garde material like the title track and "Set the Controls for the Heart of the Sun."

Ummagumma, the follow-up to *Saucerful,* reflects the difficulties the band had without Barrett in the lineup as chief composer. They exerted great energy in coming up with new material, but no one in the band had asserted himself as a confident writer. As a result, they made *Ummagumma,* a double LP consisting of one live disc and one studio disc. The studio material came from each of the band's four writers, separately, not collaborations, making it something of a transitional effort while the artists got their footing as songwriters.

Atom Heart Mother, released in 1970, continued to reflect that transition. Side One is composed of the title track, a full-length collaboration with an outside writer, Scottish experimental composer Ron Geesin. Side Two features a song each by Waters, Wright, and Gilmour, and it ends with an ensemble piece. But, the group's small recording budget wasn't commensurate with their ambition, especially on the Geesin collaboration, and even after hiring a full orchestra and choir, they ran out of studio time and money enough to complete the piece to everyone's liking.

Meddle followed *Atom Heart Mother,* and found the band sharpening its focus. Pink Floyd trimmed its orchestral excesses and snapped back to a slightly more rock sound. Gilmour stepped up his presence on the album, both as a guitarist and as a singer, and his increased accountability boded well for the future of the band.

Of course, nothing could prepare the general public for the next Pink Floyd album. *Dark Side of the Moon,* issued in 1973, came virtually out of nowhere. In retrospect, explanations exist to help determine how the band got from *Meddle* to *Dark Side.* Music critics point to how the *Meddle* explorations were simply condensed into songs, trimmed again of excess and far more concrete musical expressions. In fact, this concreteness, this focus, signaled a turning point in Pink Floyd's studio machinations.

"But what gives the album true power is the subtly textured music, which evolves from ponderous, neo-psychedelic art rock to jazz fusion and blues-rock before turning back to psychedelia. It's dense with detail, but leisurely paced, creating its own dark, haunting world" (Erlewine, Stephen Thomas, allmusic.com).

All of a sudden, the band's cosmic rock became completely approachable and accessible. It had state-of-the-art production and just enough creative flourishes to please fans of both mainstream and progressive, space-rock. Gilmour's work on songs like "Time," "The Great Gig in the Sky," and the lyrical "Breathe" featured the guitarist carving out a more distinctive style, with blues-based chords and solos. The rock framework of the album suited Gilmour well and his coloring throughout is exquisite.

Its creative triumphs catapulted the band into commercial success, vaulting them to incredible heights and turning them, nearly overnight, into rock superstars. Pink Floyd became one of the world's most popular bands, thanks to this single album. It remained on the charts for an inscrutably long time; the last tally had it on the *Billboard* album chart for over 470 weeks. To this day, the album remains one of the most popular recordings of all time.

It also proved to be a very difficult act to follow.

But follow it they did, with another chart-topping album, *Wish You Were Here,* in 1975. This album, a loose concept piece based on their friend Syd Barrett, unfolds beautifully. Its centerpiece is "Shine On You Crazy Diamond," a candid tribute to Barrett and a song that yearns to regain the emotional and creative connection to their ex-partner during the band's soaring success. The working title of the album is telling: *Variations on a Theme of Absence.* Gilmour distinguishes himself on the album as well, especially on the modulating riff of "Have a Cigar," a funky interlude that serves to distance Pink Floyd from its prog rock roots.

Wish You Were Here is a far more sincere and passionate record than its predecessor and also features something of a refinement in Roger Waters' songwriting contributions. Waters, a sardonic and intellectual talent, began to hone his vision and his progress, and product, began at this point to dominate within the band.

With *Animals* (1977) and *The Wall* (1979), Roger Waters took the reins of Floyd and turned the process into a dictatorship. Waters' bitter worldview on *Animals* stands in stark contrast to the warmth and passion of *Wish You Were Here.* It is Pink Floyd's strangest and darkest record, resting not on hooks and vocal melodies but on atmosphere and message. "Pigs," "Dogs," and "Sheep" all become metaphors for people and Waters communicates with effective immediacy; his songs beautifully capture his bleak perspective.

But if Waters steps forward on *Animals* as the band's visionary leader, Gilmour comes forth as its musical heart. His guitar lines dominate; Waters' songs are brittle, moody, and dark, perfect for Gilmour's expressionist blues flourishes.

The extensive *Animals* tour also found Waters in a foul, almost misanthropic mood. He began to distance himself from the band and he struggled with the concept of stardom. He bemoaned the lack of an intimate connection between the band and their massive, stadium audiences.

At the Rock 'n' Roll Hall of Fame's *The Wall* exhibit, Waters wrote of an incident that happened at a gig at Montreal's Olympic Stadium on July 6, 1977. It would create the first huge fissure that formed in Pink Floyd's foundation:

> I found myself increasingly alienated in that atmosphere of avarice and ego until one night . . . the boil of my frustration burst. Some crazed teenage fan was clawing his way up the storm netting that separated us from the human cattle pen in front of the stage, screaming his devotion to the demi-gods beyond his reach. Incensed by his misunderstanding and my own connivance, I spat my frustration in his face. Later that night, back at the hotel, shocked by my behavior, I was faced with a choice. To deny my addiction and embrace that comfortably numb but magic-less existence or accept the burden of insight, take the road less traveled and embark on the often painful journey to discover who I was and where I fit. *The Wall* was the picture I drew for myself to help me make that choice.

Out of this incident, Waters realized that in order to stay sane, he needed to take complete control of the band; inside him grew an emotional need to write songs to communicate his own thoughts and feelings. *The Wall* was another bleak, overly ambitious, narcissistic double concept album concerned itself with the material and emotional walls modern humans build around themselves for survival. Essentially, *The Wall* was a rock opera about a fragile, egotistical rock star, nicknamed "Pink"—sound familiar?—that spit on a fan that was cheering during an acoustic song.

The Wall was a huge success even by Pink Floyd's standards, in part because of the music's accessible pop traits. "Another Brick in the Wall" hit #1 on both sides of the Atlantic, and fans were clamoring for tickets to an incredibly large-scale touring production of *The Wall,* which would feature construction of an actual wall during the band's performance.

Many guitar players feel that Gilmour's best work is found on *The Wall,* specifically on "Comfortably Numb," which is generally acknowledged to be one of the greatest rock 'n' roll solos in the history of the genre. It perfectly embodies the idea of a "feel solo," with its brilliant excursion, rife with crying bends, overbends, and just the right amount of space to let the notes resonate.

> At this point, the melancholy of the chorus turns to outright malevolence in tone and one of rock's greatest guitar solos enters, Gilmour's two-minute Hendrix-ian blues-rock workout with a raunchy tone that Prince seems to have copped for his excellent guitar pyrotechnics in "Purple Rain." Though Gilmour foreshadows this solo with a smaller one after the first chorus, it does not prepare for the bravura performance of the second screaming solo; it rumbles in on a low distorted chord, picking up steam quickly, a passionate rendering of the rock-solo archetype that still sounded glorious after countless listens. (Janovitz, Bill, allmusic.com)

Despite the band's success, Waters' commandeering would continue for the next six years, through *The Wall* and *The Final Cut,* both of which are considered largely Waters albums. Along the way, Waters' aggressive and exclusive new attitude left his bandmates by the wayside. First to get the elbow was Rick Wright, who, after serving in the studio

HITTING THE WALL

In 1986, fed up with the band, Roger Waters insisted that Pink Floyd was a moribund issue. He attempted to legally close down the Pink Floyd franchise forever. He insisted that it should be allowed to "retire gracefully." He lobbed in a few insults regarding the abilities of Gilmour and Mason. Gilmour rose to the occasion, explaining publicly that he considered *The Final Cut* cheap filler. " 'I'm going to fight him. I've earned the right to use the name Pink Floyd.' "

Pink Floyd, led by Gilmour, carried on recording, trying to reassemble their collective confidence. As [Pink Floyd producer Bob] Ezrin told me, "Nobody was saying, 'We're scared.' But when a key member leaves a band it's like losing a limb. You don't die, but you have to compensate. Make sure the music is as deep and interesting as it's always been" (Sutcliffe, 2006).

On July 2, 2005, Pink Floyd reunited for a gig for the first time since 1981, performing at the London Live 8 Concert, with Waters rejoining David Gilmour, Nick Mason, and Richard Wright. They reunited again for charity the next year and talks were in the works for a 2009 reunion.

In the spring of 2006, after the band hashed out an amenable agreement, and Waters and Gilmour made amends, Gilmour released *On An Island,* his first solo album in 22 years. Low key and soulful, the recording featured lyrical contributions from his wife Polly Samson.

In December 2006, Gilmour released a tribute to Syd Barrett, who had died in July that year, in the form of his own version of Pink Floyd's first single "Arnold Layne." Recorded live at London's Royal Albert Hall, the CD single featured versions of the song performed by Pink Floyd's keyboard player (and Gilmour's band member) Richard Wright and special guest artist David Bowie.

for *The Wall,* was moved out of the band and rehired as a salaried employee. Wars of the ego ensued.

"Even mild-mannered Nick Mason, who lately built his own bridge back to friendship with Waters, reckoned that back then, 'Roger made Stalin look like an old muddle-head' and that 'he was deliberately keeping Dave down and frustrating him' " (Sutcliffe, 2006).

Feeling Waters' icy wrath, Gilmour had already been preparing for his own future. In Waters' difficult arrogance, he sensed the demise of the band and began making decisions about his own career. Certainly, he felt underutilized within the context of the band.

In 1978, a year or so before *The Wall* was released, Gilmour filed his first solo project, appropriately titled *David Gilmour*. While the songs don't approach the sublime heights of his best 1970s work, the album does have enjoyable moments, like the rockin' "Cry from the Street" and the poignant "So Far Away," one of his best vocal turns. More accessible was his second solo recording. *About Face,* issued in 1984, featured more pop hooks than Pink Floyd ever cared about delivering. Neither of Gilmour's solo efforts earned the attention of a Pink Floyd release, but each one proved to the band's audience, and perhaps to Gilmour himself, that he was at least as capable a writer and performer as his then arch enemy, bandmate Roger Waters.

In 1985, Waters declared that Pink Floyd was creatively spent and he sought to disconnect himself from the outfit. In 1986, Gilmour and drummer Nick Mason issued a press release stating that Waters had quit the band and they intended to continue on without him as Pink Floyd. Gilmour wrested full control of the group from Waters, rehired Rick Wright, and produced *A Momentary Lapse of Reason* in 1987 and *The Division Bell* in 1994.

TECHNIQUE/STYLE

Asked to describe his style, Gilmour says,

My style is a mish-mash, really. A combination of blues licks, guitar solos I've learned in the past, and all sorts of lovely, lovely tunes—for instance those from musicals, like *West Side Story*. You just put it all together, bit by bit. Every time you've learned someone else's melody, from any type of music, that melody gets inside your brain a little. Eventually, something from what you've learned is going to be regurgitated into something else you do. I can sum up everything about playing guitar in about two sentences. "Play what you feel. And ignore everything else!" (Uncredited interview, Fender Players Club)

One of Gilmour's true gifts is his ability to bend a note. The skill entrances listeners and draws them more deeply into the song. Gilmour often bends a note, holds it out, and then bends it into another note even further. On "Money," for example, he does some excellent bending.

Gilmour is also a firm believer in keeping it simple. While he's demonstrated an ability to shred, or play very loud and fast, he's better known for his precise and passionate note choices. These choices accentuate his style and complement the songs in which they're featured perfectly. His melodic work within the context of his songs and solos is complex and evocative, rather than based on the cheap double thrills of speed and power. This craftsmanship is best heard on "Comfortably Numb," but also shows up on "Echoes" and "Fat Old Sun."

Another skill that Gilmour possesses is his use of tremolo for vibrato. He adds vibrato to his bent notes by using his tremolo instead of his fret hand to produce it. This technique takes practice and an adjustment from the normal concept of producing tremolo with your fret hand. But it adds depth, dimension, and uniqueness to Gilmour's solos.

When he's playing a solo, Gilmour often switches from using his lead pickups to using his neck pickups for solos. This infuses his solos with a chunkier sound and, combined with the use of his effects (see Equipment/gear), creates a rich and generous guitar tone.

In augmenting that tone, Gilmour utilizes a wide spectrum of effects, beginning with fuzz, distortion, and wah-wah pedals. He also employs the use of reverb and compressor during his solos. Back in the late 1960s and early 1970s, Gilmour developed a fondness for effects, so much so that he had a problem keeping his string of pedals problem free; they often ran out of batteries or their wiring was faulty. So, in 1972, he hired a technician to house all his pedals in a single cabinet, an invention that would become the forerunner of rack setups to come.

Anyway, while it's impossible to achieve the same exact tones through all of the effects Gilmour uses—many of the pedals he uses are no longer manufactured—he's said in interviews that players can approximate the Pink Floyd tone with Boss brand pedals.

EQUIPMENT/GEAR

Gilmour, like his predecessor Syd Barrett, initially played a Telecaster. But after losing his Tele in an airplane mishap, he replaced it with a Strat, presumably after seeing the work that Jimi Hendrix had been doing with it around the same time. Like Hendrix and Clapton, Gilmour came to favor the Stratocaster and was one of the first in Britain to create a signature sound with the instrument.

During the early Pink Floyd years, Gilmour played a Strat almost exclusively, taking full advantage of its wide tonal palette and vibrato bar. He used a Lewis 24-fret electric guitar on rare occasions for its extended range, as in the solo of "Money." He also played a lap steel or Fender twin neck pedal steel guitar for slide parts. He used various acoustic guitars on early Floyd tracks, later settling on Martin D-18 and D-35 models in the 1970s, and, depending on the song, alternated between fingerpicking and playing with a plectrum.

Originally, Gilmour played his Tele through a Selmer 50-watt amp with a 4x12 cab and a Binson echo unit. The Selmer amp eventually gave way to Hiwatt amps and he found his signature sound in 1970 when he combined a stack made of those Hiwatt 100-watt heads with WEM 4x12 cabinets. The Hiwatt/WEM combination can be heard on *Meddle* and *Dark Side of the Moon.*

In the studio for *Dark Side of the Moon* Gilmour spiced up that sound with a Fender Twin Reverb combo amp, with two 12-inch speakers to his lineup for certain parts. Gilmour set out first to create a strong, clean tone and then blend in any fuzz or other effects on top of that solid clean sound; the technique was influenced by the clean Strat tones of Hank Marvin and other early British rockers.

David Gilmour's early Floyd effects consisted of a Binson Echorec tape delay. Barrett also used this device from his first days with the band. Gilmour also employed a Dallas-Arbiter Fuzzface fuzz box, Uni-Vibe pedal, Vox Wah-Wah pedal, a DeArmond volume pedal, and Leslie and Yamaha RA-200 rotating speaker cabinets. Another vintage device he used during the 1970s was the Maestro Rover, a small rotating speaker on a stand that resembled a satellite more than a guitar effect. With the help of a crossover cable, it sent the lower-frequency sounds to his amp, while the upper-frequency tones could be miked off of the swirling, variable-speed speaker.

In 1972, his effects boxes were mounted in a custom cabinet, and his array of processors grew to include a second Binson Echorec and a second Fuzzface, an MXR Phase 90, a Crybaby wah-wah, an Electro-Harmonix Electric Mistress flanger, Big Muff fuzz, an Orange treble and bass booster, and a custom-built tone pedal.

Additionally, Gilmour used studio effects like ADT (Automatic Double Tracking, a favorite studio processor first developed at Abbey Road Studios for the Beatles), Kepex for tremolo, various tape effects, studio echo chambers, and backwards guitar.

ESSENTIAL READING

Blake, Mark. *Comfortably Numb.* New York: Da Capo, 2007.

Erlewine, Stephen Thomas, allmusic.com.

Fitch, Vernon. *The Pink Floyd Encyclopedia.* Ontario, Canada: Collector's Guide Publishing, Inc., 2005.

Janovitz, Bill, allmusic.com.

Mason, Nick. *Inside Out.* Phoenix: Chronicle Books, 2005.

Schaffner, Nicholas. *Saucerful of Secrets: The Pink Floyd Odyssey.* New York: Delta, 1992.

Sutcliffe, Phil. "And This Is Me." *Mojo*, April 2006, n.p.
Uncredited interview, Fender Players Club.
Unterberger, Richie, allmusic.com.

ESSENTIAL WORK

"Another Brick in the Wall" (1979)
"Atom Heart Mother" (1970)
"Comfortably Numb" (1979)
"Echoes" (1971)
"Money" (1973)
"Time" (1973)
"Wish You Were Here" (1975)

ESSENTIAL LISTENING

Dark Side of the Moon (Capitol, 1973)
David Gilmour (Capitol, 1978)
The Wall (Capitol, 1979)
Wish You Were Here (Capitol, 1975)

Kirk Hammett and James Hetfield

Easily the most identifiable and arguably the most influential of all heavy metal bands, Metallica dominated the genre throughout the 1980s and into the 1990s. They expanded the limits of metal, using speed, intensity, and, of course, volume to enhance their progressive and often complicated song structures. Led by guitarists Kirk Hammett and James Hetfield, Metallica blazed trails across the metal universe, setting the standard both in terms of recordings and on stage, and they became the poster boys for the commercial viability of metal as a genre.

From the beginning of the 1980s, a period that coincided with the advent of music television, rock 'n' roll became more about style than substance. Metallica, for its part, rebelled against that trend. When more and more metal and hard rock bands were teasing their hair and wearing spandex to take advantage of the television exposure, Metallica growled and spat at the camera, keeping it real in the process. For a few years, they and a handful of other bands known as the Big 4—Megadeth, Slayer, and Anthrax—kept the blowtorch of genuinely heavy music lit, with scorching riffs, flaming chords, and stadiums full of kids who identified with their approach.

The blueprint essentially began with their debut, *Kill 'Em All*. Hetfield, a founding member along with drummer Lars Ulrich, developed a signature rhythm guitar pattern and a captivating vocal growl, while guitarist Kirk Hammett weaved his razor sharp leads around Hetfield's chords, on his way to becoming the most revered and imitated guitarist in all of metal. They were a classic combination of brains and brawn, critically respected writers and performers who could pride themselves on their ability to raise the roofs of the venues they played.

They distinguished themselves from many other metal bands with deeper lyrical explorations as well, questioning justice, delving into political themes, and the insanity of war. Their fusion of noise and intelligence, brains and brawn, drove their audiences of disenfranchised kids to the brink of anarchy.

Metallica initially exploded way back in 1983. They moved to San Francisco and played their first show there on March 5 at The Stone, now a legendary venue for Metallica. Kirk Hammett's band Exodus opened for them on what was to be bassist Cliff Burton's first gig with the band. It was there that the band swapped out its first lead guitarist, Dave Mustaine, for Hammett. Mustaine would later go on to big things of his own with Megadeth, and Metallica, content to be without the self-indulgent Mustaine, also ventured onward and upward.

Each album the band released through the 1980s seemed to build on the last. The band's playing and writing and performing grew in size and depth and stature. Many feel that the band reached an early peak on *Master of Puppets*, their 1986 release. And while it made a modest splash commercially, climbing to the Top 20 on the *Billboard* charts, the recording has since grown in importance thanks to the many bands that popped up in its wake and the musicians who considered it the bible of modern heavy metal. In fact, they ended the 1980s as the decade's very best-selling rock act. All tallied, Metallica has sold nearly 100 million albums throughout its career worldwide. Unbelievably, that has made the unkempt bunch of acne-ridden rockers the seventh biggest act in the history of American rock.

EARLY YEARS

Kirk Hammett was born on November 18, 1962 in San Francisco and James Hetfield on August 3, 1963 in Los Angeles. James Hetfield and Lars Ulrich came from different worlds to form Metallica in the Los Angeles suburbs in 1981. Hetfield, whose father owned a trucking company and whose mother was an opera singer, was raised in a strict Christian Science home; Ulrich, transplanted from Denmark, had intended to become a professional tennis player like his father, Torben Ulrich. What the two teenagers shared was an interest in the gritty music of U.K. hard rockers Motörhead.

Hetfield was nine when he began his musical career, first on piano and then on his older brother's drum kit. At 14, he finally grabbed a guitar, influenced by the rock 'n' roll of bands like Aerosmith, Thin Lizzy, and Black Sabbath.

He formed his first band, Obsession, shortly after this time, one member being future Metallica bassist Ron McGovney. After his parents died, Hetfield moved to Brea where he continued to play in his own bands—Phantom Lord and Leather Charm—both with McGovney, the latter a basic hard rock band featuring James singing but not playing guitar.

The two moved into an abandoned house and jammed daily, and with the aid of a couple of local musicians, they hammered out some covers, including Iron Maiden's "Remember Tomorrow," and they played some nearby parties. One of Hetfield's bandmates, guitarist Hugh Tanner, left a mark before he departed by introducing Hetfield to Ulrich, the band's future drummer. Together, Hetfield and Ulrich would make up the heart of Metallica.

Ulrich posted an ad in a local newspaper and received a response from Dave Mustaine, a talented, confident guitarist who got the job the day of the audition. The lineup, now with Mustaine and Hetfield on guitar, Ulrich on drums, and McGovney on bass, was complete. They began writing songs immediately.

Metallica produced their first demo in January of 1982, *Hit the Lights,* with a guy named Lloyd Grant overdubbing the guitar solo and joining the band in the process. In March the band recorded their second demo, three tracks including one original song—the second version of "Hit the Lights,"—and covers of "Killing Time" and "Let It Loose." The demo earned them the opening slot for a Saxon gig at the Whiskey A Go-Go in Hollywood.

In April of 1982, they gigged as a five-piece; Hetfield had been concerned about singing and playing guitar, so they hired a singer named Damien Phillips (aka Jeff Warner) to assume vocal duties. Hetfield played his first gig on rhythm guitar when Dave Mustaine replaced Lloyd Grant on guitar. Taking on Mustaine provided the band with some real equipment, as well as a legitimate lead player, which is why Hetfield moved to rhythm.

That summer, they started recording another album's worth of material, with early versions of "Seek and Destroy," "Motorbreath," and "Jump in the Fire."

Metallica played their first San Francisco headlining gig in November of that year with Kirk Hammett's band Exodus opening for them. In the fall of 1982, bassist McGovney was replaced by Cliff Burton, a bassist Ulrich and Hetfield saw one night at the Whiskey A Go-Go in a band called Trauma. Hetfield and Mustaine felt McGovney's contributions had ended, and so a new bass player became critical. Cliff Burton joined Metallica after persuading them to relocate to San Francisco. They wanted Burton enough on bass to make the move and so the deal was sealed. Metallica's first live performance with Burton was at the nightclub The Stone in March 1983, and the first recording to feature Burton was the 1983 *Megaforce* demo.

Another significant reason for Metallica relocating concerned the work of a record shop owner named John "Z" Zazula. Zazula put the band up, he sold their first demos, and he owned a record label called Megaforce. Metallica signed to the label; it was the band's first contracted record deal.

In 1983, Hammett would replace Mustaine on lead guitar. The band's move from Los Angeles to San Francisco had exposed some of Mustaine's darker habits and the band decided to let him go. This, however, was not easy.

Dave Mustaine was really the face of the band. James was the lead singer but Mustaine did all the connecting with the fans from the stage, because James was still incredibly shy. Mustaine was certainly a character, but it just became too much for the rest of us, particularily [*sic*] with his mood swings. James and Cliff and I were happy, silly drunks, but Mustaine could get really aggressive and it just stopped becoming fun. That outweighed any fear we had of replacing him. (Ulrich, Lars, *Kerrang! Legends: Metallica*)

* * *

Kirk Hammett, native to San Francisco, had been an early player in the Bay Area thrash movement. Born to a Filipino mom and an Irish Merchant Marine dad, Hammett attended De Anza High School in El Sobrante, California in the East Bay. His older brother Rick played and collected guitars and Kirk was drawn to them at an early age. One of Hammett's earliest influences, through his brother's extensive hard rock record collection, was Jimi Hendrix. At around 15, he picked up the guitar himself, first on a 1978 Fender Stratocaster and eventually a 1974 Flying V by Gibson, teamed with a Marshall amp. He learned quickly, and when the band found Hammett he had been taking private lessons with Joe Satriani.

"Joe was a big influence back then," Hammett grants, "but not so much these days. He showed me how to use modes, and he showed me a lot of theory—like what chords to play over what scales, and vice versa. I learned a lot of finger exercises, as well. I had lessons from 1983 'till, like '87, on and off—maybe four lessons a year, sometimes. I never had enough time 'cause I was always touring! And then when he hit big with *Surfing With The Alien* he didn't have time either. In fact, I think I was probably his last student" (Gulla, Bob, *Guitar*, April 1996, n.p.).

Hammett played his first gig with Metallica on April 16 in Dover, New Jersey. Only days later on May 10, Metallica started work on their debut, to be titled *Kill 'Em All*.

"We spent six weeks up in Rochester, New York, recording the album at the Music America Studio. The actual studio is in the basement of this huge old colonial-type of clubhouse . . . The only problem is the place is f*cking haunted, so I had to have someone else up there the whole time I was recording" (Ulrich, Lars, *Metallica: In Their Own Words*, August 1983).

In interviews, Mustaine credits himself with all the leads on *Kill 'Em All* and Hammett actually corroborates that, stating he'd been instructed to use Mustaine's existing solos as a guideline.

The recording was often referred to as the birth of thrash, or that style of metal that featured high-speed riffing, percussive, low-register chords, and shredding lead work. To get to this hybrid, Metallica merged the intricate riffing of bands like Iron Maiden and Judas Priest with the intensity and velocity of hardcore and postpunk metal bands like Motorhead. Hetfield introduced metal fans to his highly technical rhythm guitar style which served as the engine of the album, setting new standards of power, precision, and stamina in the process. The band played with tightly controlled fury even at the fastest tempos and there were already several extended, multisectioned compositions foreshadowing the band's future styling.

*   *   *

Metallica toured that summer. In Boston, Massachusetts, while on tour with Anthrax, the truck with the band's equipment was stolen—the only gear left were the guitars that John Marshall stashed in his hotel room, concerned that the extreme cold outside would warp their necks. For the remaining three dates of the tour, Anthrax loaned Metallica their stage equipment. It is said that the song "Fade to Black" was inspired by this incident.

By the end of the year, *Kill 'Em All* sold over 17,000 copies, a significant achievement for an independent release. Of course, the band still struggled financially, often eating only one meal a day, and, without money for hotels, hitting up loyal fans on the road for couches and floor space.

After a short break from touring, they started back in on demos for a second album, *Ride the Lightning.* The work on the album went down at Sweet Silence Studios in Copenhagen, Denmark, the first of three albums helmed by Danish engineer Flemming

Courtesy of Neil Zlozower

Rasmussen. They finished recording the album roughly a month later and Megaforce released it.

Ride the Lightning was a huge step forward for the band, stunning in scope and staggering in growth. They had expanded their compositions, and in typical fashion, pushed the boundaries of metal outward into new territory, both musically and lyrically.

Some innovations are flourishes that add important bits of color, like the lilting, pseudo-classical intro to the furious "Fight Fire with Fire," or the harmonized leads that pop up on several tracks. Others are major reinventions of Metallica's sound, like the nine-minute, album-closing instrumental "The Call of Ktulu," or the haunting suicide lament "Fade to Black." The latter is an all-time metal classic; it begins as an acoustic-driven, minor-key ballad, then gets slashed open by electric guitars playing a wordless chorus, and ends in a wrenching guitar solo over a thrashy yet lyrical rhythm figure. Basically . . . Metallica sounded like they could do anything. (Huey, Steve, allmusic.com)

Twisted Sister joined Metallica for their second European tour that started on June 6 and lasted until June 10. It was soon after this tour that Metallica had their first meeting with future manager Chris Burnstein from Q Prime. This happened on August 1, 1984; Metallica let the old manager Jon Zazula go on August 2. It was also around this time that Metallica started talking to Bronze record label.

In the fall of 1984, Metallica signed with Elektra Records. The label rereleased *Ride the Lightning* on November 16, and they began touring larger venues and festivals throughout 1985. After letting their former manager Zazula go, they hired Q Prime's Cliff Burnstein and Peter Mensch. During a busy summer, they played the Monsters of Rock Festival at Castle Donington with Bon Jovi and Ratt in front of 70,000 fans.

The following fall, they returned to Copenhagen to record *Master of Puppets* with Rassmussen. Released in the beginning of 1986, the disc had a 72-week run on the album charts and became the band's first gold record.

"Even though *Master of Puppets* didn't take as gigantic a leap forward as *Ride the Lightning* it was the band's greatest achievement, hailed as a masterpiece by critics far outside heavy metal's core audience. It was also a substantial hit, reaching the Top 30 and selling three million copies despite absolutely nonexistent airplay. Instead of a radical reinvention, *Master of Puppets* is a refinement of past innovations" (Huey, Steve, allmusic.com).

Their first tour was in support of Ozzy Osbourne on the Damaged Inc. tour in the United States. It would be the first time the band made it to smaller cities on tour, especially in the Midwest, and the last time they'd serve as a supporting act on a tour of any kind.

* * *

On September 27, 1986, after a gig in Sweden, tragedy struck. The band's bus, traveling from Stockholm to Copenhagen, skidded out of control, flipped over, and killed bassist Cliff Burton in the process. Burton, 26, had been a driving force in Metallica's transition from metal band to progressive-minded loud music icon. His influence on the musical growth of the band was enormous. He fused the DIY philosophies of jamming and experimenting with knowledge of musical theory, and he opened the band's eyes to new frontiers. After a brief period of mourning, the band figured that Burton would have wanted them to continue on. They auditioned 60 bass players, asking four of them back for a second tryout. Jason Newsted, a Michigan-born player at the time with Flotsam & Jetsam, was one of them. After a night of typically hard partying and bonding, Newsted ingratiated

103

himself with the others and got the gig. The newly comprised quartet immediately jumped into a tour, and then recorded an EP of cover tunes titled *Garage Days Revisited*, released in the summer of 1987.

In the spring of the next year, Metallica started the U.S. Monsters of Rock tour with Kingdom Come, Dokken, Scorpions, and Van Halen. Thanks to blazing performances, *Master of Puppets* flew off record store shelves and went platinum. It also marked the peak of Metallica's debaucherous behavior. They drank regularly, earning their nickname "Alcoholica," especially Hetfield, who ended up entering rehab many years later.

That summer, the band released ... *And Justice for All*, the first Metallica record to enter the charts in the Top 10. It was the band's most inspired work to date, with more colorful detail and a wider sonic spectrum than ever before. Hetfield and the band appeared determined to pull out all the compositional stops, throwing in extra sections, odd-numbered time signatures, and dense guitar arpeggios and harmonized leads.

The band, with director Michael Salomon, produced their first music video, for "One," the first single off of the *Justice* record. The video, an evocative indictment of war, featured clips from the film *Johnny Got His Gun,* a film adaption of a controversial book by Dalton Trumbo. The band also performed "One" on the worldwide broadcast of the Grammy Awards, in what happened to be their first television appearance. (They had been slated to appear on "Saturday Night Live," but Hetfield broke his arm right before the show in a skateboarding accident and the band had to cancel.) They were nominated in the heavy metal category for the ... *And Justice for All* album, but they lost to Jethro Tull. The band added a sticker to their album that said "Grammy Award LOSERS." Metallica did, however, win their first Grammy for Best Metal Performance for "One."

They toured the *Justice* record for over a year, and by the end of the tour had hit all 50 states, including club dates in Wilmington, Delaware and Burlington, Vermont to complete the circuit.

Thanks to the success of ... *And Justice for All,* anticipation for new Metallica material hit fever pitch. So when the first single off the new album, "Enter Sandman," was released on video two weeks before the album, fans devoured it. The album *Metallica,* referred to as "the Black album," entered the charts at the very top and stayed there for four straight weeks. First week sales topped 600,000 copies. The record went on to win a Grammy for Best Metal Performance.

In the summer of 1992, Metallica and Guns N' Roses co-headlined a 24-date stadium tour through America's larger cities.

> The four of us are incredibly egotistical, end of story! Guns N' Roses are incredibly set in their ways too, and that's just the way it is. I don't think any of us realized, when we sat down and had our drunken talks about doing this tour together, how tough it would be to get the three months of this happening. It's down to the persistence of the band members that this is happening, because if it was left to the managers, agents and accountants, this would have never got off the ground. (Ulrich, *Metallica: In Their Own Words,* n.p.)

During a show in Montreal, Canada, on the Metallica/GNR tour, amid some confusion surrounding the band's new pyrotechnics display, Hetfield inadvertently stood in the middle of a 12-foot flame during "Fade to Black" and suffered second- and third-degree burns on his face, arms, hands, and legs. When he returned a few weeks later, he only handled vocal duties. John Marshall filled in on guitar.

"Being a frontman [without playing rhythm guitar] was weird. It reminded me how much I really loved playing rhythm guitar. Especially during some of the older songs, where there's a lot of guitar work or instrumental shit. It's like, 'What the fuck do I do?' I'd just leave. Go backstage and have a beer" (Hetfield, James, *Metallica: Unbound*, n.p.).

The band toured nearly two years straight, stretching themselves to the limit. At the end of 1995, they entered the studio again to begin recording *Load*, their sixth album, with producer Bob Rock, after a nearly six-year break from recording original material. In the interim, the band toured constantly, and underwent a period of significant change—OK, call it maturation—both personally and musically. During that time, modern rock music also made a near-complete changeover from metal to grunge to so-called alternative idioms, the latter characterized by mainstream hard rock bands like Nickleback and Three Doors Down, and nu metal bands like Limp Bizkit, Korn, and many others.

The changes profoundly affected Metallica. They were faced with the choice of transitioning with the rest of the world, or maintaining the trail they began over a dozen years earlier with *Kill 'Em All*. Progressive as they had always been, the band made a conscious effort to make changes to their sound, as well as to their appearance. They cut their hair and changed their image, in a highly publicized Anton Corbijn photo shoot that ended up on the cover of *Rolling Stone* magazine. Unfortunately, while those changes seemed like steps forward to the band, they were perceived as steps backward by fans and critics.

"Metallica's attempts at expanding their sonic palette have made them seem more conventional than they ever have before. They add in Southern boogie rock, country-rock, and power ballads to their bag of tricks, which make them sound like '70s arena rock holdovers" (Erlewine, Stephen Thomas, allmusic.com).

To support the divisive *Load*, they headlined, aptly, the alternative music caravan known as "Lollapalooza," a summer festival that had been headlined in the past by purely alt-rock bands like the Red Hot Chili Peppers, Pearl Jam, and Smashing Pumpkins. The festival, in its sixth year, helped to saturate Metallica through the mainstream rock community and, while it proved damaging to its core fan base, it ended up converting many others.

They followed up *Load* with a sequel of sorts, *Reload*, comprised of leftovers from the super-productive *Load* sessions. Both *Load* installments sold well. The first debuted at #1 and sold three million copies the first month. The second, accepted more willingly by fans and critics, didn't sell nearly as well.

Garage Inc., a double-disc collection of B-sides, rarities, and newly recorded covers, followed in 1998. In 1999, Metallica continued their flood of product with *S&M*, documenting a live concert with the San Francisco Symphony, a project that truly stretched their fans' expectations. The 100-plus members of the symphony were directed by composer/arranger Michael Kamen, whose history with Metallica dates back to 1991 when he orchestrated "Nothing Else Matters" for the band's self-titled album. For the most part, fans responded with their support. The record debuted at #2 on the album charts, reconfirming their immense popularity. At this point, Metallica cemented its place in history as one of rock's most recognizable bands heading into the new millennium.

In the summer of 1999, the band played Woodstock Festival at the Griffiss Air Force Base in Rome, New York, joining bands like Limp Bizkit, Rage Against the Machine, and Kid Rock. The event proved tumultuous and chaotic with riots, arrests, arson, and assorted vicious behavior.

The band spent most of 2000 knee-deep in controversy brought on by Napster and illegal file-sharing that allowed users to download songs from each other's computers. Metallica felt that it violated copyright agreements with the band and their label, and it constituted unlawful use of digital audio interface device and violations of the Racketeering Influenced and Corrupt Organizations Act. They even testified in front of the Senate Judiciary committee. In a prepared statement, Lars Ulrich wrote:

> We take our craft—whether it be the music, the lyrics, or the photos and artwork—very seriously, as do most artists. It is therefore sickening to know that our art is being traded like a commodity rather than the art that it is. From a business standpoint, this is about piracy—a/k/a taking something that doesn't belong to you; and that is morally and legally wrong. The trading of such information—whether it's music, videos, photos, or whatever—is, in effect, trafficking in stolen goods. (Ulrich)

So, in a very controversial and polarizing move, they went after Napster and had over 300,000 users removed from Napster's registry. Metallica's stand created widespread debate over digital music that has still not been rectified.

In July of 2001, Metallica and Napster announced a settlement of the dispute, which involved Napster paying an undisclosed amount of cash settlement, and in return Metallica would allow their music to be available on Napster's copyright-friendly subscription service.

* * *

The upheaval continued in January of 2001 when Jason Newsted, bassist since 1986, announced his departure, which by all counts was amicable. His statement read:

> Due to private and personal reasons, and the physical damage that I have done to myself over the years while playing the music that I love, I must step away from the band. This is the most difficult decision of my life, made in the best interest of my family, myself, and the continued growth of Metallica. I extend my love, thanks, and best wishes to my brothers: James, Lars, and Kirk and the rest of the Metallica family, friends, and fans whom have made these years so unforgettable. (Newsted)

* * *

The three remaining members entered the studio, again with producer Bob Rock (who'd also play bass), but it would prove to be one of the band's most contentious experiences of their lives. In the middle of demoing new material, Hetfield entered rehab to fight alcohol and other addictions. This left Ulrich and Hammett in the studio alone with producer Rock. When Hetfield returned, there was a psychotherapist on the band payroll to help Hammett, Hetfield, and Ulrich get through the making of the record. This navigation was thoroughly documented on *Some Kind of Monster,* a feature-length movie on Metallica during the making of their *St. Anger* album.

In the meantime, *Guitar World* magazine selected Kirk Hammett as the first recipient of their Hall of Fame Award. After three months of extensive auditions, the band hired bassist Robert Trujillo, formerly of Suicidal Tendencies/Ozzy Osbourne, as a replacement for Newsted.

St. Anger was released in June 2003. *St. Anger* takes listeners inside the tortured yet still vital mind of Hetfield. Written largely in the first person, the record abandoned the heavy metal baggage of the band's past and delivered simple, innovative speed metal informed by the band's considerable experience.

SOME KIND OF MONSTERS

The premise was rather preposterous. Metallica's management company hired a performance enhancement coach named Phil Towles to help the band stay together, to better understand one another as humans, as friends, and as colleagues. This entire social experiment and the emotional friction that arose as the band created the album called *St. Anger* was captured on film by directors Joe Berlinger and Brice Sinofsky.

What began as a simple documentary about the making of an album, though, turned into a profound personal exploration of the band's interpersonal relationships and their intense struggles with the creative process. The documentary also featured the chemistry in studio rehearsals and fragments of concert footage.

According to Hetfield, *Some Kind of Monster* was originally designed to be a six-part miniseries for VH1, inspired by the success of MTV's *The Osbournes* show. However, after seeing much of the footage that resulted, the band felt this was not a direction they wanted to take their careers and bought out VH1's rights to the material and made the film as you see it today. The 1,600 hours of footage the filmmakers produced in the process had to be distilled down to a mere two hours and 20 minutes.

Some Kind of Monster depicts a major rock band in near-total meltdown, which is why fans of the band were divided upon its release. Half appeared to receive it well, praising the band for its courage in revealing such a potentially embarrassing chapter in their lives. Other fans derided the movie and the band for being nothing more than insecure rock stars struggling to come to grips with age and maturity.

In 2008, Metallica delivered its fiercest and best record in two decades, *Death Magnetic*. Produced by Rick Rubin, the recording demonstrated that, despite popular belief, the band still possessed some of the anger and innovation that made its work so popular in the 1980s.

TECHNIQUE/STYLE

Over the years, Hetfield's and Hammett's guitar work has evolved considerably, less Hammett's than Hetfield's, actually. As the main songwriter of the band, Hetfield's rhythm playing does more to effect the overall sound of the band than Hammett's whose lead playing has to adhere to the structure of Hetfield's chord progressions and song structure.

Hetfield played all the rhythm guitar and most melody and harmony guitar parts, not to mention the acoustic guitar parts and the occasional electric solo. Kirk's duties on the albums were confined mostly, at least in the 1980s, to full-blown leads. As the band progressed, they divvied up their responsibilities more equally and crossed over into each other's territories more often. Both have played rhythm quite a bit, and both have played leads.

In the beginning, Hetfield more or less played thrashy, straight-up power chords. But as Metallica pushed the limits on what defined speed and thrash metal, his rhythm playing

107

grew in terms of difficulty. In the mid-1980s, ultra-technical, speedy guitar guitarists were all the rage.

"Pretty much all the early stuff was inspired by 'crunch.' You get this crunchy sound, and then you've got to play like some 'ggg-ggg' kind of thing, or slower—much slower —heavier kind of stuff. Being totally out of tune, you'll come up with something different that is pretty cool. A lot of the dropped tunings come from being out of tune." (Stix, John, "Metallica's Main Man Unloads," *Guitar One*, April 1997).

Hetfield's rhythm technique is based on precision.

"Maybe that's the German in me: 'It's got to be precise!' It's hard to escape. That's how I play. So when we wanted it looser, Kirk stepped in. But having different sounds, playing different guitars and playing through different amps absolutely makes you play differently" (Gulla, *Guitar*, April 1996).

Through the *Justice* album, the band's guitar sound was always either clean or dirty; it's either got to be shimmer-clean or completely heavy crunch. For the most part, Hetfield laid down three rhythm tracks that always served as the foundation to the Metallica sound. Later on, the band second-guessed that approach. Hetfield asked rhetorically,

> Do we need all that shit underneath? Do we need all that rhythm stuff going on while some other thing is happening? No, we've heard the riff, we know what's stuck in our head. Let's get rid of it and let something else take over. A lot of times that was a big battle in the mix. Certain parts were so cool that everyone wanted to do their thing on it. Here's the breakdown jam part and, wow, we've got this organ here, this clean sound, this bass thingy. Who's gonna take control of this part? Trying to have them all in at once won't work, so it's down to what's best for the song. (Gulla, *Guitar*, April 1996)

* * *

Kirk Hammett grew up idolizing Kiss and Hendrix, though he admits the latter held his attention longer. He loved playing "Purple Haze" and Hendrix's version of "Wild Thing," along with a few Zeppelin tunes like "Communication Breakdown" and "Whole Lotta Love." He learned Jimmy Page's solos note for note. He also experimented with all different styles, from blues and sambas to jazz and noise. "I would sit and play with feedback for hours at a time. One of the main things to hit a C# and let it feed back, because it was the intro to UFO's 'Let It Roll.' I just loved that tone. But I would play it with feedback—Hendrix did it, Jeff Beck did it" (Stix, John, "Modern Rock Hero," *Guitar One*, October 1997).

Hammett surprisingly draws much of his inspiration on solos from jazz horn players. He is passionate about the solo sounds of guys like Chet Baker and John Coltrane, and he'd been known to sneak their horn lines into his solo licks.

> The whole idea of space in my soloing totally comes from listening to Miles Davis and Chet Baker. The solo in "2x4" has a lot of quarter notes and whole notes and a lot of laid-back, slow phrasing. I just pretended I was trying to play a Chet Baker solo on a trumpet. Plus a '58 Les Paul Standard sings. You hit a note, and it's there for a long time. That has something to do with it. (Stix, *Guitar One*, October 1997)

One of the biggest guitar surprises of Kirk's solo cache comes on *Load*'s opening track "Ain't My Bitch." It's the first Metallica slide solo ever. Done on a 1963 Les Paul Junior specially set up with a high action, Kirk reeled off a spontaneous slide workout. In addition, also on *Load* and later, his soloing is based around the E blues scale at the twelfth fret, often using double-stop bends on strings two and three.

Playing like that just felt really comfortable. I didn't feel like being very modal on this album, 'cause I did five albums of modal stuff. I got modal in a few places like on "King Nothing" but the songs somehow just didn't call for that. Lars kept on telling me to "lean into" the track—I would look at him and think, "What the heck is he talking about?" And then one day when I played a lick he said, "Yeah, that's leaning into it." I was laying back and playing a little bit off the beat, maybe like Stevie Ray Vaughan did. (Gulla, *Guitar,* April 1996)

EQUIPMENT/GEAR

Kirk Hammett

Kirk's favorite guitar for shows is his original 1987 ESP KH-2. He also has an ESP KH-3 hardtail he calls the "Invisible Kid," a 1987 Gibson Les Paul called "The Tiger Stripe," then a 1959 Fender Telecaster with a blonde finish, a 1963 Fender Strat in seafoam green, a 1959 Les Paul, a Gibson ES-335, and a Martin D-28. He uses Ernie Ball strings (.011–.048). His amp rig includes Mesa/Boogie Dual Rectifier rackmount amps, Mesa/Boogie Strategy 400 amps, Mesa/Boogie Mark IV amp, Mesa/Boogie 4x12 speaker cabinets, Mesa/Boogie Triaxis preamp, Mesa/Boogie Dual Rectifier solo head, Mesa/Boogie Triple Rectifier solo head, Marshall JMP-1 preamp, Marshall 4x12 speaker cabinets w/ 25-watt speakers, Marshall 2x12 speaker cabinets, Marshall practice amps, Custom Audio Electronics preamp, ADA MP-1 preamp, Bradshaw preamp, VHT power amp, Matchless Spitfire, Vox AC-30, and Fender Tweed combos. For effects, he uses a Dunlop Crybaby Wah Wah, Roland VG-8, EMB Audio Remote Wah unit, EMB/Ernie Ball Wah Pedal, Rocktron RSB-18F pedal boards, Ibanez Tube Screamer, a Bradshaw Switching System, along with a Bradshaw Patch Bay Custom, and a Lovetone Meatball pedal (used on the opening riff of "I Disappear").

James Hetfield

Hetfield's guitar was used as the model for the ESP LTD Grynch. His ESP Explorers—in black and chrome diamond plate—date back to the *Load* tour. He decided if diamond plate was good enough for his trucks, why not his guitars? He also has an ESP LTD 7-string called "The Goblin" and an ESP LTD F-300M. His 1976 Gibson Explorer is called "Rusty," and James did the rust work himself. The 1973 Gibson Les Paul is known as "Uncle Milty"—after comedian Milton Berle—because it sounds "burly." James did all the custom work, including the racing stripe and the iron cross. It also has custom pickups made by EMG. Finally, there's a 1959 Gibson Les Paul, and he played a Fender Danny Gatton Telecaster occasionally. He uses Ernie Ball strings (.010–.046 and .013–.058) for the Viper baritone. James's amp rack includes a Mesa/Boogie Triaxis (stock and modified) and a Strategy 400, a Mesa/Boogie Mark IV, Mesa/Boogie Triple Rectifier, Mesa/Boogie Custom Graphic EQ Unit, Mesa/Boogie Amp Switcher, and Mesa/Boogie 4x12 Speaker Cabinets. He also plays a Diezel head loaded with EL34s, a Wizard, a Marshall DSL, a Roland JC-120, and a Sears Magnatone.

Hetfield's effects list is shorter than Hammett's. It includes a Bradshaw RSB-12 Switching System and Pedal Board, Bradshaw Patch Bay Custom, Boss SE-50 Stereo FX Processor, Juice Goose Rack Power 300, Aphex Parametric EQ, Morley Rack Mount Unit Custom, and a Peterson 520 Strobe Tuner.

ESSENTIAL READING

Erlewine, Stephen Thomas. allmusic.com.

Gulla, Bob. *Guitar,* April 1996, n.p.

Hammett, Kirk. *The Art of Kirk Hammett.* New York: Cherry Lane Music, 1997.

Hetfield, James. *Metallica: Unbound,* n.p.

Huey, Steve. allmusic.com.

McIver, Joel. *Justice for All: The Truth about Metallica.* New York: Omnibus Press, 2004.

Metallica, with Chirazi, Steffan. *So What! The Good, the Mad, and the Ugly.* New York: Broadway Books, 2004.

Putterford, Mark. *Metallica: In Their Own Words.* New York: Omnibus, 2000.

Stix, John. "Metallica's Main Man Unloads." *Guitar One,* April 1997.

———. "Modern Rock Hero." *Guitar One,* October 1997.

Ulrich, Lars. *Kerrang! Legends: Metallica.*

———. *Metallica: In Their Own Words,* August 1983.

ESSENTIAL WORK

"Blackened" (1988)

"Creeping Death" (1984)

"The End of the Line" (2008)

"Fade to Black" (1984)

"Master of Puppets" (1986)

"One" (1988)

"Welcome Home (Sanitarium)" (1986)

ESSENTIAL LISTENING

. . . And Justice for All (Elektra, 1988)

Death Magnetic (Warner Bros., 2008)

Master of Puppets (Elektra, 1986)

Metallica (Elektra, 1991)

Ride the Lightning (Elektra, 1984)

ESSENTIAL VIEWING

Cliff 'Em All! (Asylum, 1987)

Some Kind of Monster (Radical Media, 2004)

George Harrison

When George Harrison died from cancer in 2001, we witnessed the passing of not only a legend, but also one of the true giants of rock and roll. His passing provided rock enthusiasts with an opportunity to take a new look at his legacy and to try to put his musical contributions to the world's greatest rock band into a clearer perspective. The conclusion? While all those terrific tunes come stamped with a "Lennon/McCartney" byline, without the significant expertise of Harrison—whether it be through his suggestions, his guitar, or his magical spontaneity—they almost certainly wouldn't have been the masterpieces they are considered today.

* * *

We know this because, over the last decade or so, musical archeologists have unearthed and listened to many of the Fab Four's bootlegs and rough demos, the versions of the songs that at the time were considered works in progress. Many of these rough takes feature just John Lennon, or just Paul McCartney, and they are simply melodic skeletons of songs. But when George Harrison stepped in to flesh out those compositions, they took on a fuller, more colorful dimension. These glimpses help us better understand the role of the "Quiet Beatle" and help us add substance to the theory that George Harrison had significantly more to do with the making of the Beatles' legacy than we'd previously been led to believe.

Concrete evidence of Harrison's abilities came in 1970, when he released his first solo outing *All Things Must Pass.* Meticulously orchestrated and containing over a dozen songs remaindered from the last few Beatles albums, *All Things Must Pass* proved that Harrison could write, arrange, produce, mix, and edit material as well as play extraordinary guitar and—not to mention—reach #1 in doing so. In fact, he was the first Beatle to reach the top of the charts after the band broke up.

"Everybody talks about Lennon and McCartney and what a great songwriting team they were," says Andy Babiuk, "but when you listen to some of the original rough demos, they're just OK. Had they left them like that, would they still have become these great songs that we've come to know and love? That's where George played such an important part" (Simons, David, "The Unsung Beatle," *Acoustic Guitar,* February 2003).

As a member of the Liverpool gang, Harrison wrote some of the band's best-loved songs, including "If I Needed Someone," "Taxman," "While My Guitar Gently Weeps," "Something," "Here Comes the Sun," and "I Me Mine." As a solo artist, he produced 11 albums in all, and he was the only Beatle to start his own label in Dark Horse Records. He was also the first Beatle to tour as a solo artist.

Most important, though, was the kind of personality he brought to his work. He struggled mightily with the band's fame and its resultant life style. He regarded the glare of the spotlight as a Beatle with wary disdain. He figured prominently in the group's decision to abandon live performances, where they were routinely drowned out by screams, and instead devote their time to the recording studio. He stormed out of sessions for *Let It Be* in 1969 in frustration.

In hindsight, Harrison's solo albums reveal the conflict that was at the center of his life. On the one hand, he embraced Eastern spirituality. He immersed himself in Indian music at Beatlemania's height and became a lifelong devotee of Hindu religion, Krishna consciousness, and Vedic philosophy, the only Beatle to do so and retain it. On the other hand, his turbulent real-world existence disagreed vehemently with that Vedic philosophy of peace and meditation and nonmaterialism. He wanted desperately to withdraw from his role as a Beatle and as a recording artist to fulfill his desire to pursue spiritual goals.

He titled one of his best-selling albums *Living in the Material World,* a name that summed up his quandary. Harrison forthrightly addressed weighty matters on record and made his ruminations appealing as popular music, too.

Though understated, Harrison's legacy speaks volumes. He earned a ranking of #21 on *Rolling Stone*'s list of the 100 Greatest Guitarists of All Time. He was inducted into the Rock 'n' Roll Hall of Fame as a solo artist in 2004, and, of course, as a member of the Beatles in 1988.

EARLY YEARS

Born on February 25, 1943, George Harrison was the youngest of three sons born to Harold Harrison and his wife Louise. The only Beatle whose childhood did not include divorce or death, George had two brothers, Harold Jr. and Peter, and a sister, Louise. His father, Harold, was a bus driver, and his mother a housewife, who all the kids in the neighborhood knew and liked. He attended Dovedale Primary school two grades behind John Lennon, and then Liverpool Institute, one grade below Paul McCartney. At school, he was regarded as a poor student; contemporaries described him as slight, pimply, and very shy—someone who often sat alone in the corner. As such, George despised school.

Early in childhood Harrison developed a keen interest in music, and after buying a cheap acoustic guitar at the age of 13, he devoted most of his free time to teaching himself to play the instrument, learning chords by copying songs.

George and Paul took the same bus to school and soon found they had music and guitars in common. George, his brother Peter, and friend Arthur Kelly had formed a skiffle band called the Rebels, a short-lived group. Because they were so young, they had to sneak out of the house to play their first gig. Paul introduced George to the Quarrymen, and though he wasn't old enough to join, he still hung around with them and came to idolize John Lennon, a member of the Quarrymen. George often stood in the back of the room at their shows, holding his guitar. A few times he even filled in for the regular guitarist when he didn't show up. The boys were also welcomed into George's house by his mother to practice and for an occasional jam. Gradually, George became a member of the group, which by then had come to be called Johnny and the Moondogs.

John, Paul, and George adopted the name Johnny and The Moondogs in 1958 for the purpose of entering a talent competition. At the time, the Quarrymen had lost two of its members in late summer 1958, Len Garry and Duff Lowe, and the boys had a chance for a new start. Johnny and the Moondogs passed the preliminary audition and appeared on the stage at the Liverpool Empire Theatre, doing well enough to qualify for the area finals held in Manchester. They played there, but did not win the contest. The show was judged by the results of a "clapometer" which recorded the volume of applause for each act, during which the competitors gave a brief rundown of their performance. John, Paul, and George missed this portion of the show, as they had to catch the last train back to Liverpool. Without their presence, the applause likely didn't pin the needle on the clapometer.

George eventually dropped out of school before graduation. The Lennon/McCartney/Harrison lineup added bassist Stuart Sutcliff in January of 1960 who renamed them the Beatals. The Beatals soon became the Silver Beetles, followed in rapid succession by the Silver Beatles, the Silver Beats, and finally, the Beatles.

MUSIC

It was, of course, as the Beatles that the group traveled to Hamburg, where there was a burgeoning rock 'n' roll scene. The first time the band attempted to go to Germany, they were sent back. George was too young on their first trip to Hamburg in 1960—he was only 17—and they were sent back to Liverpool. The next attempt was successful and soon the band was packing the Cavern Club in Hamburg, Germany.

After the cementing of the Beatles' lineup with drummer Ringo Starr in 1962, the band's popularity exploded into an unprecedented pop culture phenomenon. Looking at the Beatles through the prism of Lennon and McCartney, though, is quite different than looking at the experience through the eyes of George Harrison. John and Paul were the obvious stars and spokespeople of the group. George and the band confined themselves to a background role—quiet, reserved, somewhat mysterious.

Yet there was a persistent tendency for Lennon and McCartney to take Harrison—his opinions and his contributions—much less seriously, and this led to resentment on Harrison's part. Throughout the Beatles' recording career, Harrison only placed a handful of songs on albums. Still, those he wrote and on which he sang lead ("Something," "Taxman," "Here Comes the Sun," "While My Guitar Gently Weeps," for example) were among the group's most popular.

George also released the first Beatle solo album. While *Magical Mystery Tour* climbed the charts in 1968, George worked on the offbeat score to the film *Wonderwall*. George had become enamored with Indian music and playing the sitar (first realized in 1965 on the track "Norwegian Wood" from *Rubber Soul*), and that influence now drove this entire film score. Harrison himself did not appear as a player or singer on the album—half of the cues recorded in London, the other half in Bombay, and the Indian tracks were professionally executed. At least he had an opportunity to indulge himself outside the rigid constraints of the Beatles.

After a visit to India in 1967 to attend Maharishi Mahesh Yogi's meditation camp with his bandmates, Harrison's musical and cultural interest expanded to include India's spiritual ideas. Two years later, Harrison began an association with Shrila A. C. Bhaktivedanta Swami Prabhupada, founder of the Krishna Consciousness Society. The religious practices learned from both encounters were maintained throughout the rest of his life.

* * *

Yet despite the inner peace Harrison had attained, the Beatles' friction grew exponentially. The inferiority Harrison felt as a songwriter resulted in strained band relationships, especially between him and McCartney. Others point out that the tension existed between him and John as well. George felt neither took him very seriously as a songwriter,

Courtesy of Photofest

and he really resented being pushed around by Paul in the studio. In fact, that friendship grew so strained that, in early 1969, Harrison actually quit the group. Here's what happened:

The group was filming their *Let It Be* movie in the cavernous Twickenham film studios in London. The sessions were rife with tension as they prepared to work up a set of new material for their proposed return to the stage. While Harrison's main beef was with McCartney's domination during rehearsals, he was equally peeved at John Lennon, who at that point was barely communicating to the band and letting Yoko Ono speak for him on band matters.

After running through a few songs that day, including a brief rendition of the group's "All Together Now" and "Get Back," Harrison nonchalantly announced that he was leaving the band immediately and sarcastically told them as he walked out, "See you around the clubs."

George later told a journalist that while he had a growing backlog of new material, he constantly had to work on Lennon and McCartney's songs before the group could work on his. In fact, it wasn't until the year prior to the dissolution of the Beatles that one of his contributions was released as a single. The track in question, "Something," eventually became one of the band's most covered songs.

Released as a single in October of 1969, "Something," appearing on the *Abbey Road* album, was the first Harrison track to appear on the A-side of a Beatles single and the only Harrison composition to top the American charts while he was a Beatle.

Initially, Harrison himself had been dismissive of the song, calling it too easy to write. Lennon and McCartney both held "Something" in high regard even though both had largely ignored Harrison's compositions prior to "Something." Lennon later explained: "There was an embarrassing period when George's songs weren't that good and nobody

114

wanted to say anything. He just wasn't in the same league for a long time—that's not putting him down, he just hadn't had the practice as a writer that we'd had" (www.beatles-discography.com).

Harrison would move forward, despite what the others thought of him. In 1969, he released *Electronic Music,* a groundbreaking experimental album featuring two lengthy, abstract tone poems for early vintage Moog synthesizer reveal. The album, the second to be released on the Beatles' offshoot label, Zapple, never made a chart impact, but it did demonstrate the courageous nature of Harrison's progressive creativity.

After a series of unfortunate events that began around the beginning of 1970 and lasted through the year, the Beatles announced their breakup after 10 years together.

SOLO WORK

Harrison wasted no time launching his solo career with the triple-record set *All Things Must Pass.* Produced by the eccentric talent Phil Spector, the recording drew on his backlog of unused compositions from the late Beatles era, when he truly came into his own as a songwriter. Harrison crafted material that managed the rare feat of conveying spiritual mysticism without sacrificing his gifts for melody and grand, sweeping arrangements. Spector, noted for his "wall of sound" arrangements, frames the material with lush perfection.

The record's first single, "My Sweet Lord," was the first track by any of the former Beatles to reach the top of the charts. George jumped into his solo career with vigor, now freed to fill entire albums with his own creations. After years of rejection from John and Paul, George possessed a backlog of material just aching to be released. Indeed, *All Things Must Pass* took the form of a triple-album set.

Next, Harrison organized a major charity concert. His Concert for Bangladesh on August 1, 1971, drew over 40,000 people to New York's Madison Square Garden and raised millions of dollars to aid the country's starving refugees. The show included Eric Clapton, Bob Dylan, Leon Russell, and many other luminous guests, accompanying each other on a variety of classic material. Indian classical sitar maestro Ravi Shankar, a guru of sorts for Harrison, opened the proceedings. The second night of the two-night stand also became a triple-album live set. Harrison's magnanimous intentions proved that he and the other stars sensed they could make a difference. It would be the first time a rock star organized a charity event of this incredible magnitude.

Two and a half years later, Harrison released *Living in a Material World,* a solid recording that didn't benefit from the backlog of Beatles-era material that Harrison enjoyed when he recorded *All Things Must Pass.* In retrospect, the record does seem like Harrison narrowed his vision and objectives for the project. But it does feature some great songs, as well as some of his best guitar work. He's the only player throughout *Material World,* and it does represent his solo playing extremely well. Most notable are his bluesy moments and his vastly underrated slide playing, glimpsed on some of the later Fab Four sessions but often overlooked by fans.

He recorded consistently throughout the 1970s but lost his dramatic gifts the further he ventured from his Beatles songwriting roots. Still, his music had fans, and he indulged in some quirky concepts, like his group of Hoagy Carmichael covers on 1981's *Somewhere in England,* and spiritual material, as well as blues and ballads.

In 1987, Harrison made an unexpected return to the top of the charts with his album *Cloud Nine,* which featured his most inspired pop rock of his solo career, particularly a

THE TRAVELING WILBURYS

The Traveling Wilburys were a supergroup consisting of George Harrison, Tom Petty, Bob Dylan, Roy Orbison, and Jeff Lynne. Lynne had been producing Harrison's *Cloud Nine,* and the two were dining with Roy Orbison when the idea for the group arose. "Wilburys" was a slang term coined by Harrison and Lynne during the recording of *Cloud Nine* as a reference to recorded "flubs" that could be eliminated during the mixing stage.

Calling themselves Lucky, Lefty, Otis, Nelson, and Charlie T. Wilbury (you figure out who was who), they released a hit album, *Traveling Wilburys Vol. 1,* with a couple of successful songs—"End of the Line" and "Handle with Care"— and a good-time, homespun feel to it. Written by all the members, the album was recorded over a 10-day period in May 1988 because Dylan was due to go on tour.

Roy Orbison died in 1988 during the recording of it, so full collaborations ceased. But the band finished the video for "End of the Line." In the scene where the verse is sung by Orbison, the viewer is shown Orbison's guitar in a rocking chair followed by a photo of the late artist.

Traveling Wilburys Vol. 3 begged the question of what became of Vol. 2. The first volume, ranked #70 on *Rolling Stone*'s list of the 100 Greatest Albums of the 1980s, was later nominated for an Album of the Year Grammy.

Released in October, *Traveling Wilburys Vol. 3* was predictably less rapturously received than its predecessor, yet still saw a fair measure of success, with both "She's My Baby" and "Wilbury Twist" becoming radio hits as the album reached #14 in the United Kingdom and #11 in the United States, where it went platinum. Although there has since been speculation about further Wilbury releases, Harrison's 2001 death is considered to have ended any possible future projects, with Harrison having been the unofficial leader of the group and with his estate owning the rights to both albums.

cover of an old gospel number called "Got My Mind Set on You," which reached #1 on the charts. The recording was produced by Beatles' scholar and disciple Jeff Lynne.

In the late 1980s George formed his own band, a true "supergroup" of famous artists representing three generations of rock 'n' roll history. The band, called the Traveling Wilburys, consisted of Bob Dylan, Jeff Lynne of the Electric Light Orchestra, Tom Petty, and Roy Orbison (see sidebar).

The Traveling Wilburys released two successful recordings, *Volume 1* and *Volume 3.* The second title was the band's joke on its fans, as *Volume 2* never existed. In the 1990s, Harrison grew more comfortable with touring. Since the Beatles' harrowing tours of old, gigs in which the crowds drowned out the music, Harrison had refrained from doing much performing. A tour of Japan yielded *Live in Japan,* with a supporting band that featured Eric Clapton.

In the latter part of the 1990s, Harrison withdrew from public life. In 2001, he and his label began a string of reissues, including a remastered and expanded edition of his magnum opus, *All Things Must Pass.* In 2001, he also revealed that he'd been diagnosed with inoperable throat cancer. He had been treated in the late 1990s for the same disease. He died on November 29, 2001 at the age of 58.

TECHNIQUE/STYLE

George Harrison began playing guitar in the late 1950s and early 1960s in the style of Chet Atkins and Chuck Berry, playing his big Gretsch Country Gentleman. The Beatles packed an enormous amount of musical dexterity into their seven-year recording career, and quite a few of those finer musical moments belong to Harrison. As a guitarist, he was neither fast nor flashy. Yet, ultimately, he defined the role of lead guitarist in the flourishing world of rock 'n' roll in the mid-1960s.

Harrison innovated as a rhythm guitarist too. He used a capoed acoustic guitar, in particular, as a distinctive songwriting tool, working out classics like "Here Comes the Sun," "I Me Mine," and "For You Blue." His shimmering acoustic added new hues to the Beatles sound.

> Time and time again, Harrison crafted intros, fills, and lead lines that were nearly as hooky as the songs themselves. Putting his newly minted Rickenbacker 360/12 electric 12-string to the test, Harrison opened John Lennon's rocker "A Hard Day's Night" with a single ringing G7sus4 chord, in the process creating one of the most celebrated intros in rock.... Throughout 1964 and '65, Harrison uncorked one Rickenbacker riff after another, from the descending fills of "Help" to the ear-grabbing opening in "Ticket to Ride." (Simons, 2003)

In fact, thanks to Harrison, the Beatles were the first act to turn an acoustic guitar into a prominent part of a pop rhythm section. His acoustic guitar parts were central to the development of the band's approach to songwriting. Lennon and Harrison both strummed a Gibson J-160E (with electric pickup) early on, using it on such tracks as "Love Me Do" and "I'll Be Back."

Harrison's acoustic direction was, in part, fostered by his friendship with Bob Dylan. Though Lennon briefly reflected Dylan's folk influence, Harrison remained a steadfast admirer and by 1968 was making regular trips to see Dylan in New York State. One visit resulted in the co-write "I'd Have You Anytime," which matched Dylan's simple poetry with a sophisticated Harrison chord progression.

"I was saying to him, 'You write incredible lyrics,' and he was saying, 'How do you write those tunes?'" Harrison later told *Crawdaddy*. "So I began showing him chords like crazy, because he tended to just play a lot of basic chords and move a capo up and down" (Simons, 2003).

From the beginning, Harrison took the raw material of the Lennon/McCartney songs and spun them into gold, adding simple guitar counterpoints, echoing melody lines and brilliant guitar hooks. His Gretsch infused colors of country, rockabilly, and even jazz chord voicings into the traditional pop/rock compositions of his colleagues.

George Harrison's brief, song-oriented guitar solo in "All My Loving" is a mini-masterpiece of early Beatle guitarwork. In it he adopted a Chet Atkins-inspired country guitar approach, exploiting his familiar pick-and-finger articulation and parallel double stops as a deliberate theme. He also employed the twangy tone of his familiar Gretsch Chet Atkins Country Gentleman guitar for a bona fide rockabilly/country result.

Harrison's versatility was the key to his success. He was the biggest R&B fan in the band. But with his acoustic, he echoed the sound of the singer-songwriter movement of

Greenwich Village he had heard going on across the ocean. Of all the Beatles, Harrison had his ear to the ground the most, and he absorbed the various styles that were happening in music's most explosive decade.

A list of Harrison's finest moments as a guitarist almost equals the roster of great Beatles songs. His breadth was amazing—he could range from the raw blues overdrive of a Clapton for his solos in "Helter Skelter" and "Sgt. Pepper's Lonely Hearts Club Band (Reprise)" to the rockabilly strut of Carl Perkins ("Honey Don't") to the tightly wound sexual squawk that later gave punk its edge ("Got to Get You into My Life") to the delicate acoustic filigree of "Here Comes the Sun." It could even be argued that several of the Beatles' less perfectly conceived songs, such as "Nowhere Man" and "Fixing a Hole," were salvaged by Harrison's incisive Stratocaster solos.

As the 1960s progressed, Harrison proved he was not content to sit back and remain merely a creative session man. His own songs, "Think for Yourself," "I Need You," and "If I Needed Someone" showed he had begun to emerge as a writer, even if he wasn't taken seriously by his mates.

Any discussion of the Beatles archive typically revolves around two major themes: that the Beatles wrote great songs and that they turned them into great-sounding records. It's a point that becomes especially relevant during the band's post-1966 efforts, the period of Harrison's greatest achievements in the studio.

As any guitarist with a keen ear knows, it's not just the parts Harrison played—it's the way he made them sound—his tone, phrasing, and ability to articulate the details are magical. At the time, rock had turned more aggressive, especially in the United Kingdom, with bands like Cream, Hendrix, and the Yardbirds kicking up a racket. When rock upped the decibels in 1966, so did Harrison, acquiring a Gibson SG and announcing his presence with authority on McCartney's "Paperback Writer," the toughest-sounding A side in the Beatles' collection.

* * *

As the decade progressed, Harrison drifted toward the sitar, having bought a good one in India, and then received some lessons from sitar master Ravi Shankar. "Love You To" on *Revolver* was the first Beatles tune that he wrote purposely for the sitar. Later, "Within You Without You" on 1967's *Sgt. Pepper's Lonely Hearts Club Band* would be a full-blown Indian music piece with tablas and the works. He also began writing songs on organ and harmonium.

Harrison returned to the guitar in peak form, saving some of his best work for last during the marathon medley that closes *Abbey Road,* the band's final studio album. Harrison had distanced himself from Lennon and McCartney, but his guitar work continued to crest, and his work gave the impression that the Beatles were still somehow unified.

"From *Sgt. Pepper's* forward, it was really Lennon songs or McCartney songs," says Babiuk, "but George helped keep the cohesion because he'd put his signature parts on all of them. If you want proof, all you have to do is listen to any of McCartney's first few solo albums right after the break. Harrison wasn't on them, and consequently they just didn't sound the same" (Simons, 2003).

Coincidentally or not, Harrison's most remarkable stretch of songwriting—from 1968 through 1970—began with the purchase of a Gibson J-200, the big-bodied acoustic heard on White Album cuts "Long, Long, Long," "Piggies," and the tour de force "While My Guitar Gently Weeps."

With his premiere solo single "My Sweet Lord," Harrison elevated the sound and scope of recorded acoustic guitar to even greater heights. Over a basic F#m-B progression, he created a lush bedrock of rhythm, enlisting the guitar services of Peter Frampton as well as Badfinger's Pete Ham, Tom Evans, and Joey Molland. "They put us inside this huge blue wooden box made out of plywood, with doors in the front of it," says Molland of the *All Things Must Pass* sessions. "We'd go in there and get on these tall stools, they'd mic us up, and we'd begin recording. I remember hearing the rough-mix playback of 'My Sweet Lord.' The balance was all there. It was so incredibly full, an enormous acoustic guitar sound without any double tracking or anything. Just all of us going at once, straight on" (Simons, 2003).

EQUIPMENT/GEAR

George Harrison bought his first Gretsch in the early 1960s in Liverpool. His black Duo Jet with a Bigsby vibrato arm reportedly was his favorite Gretsch guitar. Harrison used this guitar for years in the recording studio. The Duo Jet sported "humped block" inlays and two single-coil DeArmond pickups. When the Beatles started to get famous in the early 1960s, George bought a 1962 Chet Atkins "Country Gentleman" Gretsch guitar.

In 1964, while on the first official Beatles U.S. visit, George Harrison was presented with a brand new Rickenbacker that was an experiment at the time, but set the standard for all future electric 12-string guitars: the 360/12. This guitar was unique in its sound, mainly due to the "reverse" stringing (octave string strung second instead of first) and soon became synonymous with a 1960s jangle sound.

In February of 1965, John and George received matching Sonic Blue Stratocasters. George used his immediately to lay down his solo to "You're Gonna Lose That Girl" on the *Help!* album. He also used it almost exclusively on *Rubber Soul.*

In early 1966, George Harrison acquired a 1964 Gibson SG Standard to use as his main guitar on *Revolver*. It was cherry red with two humbucker pickups and a Maestro Vibrola. George used this guitar on "Paperback Writer," "And Your Bird Can Sing," and "Lady Madonna," to name just a few. Later in 1966, John and George purchased Epiphone Casinos to use on *Revolver* and on their last world tour. George's was finished in sunburst with a B7 Bigsby tremolo and was his main guitar for the last tour and also showed up on *Sgt. Pepper*. In preparation for the recording of *Sgt. Pepper's Lonely Hearts Club Band* in 1967, all four band members gave their instruments psychedelic paint jobs. Harrison chose to repaint his Sonic Blue Strat in a Day-Glo paint, which was a new thing at the time, and he renamed it "Rocky" in 1968.

In August 1968, Eric Clapton gave George a 1957 Les Paul Gold Top refinished in cherry red, which he named "Lucy" (after the popular Hollywood star Lucille Ball). He used "Lucy" extensively on the demos for the Beatles' "White" album, and he also played it on *Let It Be* and *Abbey Road*.

* * *

The venerable music company Vox got a hold of the Beatles early in their career and struck a deal to provide them with Vox equipment exclusively for use on stage. John Lennon's first piece of Vox gear was a light brown twin-speaker AC15, while George's was a similar colored AC30 with a top boost unit installed in the rear. The two guitarists were also provided with two black-covered AC30s with the rear panel top boost units. As the crowds at Beatles shows began to make more and more noise, the band needed louder amps to be heard. Lennon and Harrison were given the first AC50 "Piggyback" units. They eventually received their own AC100 rigs, with 4x12"/2-horn configurations. From 1963 through 1966, the Beatles tried out many prototypes or exclusive Vox amps, including hybrid tube/solid-state units from the 4- and 7-series, both of which were unsuccessful products. Vox manufactured a solid-state amp known as the "Super Beatle" to cash in on the public's obsession with the Beatles and the band's Vox affiliation, but it was not nearly as successful as the tube-based AC-30 and AC-15 models.

ESSENTIAL READING

Babiuk, Andy. *Beatles Gear.* San Francisco, CA: Backbeat Books, 2002.
Leng, Simon. *George Harrison: While My Guitar Gently Weeps.* London: SAF Publishing, 2002.
MacDonald, Ian. *Revolution in the Head: The Beatle's Music and the Sixties.* New York: Pimlico, 1995.
Simons, David. "The Unsung Beatle." *Acoustic Guitar,* February 2003.

ESSENTIAL WORK

"Here Comes the Sun" (1969)
"If I Needed Someone" (1965)
"My Sweet Lord" (1970)
"Something" (1969)
"Taxman" (1966)
"While My Guitar Gently Weeps" (1968)

ESSENTIAL LISTENING

Abbey Road (Capitol, 1969)
All Things Must Pass (Capitol, 1970/2001)
The Best of George Harrison (Capitol, 1976/1990)
A Hard Day's Night (Capitol, 1964)
Help! (Capitol, 1965)
Revolver (Capitol, 1966)
Rubber Soul (Capitol, 1965)
Sgt. Pepper's Lonely Hearts Club Band (Capitol, 1967)
Traveling Wilburys, Volume 1 (Wilbury, 1988)

ESSENTIAL VIEWING

A Hard Day's Night (MPI, 1964/2002)
Concert for Bangladesh (Rhino, WEA, DVD, 2005)
Concert for George (DVD, 2003)
The Dark Horse Years, 1976–1992 (Capitol, DVD 2004)

Jimi Hendrix

It is hard to overstate the impact Jimi Hendrix had on the electric guitar. He single-handedly expanded the vocabulary of the instrument by taking what came before and bringing it into uncharted territory. Many, if not most, experts on the subject claim that Hendrix was the best, most important player in the history of popular music. If not that, then his creative innovations on the instrument and his courageous experimentation were second to none. More than any other musician, Hendrix maximized and stretched the potential of the electric guitar, by driving his instrument, his effects, and his technique to obtain greater heights than anyone who had come before him.

In a relatively short time, from his 1967 debut until his death in 1970, over the course of just a small handful of official studio albums, Hendrix ushered in wholesale changes in popular music with his Stratocaster. He realized its full range of sound by fusing elements of funk, R&B, soul, psychedelia, acid rock, blues, and singer-songwriter styles. By bringing such elements together, he revolutionized modern music and created an amplified and electric sound no one had ever heard before.

Of course, players before Hendrix like Jimmy Page and Jeff Beck, among others, had experimented with feedback and distortion. But Hendrix turned those effects and others into a controlled, fluid vocabulary every bit as personal as the blues with which he began. His vehicle for these heady achievements came largely with his power trio, aptly named the Jimi Hendrix Experience, or the Experience for short. Costarring bassist Noel Redding and drummer Mitch Mitchell, the Experience recorded three landmark albums in the span of a year and a half: *Are You Experienced?, Axis: Bold as Love,* and *Electric Ladyland.* These recordings—featuring classics like "Purple Haze," "Hey Joe," and "Foxey Lady"—told only part of the Hendrix story.

The rest of the legend comes from his unforgettable live appearances at festivals, namely, Monterey Pop and Woodstock, which highlighted Hendrix at his majestic peak in front of hundreds of thousands of fans. These performances are considered—like the Beatles at Shea Stadium and Elvis on "The Ed Sullivan Show"—integral episodes in the canon of rock 'n' roll. When Jimi torched his guitar on stage at the Monterey Pop Festival, it became one of, if not the single greatest iconic moment in the first half-century of rock; his image as the psychedelic voodoo child conjuring uncontrollable forces is a rock archetype.

His brief, incendiary work with the Experience took an exhausting toll on Hendrix. He felt excessive pressure to produce and his nonstop touring and sudden celebrity status wore him down. The stress forced him to break up the trio and start something fresh in 1969.

The Band of Gypsys was the result. Originally called Gypsy Sun & Rainbows, Hendrix's new band debuted at Woodstock in 1969. The group included Billy Cox on bass, Mitch

Mitchell on drums, second guitar player Larry Lee, and percussionists Jerry Velez and Juma Sultan. They would later record, just as notably, at the Fillmore East—with Cox on bass and Buddy Miles on drums—with the name Band of Gypsys.

Hendrix performed his last official show at the Isle of Fehmarn, Germany on September 6, 1970. On September 18, he died from suffocation, after inhaling vomit following barbiturate intoxication. His death at age 27 is one of rock's great tragedies. His premature departure deprived his fans and subsequent fans of electric guitar the joy of seeing him perform and left us wondering what could have been.

Still, there is his legacy. His expressively unconventional, six-string vocabulary lives on in the work of the guitarists who've followed his lead, players like Eddie Van Halen, Stevie Ray Vaughan, and Vernon Reid. Hendrix's studio innovations and his outright virtuosity in both conventional and unconventional areas have been imitated, adopted, and pushed. Hendrix's unprecedented musical vision profoundly affected both black and white performers, everyone from Sly Stone and George Clinton to shredders Yngwie Malmsteen and Steve Vai, from soul (Prince) to jazz (Miles Davis).

He unleashed hard rock, dug deeply into the blues, and created towering monuments to noise and high-powered psychedelia. But he also played tender ballads, "The Wind Cries Mary," "Little Wing," and "Angel," with incredible emotional power. And let's not forget his voice. Although he did not consider himself a very good vocalist, his singing ranged almost as widely and as evocatively as his playing.

Since his death, over a dozen books have been written about Hendrix; every note he ever recorded has been released and rereleased; and every aspect of his career has been debated, scrutinized, analyzed, fought over, and often, brought to court. Bootlegs, session work, radio appearances, interviews, jams, and live shows have been released to the public, often unauthorized. Jimi Hendrix's estate, under the aegis of Experience Hendrix and Jimi's sister Janie, has fought constantly against unauthorized release of material. Still, approximately 100 albums have been stamped with the Hendrix name, flooding the marketplace and diluting the strength of Jimi's recorded oeuvre.

Hendrix earned many of rock's most prestigious awards during and following his lifetime. He was inducted into the Rock 'n' Roll Hall of Fame in 1992 as well as into the U.K. Music Hall of Fame in 2005. (He first broke through in the United Kingdom.) His star on the Hollywood Walk of Fame was dedicated in 1994 and *Rolling Stone* magazine named Jimi the top guitar player on their list of the "100 Greatest Guitarists of All Time."

EARLY YEARS

Johnny Allen Hendrix was born on November 27, 1942 in Seattle. His birth mother, Lucille Hendrix Jeter was only 17 at the time, and, because her husband was in the army, she put her baby in the care of friends. When the father, James "Al" Hendrix, returned from World War II, he retrieved his child and renamed him James Marshall Hendrix. His family nicknamed him "Buster."

Jimi had two brothers, Leon and Joseph, and two sisters, Kathy and Pamela. But his family didn't stay together long. His father had trouble gaining meaningful employment after returning from the service, creating a turbulent household. Joseph, Jimi's brother, was born with physical difficulties and at the age of three was given up to state care. His two sisters were both given up at a relatively early age as well, to foster care and subsequent adoption. His brother Leon was also temporarily put into foster care.

Hendrix was shy and sensitive, deeply affected by the conditions of poverty and neglect that he was raised in. The Hendrixes ultimately divorced when Jimi was only nine, and his mother died when he was 15. About that time, Jimi bought his first acoustic guitar, acquiring it for $5 from a friend of his father. He immersed himself in learning and suddenly found a focal point for his life.

His father enjoyed the sounds of Muddy Waters and B.B. King and so Jimi grew up listening to those same blues. The Hendrixes were also fond of Elvis Presley; they saw him perform in Seattle in 1957. In the summer of 1959, Jimi received a white Supro Ozark, his first electric guitar, from his father. He began to absorb blues, R&B, and early rock techniques, not to mention performing antics—playing with his teeth, behind his head, and so forth—which his Seattle bandmates said he got from a local youth named Butch Snipes.

About this time, he began playing guitar in local bands. His first experience was with the Velvetones. They performed regularly at the Yesler Terrace Neighborhood House without pay, but even then Jimi's flashy, unorthodox style—playing left-handed on a right-handed guitar upside down—made him stand out from his bandmates. His next band, the Rocking Kings, gigged for money, though not much. He received $.35 for his first gig with the band.

When his Supro was stolen, his father replaced it with a white Silvertone Danelectro he painted red and emblazoned with the words "Betty Jean" (Morgan), the name of his Garfield High School sweetheart.

Jimi underachieved in school. In fact, he failed to graduate from Garfield. He argued later in an interview that the school expelled him for holding hands with a white girl, but school officials insist his grades and attendance were unacceptable. His expulsion was rectified posthumously when he was awarded an honorary diploma and a bust of him was installed in the school's library.

At the age of 17, he dropped his rock 'n' roll dream to join the U.S. Army. But Jimi didn't voluntarily join. He was caught not once but twice riding in a stolen car. As a result of this, a judge gave him the choice of serving two years of jail time or serving two years in the military. Jimi opted for the latter.

Stationed at Fort Ord in California, Jimi adjusted surprisingly well to the army, at least early on. In 1961 he was transferred to Fort Campbell, where he trained as a paratrooper. He learned how to fly and how to jump out of airplanes. He was considered a poor marksman.

The circumstances surrounding Jimi's discharge from the military are murky. One account, Jimi's own, holds that he broke his ankle during a parachute jump and was given a discharge based on this disability. Another, the military's perspective, states that Jimi required constant supervision and that he showed little merit. Commanding officers suggested he be discharged. A third excuse comes in the 2005 *Room Full of Mirrors* biography by Charles Cross, which claims that Hendrix faked falling in love with a fellow soldier and was discharged for this overt exhibition of homosexuality. Whatever the case, Jimi served a little over one year in the military, and then he set out to resume his music career.

MUSIC

During his brief tenure in the military, Jimi befriended a fellow musician named Billy Cox. They met on the base in a club recreation room. Cox recalled hearing a strange sound coming from a club room, and he followed it.

Michael Ochs Archives/Getty Images

"My buddy thought it sounded like shit, but I disagreed and I followed it. It was Jimi" (Gulla, Bob, "High Times," *Guitar World's Bass,* October 2006, n.p.).

Cox and Hendrix struck up a friendship based on their mutual love for music, and Hendrix convinced Cox to get back to playing bass. A few months after jamming with Jimi, he scooped up a bass of his own.

"Before heading out, I bought my first bass, a P-Bass, at the Gate 5 pawn shop," he says. "It cost me $100. We were poor for a long time, but we sounded good together" (Gulla, *Guitar World's Bass*).

Following the service, Cox and Hendrix moved together to nearby Clarksville, Tennessee, and later to Nashville, where they formed a band called the King Kasuals. They played low-paying gigs on the chitlin' circuit in 1963 in what was a lively R&B scene. Soon, Jimi, Cox, and a couple of other local musicians became essentially the house band at a venue called Club Del Morocco. For two years, Hendrix built his performing chops in the South, with King Kasuals, and for various sessions, until 1965. He backed performers such as Sam Cooke, Jackie Wilson, Chuck Jackson, and others during that period. The demanding chitlin' circuit served a critical role in Jimi's career, since it helped refine his style and solidify his blues roots.

In February of 1964, Hendrix won first prize in an amateur contest sponsored by the Apollo Theater in Harlem. That spring the Isley Brothers, a huge R&B act out of Cincinnati, hired him on guitar, and he joined their national tour. He recorded the Isleys hit "Testify," his first successful studio session. A few months later, Little Richard hired Jimi for his backing band, the Royal Company. But the two personalities clashed over discipline, wardrobe, playing style, and stage antics, which the artist deemed were stealing some of his spotlight. His stint with Little Richard ended quickly.

In 1965, he participated in dozens of sessions and a handful of bands, including Curtis Knight and the Squires and Joey Dee and the Starliters. Later, in 1966, he formed his own band in New York City, Jimmy James and the Blue Flames. That lineup featured Randy Palmer (bass), Danny Casey (drums), a 15-year-old guitarist who played slide and rhythm named Randy Wolfe and the occasional stand-in. Since there were two musicians named "Randy" in the group, Hendrix dubbed Wolfe "Randy California" (as he had recently moved from there to New York City) and Palmer (a Tejano) "Randy Texas." Randy California later went on to form his own successful band, Spirit. Hendrix and his new band performed around the flourishing Greenwich Village folk scene.

THE EXPERIENCE

During his time in the Village, Hendrix's network expanded. One of the music industry people he met was Chas Chandler, a musician formerly of the Animals who was looking to manage talent. Chandler helped Hendrix form a new band; he introduced him to two British musicians, drummer Mitch Mitchell and bassist Noel Redding. Chandler also escorted Hendrix to London, to introduce him to influential tastemaker friends like Eric Clapton, who had just formed Cream, and Pete Townshend, who was launching the Who. Clapton and Hendrix hit it off, and Chandler's exposure of his new artist helped establish him on the London scene.

In late 1966, word of Hendrix spread quickly, thanks to a couple of well-received gigs and a handful of television appearances. His showmanship made instant fans of already idolized guitarists like Clapton and Jeff Beck. When his first single came out, "Hey Joe" b/w "Stone Free," the London scene responded enthusiastically.

The first Experience album, *Are You Experienced?*, came out in the spring of 1967 in the United Kingdom, and it shot straight to the top of the charts, almost. Only the Beatles' *Sgt. Pepper's Lonely Hearts Club Band* kept it from #1. It was released in August of 1967 in the States, where Jimi's reputation as a star had yet to become widespread.

American executives had decided to start the album with "Purple Haze," whereas the British version commenced with "Foxey Lady." Whatever the case, *Are You Experienced?* single-handedly changed the landscape of the electric guitar in rock music. The album was recorded on four tracks, mixed into mono, and modified by a "fuzz" pedal, reverb, and a touch of the "Octavia" pedal on "Purple Haze." A remix using the mostly mono backing tracks with the guitar and vocal overdubs separated and occasionally panned to create a stereo mix was also released in the United States and Canada.

Though the album didn't sell particularly well, and the single didn't create the sudden impact it did in the United Kingdom, Hendrix, thanks to the recommendation of Beatle Paul McCartney, did clinch a spot at the Monterey Pop Festival in June of 1967. His performance at Monterey was epic, climaxed by the now famous guitar burning for his finale.

Hendrix returned to New York City for more club gigs. In July he saw Frank Zappa, whose band the Mothers of Invention was playing at an adjacent club. Hendrix developed a fascination with Zappa's wah-wah pedal, and he went out to buy one of his own. The pedal became a notable weapon in his arsenal.

Hendrix released his second album, *Axis: Bold as Love,* at the end of 1967. The recording reflected a more mature and melodic songwriting technique as well as some studio innovations, particularly with stereo phasing. This album also marked the first time

Hendrix recorded the whole album with his guitar tuned down one half-step, a tuning he used exclusively thereafter. It was also his first work to feature his wah-wah pedal.

The third and final Experience album, *Electric Ladyland,* came out in October of 1968. It finds Hendrix taking his space-age guitar funk and psychedelia to the limit and is considered one of the best rock albums of all time.

Working with engineer Eddie Kramer, Hendrix achieved once and for all his extraordinary vision, with odd use of mics, echo, backward tape, flanging, and chorusing, all new techniques at the time—at least the way Hendrix used them. The recording influenced a generation of players and beyond. Taken as a whole, his three Experience albums became his ultimate statement and proof of his otherworldly power on the electric guitar.

THE BAND OF GYPSYS

In discourse about Jimi's impact on electric guitar, his juggernaut effort with the Experience gets most of the headlines. Indeed, he created a tough act to follow. But Jimi's follow-up trio the Band of Gypsys, together from April of 1969 to his death, doesn't receive nearly the praise it deserves. In fact, when the discussion turns to Jimi's principal recordings, *Band of Gypsys,* the only album he made with this group, is rarely mentioned, if at all. It's as if it's some sort of afterthought, an unofficial entry in Jimi's canon.

Band of Gypsys and its more fully realized cousin *Live at the Fillmore East* are logical steps forward from his work with the Experience. Rather than any sort of redheaded stepchild, *Band of Gypsys* has more moods, hues, and dimensions in style than does his work with the Experience. And it clearly hints at directions Jimi would have explored had he survived to tell the story. Not only that, the four Fillmore Concerts—the quartet of sets that spawned the *Band of Gypsys*—serve as the third and critical pillar of his celebrated live triumvirate, right alongside his gigs at Monterey (1967) and Woodstock (1969).

Understandably, his fans at the time considered the live disc nothing more than a contractual obligation, which it was. *Band of Gypsys* was recorded to fulfill an early contract Jimi, along with his band Curtis Knight and the Squires, inked with PPX Industries for a single dollar. Still, regardless of that ill-advised signature, Jimi was desperately hungry to make music.

At the time he recruited Cox to help him in the spring of 1969, Jimi's mood was somber. He had become unmoored from his manager Chas Chandler, who at the time was pressing him for a follow-up to *Electric Ladyland.* His relationship with bassist Noel Redding had broken down, and the trio's relentless schedule of touring, recording, and personal appearances had grown tiresome. Jimi also had drug charges to answer to. The turmoil dimmed future prospects for the Experience.

To ease his discontent, he phoned his Army buddy Billy Cox. At the time, Cox was playing sessions, touring the "chitlin' circuit" with artists like Gatemouth Brown and Freddie King, and running a publishing company. The two friends hadn't been in touch in a few years and Cox, far removed from the commercial rock scene, was unaware of Jimi's success. "When he called me," Cox recalls, "I realized he was way up *there* and he could choose the best bass player in the world to work with. Jimi said, 'That's why I chose you!' "

Not long after that call, Jimi invited Billy backstage following an Experience gig in Memphis. Cox was blown away by the show. Something remarkable had happened to his old friend's artistry in the time they'd been apart. "Jimi put 25 years on a guitar in five years," he marvels. "Jimi's guitar became a part of him." U.S. dates for the Experience were scheduled into June of that year, but that didn't stop Jimi from setting in motion a new musical direction with Billy at his side (Gulla, *Guitar World's Bass*).

That summer, during a break from Jimi's touring, the two retreated to a home in upstate New York to jumpstart a band, work up new material, and prepare for Woodstock. If his hyperproductivity was any indication, the time away from the Experience and the frantic rehearsals working on a sequel to *Electric Ladyland* did him good. The band Jimi assembled to headline Woodstock, Gypsy Sun & Rainbows, included Cox on bass, Mitch Mitchell on drums, second guitar player Larry Lee, and percussionists Jerry Velez and Juma Sultan. Incredibly, Woodstock was Cox's first paying job for Jimi.

After Woodstock the six-piece band concept didn't stick. Jimi had difficulty controlling the creative environment and the material, generally written for smaller combos, wasn't gelling. To make matters worse, in October of 1969, his drummer Mitchell returned to London. Cox, unhappy with the situation and eager to return to a more stable environment, left for a while until Jimi figured things out. "There was just a lot of things I was unhappy with," says Billy, "so I left." A few months later, and with a few concessions, Jimi convinced Billy to return. Together, they decided to start anew. They turned up a mutual friend, Buddy Miles, to play the drums. Buddy had done some time with Jimi during the *Electric Ladyland* sessions (Gulla, *Guitar World's Bass*).

In the fall of 1969, the Band of Gypsys came together. Cox and Miles, sensing the increasing pressure their bandleader was feeling from his label, Capitol Records, pressed Jimi to pull together something fresh. Concert promoter Bill Graham arranged a two-night stand at the Fillmore East for the end of the year. In part to fulfill the aforementioned contractual obligation and in part to record the live album Jimi had always wanted to make, plans were made to record all four shows.

That fall, the outlook grew rosier and the mood lighter. Jimi was acquitted of his drug charges. Cox and Miles provided him with comfortable new surroundings and the prospect of uninterrupted productivity lie ahead. Because of their diverse backgrounds, Billy and Buddy pushed him stylistically. Jimi experimented deeply with funk, R&B, blues, and soul like he'd never done before. The group plunged into rehearsals at a Lower Manhattan warehouse called Baggy's Studios. (The tapes from those rehearsals, called *The Baggy's Rehearsal Sessions*, are available at www.daggerrecords.com.) It was here that the band created the bulk of the originals they'd debut at the Fillmore shows, from "Machine Gun" and "Stepping Stone" to "Earth Blues" and "Burning Desire," none of which had ever made it onto a studio recording or a set list. For three months the band jammed in the warehouse, firming up loose rhythm patterns into usable songs.

There were several salient changes in Jimi and the band's new material. Most importantly, Jimi's playing took on a bluesy flair. The soulful swing of the rhythm section sent him off into bold exploration. Even on an Experience standard like "Stone Free," the insistent rhythms of Cox and Miles inspired Hendrix to go places he had never been. Focused less on theatrics and pyrotechnics and more on playing, Jimi probed funk, soul, blues, flamenco, jazz, and many stops in between. Cox, for his part, provided superb, fatback bass lines on tunes like "Machine Gun" and "Izabella" for Hendrix to launch his solos.

In a technical attempt to alter his sound, Jimi complemented his playing by tinkering with his effects chain. For the first time he ran his black Strat signal through a Vox wah pedal, a Roger Mayer Axis fuzz, a Fuzz Face, a UniVibe, and a Mayer Octavia. The Octavia debuted on *Are You Experienced?*, and its upper octave generation shows up on "Purple

LEGAL HASSLES

Jimi's recorded legacy has been tied up in legal hassles through four decades, since before his death. At just 27 years old, Jimi Hendrix died without a will and because of that his estate has been contested around every corner. For two decades, beginning in the 1970s, a California attorney managed the Hendrix estate. Jimi's father, Al Hendrix, sued for the rights to Jimi's music and won in 1995.

Under the name of the estate, Al created multiple trusts, partnerships, and corporations, notably Experience Hendrix, L.L.C. based in Seattle. This company, in conjunction with MCA Records, helps allow Jimi to live on through newly released DVDs, videos, CDs of previously unreleased material, and even the "Jimi Hendrix Red House Tour," a traveling museum of replicas of Hendrix memorabilia.

Another court battle has to do with entrepreneur Ed Chalpin. Chalpin signed Hendrix to a three-year recording contract, receiving $1 and 1 percent royalty on records with Curtis Knight. The Knight masters numbered 33 performances. The contract never officially lapsed, which caused considerable problems for Hendrix later on in his career as well as posthumously.

Chalpin ultimately was ordered to pay Experience Hendrix, Jimi's official estate, a percentage of the royalties he made on those masters. The case is still pending.

Things grew more complicated when Al died in 2002. At the time, the Hendrix estate was worth about $80 million, which went almost entirely to Al's adopted daughter Janie. Al had divorced Jimi's mother in the late 1950s and adopted Janie when he married her mother in 1968. Jimi's brother, Leon, alleged that Janie manipulated Al into writing Leon and his children out of the will, and he sued to be written back in. In the same suit, other beneficiaries claimed that they received nothing while Janie and a cousin in charge of the estate grossly mismanaged and abused trust funds (Kaminsky, Michelle, Esq., "The Battle Over the Jimi Hendrix Estate," www.legalzoom.com).

In the end, a judge in Washington didn't believe that Janie preyed on Al's weakened state to persuade him to excise Leon from the will. Instead, the judge noted Leon's drug use, demands for money, and threats of litigation were reason enough for Al to change his estate plan.

Despite all of the recent legal wrangling over his estate, some claim that those who had been closest to Hendrix during his life, particularly relatives on his mother's side, never benefited from his body of work. This is unfortunate, and almost guarantees that the disagreements and accusations will persist among the various factions of the Hendrix family. And one other thing is certain: the court system has played far too big a role in the Hendrix Experience, and the lingering malice of those involved has detracted considerably from his legacy.

Haze" and other classics. The UniVibe first appeared at Woodstock and would go on to play a significant role at the Fillmore concerts and beyond.

All of the original *Band of Gypsys* tracks came from the second day—"Who Knows" and "Machine Gun" from the first set, and "Changes," "Power of Soul," "Message to Love," and "We Gotta Live Together" from the second. "Machine Gun," specifically, is hailed as one of his greatest guitar performances, with an intricate solo at its center and percussive riffs and controlled feedback generated to mimic the violence and chaos of a battlefield. And yet, despite his explosive noise—the helicopters, bombs, and automatic weapons—Jimi never buried his brilliant tone or the melodic core of the song. He'd go on to make "Machine Gun" the main attraction of shows until his death, but it was this particular performance that demonstrated the visceral intensity and dazzling invention of his best work. Indeed, the second set on New Year's Day 1970 has come to be known as one of Jimi's greatest performances.

"In December of '69, Jimi made extraordinary advances," says McDermott. " 'Machine Gun' represents an extraordinary, almost unfathomable advance. He took the Delta blues to a whole different place. He had a real passion to push it as far as he could go. The work in *Band of Gypsys* tells you that Jimi's train never stopped" (Gulla, *Guitar World's Bass*).

As soon as the dust had settled from the Fillmore shows, Jimi's manager Michael Jeffery began badgering him to reform the Experience, get back on the road, and make some money to finish the construction on Electric Lady Studio. Jimi hesitated and lashed out. A late January show at Madison Square Garden proved disastrous, when a clearly disturbed Hendrix stormed off the stage after just two plodding numbers. "Backstage, amid the chaos and confusion," writes McDermott in the liner notes to the *Band of Gypsys* album, "Jeffery fired Buddy Miles and the Band of Gypsys were no more" (McDermott, *Band of Gypsys* liner notes).

The end, coming as it did after such an incredible triumph, shocked many who were involved. But despite the second-nature chemistry of the Band of Gypsys, and despite the success of the subsequent album, it always felt like Jimi's handlers were intent on reassembling the Experience. Immediately after disbanding, Cox went home, only to be persuaded to return soon after to become a part of the Experience with drummer Mitchell. In the spring of 1970, the band toured the United States successfully, and inspired by that success, they went into Jimi's brand new, finally completed cutting-edge studio to begin work on a new album. The material they were working up? Songs that Jimi had conceived with Billy and Buddy as the Band of Gypsys: "Izabella," "Ezy Rider," "Room Full of Mirrors," and "Earth Blues." Those songs would end up on the list for *First Rays of the New Rising Sun*, the album Jimi was making at the time of his death.

DEATH

Jimi Hendrix died in London, but the circumstances of his death have never been satisfactorily laid out. The night he died, he had been at a party and was picked up by his current girlfriend Monika Dannemann. She drove him to her apartment at the Samarkand Hotel. According to the coroner's estimated time of death, Hendrix passed away not long after arriving at Dannemann's.

She claimed in her testimony that she had no idea he had consumed a total of nine of her prescription sleeping pills. The doctor that attended to him first explained that the guitarist drowned in his own vomit, which appeared to consist mainly of red wine. Statements from police and ambulance staff show Hendrix was home alone at the time and was discovered dead on the scene. Not only that, statements say, but he had been dead for a while before authorities discovered him. In the aftermath of his death, additional statements arose saying that Hendrix had overdosed on heroin, that there were needle marks on his arm to prove it. These statements were all subsequently disproven, although it remains unclear whether Dannemann played some kind of role, accidental or otherwise, in Hendrix's death.

Hendrix had verbally requested to be buried in England, but relatives had his body returned to Seattle, where he was interred in Greenwood Memorial Park in Renton, Washington. As the popularity of Hendrix and his music grew over the decades following his death, the remains of Jimi Hendrix, his father Al Hendrix, and grandmother Nora Rose Moore Hendrix, were moved to a new site. The headstone contains a depiction of a Stratocaster, although the guitar is shown right side up, not upside down as Hendrix played it.

TECHNIQUE/STYLE

After four decades, and thousands of guitarists, Hendrix remains atop the player pyramid, miraculously unsurpassed as rock's most revolutionary guitarist. Indeed, Hendrix devotees, dismayed at having lost their hero before he completed his body of work, crave more; one note or an entire guitar solo will do. Students of the guitarist know that every piece of work he did is essential, and it seems there's always something new to discover, something new to surface, something new to learn. Of course, playing it, and playing it well, takes some a lifetime.

He played the Strat almost exclusively, though he'd occasionally be seen playing a Gibson, either a Les Paul or a Flying V. The Strat's easy action and narrow neck were well suited to Hendrix's evolving style and enhanced his tremendous dexterity. He had large hands, and he could fret across all six strings with his thumb, leaving his fingers to play the melodic fills on top. This enabled him to play lead and rhythm parts simultaneously.

Another critical fact about Hendrix is that as a left-handed player, he used right-handed Strats. But instead of playing the guitar as a traditional left-hander, he played his upside down. He restrung his instruments so that the heavier strings were in their standard position at the top of the neck. This configuration allowed him to manipulate the tremolo arm and volume/tone controls, and it also had an important effect on the sound of his guitar. Because his pickups' pole pieces were staggered, Jimi's lowest string rang out with a bright sound, while his highest string was rather mellow sounding, a result that is in fact the opposite intention of the Strat's design.

When you compare Hendrix's early session recordings to his playing when he exploded on the London scene, the two are not far apart. Hendrix was always grounded in R&B and soul, and never too far removed from his roots on the chitlin' circuit. Certainly, his technique grew more sophisticated, but it still maintained the rhythmic foundation that others who copped his licks, like Clapton and Beck, never truly mastered.

Hendrix came up from the bottom of the music ladder. He spent years playing chords and absorbing rhythms before he could come into his own as a solo player. Lead players like Beck and Clapton started as lead players and refined their soloing styles above everything else. Most blues bands require a competent soloist, and they leave the rhythm to the rhythm section.

But Hendrix led with his rhythm and his songs are more riff-oriented. In live performances, this meant that his solos were nearly always patterned after the chord progression or riff pattern. He never allowed his solos to veer too far from the core song.

On an interesting note, Hendrix didn't begin tuning his guitar below standard pitch until after the *Are You Experienced?* sessions. That entire album is in standard tuning, but all of the guitars that followed on the two remaining Experience albums—*Axis: Bold as Love* and *Electric Ladyland*—are tuned down one half-step.

Hendrix also mastered his Strat's whammy bar. Generally utilized as a way to gently manipulate a note or a chord, Hendrix combined his use of the whammy with feedback to gain dramatic drops in pitch on certain notes and chords. On a song like "Machine Gun," he uses the whammy's dramatic effect to imitate the sound of weapons and war. He also used his pick and his fingers to create grinding noises, and he'd often thump the body of his instrument to create strange moments of feedback and noise.

Often Hendrix is equated with his antics on the guitar. That is, he's often pictured burning his guitar, playing it behind his head, or with his teeth. These were all ploys he learned very early on to retain the attention of his audience and entertain difficult crowds.

In reality, though, while these skills may be on the challenging side, Hendrix's real talent lie in his manipulation of sound— the way he looked differently at his upside down, reverse-strung guitar and perpetrated the kinds of tones and effects that no one had ever heard before.

EQUIPMENT/GEAR

Guitars

Hendrix played Strats almost exclusively, but he could be seen occasionally with a Les Paul or a Flying V, both Gibson models. Jimi was also seen playing Fender Jazzmasters, Duosonics, Gibson SGs, and a Gretsch Corvette he used in a 1967 TV appearance with Curtis Knight's band. In another TV appearance, this one in 1969 on "The Dick Cavett Show," and again that year at the Isle of Wight concert, he was seen using a white Gibson SG Custom and a Gibson Flying V. The latter guitar was a unique custom left-handed model with gold-plated hardware, a bound fingerboard and "split-diamond" fret markers not found on other Flying Vs in the 1960s.

His loyalty to Fender—as well as Clapton's and Jeff Beck's—made it the biggest selling guitar in history. Jimi started playing the Strat in 1966 or so and bought many Strats along the way. Jimi liked his Strats to sound bright, and so he chose a light-tone maple fretboard over the darker rosewood to balance the power chords of his playing with flexibility and speed. In early 1969 he restrung his guitars with heavier strings and tuned them lower by a half-step. This enabled Jimi to play his R&B/funk/soul-influenced rhythms with searing rock solos more effectively.

The configuration also required Jimi to retune frequently in concert, because his aggressive use of the tremolo bar often threw his strings out of tune.

Amplifiers and Effects

Hendrix's enthusiasm for effects, and his ability to maximize and push them beyond what they were likely intended to do, made him a catalyst in guitar electronics and pedals. Technically, in his desire to expand his vocabulary, Hendrix employed nearly every effect available to him.

But among the effects he used consistently were an Arbiter Fuzz Face, Vox wah-wah (which he was inspired to use when hearing Frank Zappa), a Roger-Mayer produced Octavia, an Axis Fuzz unit, a UniVibe, and a Leslie rotating speaker. He also manipulated his sounds extensively in the studio, especially on his last Experience album, *Electric Ladyland*. The Japanese-made UniVibe was designed to simulate the modulation effects of the Leslie; it provided Jimi with a phasing sound on a speed control pedal. The aforementioned Band of Gypsys' track "Machine Gun" highlights many of these pedals with spectacular results.

Jimi's high-volume stage presentation required amps that were up to the task. At first he employed Vox and Fender amps, but in his experience with Cream, in which he sat in with Eric Clapton, he saw the potential of the Marshall amplifiers. Along with his Strat, the Marshall stack and amplifiers helped shape his overdriven sound. They also allowed Jimi to perfect the use of feedback as a musical effect.

ESSENTIAL READING

Gulla, Bob. "High Times." *Guitar World's Bass*, October 2006, n.p.
Kaminsky, Michelle, Esq. "The Battle Over the Jimi Hendrix Estate," www.legalzoom.com.

McDermott, John. *Band of Gypsys* liner notes.
McDermott, John. *Jimi Hendrix: Sessions: The Complete Studio Recording Sessions, 1963–1970.* Boston: Little, Brown, 1996.
Murray, Charles Shaar. *Crosstown Traffic: Jimi Hendrix & The Post-War Rock 'N' Roll Revolution.* New York: St. Martin's Griffin, 1991.
Shapiro, Harry. *Electric Gypsy.* New York: St. Martin's Griffin, 1995.

ESSENTIAL WORK

"All Along the Watchtower" (1968)
"Castles in the Sand" (1967)
"Crosstown Traffic" (1968)
"Little Wing" (1967)
"Purple Haze" (1967)
"Voodoo Chile" (1968)

ESSENTIAL LISTENING

Are You Experienced? (MCA, 1967)
Axis: Bold as Love (MCA, 1967)
Band of Gypsys (MCA, 1970)
Electric Ladyland (MCA, 1968)
Live at Woodstock (MCA, 1999)

Tony Iommi

In the 1960s, Tony Iommi was just another guitar player influenced by popular U.K. phenom Hank Marvin, leader of his band the Shadows. Like so many of his fellow Brits at the time, Tony played a lot of blues and he dabbled in jazz and pop as he came of age as a player. At the time, Iommi played in a band with future Sabbath drummer Bill Ward called Mythology that was primarily into a bluesy, jazzy vibe. But amid the standard blues progressions and "jazzy bits" Tony was playing one night at a Mythology rehearsal, a few notes—dark, moody, chilling notes—emerged, raising the hairs on the neck of those who heard them. Those notes, patiently played, combined with a clutch of downtuned power chords, (tuned to help Iommi compensate for the fingertips he was missing on his fret hand from an accident), resonated in the night and many nights thereafter like the creaking, dusty door of a castle dungeon.

"It was such a different vibe, I knew that was it," he told me. That tune was "Wicked World," and another signature song, "Black Sabbath," came soon after. Iommi's "Wicked World" still had the jazzy feel of his previous material. But "Black Sabbath" took a total turn from the band's traditional sound and grabbed the attention of everyone in the band, seizing their imagination and making their hairs stand on end. What would happen if they followed that dark, downtuned songwriting slant? Where would they end up? Could they leave the blues- and jazz-inflected material of their youth? If they did, and ventured off in search of unexplored territory, would the risk yield a reward?

The young rockers decided to abandon their past and blaze a new trail. They renamed their band after that second riff, "Black Sabbath," and remade themselves in a new image. From there, the sleeping ogre had awakened. Tony, along with Ward, singer Ozzy Osbourne, and bassist Geezer Butler, embarked on a sonic rampage for nearly a decade, highlighted by the 1971 release of *Paranoid*, the album many cite as the first real heavy metal album.

"Heavy 'f*cking' metal!" Pantera's Dimebag Darrell once said about the towering glory of Sabbath. "Without *Paranoid* it would have been just plain metal" (Gulla, Bob, unpublished *Guitar* magazine interview, April 1999). Dime was right. More than any other record in rock history, *Paranoid* was the blueprint for heaviness, and its freakish sounds gave disaffected teens throughout the galaxies an escape from themselves and those bleak, unforgiving years when nothing else made sense.

There were other milestones for Iommi and Sabbath, of course. The band, led by Iommi's stomping riffs and Ozzy Osbourne's maniacal vocal performances, became a blueprint, a prototype, for all deep and loud bands to follow, so much so that it has become impossible to talk at any length about the origins of heavy metal music without bringing up the name of Black Sabbath.

EARLY YEARS

Tony Iommi was born in 1948 in the city of Birmingham in England's industrial mid-section. Inspired by the quirky and versatile sounds of Hank Marvin and the Shadows, Iommi played in several blues and rock bands throughout the 1960s. His first viable, paying rock gig came at the hands of a pub band called the Rockin' Chevrolets when Tony was only 16. The band had regular live bookings and, when they were offered work in Germany, Iommi opted to leave his factory job and go on the road with the band. But on the day before he was set to leave England with the band, tragedy struck. While working in a sheet metal factory, Iommi lost the tips of the middle and ring finger of his right hand in an industrial accident. He was only 17 when it happened. They told him at the hospital that he may as well forget about playing guitar again. Distraught, he thought his music-making was over before it even began.

A supervisor at the factory, a friend who was familiar with his after-hours guitar exploits, empathized with Iommi's tragic plight. He visited one day while Tony was recovering and brought along with him a recording by Django Reinhardt, a gypsy guitar player who lost mobility in the third and fourth fingers of his fretting hand in a caravan campfire.

Iommi accepted his friend's encouragement and decided that he'd do what he could to relearn the instrument. At first, he attempted to learn the guitar as a right-hander. This opposite side didn't feel comfortable, and certainly did not work as well. Back at the drawing board, Iommi thought to string his guitars with extra-light strings—using banjo strings, which were a lighter gauge than most guitar strings at the time. He also fashioned plastic caps on his two damaged fingers. He did this by melting plastic bottles into a ball and then using a soldering iron to make holes for his fingers. He fit his fingers into the plastic while it was still pliable enough to be shaped. He then trimmed and sanded away the excess plastic and covered them with leather to provide a better grip on the strings. The jerry-rigged solution held remarkably well and soon enough Iommi was back on stage.

Between 1966 and 1967, Iommi played in a psychedelic band named the Rest with his schoolmate and future Sabbath drummer Bill Ward. In January of 1968, Ward and Iommi left the Rest and formed Mythology. But a few months later, police raided the group's practice space and discovered marijuana. The bust resulted in a fine and a two-year probationary period for the entire band. But that band too was short-lived, breaking up in the summer of the same year.

At about the same time as the dissolution of Mythology, another Birmingham band, Rare Breed, featuring vocalist John "Ozzy" Osbourne and rhythm guitarist Geezer Butler, also broke up. Iommi and Ward joined forces with Butler and Osbourne, along with slide guitarist Jimmy Phillips and saxophonist Alan "Aker" Clarke, and named themselves the Polka Tulk Blues Company.

After just two gigs, Phillips and Clarke were given their pink slips, and the band shortened its name to Polka Tulk. The band combined their blues roots with a harder rock sound, stemming from the influence of the British blues explosion happening in the United Kingdom at the time. Bands like John Mayall and the Bluesbreakers, Cream, the Yardbirds, and many others were taking American blues and electrifying it.

Polka Tulk, aspiring to do the same, lasted in name until the fall of 1968. Iommi and the band chose to relabel themselves Earth soon thereafter. The band featured what would soon become the classic Sabbath lineup of Iommi, Ward, Butler, and Osbourne.

The quartet evolved for a few months before Iommi got a phone call. Ian Anderson, leader of a premier blues and rock band called Jethro Tull, said his band was looking to fill

Tull's guitar slot. The offer, coming as it did when Iommi desperately sought to abandon life in the factory and become a famous rock 'n' roll guitarist, proved too tempting to resist. He left his friends and accepted the gig.

For whatever reason, the gig lasted just a single night.

Jethro Tull was slated to appear on the Rolling Stones' *Rock and Roll Circus,* where they would perform their hit "Song for Jeffrey." Iommi, hiding under a white hat and playing a matching white Stratocaster, looks sheepish and rather undemonstrative on the DVD version of the show. For his first high-profile gig, this one must have seemed disappointing.

He left Tull immediately after. While it's not entirely certain why he ditched the band, Iommi did bring back some valuable information. Having only spent a few weeks with the band, Iommi learned the importance of establishing a routine for the band. Rather than rolling out of bed sometime in the afternoon and drifting into practice, Iommi thought that setting a rehearsal schedule the way Tull did would benefit Earth.

Iommi and Earth reunited following his short-lived dalliance with Jethro Tull. In the early half of 1969, they were confronted by a marginally successful band, also called Earth, who had dibs on the moniker. Iommi and company backed down and chose the name Black Sabbath, after a song Iommi had written back when the band was called Mythology.

Music

Thanks to the sound Iommi had developed with his physical deformity—he downtuned three half-steps down, from E to C# to ease the tension on his fingers—Sabbath devised what would become a staple of the heavy metal sound to this day: downtuned guitar riffs. From late 1969 to early 1979, Black Sabbath, with its classic lineup, turned the loud rock world upside down with its unorthodox decibels.

In fact, the success of Sabbath marked a paradigm shift in rock 'n' roll. "Heavy metal," hinted at with bands like Iron Butterfly and Cream, gained legitimacy in their hands. The term entered the musical lexicon to describe the denser, more electrifying tributary of rock, over which Black Sabbath had become early kings.

The band's legitimacy was emphasized by the overwhelming success of Sabbath's first two recordings, *Black Sabbath* and *Paranoid. Black Sabbath* may just be the most stunning debut album in rock 'n' roll history. It is characterized by the doomy guitar notes resonating from Iommi's Gibson SG. The sound on early tunes like "Black Sabbath," "Wicked World," and "N.I.B." riveted audiences in the months leading up to their first official studio sessions. They could see clearly that their unusual sound was captivating, and their image—with long, unkempt hair and black the dominant clothing color—did the same. The formula during these first few months of playing and recording in 1969 and 1970 emerged, coming quickly into crisp relief.

It was odd then, that once the band began sending out its material, it was very poorly received. No fewer than a dozen record companies rejected Sabbath's first demos. Perhaps the band's haunting image scared people off. Certainly, when the band played out and came to tunes like "Black Sabbath," audiences had no idea what to think. Sabbath was taking the blues rock style in a decidedly radical and profoundly loud direction.

When *Black Sabbath* came out in the United Kingdom, it sold very well and remained on the charts for months. The same happened in the United States when it was released there sometime later, selling 40,000 copies in two weeks and going on to spend 18 months

THE MAKING OF *PARANOID*

Tony Iommi Explains "The Greatest Heavy Metal of All Time"

When did the material for *Paranoid* first start to appear?

When we were on tour for a bit after the first record. We had a six-week stint in a club in Zurich, where we'd start at 3 p.m. and play seven 45-minute sets. For six weeks! Well, we didn't have enough songs, so we'd keep playing the same things, which got really boring, as you can imagine. So we used that time to start jamming and making up things, especially in the off hours when there were only a few people in the club. That's when "War Pigs" came about. At the end of the six-week period we had two or three real songs to start the new album with.

So then you went in to record *Paranoid*.

Right. The recording of *Paranoid* was very quick. We went in and five days later it was finished. Most of my ideas came from gigs and I'd throw something in, a little riff, or another kind of idea. It was tricky, though, because you had to remember it in those days. There were no recording devices then. A lot of the ideas were structured at shows and when it came time to do an album we'd put all those ideas together.

There must have been a lot of pressure on you to come up with material.

They looked to me to come up with the music. If I didn't come up with something we didn't do anything. You couldn't start with the drum thing, that didn't work for us. The guitar was the most tuneful element in the band so everything stemmed off of it.

It's been written that you worked well on the spot.

I tended to come up with stuff on the spot all the time. I wasn't the type to go home and think about it and work on something. I don't know why I couldn't do that. I'd go in with nothing and took it upon myself to not let anyone else down. I couldn't tell them, "I can't think of anything, guys, sorry." I had to come up with something. (Gulla, Bob, *Guitar One,* July 2006)

on the American charts. Iommi insisted that he would have been happy had the album done well in Birmingham . . . .

The cover, with a spooky, white-faced woman enrobed in black set against a stark landscape, captured the mood perfectly.

Paranoid, the follow-up to *Black Sabbath,* would be the album that truly put the band on the metal map. The album was originally going to be titled *War Pigs,* but because the band now had commercial interest in the United States, they refrained from getting too mixed up in the controversy surrounding the Vietnam War. The image on the cover, more coincidental with the "War Pig" title, remained.

"When we first saw the album cover we thought, 'Blimey, what's this?' " says Tony. "It was a record company thing. The album cover was done for us and we had nothing to do with it. We had no control over anything at the time. There was no time to change the cover image" (Gulla, 1999).

Regardless of the cover image, the music held inside *Paranoid*'s grooves did most of the talking. It is generally regarded as the quintessential Sabbath album, thanks to such classic tracks as "Iron Man," "Paranoid," and "War Pigs." Released only seven months after *Black Sabbath, Paranoid*—containing works that pointed rock in a heavy new direction —set the band on a frenetic climb to the top of the charts. Both albums were certified gold within a year of release, and Sabbath became a ubiquitous presence on the road.

Black Sabbath played many of the early 1970s biggest rock festivals, and the indefatigable roadwork improved them all as musicians and songwriters. Their next two albums, *Master of Reality* (1971) and *Vol. 4* (1972), demonstrated this expansion of range and ambition. They began delving into quieter, more evocative changes of pace, including balladic instrumentals like "Changes" and "Orchid." These songs, existing alongside devastating Sabbath eruptions like "Children of the Grave" and "After Forever" (from *Master of Reality*) and "Snowblind" and "Supernaut" (from *Vol. 4*) came to embody the yin and yang of the classic Sabbath sound.

In 1974 the band toured endlessly throughout America, playing to enthusiastic crowds. The tour was punctuated by festivals, and capped by California Jam with Deep Purple and Emerson, Lake and Palmer, enjoyed by 200,000 people. Sabbath's set, marked by no special effects and blistering performances, came after a heated debate as to which band should headline. "It was really nerve-wracking," Tony recalls. "We went down great while the others were still arguing about who should headline" (Welch, Chris, liner notes, *Black Box*, 2003, p. 13).

Courtesy of Neil Zlozower

For their part, Sabbath rarely argued. "If we'd had an argument in those early days, we'd have broken up. That's the way we were. There'd be moans and groans, but in the early days we never had any rows. We felt so lucky to be a successful band" (Welch, *Black Box*, p. 21).

*   *   *

The luck would continue, but not without a struggle. On *Vol. 4*, recorded in Los Angeles, the band shifted from England to Los Angeles, renting a mansion in Bel Air with the proceeds from their tour and their first three successful recordings. The rock star mentality set in—with its various vices—and when the band decided it was time to record their fifth album, *Sabbath Bloody Sabbath*, in 1973, they had a difficult time focusing. Cocaine became a hobby with the band, a habit reflected in the song "Snowblind," on *Vol. 4*.

In fact, Iommi, the band's riff writer and principal composer, encountered a frightening case of writer's block. Sabbath let the distractions win out. They moved out of Los Angeles momentarily to allow the creative flow to begin again. Iommi retreated to a castle in Wales, where he worked in the dungeon to take advantage of the creepy vibe.

Oddly, the vibe was too creepy for Iommi and the band; they insisted Clearwell, the Welch castle, was haunted. But the ghostly presence there helped Tony work through his writer's block, and *Sabbath Bloody Sabbath* came roaring into existence. The riff to the title track proved to be the end of his dry spell. "It was like seeing your first child born; it was the beginning of a new direction and an affirmation of life. It set the level for the album and we were rolling again" (Ives, Brian, liner notes, *Black Box*, p. 31).

The album did very well throughout the world and enabled Sabbath's rise to super stardom. But the band began to fall apart. Drugs were taking their toll on each member, and egos factored heavily into their relationships. *Sabotage, Technical Ecstacy*, and *Never Say Die!* were recorded under very stressful circumstances. With relations deteriorating, it was Tony Iommi's material that kept everyone coming back together to the studio.

On tour following *Technical Ecstasy*, the crisis exploded and Ozzy quit. The move was temporary at first. Ozzy said when he initially left, he felt like a "fish out of water." At the time, Tony had rushed in another singer, longtime friend Dave Walker, to help Sabbath soldier on. But when Ozzy decided to return, pushing Walker back out, Ozzy refused to work on any of the songs Walker had helped the band with while he'd been in the lineup. This posed another problem for Sabbath; the band was due to enter the studio in just days, and so had no original, Ozzy-related material to record. The ensuing turmoil essentially put an end to the productivity of the band's classic lineup. It was 1979.

*   *   *

Iommi kept the Sabbath name alive with several inspired releases not featuring Ozzy Osbourne (1980's *Heaven & Hell* and 1981's *The Mob Rules*). He also released some albums throughout the 1980s and early 1990s billed as Sabbath albums, but they were essentially solo outings. A case in point was the 1986 album *Seventh Star*, which was labeled a Sabbath album at the eleventh hour by Iommi's label Warner Brothers.

Along the way there were many creative missteps. After Osbourne left, drummer Bill Ward was the next to go, and then bassist Butler, leaving Iommi holding the bag. Sabbath became a revolving door of temporary members in all of the band positions, with only Iommi remaining constant. Obviously, the fleeting nature of these lineups and requisite songwriting inconsistencies turned most of these projects into a forgettable blur.

But all was not lost for Iommi, who was clearly discouraged, if not outright uninspired by his work through the 1980s and much of the 1990s. The original Sabbath lineup reunited for several highly successful and highly publicized tours in the late 1990s. This, along with several Ozzy-related projects, helped to elevate Black Sabbath's profile with a new legion of fans. They had what was billed as their swan song in 1999, with a live album and a very successful tour. But the group announced yet another tour, as a headliner of the 2001 version of Ozzy's rock 'n' roll road show, Ozzfest.

Tony issued his first true solo release in the form of 2000's *Iommi*. The 10-track disc starred many of rock's top voices lending their talents as front men, including the Foo Fighters' Dave Grohl, the Smashing Pumpkins' Billy Corgan, and Pantera's Phil Anselmo. He also worked briefly in the late 1990s with former Deep Purple singer and bass player Glenn Hughes.

Technique/Style

Because of Iommi's handicap—with two fingertips missing from his right hand—there are many things he cannot do that most guitar players can do quite easily. On the other hand, the sound he did end up making, by changing the gauge and height of his strings, became unique by default. His nightmarish incident at the factory made him more determined than ever to play with discipline and focus.

He explained to me, in an unpublished interview, his thought process while coming up with such an unexpected and mysterious sound. "We never thought about commercialism. It was just that the style grabbed us. We tested that sound out at a blues club, of all places, and it was interesting to see the shock on peoples' faces in the middle of our blues set. But they seemed turned on by it, from what we gathered. We knew *we* liked it."

In 1969, when Earth traveled to Hamburg, Germany to play a few shows, they encountered some testy, combative audiences. To counteract them, in something of an act of defiance, they began emphasizing their louder, heavier material over their more creative, bluesier, and jazzier sides. They cranked up their amps, fuzzed out their performances with distortion, and began defying the rude crowds. This tactic helped the band cope with adverse circumstances, not to mention define their own sound further.

The first two Black Sabbath albums are actually in E tuning, however, as Iommi didn't start tuning down to C# until 1971's *Master of Reality*. Black Sabbath bassist Geezer Butler also tuned his instrument down to match Iommi's. It may be argued that Tony Iommi was a pioneer of heavy metal riffing, due to his guitar playing on now famous tracks such as "Paranoid," "War Pigs," "Iron Man," and "Into the Void." Iommi combined blues-like guitar solos and dark, minor key riffing with a revolutionary high-gain, heavily distorted tone, with his use of a modified treble-boosting effect-pedal and a Gibson SG, as well as plugging his guitar into his amp's bass socket.

Equipment/Gear

In 1961, Tony heard "Shakin' All Over." It was different. It had a good solo in it and when he first heard it, he couldn't play it the way he heard it. At the time, he was playing with some local folks in Birmingham, and rock 'n' roll was just beginning to take hold. The first guitar Tony had was called a Watkins, a cheap axe made in England. It was also one of the few instruments he could buy that was made for a lefty player. The next guitar he bought was a Burns, one of the better models available at the time. And finally, just a few years later, still in the early 1960s, he laid his eyes on his first left-handed Strat. When he played it through his Vox AC-30, he knew immediately that was the sound he'd been looking for.

Tony Iommi loved his Strat. As a fan of Hank Marvin and the blues, all of his favorite players worked with the Strat. But then, how did he come to play, and be famous for his use of, the Gibson SG? Simple, during the first few days of recording their debut album, the pickup on the Strat began to malfunction. Without the means, or the time, to repair it, Iommi resorted to his backup axe, the SG. Since then, Iommi has become, alongside AC/DC's Angus Young, one of the SG's principal heroes.

Tony also has a long-standing relationship with Laney amps. He uses Laney 100Watt Supergroup Head, Laney Straight Cabinet/4x12, and for effects, Dallas Arbiter Rangemaster and a Tychobrahe ParaPedal Wah.

ESSENTIAL READING

Bushell, Gary, Mick Wall, and Stephen Rea. *Ozzy Osbourne: Diary of a Madman.* London: Omnibus Press, 1990.

Christe, Ian. *Sound of the Beast: The Complete Headbanging History of Heavy Metal.* New York: HarperCollins, 2004.

Gulla, Bob. *Guitar One,* July 2006.

———. Unpublished *Guitar* magazine interview, April 1999.

Ives, Brian. Liner notes, *Black Box,* p. 31.

Welch, Chris. Liner notes, *Black Box,* 2003.

ESSENTIAL WORK

"Iron Man" (1971)
"Paranoid" (1971)
"Sabbath Bloody Sabbath" (1973)
"Sweat Leaf" (1972)
"Symptom of the Universe" (1975)

ESSENTIAL LISTENING

Black Sabbath (Warner Bros., 1970)
Master of Reality (Warner Bros., 1971)
Paranoid (Warner Bros., 1971)
Sabbath Bloody Sabbath (Warner Bros., 1973)
Sabotage (Warner Bros., 1975)
Vol. IV (Warner Bros., 1972)

Yngwie Malmsteen

The young Swede with a nearly unpronounceable name redefined the way people approached the electric guitar in the 1980s. By ramping up the speed of his technique in a manner no one had ever heard or seen before, he reinvented heavy metal and popularized a style known as "shred."

There had been technically fast players on the scene before Malmsteen, including speedy alchemists like jazzer Tal Farlow, country pickers like Roy Clark and Joe Maphis, and finger stylists like Bert Jansch and Richard Thompson. But with his heavy amplification and a metal backdrop, Malmsteen's drag-racing speed simply left all the others behind.

His style, built atop a foundation of classical music and progressive rock, provided him with sophistication and elegance. He derived much of his technique from classical composers like Bach and Paganini and blended that technique with a maxed out Marshall stack. The result came to be known as neoclassical shred, Malmsteen's own thumbprint on popular music.

Make no mistake about it, Malmsteen is over the top. In fact, he'll be the first one to admit it. He is something of a caricature; but he loves it. He thrives on being larger than life. But it is in this way that he has developed a true identity, a unique sense of style, and something that few guitar players ever achieve on their own: authenticity.

The great debate surrounding Malmsteen's overwhelming technical skills can be split into two camps: those who feel he has drained the passion and emotion from guitar playing, and those who feel like he has simply elevated the artistry of the instrument to sublime heights. Old school players accustomed to hearing the bent notes and searing tones of the blues and blues-rock influenced players likely find Malmsteen's expression empty; some would go so far as to describe it as "soulless." Critics called him an egotist whose emphasis on blazing made for masturbatory product with no room for subtlety.

In his defense, Malmsteen countered that he loved the music he played, and so it couldn't possibly lack emotion. He insisted that his imitators, not him, copied his style and drained it of substance. Malmsteen's many fans, of course, also stood by his side. They noted that his soaring technique was, at the time, unparalleled. The speed with which he played had heretofore never been seen. And his pure expertise, the fluency with which he attacked his Strat, set the bar higher than ever for technically minded guitar players. For that, his legions were thankful.

Toward the end of the 1980s, Malmsteen fell out of favor with the metal community; his musician fan base tired of his consistently torrid licks, not to mention the incredible amount of practice it would take to emulate him. Following a series of personal setbacks, tragedies, and even injuries, Malmsteen resurfaced on indie labels, recording at a prolific pace and continuing to issue the music he loved in his signature neoclassical brand.

EARLY YEARS

Yngwie (pronounced "ING-vay" and meaning "young Viking chief") Malmsteen was born Lars Johann Yngwie Lannerback in Stockholm, Sweden, in 1963. The youngest child in a household that included his mother Rigmor, sister Ann Louise, and brother Bjorn, he was a difficult child, a behavioral monster, and early on, despite his mother's attempts, he had no interest in music.

Malmsteen had a very musical family. His sister played the flute and piano, and his brother played multiple instruments, including guitar, drums, piano, violin, and accordion. His father even played guitar, though he wasn't at home to help bring Yngwie up. The Malmsteens were divorced when Yngwie was an infant.

He received his first guitar as a gift when he was just five, a cheap Polish guitar. Even then, though, he never sat down and played the same licks over and over in a conventional way. At seven years old, he saw a TV show on Jimi Hendrix at the Monterey Music Festival, with the now iconic footage of Hendrix coaxing fire from his Stratocaster. After that, the young Yngwie became obsessed with the guitar. "It was a revelation. I really started playing the day Hendrix died," Malmsteen recalls (www.yngwie.org).

From the very beginning, from the first day he picked up a guitar, he was prone to improvising and creating music. Those who knew him then said he had perfect pitch from the beginning, so he could decipher notes and chords easily simply by listening. His mother and sister recognized his unique musical gifts and gave him support and encouragement. His mastery of the instrument progressed rapidly. After catching the bug, he played up to nine hours a day—only because he wanted to keep improving.

In his early teens, Yngwie saw a television performance of Russian violinist Gideon Kremer, who performed the highly difficult "24 Caprices" of nineteenth-century virtuoso violinist Niccolo Paganini. He became infatuated with the composition and with the composer himself, who possessed a showy, flamboyant side and enjoyed a reputation as classical music's "wild man." The effect Paganini had on him was profound, and Yngwie understood at last how to combine his love of classical music with his burgeoning guitar skills and onstage charisma.

As a young man, Yngwie worked in a music instrument repair shop where he was introduced to many old instruments, including fretted, scalloped necks like that on a lute. (To this day, he still does much of the work on his own guitars.) About the same time, he discovered Deep Purple—his first album was that band's *Fireball* at the age of eight—and began listening obsessively to them as well. Deep Purple's Ritchie Blackmore employed diatonic minor scales over simple blues riffs, and the combination excited Malmsteen.

His sister exposed him to the music of classical composers like Vivaldi, Bach, and Paganini, and he began to see a crossover in the work of Blackmore and his sister's classical music. He practiced constantly, often until his fingers bled, so thorough was his obsession. Finally, by the time he turned 14 his mother allowed him to stay home from school, not only to work on his guitar for the entire day, but to stay out of the trouble he constantly found himself in.

Malmsteen was a young warrior during his school years. When he was a teen he drove his motorbike inside the school. He fought with other kids a lot and rarely did his school work. In class he became frustrated easily, especially with kids who didn't have the same aptitude he did. "Fights would start whenever I told someone how stupid they were" (Unattributed interview, *Guitar World,* January 1986).

Classical music dominated his listening, and he discovered early on how to combine his love for Hendrix with his souped-up version of classical composing. The synthesis supplied the template for Malmsteen's singular, neoclassical hybrid.

* * *

In his early teens, Malmsteen played in his first few bands. But at 18, he had to enlist in the army. He stayed for just two days. The extensive testing they did on him didn't do him any favors.

> When they realized I had a high I.Q. they wanted me to be an officer, but I didn't want to. They didn't want to let me go, but I acted very insane to them. I told them I could never get along with my mother, I never worked a day in my life and I never used to go to school. All I did was play guitar all day long. There were plenty of guns there, so I made a threat. I told them I would shoot myself if they didn't let me go, and they fell for it. (*Guitar World,* January 1986)

Back on the pop scene in Sweden, Malmsteen was getting frustrated. He wanted desperately to make it, but since the music he was playing wasn't commercial, the record companies turned up their noses. As a bandleader, he took control of his acts' music and continued on his jag of splashing technical virtuosity on a metal or hard rock canvas. At the time, at least in Scandinavia, pop music ruled, and so Malmsteen had a hard time winning over audiences with a hunger for simple pop.

* * *

Frustrated, he looked overseas for a more suitable audience. He decided to send a demo tape in to *Guitar Player* magazine, one of the only instrument mags at the time that Malmsteen could buy in Sweden. They had a "Spotlight" column, and he sent music in care of that column's writer, a guitarist named Mike Varney.

"I didn't expect anything. But, two weeks, three weeks later, my phone is ringing off the hook, man. I got phone calls like it's ridiculous and all times of the day. Cause they didn't know Sweden was 9 hours different. [laughs]. I was like, 'What the [heck]?' " (Ochoa, Hugh, www.modernguitars.com).

The calls came in from bands, magazines, and labels. One of those phone calls came from Varney himself who had recently started his own imprint called Shrapnel. "He basically called me up and said, 'Dude, pack your shit and come on over, man!' And it was weird. I had a life, I had a band, I had a girlfriend, I had a cat, I had an apartment. You know, I had family, a studio. And I said, 'OK. [Screw] it. I'm in' " (Ochoa, www.modernguitars.com).

MUSIC

"I've always been a logical thinker, and I've always come to the conclusion that less equals less and more equals more. And I've always thought that 'less is more' is a weird thing to say. Sometimes less *is* more, but very rarely; most of the time, more is more" (Perlmutter, Adam, "A Private Lesson with Yngwie Malmsteen," *Guitar One,* January 2006, p. 74).

When Malmsteen discovered Varney at Shrapnel, he knew he had met a kindred spirit. Varney heard Malmsteen's demo tape and, in 1981, invited the Swede to fill the guitar slot

SHRAPNEL RECORDS

Yngwie Malmsteen had trouble finding a label willing to commit to his uncompromising style. The Swedish music scene of the late 1970s, dominated by pop, would have nothing of him. Actually, he did get into the CBS Studio in Stockholm to lay down some sides, but those tracks were never finished or released. Desperate to jumpstart his recording career, Malmsteen looked to America. Right around the outset of the 1980s, he sent out dozens of demos to the States, one of which landed in the hands of a *Guitar Player* columnist named Mike Varney. The journalist, himself a skilled guitarist, was blown away. Yngwie had finally found the outlet he was seeking.

A short time before Varney heard Malmsteen, Varney had started a label called Shrapnel, an indie imprint dedicated to releasing heavy metal, the first of its kind in the United States. As the world of independent labels flourished in the early 1980s, Varney distinguished himself by signing bands with extraordinary guitarists. Shrapnel was at the forefront of the neoclassical electric guitar and shred movements. Worldwide, there was a growing interest in virtuoso guitar playing, and Varney was pivotal in introducing this style to international audiences, helping to launch the careers of Marty Friedman, Jason Becker, Paul Gilbert, Racer X, Tony MacAlpine, Vinnie Moore, Greg Howe, Richie Kotzen, and many others. In the 1990s, Shrapnel continued to make an impact despite an unfavorable climate. Fans of alternative music and grunge preferred less technique and showmanship from their guitarists. Varney also helped George Lynch (Dokken, Lynch Mob) and Michael Schenker (MSG, Scorpions) continue their careers with new works.

Today Shrapnel continues to record guitarists of extraordinary ability and has also returned a bit to its metal roots in releasing some classic metal and hard rock records. The turn of the new millennium has brought a resurgent interest in virtuoso guitar work and this groundswell continues to build, so you can continue to look to Shrapnel to be at the forefront of a whole new generation of guitar excellence. Recent signings include Marc Rizzo (Soulfly), John 5ive (Rob Zombie), and a few others. Varney also formed a couple of sublabels, Tone Center and Blues Bureau International.

in a band called Steeler. One of the first acts to be signed to Shrapnel, the LA-based Steeler was a rather generic metal/hard rock act characteristic of the prevailing party vibe on the city's Sunset Strip. Malmsteen settled down for one album—a self-titled album released in 1983—with the band and then looked elsewhere for his kicks.

Malmsteen's next band was Alcatrazz. Originally, Alcatrazz was formed to showcase the vocals of Graham Bonnet, the former singer who replaced Ronnie James Dio in Blackmore's Rainbow in 1979. But Blackmore was disappointed with Bonnet, and he was released after a single album. Bonnet formed Alcatrazz immediately after. He recruited Malmsteen, who immediately took to Bonnet and the band's more elaborate, neoclassical approach.

Their first album, *No Parole from Rock and Roll,* released in 1983, was an impressive collaboration. But young Malmsteen developed quite an ego for himself, which resulted in a clash over control between him and Bonnet. Malmsteen left after the band's subsequent tour to go it alone. Incidentally, the guitarist tapped to replace Malmsteen was none other than Steve Vai, another phenomenal shredder.

Malmsteen pulled his own band together and called it Rising Force. The band's first album, a predominantly instrumental work called *Rising Force,* would turn the world of rock guitar upside down. Eddie Van Halen had upped the speed and virtuosity of rock in his band Van Halen, and Randy Rhoads, Ozzy Osbourne's lead guitarist, introduced neoclassical elements into heavy metal, but no one before Malmsteen's Rising Force was able to combine these traits in a single vehicle.

The album made an immediate impact in guitar circles; instrument magazines and readers' polls draped it with accolades. It made such an impression that it impacted *Billboard*'s album chart as well, reaching #60. To top it off, *Rising Force* received a Grammy nomination for Best Rock Instrumental Performance. Rising Force blazed a trail on the concert circuit that established Yngwie as one of rock guitar's brightest new stars and added a new genre to the music lexicon: neoclassical rock.

*   *   *

Controversy began arising almost immediately about aspects of Malmsteen's personality: his ego, his confidence, his arrogance.

> People describe me as being a big-headed guy who sucks up attention, which is totally wrong. The biggest mistake people make about me is that they see me as some sort of God-like figure with a big ego. If I see a button or a t-shirt that says "Yngwie Is God," I just look at it as a complimentary way of people telling me they like me. Although it's very flattering, it doesn't change the way I look at myself. I'm just a normal person completely devoted to my art as a guitarist and musician. (*Guitar World,* January 1986)

Over the next few years, Malmsteen toured and solidified his reputation as the rock scene's most formidable talent. His next two albums, *Marching Out* and *Trilogy,* extended Malmsteen's reach. His inclusion of more lyrics, and fewer instrumentals, helped to make his music more accessible to a wider audience, though purists had trouble with his subject matter, which addressed black magic, the occult, and other such dungeons and dragons.

Malmsteen produced both the *Marching Out* and *Rising Force* albums. Not surprisingly he felt he could do a better job than an outside producer. . . . "They obviously don't know the song as well as I do. I mean, I don't think a painter would do the background and let someone else finish the rest of the painting. I want to write the songs, produce them and control it until the record is in the stores and on the turntable" (*Guitar World,* January 1986).

Jeff Scott Soto filled vocal duties on these initial albums. His third album, *Trilogy,* featuring the vocals of Mark Boals was released in 1986. In 1987, another singer, former Rainbow vocalist Joe Lynn Turner joined his band. That year, Malmsteen was in a serious car accident, wrapping his Jaguar XKE around a tree and landing him in a coma for a week. He also suffered nerve damage to his right hand, a frightening affliction for a guitar player. During his time in the hospital, Malmsteen's mother died from cancer.

He recovered fully from his hand injury and vowed, in his own inimitable way, to drive even faster cars, which he does. Malmsteen is especially, and not surprisingly, partial to vintage Ferraris.

In the summer of 1988 he released his fourth album, *Odyssey.* His comeback album, *Odyssey* would be his biggest hit, thanks to its first single, "Heaven Tonight." Malmsteen also toured extensively in support of the recording and performed epic, groundbreaking

Courtesy of Neil Zlozower

gigs in the former Soviet Union in February 1989. The concert in Leningrad was the largest ever by a Western artist in the Soviet Union.

Subsequent 1990s albums included *Eclipse, Fire and Ice, The Seventh Sign,* and *Inspiration.* In 1993, Malmsteen's mother-in-law, who had been vehemently opposed to the guitarist marrying her daughter, had him arrested for threatening her with a shotgun and holding her daughter against her will. The charges against Malmsteen were dropped when he denied the incident.

Malmsteen released his first completely classical work, *Concerto Suite for Electric Guitar and Orchestra in E Flat Minor Op. 1,* performed with the Czech Philharmonic Orchestra, in 1998. *Face the Animal* also appeared that year, as did Fender's Artist Series Yngwie Malmsteen Stratocaster guitar. A DVD of the Concerto Suite, performed in Tokyo with the New Japan Philharmonic Orchestra, was released in 2002, as was the album *Attack.*

In 2003, Malmsteen joined that year's G3 tour, which also featured Steve Vai and Joe Satriani in what amounted to a dream for fans of technically minded guitarists. After several years of fading from view, Malmsteen returned to the headlines in 2002, after a fellow airline passenger threw water on him, accusing him and his bandmates of making lewd and slanderous remarks about homosexuals. This incensed Malmsteen and his band, who had to be escorted away by security, all the while screaming to the passenger that she had "unleashed the f*cking fury" of Malmsteen. This stint proved to be so popular in revitalizing his career that he used the phrase as the title of his comeback album in 2005.

In the United States, Malmsteen's popularity faded, largely because the whole idea of guitar shred ebbed from the spotlight, a result of the antiguitar heroes of grunge and alternative music. But Malmsteen still finds audiences in Europe and is more popular in Japan and Asia than ever. *Instru-Mental* was released in February 2007.

I'm not the kind of guy that likes to rest on my laurels. In other words, whatever I've done in the past . . . that was then. This is now, you know. That, I don't do. So that means that every day is a new day and time to f*cking rock, you know. That's just my personality. That's who I am. And the other thing is that um . . . it never gets boring to me, you know. (Unattributed interview, www.yngwie.org)

TECHNIQUE/STYLE

Malmsteen's need for speed is legendary, but . . .

I don't consider myself to be a very fast player. I'm sure there are other guitarists who can play faster. What I do that a lot of other guitarists don't do is I don't play things that are rubbish. If you would slow down the fast licks that a lot of other guitarists do, people would puke. I play classical runs, arpeggios and broken chords that if played at a slower speed would sound very nice as well. But if you do it very fast and very clean, but not necessarily as fast as someone else, you appear much faster because what you're playing actually makes more sense. (*Guitar World*, January 1986)

Yngwie says he developed a fast technique simply because he didn't want to be limited. He was obsessed with improvement, with being excellent. He was determined to take what he played one day and improve it in a particular way the next. Here's how Malmsteen developed his technique. He had two cassette decks that he used to record his music on, one at the rehearsal studio and one at home. The one at the rehearsal studio was slower than the one at home. So when he went home and listened back to the tape he recorded at rehearsals, his guitar sounded so much faster than he actually played it. The speed and facility pleased him. And since it was his goal to improve on everything he'd played the day before, he developed a lot of speed, and he began playing faster and faster.

He also made it look easy. At 19, Malmsteen was reeling off alternate-picking phrases easier than most guitar players find their way through a harmonic minor scale. He specialized in part in diminished arpeggios, but filtered them through rock 'n' roll tradition as well as the blues. While his style wasn't so blues-like—way too many notes to be considered in the same breath as many emotive blues players—he did take the idiom, as well as classic rock, and use it as his foundation. Malmsteen dipped generously into the darker side of classical obsessions, setting up gothic ambience and rhythms over which he'd lay down a frighteningly fast and fluid flurry of notes. The age of the shredder had arrived.

Rising Force, his first album as a bandleader and largely instrumental, became a blueprint for all 1980s metal guitar players to follow, with its classical chord progressions and harmonic minor scales, a classically influenced vibrato technique, and what is called "sweep-picking," a hybrid technique of strumming a chord and picking individual notes.

Malmsteen style has influenced players from Racer X's Paul Gilbert to the more sophisticated Tony MacAlpine, Jason Becker, Marty Friedman, and Vinnie Moore. MacAlpine came to the neoclassical/shred field by applying his classical piano training to his guitar playing, and Moore arrived at a similar style because he shared Malmsteen's major influences. Not since Eddie Van Halen has a guitar player been as influential to the prevailing sound of rock music.

Malmsteen's guitar style includes a wide, violin-like vibrato inspired by classical violinists. He employs the use of minor scales, including the harmonic minor, and minor modes like the Phrygian and the Aeolian.

In interviews, he admits to being influenced himself by the playing of Brian May of Queen, Steve Hackett of Genesis, Ritchie Blackmore of Deep Purple, and Uli Jon Roth.

EQUIPMENT/GEAR

Yngwie's best-known guitar is his 1972 blonde Stratocaster known as "Play Loud." Bought in Sweden when he was a teenager, the guitar has been responsible for much of Yngwie's noise since, both in the studio and on the stage.

In 1988, Malmsteen released his own signature Fender Stratocaster. He was only the second player to be bestowed with that honor by the legendary guitar maker. The first was none other than Eric Clapton. His signature model is an important weapon in his arsenal. It's templated after that 1968 Strat. It has stock Fender tuning keys and a brass nut, because, he feels, brass doesn't wear out very quickly. It has single-coil pickups, his own YJM pickups.

He also uses a custom-designed DiMarzio guitar with vertically stacked humbucker mounted in a single-coil housing for less noise. Malmsteen briefly used Schecter guitars in the 1980s; the company constructed him Strat-style guitars with scalloped necks, but the relationship was short-lived.

All of his necks are scalloped, which means between the frets is carved out concavely. Malmsteen says that the scalloping helps him with control over his vibrato and bending because he has a better grip on the neck. The guitar has wide Dunlop frets and DiMarzio Yngwie Malmsteen pickups. The vibrato bar is set up so that it can move in both directions.

Malmsteen prefers thin-gauged Dean Markley strings that run .008 to .048, an unusual configuration for such a powerful player. For effects, he uses his own signature Digitech overdrive pedal and a Boss Noise Suppressor.

Malmsteen is a stickler for tone, and he gets his own monster version of it through a fairly simple setup. He uses his 1968 Fender Strat through vintage Marshall amps. Though he may seem to use some slight of hand to achieve his sound, Yngwie's gifts come from his fingers, and his tone, through patience and his basic rig.

Malmsteen's live rig consists of vintage 1971 Marshall amplifiers with a wall of up to 27 Marshall cabinets, also vintage, with Celestion G12T-75 watt speakers. All of the 24 heads on the cabinets are Vintage 1971 Mark II Marshall 50 Watt heads. Floor effect pedals consist of a BOSS CS-3 Compression Sustainer, Roland DC-10 analog echo pedal, vintage Dunlop Cry-Baby Wah pedal, BOSS OC-2 Octave, DOD 250 Overdrive Pre-Amp pedal, BOSS NS-2 Noise Suppressor, and a Custom Audio Electronics switching system for his effects rack.

Malmsteen's guitars onstage are 1968–1972 Fender Stratocasters. For his acoustic sets, Malmsteen uses a nylon strung electroacoustic black or white Ovation Viper. Prior to the Ovations, Malmsteen used Aria, Alvarez & Gibson classical acoustics on stage. Malmsteen regularly performs onstage with a custom light top, heavy bottom string gauge ranging from 0.08 through 0.48 gauge, which are considered by most guitarists to be very thin, especially with the downtuning used. Malmsteen's picks are Jim Dunlop 1.5 white.

Malmsteen also played bass on the *Rising Force* and *Seventh Sign* albums, a Fender Telecaster bass with a tremolo. "The bass parts are pretty straightforward," he says, "so after a while I got bored. I could have played very technical and complex if I wanted to, but I didn't think fancy bass playing would have sounded good. I did a few cool-sounding runs, though" (*Guitar World,* January 1986).

Made by Fender of Japan, this specialty guitar features a 12-string acoustic Malmsteen Signature top, with the Malmsteen Japanese Signature Strat on the bottom. The controls are separate for the two guitars.

Mike Eldred and John Cruz, Master Builders at the Fender Custom Shop, did extensive studies of Malmsteen's "The Duck." They measured and videotaped it, so they could re-create it precisely in a batch of 100. It has the same scratches, the same rust, even the same cigarette burns.

ESSENTIAL READING

Ochoa, Hugh. www.modernguitars.com.
Perlmutter, Adam. "A Private Lesson with Yngwie Malmsteen." *Guitar One*, January 2006, 74.

ESSENTIAL WORK

"Black Star" (1984)
"Far Beyond the Sun" (1984)
"Queen in Love" (1986)
"Trilogy Suite Op: 5" (1986)

ESSENTIAL LISTENING

Concerto Suite for Electric Guitar and Orchestra in E Flat Minor Op. 1 (Pony canyon, 1998)
Concerto Suite Live with Japan Philharmonic (Pony Canyon, 2002)
Marching Out (Polydor, 1985)
Rising Force (Polydor, 1984)
Trilogy (Polydor, 1986)

Jimmy Page

Thanks to his immense and enduring commercial success, as well as his spectacular innovations on the instrument, Jimmy Page is, arguably, the best-known electric guitarist of the rock 'n' roll generation. Supporting that reputation, Page enjoyed induction into the Rock 'n' Roll Hall of Fame twice, first as a member of the Yardbirds in 1992 and then as a member of Led Zeppelin in 1995.

* * *

Definitive in many ways, Led Zeppelin established the template for blues-based hard rock and metal acts to this day. They also set forth the blueprint for album-oriented rock by not releasing their more concise, popular songs as radio singles. (Hence, the emergence of "Stairway to Heaven.")

Zeppelin, and Page in particular, had an intriguing mystique about them that lured audiences the way a scent lures bees to flowers. The band refrained from speaking to the press or doing interviews of any kind, in part because the press panned them every chance they could get, but also because they didn't want to reveal too much information about themselves. The absence of publicity and promotion only enhanced their reputation; no one knew who they truly were. With that mystery in their grasp, Zeppelin climbed to mythical status.

Jimmy Page, a blues and post-blues guitarist, served as the engine behind the music of Led Zeppelin. His riffs, crushing and psychedelic renditions of the blues of his youth, became the foundation of heavy metal, and his playing influenced rock guitarists for decades. But Page also defied pigeonholing. Throughout his career, he dabbled in many different musical genres, most interestingly, folk, funk, and country styles. This versatility kept his listeners off balance and impressed his fans even more.

Jimmy Page is acknowledged as one of the great psychedelic guitar players in rock. Page's underrated work with the Yardbirds and on countless sessions (take note of his hypnotic work with Donovan in particular) prior to Zeppelin, illustrate that he set the standard for hallucinogenic discord unlike any other.

And in light of the fact that Page played on hundreds of uncredited session tracks in Britain between 1963 and 1966, and was instrumental in the Yardbirds and Led Zeppelin, he likely ranks as *the* most recorded major rock guitarist ever. Mystery appearances as teenage session guitarist on records by the Rolling Stones ("Heart of Stone"), the Who ("I Can't Explain"), Them ("Baby Please Don't Go"), Lulu ("Shout"), Tom Jones, Donovan, the Tremolos, and Herman's Hermits are but another chapter in Page's historical legacy. Even on the lightest-weight session material he appears on, Page's guitar playing is noteworthy, "I was fortunate enough to turn it into my career, with the added good fortune that it made people happy and inspired some of them to pick up a guitar," he says.

"That makes me a very fortunate man" (Cooper, Tim, "The Godfather of Rock," *The Independent* online, August 27, 2004, London, UK).

EARLY YEARS

James Patrick Page was born on January 9, 1944 in Middlesex, England, north of London. His father worked as an industrial personnel manager and his mother was a doctor's secretary. Jimmy was an only child.

He took his first guitar lesson at 12 years old, but didn't adjust well to instruction and so became mostly self-taught. He listened passionately to early rock 'n' roll, especially musicians like Elvis Presley, whose guitarists Scotty Moore and James Burton caught his ear. He also listened to skiffle artists like Lonnie Donegan and British folk guitar players: Bert Jansch, who supplied him with inspiration to future Zeppelin tunes, and John Renbourne. When blues migrated from Chicago and Mississippi across the Atlantic to the United Kingdom, Page was there to accept it. He plunged into the seminal work of Elmore James, Freddie King, and Howlin' Wolf's guitarist Hubert Sumlin.

In 1958, he formed a skiffle trio and played local talent shows. In 1959, he bought a secondhand Futurama Grazioso electric guitar and started digging in. Contrary to the wishes of his schoolmaster, he began bringing his guitar to school, only to see it confiscated daily. He'd get it at the end of the day when classes were over. He was nothing if not persistent. Eventually, his persistence paid off.

In school, Page also enjoyed science and, following school, he interviewed for a job as a lab assistant. But the prospect of being cooped up in a laboratory all day didn't excite him. He turned the job down and chose to leave school altogether to pursue music.

Early on, Page accompanied local artists like Beat poet Royston Ellis and Red. E. Lewis and the Red Caps, pickup gigs that he readily agreed to. A man named Neil Christian, who had a band called the Crusaders, offered him a slot in his group in 1961. Page agreed and he began touring and recording with Christian. He toured with them for two years and played on a handful of records, including the November 1962 single, "The Road to Love."

Unfortunately, Page grew seriously ill while with the band with something called glandular fever, a recurring illness that prevented him from engaging in the rigorous process of touring. Reluctantly, but necessarily, Page had to halt his involvement with Christian and the Crusaders. Once well enough, he returned to school, this time to the Sutton Art College in Surrey. While still a student of painting there, he gradually got on his feet and regained his strength. After a while, he returned to music.

MUSIC

The emergence of such bands as the Rolling Stones in the early 1960s stimulated Page's interest in music once again. However, instead of establishing his own band, he chose to perfect his craft by becoming a session guitarist. While at Sutton pursuing his art degree, Page often jammed at a place called the Marquee with bands like Alexis Korner's Blues Incorporated and Cyril Davies's All Stars. The Marquee also hosted the likes of young enthusiasts Jeff Beck and Eric Clapton, so Page was in good company.

One night, John Gibb from a band called the Silhouettes asked him to help him in the studio on behalf of EMI Records. It would be his first big break and the beginning of a successful stint as a session guitar player. Initially, he cut sides like Jet Harris & Tony Meehan's "Diamonds," which went to #1 on the singles chart in early 1963.

After a few brief excursions with bands like Carter-Lewis and the Southerners, and Mickey Finn and the Blue Men, Page began to work in music full time. Known as "Little Jim," his studio products in 1964 included the Rolling Stones' "Heart of Stone," Marianne Faithfull's "As Tears Go By," the Nashville Teens' "Tobacco Road," Brenda Lee's "Is It True," and Dave Berry's "The Crying Game" and "My Baby Left Me."

Under the endorsement of producer Shel Talmy, he lent his talent to a 1964 debut album by the Kinks, including their classic "You Really Got Me" (this is not debatable) and the Who's legendary first single "I Can't Explain." Throughout his session work, Page had invitations to join legitimate touring bands, but he rejected them in favor of the money session work generated. In 1965, Rolling Stone manager Andrew Loog Oldham recruited Page as house producer and A&R man for Immediate Records, an ambitious new imprint. The responsibility permitted him to play and produce tracks by artists like Clapton, Mayall, and Nico. In fact, Page was everywhere. One music critic half-joked that Page, unofficially, appeared on 60 percent of the rock music recorded in England between 1963 and 1966.

THE YARDBIRDS

One of the band offers Page received was from the Yardbirds, who were searching for a replacement for their lead guitarist, Eric Clapton. Clapton, following his stint with Mayall and the Bluesbreakers, jumped to join the up and coming Yardbirds. But Clapton left that band soon after because the Yardbirds had strayed from their blues roots and gone in a pop direction with "For Your Love." Initially, Page turned the slot down, instead suggesting they speak with his friend Jeff Beck, who ended up accepting the position.

By 1966, Page had grown tired of session work and he was looking for a change. Fortunately for him, the Yardbirds, now the most popular band in the United Kingdom, were once again in need. Paul Samwell Smith, the band's bassist, left the lineup, leaving the bass slot open. When approached to fill it, Page agreed and he put down the guitar to take up the bass. Eventually, the band lineup shifted again and Page returned to lead guitar alongside Beck. While they lasted, the duo made the Yardbirds the greatest one-two guitar combination in the history of rock 'n' roll.

With incredible talent, the Yardbirds ascended quickly. But Beck was temperamental, and this stellar lineup only recorded three songs together. One of them, a towering masterpiece of psychedelic pop called "Happenings Ten Years Time Ago," occupies the pinnacle of the entire psychedelia genre. Within six months, though, and under mysterious circumstances, the volatile Beck left the band. The Yardbirds decided to carry on, but their subsequent studio work didn't achieve the standards of the Beck era. Page recorded a classic with the Yardbirds, *Little Games,* and the Yardbirds, spent, called it quits.

In the spring of 1966, Beck assembled a super group, including drummer Keith Moon, bassist John Paul Jones, keyboardist Nicky Hopkins, and Page. Lack of a capable lead singer sank the project, though the seeds for Zeppelin and the Who were planted.

LED ZEPPELIN

When the Yardbirds disbanded in early 1968, Jimmy Page was left with the rights to the name, but no band to speak of. So he set to recruiting new Yardbirds. He sought something the Yardbirds didn't have, a powerful belter, a singer that could reach the heavens with his wail. A friend of his, Terry Reid, happened to be Page's first choice, but Reid

Courtesy of Neil Zlozower

begged off. He did direct the guitarist to seek out a friend of his named Robert Plant. A big-voiced belter from Birmingham, Plant responded positively and signed on with the band. He also brought along with him a drummer, John Bonham, with whom Plant played in Band of Joy. John Paul Jones, a London session player known to Page from their studio projects together with U.K. folksinger Donovan, rounded out the lineup.

Page recalls with perfect clarity their very first rehearsal and the first song they played together, "Train Kept a Rollin'," along with his reaction.

"When it finished it was scary. None of us had played with our musical equals until that point" (Cooper, "The Godfather of Rock," August 27, 2004).

The band scooted quickly past where the Yardbirds had ended, and these "New Yardbirds" embarked on a contractually obligated tour of Scandinavia that the original Yardbirds had booked. But in performance the band felt like something completely different. Page, in particular, felt like he and the band needed to establish an independent identity. They hammered out a new contract to formulate Led Zeppelin, and, when they returned to the United Kingdom, recorded their debut album. It took them roughly 30 hours.

Led Zeppelin *was* something entirely new: a band in control of its own destiny, beyond the reach of record company manipulation and other industry restriction and constraints.

"Musically, we weren't afraid to go in any direction whatsoever. I guess that was the way we kept ourselves really alive as musicians. The band wouldn't have existed if it hadn't been like that" (Palmer, Robert, "Led Zeppelin: The Music," liner notes, *Led Zeppelin,* Atlantic Recording Company, 1990).

They had an insatiable appetite for music. Page, especially, attempted to tackle everything from hard blues to acoustic folk, to Indian-style raga. The guitarist led the band with this versatility, but he was by means a dictator. In Zeppelin's music, the song was most important, followed by the ensemble arrangement, overall sound and mood, then the solo turns. Says Page: "No matter how many guitar parts I might layer on in the studio, I followed the tune's overall theme and ambiance in my mind" (Palmer, liner notes, 1990).

Led Zeppelin was a band in the truest sense. The ensemble approach and generous range appeared immediately on *Led Zeppelin,* their debut, and signaled a rapid rise. The album was produced by Page and engineered by Glyn Johns, who had previously worked with the Beatles, the Stones, and the Who, and recorded on an analog four-track machine. The analog feel warmed the record's sound, and Page reportedly used natural room ambience to enhance the reverb and recording texture on the record.

The blues influence was immediately evident, not surprising, considering Page's background. He loved American blues artists like Skip James, and especially Howlin' Wolf. "I've often thought that in the way the Stones tried to be the sons of Chuck Berry, we tried to be the sons of Howlin' Wolf" (Palmer, liner notes, 1990).

The abrupt, nonfluid country blues lines of Wolf did show up in the sounds of Zeppelin. But they always found the right grooves as well. As an aside, Zeppelin, and Page specifically, were often fingered as plagiarists of the blues. Page did absorb everything he heard and spewed it back at various times in his career; only the spirit would know when something of a derivative nature would emerge. Page was a prolific artist who churned out ideas. Occasionally, some of those ideas appeared pilfered. Popular Zep work like "Dazed and Confused" and "Stairway to Heaven" are rumored to have non-Zep roots. That controversy arose much later on in the band's career.

Upon its release, *Led Zeppelin* hit the Top 10 on the album charts, starting a streak of platinum studio albums that lasted through the band's dissolution. Over the course of the next three albums, Page and Zeppelin demonstrated an impressive grasp of musical idioms, from blues, of course, which formed the band's foundation, to British Isles folk, another integral element, R&B, rockabilly, and soul. But the music of India and Arabia, which informed the work of both Page and singer Plant, also played a central role in Led Zeppelin's creative development.

Zeppelin soon began selling out tours, and doing it frequently. They were met with enthusiasm both at home and abroad, and demands on their time quickly became great. They recorded *Led Zeppelin II* during a brief point between gigs in the States. Because of that, the riffs and tunes were essentially recorded versions of the songs they were playing onstage while on tour, mainly reworked blues riffs and simple rock songs, only amplified. Because of the simplicity and utter intensity of the material, the album is seen as a blueprint for hard rock and metal. It is not as eclectic, but it is, many say, more influential, with enduring tracks like "Moby Dick" and "Whole Lotta Love."

For *Led Zeppelin III*, Page and the band briefly put their blues power on hold, with a folk-oriented shimmer of an album. It stands in stark contrast to the first two albums in that it lays back frequently, as if, when given the luxury to think things through, their material becomes more reflective and intricate.

Led Zeppelin IV, released in November of 1971, is Zep's towering masterwork, the rock album that inspired millions and which served, then and now, as the template for so much hard rock and metal. Rock standards like "Stairway to Heaven," "Rock and Roll," and "Black Dog," songs that lie embedded in the foundation of the high-decibel genre all appear here, as does the band's best folk song, "Going to California," and a handful of others.

Certainly, it is Page's and Plant's "Stairway to Heaven" that has come to be synonymous with the band. Its fingerpicked intro segue into a juggernaut of cascading guitars is now something of a rock 'n' roll cliché. Few bands have ever approached this kind of majesty. It has qualified as the most played song of all time on rock radio.

Houses of the Holy and *Physical Graffiti* met with similar innovation and success. The first is a lushly executed suite of songs, all produced brilliantly by Page, and featuring what many feel to be the band's best arrangements and best performances. *Physical Graffiti*, a

OCCULT OF PERSONALITY

In the early 1970s, Jimmy Page owned an occult bookshop and publishing house, "The Equinox Booksellers and Publishers" on Kensington High Street in London. But Page eventually had to close due to him not having sufficient time to devote to it. Page himself was a devout follower of alleged Satanist, Aleister Crowley, who proclaimed himself as "The Beast 666" and is recognized as the master Satanist of the twentieth century. In 1971, Page bought Crowley's Boleskine House on the shore of Loch Ness where Crowley practiced his supposed Satanic rituals. Page actually performed Crowley magical rituals during their concerts. In fact, many scholars feel that Zed Zeppelin's songs are saturated with Aleister Crowley's Satanic doctrines.

On a related note, Page was commissioned to write the soundtrack music for the film *Lucifer Rising* by occultist and Crowley follower Kenneth Anger. Excited, Page permitted Anger to use the basement of Tower House (Page's London residence) for filming. But time constraints and disciplinary issues arose, and Page didn't meet the deadline. Actually, he only managed to produce 23 minutes of music for a 28-minute film.

Disappointed and enraged, Anger claimed Page took three years to deliver 23 minutes of music, material the director slagged as being useless noise. In the press, Anger accused Page of being too strung out on drugs to complete the project, which may have been true. Page countered by saying he had fulfilled all his obligations to Anger, even going so far as to lend Anger his own film editing equipment to help him finish the project. In the end, Page's music was dumped, replaced by a composition completed in 1980 from prison by Bobby Beausoleil, a Charles Manson family member and convicted murderer.

Bootlegs of Page's soundtrack, prized among fans, were in great demand, until the album of the same name, *Lucifer Rising,* was released by Boleskine House Records in 1987. The blue vinyl disc contains all 23 minutes of the soundtrack music Page composed.

double-album set released in 1975, is a hodgepodge of material, by turns genius and head-scratching, but mostly the former.

At this point in the band's career, they began to absorb the influences of American R&B and funk. Jimmy Page dug the seminal work of James Brown and Stevie Wonder, and so it began to show up in subtle ways on *Physical Graffiti.* Without a doubt, Page showed ample mastery in this style of guitar playing as well.

Presence followed, then the live album, *The Song Remains the Same,* and then *In Through the Out Door.* The recording came out in 1979, after a hiatus in which singer Plant grieved the loss of his six-year-old son Karac, who died from a stomach infection.

Tragedy beset the band again when in September of 1980 drummer John "Bonzo" Bonham—a critical element to the Led Zeppelin sound and its muscular engineer, not to mention one of the best drummers to ever sit behind a rock 'n' roll kit—died after a binge of drinking. The remaining three remembers unanimously voted to disband, avowing that Zeppelin would never be the same without Bonham.

POST ZEPPELIN

Page went into hiding for quite a while following the death of Bonham and the dissolution of his beloved band. He later admitted that he didn't pick up the guitar for over a year.

Colleagues coaxed him out of his seclusion and convinced him to perform, which he did, with the three remaining members of Zeppelin and special guests. He formed a band called the Firm, which released two albums. He also appeared on Plant's Honeydrippers album, and formed a short-lived band with Deep Purple and Whitesnake vocalist David Coverdale called, unimaginatively, Coverdale-Page.

In 1994, Plant and Page finally agreed on a Zep reunion once again (although John Paul Jones wasn't invited), leading to the release of the acoustic set *No Quarter* the same year, plus a highly popular MTV "Unplugged" special and sold-out world tour. A year later the band was voted into the Rock 'n' Roll Hall of Fame, the second time a Page-related band received an induction. The first was in 1992, when the Yardbirds were invited. In 1998, Plant and Page issued an album of all new material, *Walking into Clarksdale,* and in 2003, Led Zeppelin released the epic set, *How the West Was Won,* a live album of vintage material that filled a gaping hole in the Zeppelin catalog.

"For those who never got to see Zeppelin live, this—or its accompanying two-DVD video set—is as close as they'll ever get. For those who did see them live, this is a priceless souvenir. For either group, this is absolutely essential, as it is for anybody who really loves hard rock & roll. It doesn't get much better than this" (Erlewine, Stephen Thomas, "How the West Was Won," allmusic.com).

TECHNIQUE/STYLE

Describing the technique of Jimmy Page is akin to explaining to someone who's never traveled what "the world" is like. Where to begin? Page explained in later interviews, in which he finally opened up to the press, that he wanted Led Zeppelin to be a marriage of blues, hard rock, and acoustic music, topped with heavy choruses, with lots of light and shade in the music. They achieved this blend early on, before later grasping at other modes of sound from Jamaica, Morocco, and the Arabic world.

"I started to digest the whole system of Indian music and learned what was involved. I realized it was far too complicated for a rock 'n' roll guitarist. But ideas from Indian music were well worth incorporating, tunings and such" (Palmer, liner notes, 1990).

Some worldly blends like "White Summer/Black Mountain Side" or "Kashmir" are perfect unions of lyric, tradition, innovation, and magic. Later Zeppelin albums showed an adventurous mix of influences like the funky backbeat of "D'yer Maker" and the exotic, swirling synthesizer of "Carouselambra."

Page's biggest pool of inspiration came from the blues and the blues rock of the U.K. bands that co-opted the blues and made it their own. Zeppelin reshaped Chicago blues, and even some Delta stylings, into their own image, adding texture, amplification, mysticism, and then some. Like Cream and Hendrix, Jimmy Page was at the fulcrum of blues and rock, and his material reflected that fiery connection. The first album is perhaps the best example of this, with two Willie Dixon songs, "You Shook Me" and "I Can't Quit You Baby." (The former disappointed Page when it unexpectedly emerged on colleague Jeff Beck's debut album that same year.) It's interesting to note that Dixon sued the group successfully for infringement on the song "Whole Lotta Love" on the second album, copped from his own song, "You Need Love."

Right behind the blues came Page's rock 'n' roll inspiration. After all, he did grow up listening to Buddy Holly and Elvis Presley before picking up the guitar himself. To put his stamp on rock 'n' roll, Page yanked the blues out by the roots and twisted it up to make it nearly unrecognizable. His experimentations early on with the Yardbirds and Jeff Beck are now legendary and provide the yang to his blues/folk yin. Page's distinctly muscular wailing sound is quite literally *the* sound of rock 'n' roll. Together with his creative production and recording techniques and liberal use of overdubbing, he also forged a Marshall-stack-driven concert sound that has also become standard with the majority of big-time rock groups. The frenzy and ferocity in tracks like "Dazed and Confused," "Communication Breakdown," "Black Dog," and "Houses of the Holy" incited audiences and urged kids to pick up guitars themselves.

On the flip side of all that wailing, Page was also, without a doubt, overwhelmed by the new breed of English folk guitarists, whose ranks include Bert Jansch, John Renbourne, and Davey Graham. Many Zep classics featured acoustic fingerstyle parts on them, beginning with the very first album. Page often allowed the acoustic part to yield to an electric crescendo later in the song.

Page was also a great rhythm player. He could alternate between explosive power chords to barely strummed triads or arpeggios. He also mastered acoustic guitar strumming as well on tunes like "Over the Hills and Far Away" and "Ramble On." If you observe his playing closely, you can see that the keys to his effective acoustic and rhythm playing are dynamics (accents; loud, soft strums), switching up single notes and chords, and skipping strums.

Page also perfected his hammer-on technique, that is, playing two or more notes for every one note that you strike with the picking hand. Page honed this skill so that he could play fluidly without having to increase his picking speed. Spend some time playing scales and riffs with only your left hand (or right hand if you're left-handed). Hammer-ons are a staple of rock 'n' roll guitar playing, so it is an important technique to master.

Much of Zeppelin's gargantuan sound can be attributed to the care Page took ensuring that the rhythm section was the foundation of the band's recordings. He based everything around the band's bass and drum combination.

Yet while Bonzo's drums typically have a wonderful live ambience around them, they are not washy or muddy. The kick drum stabs right through the band mix like a boxer's punch, the snare hits are solid, the toms rumble like cannons, and the cymbals sting without being overly bright. And right alongside Bonham's drums is John Paul Jones' bass—fat and clear and mixed loud enough to be clearly audible at low playback volumes. Page was also not afraid of signal leakage—where sounds from, say, the guitar bleeds into the microphones used to record the drums, and vice versa. Modern recording often strives for complete isolation of sounds, but Page typically recorded Zeppelin as if they were playing live onstage. "We would all walk around and stand around the drums," remembered Jones. "Nobody really cared how much leakage there was on anything, as long as it sounded good. That was part of the sound." (Molenda, Michael, "Epic Sounds: Jimmy Page's Production Strategies," www.guitarplayer.com)

EQUIPMENT/GEAR

Early on, Jimmy played a 1958 Fender Telecaster, a gift from Jeff Beck, and he used it as his primary guitar during the 1968–69 tours. But his most revered axe, and the one he had become attached to, was his 1959 Gibson Les Paul Standard. Page has relied on this guitar since the early days of Led Zeppelin. Another Les Paul Standard, this one from 1958 and a gift from former Eagle Joe Walsh, is also a beloved instrument. The tuners have been replaced and the neck has been shaved to resemble his 1959 Standard. The bridge has been rounded over for easier access to individual strings in use with the violin bow on "Dazed and Confused." Notably, this Les Paul features a pair of spring-loaded buttons under the scratch plate offering new pickup configurations.

Jimmy also likes a modified Danelectro guitar, which is assembled from two separate Danelectros and fitted with a Badass bridge. This guitar is often used for live performances of "Babe I'm Gonna Leave You," "White Summer/Black Mountainside," and "In My Time of Dying." Then there's the Vox 12-String, which he used in the studio for *Led Zeppelin II.*

He employed the Gibson "Black Beauty" Les Paul Custom extensively while with the Yardbirds, subsequently stolen on tour in 1970. He played a 12-string Rickenbacker in 1971, and, famously, a Gibson Doubleneck EDS-1275. This particular guitar is a twelve/ six string doubleneck, both fitted with two humbuckers and Les Paul system control assemblies. Page used it on stage from 1971 to 1980, generally on "Stairway to Heaven."

Acoustically, Jimmy had a handful of quality guitars. He used a Gibson J-200 for recording many of the band's early acoustic songs. Then there was also a Martin D28 Acoustic, played in the studio and on tour after 1970. There was also a Fender 10-String 800 Pedal Steel that Page used in the studio on *Led Zeppelin* and *Led Zeppelin III.*

As far as amps and cabinets, Jimmy was partial to a small handful, including a Fender Super Reverb in 1968 and 1969, 1x12 combo amp with 2x12 cabinet; a Supro 1x12 combo amp used for recording; a Vox AC-30, also used in recording with 36 watts output and 2x12 Celestion Greenback speakers. Then there were the Marshall SLP-1959, a 100-watt amp that Jimmy rewired to 200 watts, along with Marshall 4x12 straight and angled cabinets.

Page employed effects liberally. He used a Vox Crybaby Wah Wah from his days with the Yardbirds right through to the present. He also has remained faithful to his Sola Sound Tone Bender MkII, his Univox UD-50 Uni-Drive (after 1971), his Maestro Echoplex echo machine, an Eventide H949 Harmonizer (in guitar solos from 1977 to 1979), and his MXR Phase 90, which provides the tremolo-like wavering you hear on *Presence.* He also toyed with something called a theremin, a mad-scientist type of sound maker that creates noises from sound waves. The theremin can be heard live on "Whole Lotta Love" and "No Quarter."

ESSENTIAL READING

Case, George. *Jimmy Page: Magus, Musician, Man: An Unauthorized Biography.* Hal Leonard Publishing, 2007.

Cooper, Tim. "The Godfather of Rock." *The Independent* online, August 27, 2004, London, UK.

Davis, Stephen. *Hammer of the Gods.* Harper Paperback, repr. 2008.

Erlewine, Stephen Thomas. "How the West Was Won." allmusic.com.

Molenda, Michael. "Epic Sounds: Jimmy Page's Production Strategies." www.guitarplayer.com.

Palmer, Robert. "Led Zeppelin: The Music." Liner notes, *Led Zeppelin,* Atlantic Recording Company, 1990.

Shadwick, Keith. *Led Zeppelin: 1968–1980.* Backbeat, 2005.

ESSENTIAL WORK

"Going to California" (1971)
"Heartbreaker" (1969)
"Immigrant Song" (1970)
"Kashmir" (1975)
"The Rain Song" (1973)
"Stairway to Heaven" (1971)
"Trampled Under Foot" (1975)
"Whole Lotta Love" (1969)

ESSENTIAL LISTENING

Houses of the Holy (Atlantic, 1973)
How the West Was Won (Atlantic, 2003)
Led Zeppelin (Atlantic, 1969)
Led Zeppelin II (Atlantic, 1969)
Led Zeppelin III (Atlantic, 1970)
Led Zeppelin IV (Atlantic, 1971)
Physical Graffiti (Swan Song, 1975)

Randy Rhoads

In less than a decade on the scene, years spent with Quiet Riot and Ozzy Osbourne, Randy Rhoads changed the landscape of heavy metal guitar. Slotted perfectly between the devastating pyrotechnics of Eddie Van Halen and the equally devastating but more gymnastic shred exercises of Yngwie Malmsteen, Randy Rhoads carved out a niche previously unoccupied in metal. If his time in the spotlight was short, his influence was long, continuing to this day.

When Ozzy Osbourne plucked Rhoads from his first band, he thrust him onto one of the biggest stages in all of rock 'n' roll. Rhoads had earned his stripes with Quiet Riot, a band he formed in the mid-1970s. But he made his biggest impact with his Ozzy collaborations on *Blizzard of Ozz,* Osbourne's 1980 debut album.

In many ways, Randy Rhoads made as much of a contribution to rock 'n' roll with who he wasn't as who he was. He dedicated himself wholeheartedly to the musical side of rock 'n' roll. He rarely partied, never did any drugs, and spent more time learning the craft of the guitar than anything else in his life. Given the choice of gigging, partying, or practicing, Rhoads would opt for the latter.

He loved learning classical music, which contributed a significant amount to his abilities as a player and performer. With the first record royalties he received, he bought himself an expensive classical guitar. He sat for days and nights working on his music theories. In fact, right before he died he had been up for four days and nights, gigging too, working on his musical theory. His goal was to get admitted to a university in a music program.

All his hard work paid off. Though he was only on the scene for a short time—he died at 25—Rhoads injected rock with a dazzling array of techniques. He exerted influence on popular rock music that endures to this day.

Accolades were mainly posthumous. He broke into the Top 100 in *Rolling Stone* magazine's "100 Greatest Guitarists" list, coming in at #85. Guitar magazines worshipped Rhoads' work the first time they heard it. *Guitar World* placed Rhoads fourth on the list of "100 Greatest Heavy Metal Guitarists." He was also named in the same magazine's list of "50 Fastest Guitarists." Rhoads' guitar solos for the songs "Crazy Train" and "Mr. Crowley" placed ninth and twenty-eighth, respectively, on *Guitar World*'s "100 Greatest Guitar Solos" readers poll.

In 1987, five years after Rhoads' death, Osbourne released *Tribute,* the only official live album featuring Ozzy and Randy playing together. Rhoads was inducted into the Guitar Center Rock Walk on Sunset Boulevard in Hollywood in March 2004. More recently, as a tribute to Rhoads, Marshall Amps released the 1959RR at a popular music industry trade show in 2008. The amp is a limited-edition, all-white Marshall Super Lead 100-watt head modeled after Randy's own Super Lead amp, right down to the high-gain modification Randy specified when he first visited Marshall in 1980.

Randy was an all-encompassing player. He was slight in stature, but his guitar sound was huge. Occasionally, he'd seem to be playing three parts at once, which made it particularly difficult for his bandmates to keep up. Still, he pushed everybody around him by virtue of what he could do, and he elevated the expectations of fans of rock 'n' roll guitar. During his career, he became the new standard.

"My strength is my determination—I just want to keep getting better. I want people to know me as a guitar player, the way I knew other people. I don't want to be satisfied with myself" (Stix, John, www.randy-rhoads.com, 1981–1982).

EARLY YEARS

Randall William Rhoads was born on December 6, 1956 at St. John's Hospital in Santa Monica, California. With an older brother and sister, Randy was the youngest of three. Randy's father, William Arthur Rhoads, a public school music teacher, left the family when Randy was just 17 months old. Randy's mother, Delores, raised the three kids by herself in a religious environment. Randy went to First Lutheran Day School through sixth grade, and then to John Muir Junior High.

Delores, a former concert trumpeter, couldn't afford a TV or a stereo, so the family contented itself with learning to play music.

"I didn't own any rock guitar albums. I listen to a lot of background music that I don't have to think about. I didn't listen to music to achieve anything from it. I just listened to relax and be social. Mostly I liked mellow jazz and classical. If I'm out in public, I like to hear blaring loud rock, but never in my own house" (Stix, 1981–1982).

Randy started taking guitar lessons around the age of six or seven at his mother's music school in North Hollywood called Musonia. His first guitar was a Gibson acoustic that belonged to his grandfather. Randy and his sister both began taking folk guitar lessons, and Randy took piano lessons as well to enhance his ability to read music.

At the age of 12, Randy started listening to rock music and taking an interest in playing electric guitar. His mother had an old semi-acoustic Harmony Rocket, on which Randy took lessons at his mother's school. His instructor, though, a man named Scott Shelly, told Randy's mother that he could not teach his student anymore; Randy knew as much as his instructor.

"I tried lessons on and off when I was real young, but I couldn't stick with it. I didn't have the patience," said Randy.

But when I went back to lessons in my teens, I took classical guitar. It did wonders for me. When I was 12 or 13, I started jamming, and that's when I said I wanted to do this for real. When I first got up and played for people, it was a fluke. These guys used to jam on a mountain in Burbank, and I thought I wanted to get up and play. When I first did it, people started clapping. A friend had shown me the beginning blues scale. That sort of showed me how to connect the barre chords to a little scale. From then on, it was just add-ons. (Stix, 1981–1982)

By the time he was 13 or 14, Randy's group was playing frequently, for parties and picnics, in the park, and down on the Burbank Mall. As he got older his tastes changed. At the end of the 1960s and the beginning of the 1970s he discovered Alice Cooper, the original "shock rocker," and his sensibilities changed.

His older brother took Randy to see Cooper in 1971. The experience altered the way he perceived guitar playing. "He never saw anything like it, and he couldn't talk for four hours. I think that kind of showed him what he could do with his talent, and that's partly what made him decide to play rock. Before that, he played rock guitar and I played drums, but we never really thought about it" (Obrecht, Jas, "Randy Rhoads: 1956–1982, a Biography by Family, Friends, and Fellow Musicians," *Guitar Player,* November 1982).

MUSIC

At the age of 11, Randy met Kelly Garni, a kid who'd later become his best friend. The two began their relationship largely based on their fondness for music. At that time, Randy knew his guitar chords already and was just starting to learn his leads. Randy taught Garni to play the bass, and they started jamming after school.

The two began to practice and perform at the recital room at Musonia. At the age of 14, Randy formed Violet Fox, named after his mother's middle name, with Kelly on bass and his brother Doug on drums. Randy hadn't yet worked with a singer, and the slot proved to be a difficult one to fill. There were other bands around at the time, including the Katzenjammer Kids, but they were largely trios without a front man.

Randy and Kelly gigged frequently at a club called Rodney's English Disco in Hollywood. They met Kevin Dubrow, 18, through a friend of a friend. Randy and Kelly were unimpressed at first. They went into Randy's garage to jam with him, and they believed Dubrow was a horrible singer. But Dubrow didn't think so, and he persisted. For months, Rhoads and Garni tried to avoid Dubrow, but they ultimately relented, finally inviting him to a rehearsal and giving him musical pointers to polish his act.

Courtesy of Neil Zlozower

As time went on Dubrow became a good singer, and once he was accepted into the band he took over all the business and management responsibilities. Drew Forsyth, one of the drummers that Randy had used through the years, rounded out Quiet Riot, a name Kevin came up with.

Quiet Riot played its first show at what was to be Randy and Kelly's high school prom, a strange experience considering most of the kids in their class didn't really accept them at school. Of course, after they heard them play, the story changed. The second show they performed was at a Halloween party in Burbank, then a Chili Cook Off festival.

From then on they quickly became a popular Hollywood band, giving acts like Van Halen competition for local club slots. Stress from management forced Quiet Riot to take on a glam look, with teased up hair and a greater fashion emphasis, which is also where Randy's signature polka-dotted bow tie came from.

At the same time, Randy began teaching guitar lessons at Musonia, in the same way he had taken them himself as a kid. Randy would teach during the day up to the time when he had to go play, which was until around 7 pm, and on days he didn't play he'd teach until late in the night.

"He always said that was one thing that built him up strongly, because he played with the students, which encouraged them so much. He was a very successful teacher who built up a large group of students because he could relate well with them. He had his own way of presenting material, even in the rock field. His playing inspired the students a great deal" (Obrecht, 1982).

*   *   *

Initially, Quiet Riot secured a record deal with the popular Casablanca label, the home of Kiss. But the company eventually backed out. Next, they signed to Buddah records, another popular label from the 1960s, but their financial fortunes had dropped quickly and they went bankrupt before working with the band. In fact, Quiet Riot struggled with record deals and only managed to release two albums in Japan, under a CBS/Sony imprint. They released *Quiet Riot I* (1978), and *Quiet Riot II* (1979).

They were meant to eventually tour in Japan, but that never came to be. In 1978, Kelly Garni decided to leave the band, to be replaced by bassist Rudy Sarzo. Kelly's last gig with the band was at the Santa Monica Civic Center, opening for Angel. Five months before Randy would leave Quiet Riot, he had his signature Polka-dot V made by Karl Sandoval for $738, which he received on September 22, 1979. Later that same year, Randy would audition for the gig with Ozzy Osbourne.

Quiet Riot would go on to much bigger and better things, when their 1983 album, *Metal Health*, featuring guitarist Carlos Cavazo, became a monster smash.

THE OZZY OSBOURNE YEARS

After the 1978 album *Never Say Die*, Osbourne was canned from his star-making band, Black Sabbath, for a variety of reasons. His sacking led Osbourne to form his own solo project, one with his new manager and wife, Sharon Arden. They started by calling the act the Blizzard of Ozz.

In late 1979, after scouring Los Angeles and New York for guitarists, Ozzy Osbourne was finally introduced to the guitarist that would revitalize his career. Rhoads was an unlikely candidate for Ozzy's band. He never liked the Sabbath sound and was hardly interested in the kind of rock star indulgences for which Ozzy had been notorious.

Garni remembers Randy's feelings toward Black Sabbath: "When we were growing up, we thought Black Sabbath was a ridiculous thing. It was something we made fun of. Here were these guys out there, and then there's the devil and all this. It was goofy. We parodied it all the time. We would act all heavy, y'know, do pre-headbanging moves and act all dark and everything. We thought it was funny. It was a joke" (Obrecht, 1982).

But of all people, his mother Delores, exhorted him to take the audition. She told him it might be worth making the trip to Hollywood just to meet some people and make some connections. Later that same night, he went down to meet up with Ozzy Osbourne. He plugged into a small practice amp, ran through some scales, and got the gig.

> I thought I was going to go play with a band. I met him at a recording studio and I had just brought a tune up amp. If you've ever been in a recording studio, they have the glass booths up there. Well, through the tune up amp, no effects or nothing, straight through that and mic'd, they were all listening and said, "OK, play." You've got to be joking. What can I play? I didn't know what to do so I just started warming up and he said, "Yeah, you're good." I had only played for a couple seconds, and then I got kind of mad 'cause I thought, "You haven't even heard me yet." (Stix, 1981–1982)

* * *

In the fall of 1979, Randy and Ozzy left for England to begin work on Ozzy's debut album, *Blizzard of Ozz*. On March 20, 1980, the band—Osbourne, Rhoads, bassist Bob Daisley (Rainbow), and drummer Lee Kerslake (Uriah Heep)—entered Ridge Farms studios to record their first album, with producer Max Norman. Norman remembers very well recording with Randy, "Randy was always very nervous in the studio. He was extremely careful about what he played. If there was one thing out, he would go back and do that again. That's a pretty good policy, really, because a lot of those tracks—especially the lead guitar tracks—were triple-tracked" (Obrecht, 1982).

The group's self-titled first album was released in September 1980 in the United Kingdom and in early 1981 in the United States. *Blizzard of Ozz* featured many of the same elements found in Sabbath's material: occult lyrics, loud, heavy guitars, mid-tempo rhythm section. Yet, thanks to the presence of Rhoads, the band was more technically proficient and capable of pulling off variations on standard metal formulas. Featuring the hit singles "Crazy Train" and "Mr. Crowley," the disc reached #7 on the U.K. charts; it peaked at #21 in the United States, continuing to sell for over two years and becoming a huge success.

On September 12, 1980, the Blizzard of Ozz played their first show at the Apollo Theater in Glasgow, Scotland on a tour designed to promote the recording. They would play a total of 34 gigs right up to Christmas. It was at this time that Randy returned home to California and had his custom white flying V built with the help of Grover Jackson (see Equipment/Gear). Jackson finished the instrument two months later and had it shipped to Randy in England.

* * *

From January to March of 1981, the Blizzard of Ozz entered Ridge Farm Studios again to begin work on a follow-up, called *Diary of a Madman*. The recording felt rushed in comparison, but sales were brisk. Ozzy obviously maintained his audience appeal, while the fortunes of Black Sabbath sank precipitously. The new album, thanks in part to the drug anthem "Flying High Again," charted at #16 in the United States and became another huge seller. It went gold in just over three months.

The tour, on the other hand, didn't go quite as well. Ozzy's behavior grew erratic. He had been indulging in drugs and alcohol, and the mood of the tour felt stressed. To compound matters, ticket sales lagged.

It was also during this time that Randy petitioned Grover Jackson to build another flying V, this time with a more distinctive design. Randy asked for three, but only received the first of them. The U.K. leg of the *Diary* tour ended abruptly in early December of 1981 when Ozzy experienced a nervous breakdown.

After a few weeks of rest and recovery, the tour picked up again and the band's fortunes, including Rhoads' reputation, began turning around. Randy was voted the "Best New Talent" by *Guitar Player* magazine in 1981.

> There's so much going on and there's not enough time to do anything. I'm not confident about everything yet. I haven't had time to sort everything out. Since I've started this, great things haven't stopped happening. It gets to the point to where you don't know how to handle any good news anymore. Everything is great. When you dream of things you don't dream of that, you just dream of being in a band and getting your chance to do it. (Stix, 1981)

During this time, Randy's obsession with classical guitar increased. Friends noticed that he withdrew slightly from the band dynamic just as he was drawn toward his pursuit of classical music and the prospect of going to school and pursuing a master's degree to enhance his musical abilities. Band members recall the tension between Randy and Ozzy, both of whom had collaborated closely on the band's material and had gotten along very well in the first year or so of their working relationship. But the band's schedule prevented him from working on his first love, and so a conflict grew between his desires and his commitment to Ozzy.

Bassist Tommy Aldridge witnessed Randy's dynamic firsthand:

> Towards the end there, Randy wasn't very happy. I don't know so much if it was the road he became disenchanted with, or if it was what he was doing. He was so young and he had so much ability. His vocabulary was so vast, and his potential was so much bigger than he even knew. He definitely wanted to be elsewhere, to move in a new direction. He wanted to go back and teach, to write some pieces out, and to take advantage of some of the classy session offers and flattering invitations that he was getting. With our schedule, he just didn't have the time. He was always asking me about lawsuits: How can I get out of this? How can I get out of that? I felt so much for what he was going through, but I honestly couldn't think of a way that he could get out of his situation, you know? (Obrecht, 1982)

TECHNIQUE/STYLE

Rhoads had an unprecedented drive to be the best. How could he become great? His ambition pushed him every time he picked up the guitar. It was central to who he was as a person and as a player.

And he played constantly. He couldn't put his guitar down. Being on the road, in fact, disappointed him because it meant he had less time to practice. So when the band went on the road, he used to book a guitar lesson every day. He toyed with the idea of bringing an instructor on the road, but it would cost too much. So he'd flip through the local yellow pages to find an instructor, usually a classical guitar teacher at a local music school, and have a lesson. In many unfamiliar cities, he'd often get lost, or choose an inappropriate instructor. Occasionally, he would have to face some young, 18-year-old teacher who couldn't possibly teach Randy anything. Still, many of these times he wound up giving *them* lessons and paying for it out of his own pocket.

Randy is often credited with bringing a classical music influence to the guitar. Indeed, his neoclassical-influenced harmonic phrasing, repeating licks that moved up and down the fretboard, legato technique, and modal mastery all pointed to his intense classical training as a kid. He was actually given a chance to exhibit his classical, nylon-stringed chops with "Dee," a tribute to his Mom, and it most likely was the first exposure to classical music for millions of teenager guitar players in 1980.

"I think the relationship between heavy metal and classical music is great," said Rhoads. "It has been going on like that for a long time. Look at Deep Purple: It's heavy, but it's a way to bring a melody in there, too. Leslie West was one of my all-time favorite guitar players. I love his feel. He used a lot of classical lines, but he was really into it when he did it" (Stix, 1981).

Randy believed that the way he developed his technique came through teaching others.

> When you teach something to a student, it clicks in your head. You may find the answer to another problem you may have been trying to figure out. So I started combining what they wanted to learn with a bit of technique. Every day with every student I'd learn something. When I started to get a lot of students, I thought, "Enough with the licks. I'm going to have to get them to learn to find themselves." (Stix, John, "Randy Rhoads Interview," *Guitar for the Practicing Musician*, October 1981)

He instructed young guitar players eight hours a day, six days a week, and everyone from toddlers to teenagers. He played all day, developing his technique, his speed, and his sight reading.

> I think half of your sound comes in the way you play. A lot of it is in your hands. If you practice with a lot of muting and then go out and do it louder onstage, you've still got the same sort of sound. You can't be lazy. You have to want to play. You have to love the guitar. I did. As a matter of fact, I was afraid of competition because I thought that everybody was better than I was. It was so close to me, I thought everybody was great. Therefore I couldn't copy licks; I just learned on my own. (Stix, 1981)

In the studio, Randy demanded perfection. After a solo, if there were a couple of mistakes, no matter how small, he would go back and do the whole thing again. A lot of Randy's outro solos, that is, solos on long fades at the end of the tracks, were first takes. Most of his other solos were written out beforehand; he would work on them for a few days, playing a few, listening back, and then identify his aim. He would study a tape loop of his various work and then try another one. When it came time to record his now famous solos—as on "Revelation" and "Mr. Crowley"—he'd be able to play the whole thing through.

* * *

Randy Rhoads had an accurate and powerful picking technique. He created a variety of attacks, from lightning-fast fully picked runs to smoothly executed legato phrases. To achieve this fluency, he possessed precise synchronization of left and right hands. He used a standard medium gauge pick, held between the thumb and index finger, with the rest of the fingers slightly fanned out over the strings. He varied his point of balance from resting on the bridge or low E string to playing free hand with no palm support whatever. By

FATAL FLIGHT

Randy Rhoads' last show was in Knoxville, Tennessee on March 18, 1982 at the Knoxville Civic Coliseum. The next day, the band headed to a festival in Orlando, but the bus stopped at the home of the bus company Jerry Calhoun, and the bus driver, Andrew Aycock, took the liberty of inviting Rhoads and one other person, hairdresser Rachel Youngblood, on a flight in a small plane, a Beechcraft Bonanza. Aycock had little flying experience, but enough to convince Rhoads to come along for the ride.

During this trip the plane began to fly low to the ground, at times below tree level, and "buzzed" the band's tour bus three times. The plane was an estimated 10 feet off the ground traveling at approximately 120–150 knots.

On the fourth pass, the plane's left wing struck the left side of the band's tour bus, puncturing it in two places approximately halfway down on the right side of the bus. The plane, with the exception of the left wing, was thrown over the bus, hit a nearby pine tree, severing it approximately 10 feet up from the bottom, before crashing the home owned by Calhoun.

Ozzy Osbourne, Tommy Aldrige, Rudy Sarzo, and Sharon Arden, who were all asleep on the bus, were awoken by the plane's impact and (at first) thought they had been involved in a traffic accident. Rhoads, age 25, Aycock, 36, and Youngblood, 58, were all killed instantly. It was determined in an autopsy that Aycock had traces of cocaine in his system.

Randy's funeral was held at the First Lutheran Church in Burbank, California, which he attended as a child. He was buried at Mountain View Cemetery in San Bernardino, California, where his grandparents are also buried. Ozzy and the rest of the band went to the funeral, as well as all of the people from Jet Records, Ozzy's label. Members of Ozzy's band and Quiet Riot were pallbearers. Music teacher Arlene Thomas, a close friend of Randy's, sang and played acoustic guitar. There is a small bronze guitar on one side of his name on the gravestone, and on the other the "RR" signature that he used.

Ozzy Osbourne found some words to describe the tragic figure's legacy.

Randy was so unique that I don't think people will ever fully realize what a talent that guy was, not only in rock and roll, but in every other field. He was phenomenal in the classics. We loved each other very dearly. I swear to God, the tragedy of my life is the day he died. I've been doing this for a long, long time now with my life, and if ever I could say that I met a natural born star, it was a guy called Randy Rhoads, God bless him. Long live Randy Rhoads! If I could only put it in one word and people would believe me, as crazy as a reputation as I have, he was the most dedicated musician I ever met in my life. He was a master of his art. (Obrecht, 1982)

varying his pick hand posture, he could attack in different ways, from fully picked lines, muted tones, arpeggiated movements, and flowing, hammered approaches. He used strict alternating picking for quick scales and patterns unless a special pick effect was desired. He also muted, an important stylistic aspect, by lightly resting the palm and lower edge of the hand against the string surfaces. This requires intense control to produce a staccato tone without deadening the note's vibration entirely.

Randy Rhoads' left hand/fretting technique was particularly effortless. He had a thorough knowledge of the fretboard and the ability to move scale and pattern formations from position to position in a variety of ways. The wrist was brought out to be perpendicular to the neck for wide finger stretches and complete finger independence. Every finger of the left hand was used.

EQUIPMENT/GEAR

Four or five months before he left Quiet Riot, Randy brought pictures and petitioned custom guitar maker Grover Jackson to make him an instrument. They met several times to discuss details; he wanted a slightly offset Flying V shape, tremolo unit, double humbucking pickups, and one volume and one tone control per pickup. The tuners were standard Schallers. There was a Strat-style side-mount jack underneath the V section and toggle switches at the end of the wing.

The guitar had an old 1960s nonadjustable Danelectro neck shaved and modified to look somewhat like an arrowhead, with a rosewood fingerboard and wide, flat feel. The instruments have fairly small bodies that are easy to get around. They have a neck-through solid maple construction, 22 frets, a 25 1/2″ scale, and Seymour Duncan pickups: a jazz model in the neck position and a distortion model.

Polka dots, his trademark, were used, and the inlays on the fingerboard resembled bow ties. Rhoads liked small frets on his guitars, which he customized every one of his guitars with. Jackson created two guitars for Rhoads, a white one and a black one. The white one had one of Jackson's standard tremolo units on it. One of the main differences between the white one and the black one is that the black one has a pickguard and a lengthened, thinned-out rear wing. Randy complained that too many people thought the white one was a Flying V, and he wanted a more distinctively shark-finned design, more off-center.

Interestingly, Jackson's "white" guitar would be the beginning of the Jackson Guitars, a successful instrument-making company. Randy also occasionally used a 1964 cream-colored Les Paul. He played them all through a very simple amp setup: three 100-watt Marshall cabinets and Marshall heads, two of them from 1959.

He used regular GHS strings (.010s) and a medium-gauge pick.

As for effects, Randy was a wizard and he enjoyed combining a number of them to get a desired sound. Ozzy's music didn't require a lot of effects, so Randy felt a little limited in his use of them. But he applied them whenever he could. His pedalboard, used both in the studio and on stage, housed the array of boxes and pedals, including an MXT Distortion Plus, an MXR equalizer, a Cry Baby wah wah, an MXR chorus, an MXR flanger, and Korg Echo.

Of all these effects, Randy used the distortion unit most; it was chiefly responsible for producing the thick, overdriven tone associated with his sound. Often, the distortion was combined with heavy midrange boosting from the EQ and/or filtering from the wah pedal.

Randy had a thoughtful approach to effects; the processors were always used to add dimension and complement the guitar sound. Sustain, controlled feedback, boosting and filtering, and delay/doubling/stereo simulation contributed to his musical statements and never diluted the song's impact.

ESSENTIAL READING

Bene, David. *Randy Rhoads: A Life.* Self-published, 2008.
Obrecht, Jas. "Randy Rhoads: 1956–1982, A Biography by Family, Friends, and Fellow Musicians." *Guitar Player,* November 1982.

Osbourne, Ozzy, Randy Rhoads, and Aaron Rosenbaum. *Ozzy Osbourne: The Randy Rhoads Years (Guitar Legendary Licks)*. New York: Cherry Lane Music, 2002.

Sarzo, Rudy. *Off the Rails*. New York: Booksurge, 2006.

Stix, John. "Randy Rhoads Interview." *Guitar for the Practicing Musician*, October 1981.

———. www.randy-rhoads.com, 1981–1982.

ESSENTIAL WORK

"Crazy Train" (1980)
"Flying High Again" (1981)
"Mr. Crowley" (1980)
"S.A.T.O." (1981)
"Suicide Solution" (1980)

ESSENTIAL LISTENING

Blizzard of Ozz (Jet, 1980)
Diary of a Madman (Jet, 1981)
Quiet Riot (CBS, 1977)
Tribute (Epic, 1987)

Keith Richards

Keith Richards, lead guitar for the world's greatest and longest-lived band, is responsible for some of rock 'n' roll's most memorable riffs and is widely acknowledged as perhaps the greatest rhythm player in the entire genre. Richards is also legendary for his ability to navigate through and around the treacherous excesses of the superstar lifestyle. Having been in the rock arena since the early 1960s, Richards is, if nothing else, a survivor. But, in fact, he is so much more.

Back in 1962, when the Stones originally formed—inspired by the title of a Muddy Waters tune—they likely had no idea how perfect their moniker would be. Across four decades of dramatically shifting trends in popular music, the Stones have indeed rolled. They've adjusted and adapted to the changing times with nimble dexterity without really disconnecting themselves from their blues roots, thanks to the distinctive styles of Richards and his Telecaster.

Not since Chuck Berry knocked out his proto-rock riffs in the late 1950s and early 1960s, like "Maybellene" and "Johnny B. Goode," has there been a player as inimitable as Keith Richards. He invented so many fabulous riffs and chord progressions that rock 'n' roll has up till now taken him and his songwriting dexterity for granted. Only today, given his incredible endurance, do we recognize him for what he is: one of rock 'n' roll's true treasures.

His tough, sinewy sound and impeccable musical instincts played a major role in establishing the foundation of hard rock. Rather than soloing, he preferred to work a groove using open-chord tunings drawn from his passion in Delta blues.

Richards' role in the Rolling Stones picked up in 1969, after the death of founding guitar player Brian Jones. He stepped up in terms of playing and in terms of songwriting partnership with singer Mick Jagger. He and Jagger have together written hundreds of songs, 14 of which made *Rolling Stone* magazine's list of the "500 Greatest Songs of All Time."

He was also inducted into the Songwriting Hall of Fame. Among the most prominent songs in the Richards catalog include "Jumpin' Jack Flash," "Satisfaction," "Ruby Tuesday," "Start Me Up," "Happy," "Miss You," "Brown Sugar," "Gimme Shelter," "Wild Horses," "It's Only Rock n' Roll (But I Like it)," and "As Tears Go By," the latter popularized by the British singer, Marianne Faithfull, and one of the few songs by Richards and Jagger to become a major hit for another artist.

In 2003, Richards earned another feather for his cap, a #10 ranking on *Rolling Stone*'s "100 Greatest Guitarists of All Time" list.

In the 1970s, the band continued making important and best-selling albums like *Sticky Fingers* and *Exile on Main Street,* two of its masterpieces. Later on in the decade, *Some Girls,* featuring a newly cleaned up Richards, was one of their most focused efforts of the period and yielded their #1 single, "Miss You," a danceable tune that demonstrated the band's ability to swing with the times. The song spent a solid five months on the radio.

The 1980s yielded the group's best-selling album, *Tattoo You,* which hung at #1 for nine weeks in 1981, thanks to songs like "Start Me Up" and "Hang Fire." Touring and records continued throughout the 1990s; somehow the Stones found time to conveniently accommodate the solo careers of both Richards and Mick Jagger. At the same time, the Stones won a Best Rock Album Grammy, their first, for *Voodoo Lounge* in 1994.

Keith and the Rolling Stones were inducted into the Rock Hall of Fame in 1989, part of the museum's fourth class. Since then, the band has maintained, if not increased, their productivity, touring in 1994 (for *Voodoo Lounge*), in 1997 (for *Bridges to Babylon*), in 2002 for a greatest hits tour ("Licks"), and in a two-year jaunt (2005–2007) called "A Bigger Bang." They gigged and released records as if they were still teenagers in their first lively decade as a band.

Rolling Stone: Why have you been able to survive, physically and otherwise, the excesses that have killed so many of your peers and followers?

Richards: I don't know. I have an intuitive sense of my own body and my inner workings. I don't push it for the fun of it. I have a lot of energy, and I gotta burn it one way or another. And I'm trying to burn it in the best way—for my life, for what I think should be done. (Fricke, David, "Keith Richards Uncut," *Rolling Stone,* October 17, 2002)

EARLY YEARS

Born in 1943 in Dartford, Kent, Keith Richards was the only child of Bert Richards and Doris Dupree Richards. Richards' father worked in a factory. His paternal grandparents were civic leaders, while his maternal grandfather (Augustus Theodore Dupree) toured Britain in a Big Band, called Gus Dupree and his Boys, during the late 1940s and early 1950s. Of course, this exposure to popular music proved to be an early influence on Richards' musical ambitions.

Richards' mother enhanced that exposure by playing him the music of Billie Holiday, Duke Ellington, and Louis Armstrong. His first instrument was a Rosetti acoustic guitar, and his mother encouraged him to practice frequently. His father, though, didn't have the same warm feeling about it. He'd come home from work at night, tired and beleaguered, and see young Keith banging noisily on the guitar.

In 1955, Richards heard the strains of Elvis and his guitar player, Scotty Moore, float their way across the Atlantic from Memphis. Moore would become his first guitar inspiration.

Richards attended Wentworth Primary School with a boy named Mick Jagger; the two lived in the same neighborhood briefly until Richards' family moved to another section of Dartford in 1954. He attended Dartford Technical School, where the choirmaster recruited him to sing as a boy soprano. In this capacity, he actually sang for Queen Elizabeth II at Westminster Abby.

Richards didn't like school much, and he ended up getting expelled for bad attendance. The headmaster suggested he go to art school in the town of Sidcup. It would be the best move he ever made. At Sidcup Art College, he played guitar most of the time. He traded some records for his first electric guitar, a hollow-body Hoefner cutaway. He then discovered and delved into American blues, including artists like Big Bill Broonzy, Sonny Terry and Brownie McGhee, and Lightnin' Hopkins. He also studied the riffs and technique of Chuck Berry.

Richards reconnected with his boyhood friend Jagger when the two ran into each other at a train station in the fall of 1960. (As the story goes, Keith noticed the imported blues albums that his old friend Mick carried onto the train.) As it turned out, Richards discovered that Mick, a student at the London School of Economics, loved the blues as much as he loved early rock 'n' roll. He even had a group together, Little Boy Blue and the Blue Boys. Jagger recruited Richards for his band, and they had soon rekindled their friendship.

MUSIC

Together, Jagger, Richards, and their upstart act began hitting the nascent blues circuit around London. It didn't take them long to encounter Alexis Korner's Blues Incorporated, a key player, as it turns out, in London's burgeoning scene. Korner had hired a guitar player, Brian Jones, who floored Richards. Jones had the kind of grasp on American blues that Richards and Jagger had set their own sights on; his slide soloing mesmerized Richards, and both him and Jagger were drawn to Jones' outstanding work.

They befriended Jones and became roommates and musical collaborators. After leaving Korner's Blues Incorporated, Jones decided to form his own group, and he invited Mick and Keith. One night, when Korner had to skip out on one of his regular Marquee gigs, the new band—also featuring bassist Dick Taylor, keyboardist Ian Stewart, and drummer Mick Avory—seized the opportunity to introduce their group. The date was July 12, 1962.

The boys, calling themselves the Rolling Stones' after a Muddy Waters' tune, did well that night, well enough to command an eight-month residency at London's Crawdaddy Club. By that time, the group's final lineup had been set, with founding members Jagger, Richards, and Jones augmented by drummer Charlie Watts (a Blues Incorporated alumnus) and bassist Bill Wyman.

At the time, the Beatles were also getting it done around London and Britain, so the band took a purposely diametrical musical approach, away from pop and toward the blues. Where the Beatles were scrubbed and sunny-sided, the Stones epitomized the opposite of all that, embodying a darker, bolder, and seamier side of popular music.

Over the next two years they toured and released a few singles, all covers, including Buddy Holly's "Not Fade Away," Chuck Berry's "Come On," and the Beatles' bluesy "I Wanna Be Your Man."

They released their self-titled debut in 1964 on the London label. They ventured to America, where they played wildly successful gigs and made the time to record at the Chess Records studio in Chicago between dates. They covered Howlin' Wolf's "Little Red Rooster," which hit #1 in the United Kingdom.

About this time they were encouraged by their manager to start writing originals. He exhorted them to sit down together and compose their own songs, largely because they'd be able to keep more of their money. He locked Richards and Jagger together in a kitchen and told them he'd let them out when they had a song to show him. In June of 1964, the group released their first original single, "Tell Me (You're Coming Back)," which became their first Top 40 hit in the United States. Indeed, from early 1965 through the end of the 1960s, Mick and Keith churned out a seemingly endless string of chart-busting singles.

HE FOUGHT THE LAW

Keith Richards is the archetypal rock outlaw. He's filled that role since the Rolling Stones first established themselves as the dangerous alternative to the Beatles in 1963. It's been a vast part of the Stones allure, and a perfect, imagistic complement to the band's bad-boy grooves. Richards has played into that image by imbibing in a smorgasbord of indulgences. He has been tried on drug-related charges five times: in 1967, twice in 1973, in 1977, and in 1978.

A February police raid on Richards' estate put he and Jagger on trial, and both were found guilty. Richards was sentenced to one year in prison. Both he and Jagger were imprisoned, but then they were released on bail the next day pending appeal. A month later, the appeals court overturned Richards' conviction for lack of evidence. Richards faced more serious charges resulting from his arrest in Toronto in 1977, when he was charged with "possession of heroin for the purpose of trafficking." He had 22 grams of heroin in his possession. His passport was revoked, and Richards and his family remained in Toronto for months before Richards was allowed to enter the United States on a medical visa for treatment of heroin addiction. The original charge was later reduced to "simple possession of heroin," but it could have been costly, as the original charge could have resulted in a prison sentence of seven years to life.

Rolling Stone: Part of the Stones allure is the way you've survived a lifetime of bad habits—the kind that can kill you. Does it bother you that people are often more interested in your mortality than in your music?

Richards: People's fascination with other people's bad habits is something you don't take into consideration when you start this thing. Yeah, it's there—the image of me with a parrot on my shoulder and a patch on the eye. But he's only one side of it. I really like a quiet life: listen to my music, burn my incense. I'm all for a quiet life, except I didn't get one. (Fricke, 2002)

In the summer of 1965, the group released "(I Can't Get No) Satisfaction," a song that elevated the Stones to superstar status. Driven by a fuzz-guitar riff designed to replicate the sound of a horn section, "Satisfaction" also heralded the arrival of a major songwriting team. Their confidence together grew, and in 1966 they released *Aftermath,* the Stones' first recording of all original songs.

Classics like "Paint It, Black," "Ruby Tuesday," and "Let's Spend the Night Together" followed, bringing them to 1967 and a very eventful year. Not only did they release three albums that year, but also they were beset with legal troubles stemming from a string of media-instigated drug busts. When the dust cleared, Jagger, Richards, and Jones had narrowly escaped serious prison sentences. However, whereas the ordeal seemed to strengthen Jagger and Richards' steely resolve, ongoing substance abuse was rapidly causing Jones' physical and mental state to degenerate.

They released another epic single, "Jumpin' Jack Flash," while Jones' condition worsened. He barely turned up for the sessions that would become their first genuine masterpiece, *Beggars Banquet* in November of 1968.

On *Beggars Banquet,* the Stones reverted back to their blues roots, from the psychedelic experimentation that everyone in the United Kingdom— Hendrix, Beck, Clapton, the Who, and the Beatles—all seemed to be indulging in. The Stones reached for it with their 1967 project, *Their Satanic Majesties Request,* an album many dismissed as mere Beatles' posturing.

Beggars Banquet was "immediately acclaimed as one of their landmark achievements. A strong acoustic Delta blues flavor colors much of the material, particularly 'Salt of the Earth' and 'No Expectations,' which features some beautiful slide guitar work. Basic rock & roll was not forgotten, however: 'Street Fighting Man,' a reflection of the political turbulence of 1968, was one of their most innovative singles, and 'Sympathy for the Devil,' with its fire-dancing guitar licks, leering Jagger vocals, African rhythms, and explicitly satanic lyrics, was an image-defining epic...At the time, the approach was fresh, and the lyrical bite of most of the material ensured *Beggars Banquet*'s place as one of the top blues-based rock records of all time" (Unterberger, Richie, *allmusic.com*).

Courtesy of Photofest

The Stones announced Jones' departure from the group on June 8, 1969, citing the typical reason: "musical differences." Less than a month later, though, those differences manifested themselves in another way, when authorities discovered Jones dead in his swimming pool. The case remains one of rock's most remarkable, unsolved mysteries; the official cause of the Jones tragedy was given as "death by misadventure."

By the time of his death, the Stones had, for all intents and purposes, replaced Jones with Mick Taylor, an extraordinary blues guitar player recently departed from John Mayall's Bluesbreakers. While Taylor didn't play much on the band's next album, *Let It Bleed,* released in 1969, Richards handled the chores with dexterity; the material extended the band's blues reinvigoration with songs like "Gimme Shelter," "Love in Vain," and the masterpiece, "You Can't Always Get What You Want."

In 1969, the group launched its first American tour in three years and broke attendance records in the process. One of the gigs on that tour, at Altamont, though, turned deadly. Based on the recommendation of the Grateful Dead in San Francisco, the Stones hired a group of Hell's Angels as security for the show. Disorganized from the start, the Angels ended up murdering a young black man, Meredith Hunter, in a scrum during the Stones'

175

performance. There was an intense public outcry, and the Stones, embarrassed and disappointed, withdrew from the public eye for a while. Many say that Altamont put a permanent end to the good vibes of the 1960s and the Woodstock era.

At that point, Stones gigs were routinely perilous events, full of violence and insanity. Keith explains his memory of the time.

> We went onstage fighting. You want to play music? Don't go up there. What's important is hoping no one gets hurt and how are we getting out. I remember a riot in Holland. I turned to look at Stu [Ian Stewart] at the piano. All I saw was a pool of blood and a broken chair. He'd been taken off by stagehands and sent to the hospital. A chair landed on his head. To compensate for that, Mick and I developed the songwriting and records. We poured our music into that. *Beggars Banquet* was like coming out of puberty. (Unattributed, "Keith Richards: Interview with Stones' Guitarist," pierresetparoles.blogspot.com, October 6, 2002)

* * *

In 1971, the Stones launched their own record company, Rolling Stones Records, with the release of *Sticky Fingers* and its legendary first single, "Brown Sugar." The album also served up epic sides like "Wild Horses" and "Sister Morphine." The next year, in what amounted to the Stones' greatest one-two punch, the band issued *Exile on Main Street,* another five-star recording that has enjoyed the reputation of being the Stones' finest release. The record also features one of Richards' signature tunes, "Happy," a sloppy but lovable tune with a driving guitar riff and Richards' mumbling, whiskey-flavored singing.

The hottest act in rock 'n' roll, the Stones toured *Exile* and proceeded to perfect the idea of a touring juggernaut, something they remain to this day. The Stones represented the yin and yang of decadence and professionalism, running their arena tour like a well-oiled machine, but also embodying the blueprint of rock 'n' roll superstars. The band released a few average recordings in the mid-1970s. Taylor left in 1974, rather abruptly, and was replaced with much pomp by former Faces guitar player Ron Wood.

With Wood now in the mix, the Stones dished out *Some Girls* in 1978, one of their hardest hitting records, driven by the insurgent challenge of punk rock and the rising tide of disco and dance music. They once again overtook the charts with songs like "Miss You" and "Shattered," funky takes on rock's latest trends.

Throughout the rest of the band's career, the Stones released solid fare. *Tattoo You,* released in 1981, emitted a pair of great singles, "Start Me Up" and "Waiting on a Friend," which enabled the album to hover at #1 for over two months. It would be the last time the group completely dominated the charts with either singles or albums.

Jagger and Richards feuded through the 1980s, quite famously, and their material suffered significantly because of it. Longtime bassist Bill Wyman left in 1991. The band assembled huge, highly anticipated, and incredibly profitable tours after that. But they had become less of an authoritative entity on the rock scene and more of an inveterate greatest hits act, serving up heavy portions of familiar singalongs, thanks to the memorable lyrics of Mick Jagger and the indelible, enduring hooks of Keith Richards, the guitar player with nine lives.

> You're talking to a madman, really. Who else in this forty or fifty years of rock has been able to sneak through the cracks like this? Which is probably why a lot of us become musicians, I think. As long as you've got a gig, it's a brilliant slide through the social structure. You

don't have to play the game that everybody else has to. It's a license to do what you want. (Fricke, 2002)

TECHNIQUE/STYLE

From the very beginning of his career as a guitarist, Keith Richards has derived his chief inspiration from Chuck Berry.

"Chuck was my man," he said in an uncredited interview.

> He was the one that made me say, "I want to play guitar, Jesus Christ!" And I'd listened to guitar players before that. I was about 15, and I'd think, "He's very interesting, nice, ah, but ..." With the difference between what I'd heard before 1956 or '57 and right after that with Little Richard and Elvis and Chuck Berry, suddenly I knew what it was I wanted to do. ("The Salt of the Earth, 1955–1960, R&B-derived Rock & Roll," www.timeisonourside.com)

His first band experience with Mick Jagger in Little Boy Blue and the Blue Boys involved learning and spewing back Berry tunes. Conversely, Jagger and Richards were later credited with bringing Berry back to prominence in later Stones' version of his songs.

Stylistically, Richards often uses guitars with open tunings, which allow for syncopated and ringing I–IV chording that can be heard on well-known tracks like "Start Me Up" and "Street Fighting Man." One of the reasons his chords are sort of difficult to play is because he liked to use only five-stringed guitars, so many of his chords are five-string variations of common chords. He was partial to a five-string variant of Open G tuning, using G-D-G-B-D without a low sixth string. The tuning shows up on many Stones cuts, including "Brown Sugar" and "Honky Tonk Women." His open tunings led Richards to the joy of discovering more ways to write, and his late 1960s material exhibits an excellent qualitative rebirth. Of course, when Jones died, leaving Keith to handle the rhythm, lead, and any other guitar tracks, including slide, his creativity and confidence multiplied.

Richards has also claimed that one of the keys to his effectiveness as a player is his ability to play something when folks least expect it. He goes on to explain that players shouldn't be afraid to play nothing. Let the sustain carry the tone for a while, then blast a reverberant power chord. On "Brown Sugar," for example, Richards plays little during the verses, so the choruses sound that much more exciting. He also changes the timing between verses, and switches chords just before or after it's generally deemed proper.

Because Keith often plays only five strings, he believes as much in playing fewer than necessary strings as he does in playing all five. Occasionally, he'll play the chord on just three strings, either the top or the bottom, often switching between the two variants. By combining these tricks with tricks in the timing, Keith has developed his very own unique approach.

EQUIPMENT/GEAR

Richards owns over 1,000 guitars, too many to list in this small space. Many of those are, of course, Fender Telecasters, his instrument of choice for the last couple of decades. In fact, Richards is the most famous of all Telecaster players, bar none. He prefers two 1950's Telecasters.

"Micawber" is the name of Keith's butterscotch Fender Telecaster. It's an early 1950s (probably a 1952) butterscotch blonde color model with a black pickguard and a stock three-way switch. The sixth string is removed, and it's always tuned to open G (G,D,G,B, D) low to high with no capo with gauges from .011 to .042 (Ernie Ball). It has replacement tuners and a brass replacement bridge with individual saddles, and the nut is cut to accommodate five strings. The strings are not evenly spaced across the fingerboard, but the first string is moved a bit to keep it from going over the edge. It's equipped with Gibson PAF humbucker pickup in the neck position and an original Tele pickup in the bridge position. It is warm, and thick sounding can be heard on such live tracks as "Before They Make Me Run," "Brown Sugar," "Mixed Emotions," and "Honky Tonk Women."

Keith's second Tele is also from the 1950s. It has a black pickguard, five strings, natural finish so that you can see the wood grain of the body. The pickups and modifications are the same as Micawber, and this Tele stays capoed at the fourth fret. Keith uses Shubb capoes. Tuned in B: B, F#, B, D#, F#, this Tele is a little louder and somewhat brighter than Micawber and can be heard onstage for "Tumbling Dice," "Happy," and "Jumpin' Jack Flash."

He uses Music Man Silhouettes guitars for standard tuning songs and has one in black and one in white. Both are nontremolo with through-body stringing; the white one has Schaller pickups, the black one DiMarzios, with both in humbucker/single-coil arrangement. He used these guitars on previous tours for songs like "Bitch," "Sad, Sad, Sad," "Sympathy for the Devil," and more.

Keith's main Fender Stratocaster is a 1958 known as "Mary Kay." It was previously owned by bandmate Ron Wood, has an all maple neck and fingerboard with a one-piece ash body, see through blond finish and all gold hardware. The pickups are stock, but a three-way selector switch has been changed to a five-way.

He played mainly Gibsons in the 1960s, prior to his changeover to Fender. In the late 1960s, he largely used stock Les Pauls. He also owned a 1959 Bigsby-sporting sunburst Les Paul Junior, nicknamed "Dice," that he acquired in 1964. It is capoed at the seventh fret and is used during "Midnight Rambler" and "Out of Control." He was one of the first major players to play a Les Paul in 1960s Britain. He plays a cherry red and ebony Gibson ES-355 as well as an ES-335.

Fender Twins are now his Richards' amps of choice. This amp is a 1957 model originally tweed, but recovered in early 1960's style brown Tolex. It has four 6L6 tubes. He used a Marshall head. There was also a Fender Bassman, 4x10, and Mesa Boogie 4x12 cabs.

In terms of effects, he used them sparingly. In 1965, Richards used a Gibson Maestro fuzzbox to get the distinctive tone of his riff on "(I Can't Get No) Satisfaction." In the 1970s and early 1980s Richards frequently used wah-wah pedals, an Ibanez UE-400 multi-effects pedal, a Fulltone Tube Tape Echo, an MXR Phase 90 and Phase 100, as well as an MXR Analog Delay.

ESSENTIAL READING

Appleford, Steve. *The Rolling Stones: Rip This Joint: The Story Behind Every Song.* New York: Thunder's Mouth, 2000.

Bockris, Victor. *Keith Richards: The Biography.* New York: Simon & Schuster, 1993.

Dalton, David. *The Rolling Stones: The First Twenty Years.* New York: Alfred A. Knopf, 1981.

Fricke, David. "Keith Richards Uncut." *Rolling Stone,* October 17, 2002.

"The Salt of the Earth, 1955–1960, R&B-derived Rock & Roll," www.timeisonourside.com.

Unattributed, "Keith Richards: Interview with Stones' Guitarist," pierresetparoles.blogspot.com;
    October 6, 2002.
Unterberger, Richie. *allmusic.com.*

ESSENTIAL WORK

"Brown Sugar" (1971)
"Gimme Shelter" (1969)
"Happy" (1972)
"(I Can't Get No) Satisfaction" (1965)
"Jumpin' Jack Flash" (1970)
"Miss You" (1978)
"Paint It, Black" (1966)
"Start Me Up" (1981)
"Sympathy for the Devil" (1968)
"Wild Horses" (1971)
"You Can't Always Get What You Want" (1969)

ESSENTIAL LISTENING

Beggars Banquet (ABKCO, 1968)
Exile on Main Street (Rolling Stone, 1972)
Let It Bleed (ABKCO, 1969)
Some Girls (Virgin, 1978)
Sticky Fingers (Virgin, 1971)
Tattoo You (Virgin, 1981)

ESSENTIAL VIEWING

Gimme Shelter (ABKCO, 1991)
The Rolling Stones Rock and Roll Circus (ABKCO, 2004)
Shine a Light (MGM, 2008)

Carlos Santana

Since debuting in 1969, Carlos Santana has sold nearly 50 million records worldwide. Despite numerous lineup changes, he's enjoyed an amazingly consistent career, playing sold-out shows in front of a whopping 25 million fans. His journey has taken him from the cantinas of Tijuana to the park festivals of San Francisco, from Woodstock to Altamont right through the legendary Live Aid show in 1985.

Carlos Santana has been recognized as the man responsible for bridging the gap between Latin music and rock 'n' roll. His intoxicating Latin vibes merged with 12-bar blues, aggressive riffs, and churning Afro-Cuban rhythms have combined to create one of the most recognizable sounds in all of popular music. And his solos? Few could mistake the guitarist's inimitable tone for anyone else's.

Indeed, Santana is one of rock's true stylists. With his beautiful use of sustain and his pitch-perfect tone, he recalls the elegance of great blues players like Buddy Guy and B.B. King. Live, he and his band made a name for themselves before they released a single record, when their promoter Bill Graham secured a slot at Woodstock for the young band. It turned into quite the coming-out party, and not surprisingly, with blistering tunes like "Savor," "Soul Sacrifice," and "Waiting." With one seven-song set, the slender, bushy-haired Chicano with one foot in the barrio and the other in the burgeoning psychedelic scene announced the arrival of a major talent.

Not only did Santana occupy an iconic place in the United States after Woodstock, but he also became a captivating presence throughout Central and Latin America, places where he still command crowds 90,000 strong. The polyrhythms of those countries resonate in much of Santana's material.

Today, Santana is one of the few stars who remain viable from those hoary days of the sixties in San Francisco, an achievement in its own right. He is now one of the lone wolves representing the open-minded cultural explosion of the hippie era. Despite going through an incredible array of difficulties and overcoming hurdles and various setbacks, he continues to represent that idealized life and those carefree times. In his speech, in his demeanor, and in his flowing white vestments, Carlos Santana symbolizes freedom, joy, and timelessness.

His guitar, of course, symbolizes something else altogether.

When he veered from his commercial rock path after this first three albums, he stayed true to his vision and viable as an artist, even after everyone implored him to stay where he was. He made records through the 1980s, through changing trends and tastes and styles and came out nothing less than a superstar, albeit a bit older. He weathered the alternative rock boom of the 1990s only to emerge a bigger star than ever at the end of the decade, when *Supernatural,* his multiplatinum, award-winning collection of collaborations with the day's pop stars, dominated the rock scene. Repeatedly he has stormed back to the forefront of popular music, all the while never falling from hipness or sacrificing his original ideals.

To this day, Santana is an inspiring presence in rock 'n' roll as a spokesperson, a role model, and a genius on the guitar. In August 2003, he was awarded the #15 spot on *Rolling Stone*'s list of the "100 Greatest Guitar Players." The next year he occupied the same slot on the magazine's "100 Greatest Rock and Roll Artists of All Time."

"Well, people give a lot of reasons," Santana says of his continuing popularity. "They say it's the merging of the congas and timbales with the electric guitar. But I feel the main reason, the prime motivation that gets people out of their houses to see us and buy our albums, is the cry" (Gill, Chris, "Carlos Santana," *MOJO*, September 1999, n.p.).

The cry. That's an apt description of the piercing, sustained guitar notes that are the immediately identifiable signature on almost every Santana record, from their first single to crack the Top 10, "Evil Ways," in 1970, to the present day.

EARLY YEARS

Carlos Santana was born in July 1947 in the small Mexican town of Autlan, near Guadalajara, into a family of four sisters and two brothers. His father, a professional musician, moved his family to Tijuana in search of gigs, played Mariachi to tourists, though his heart was elsewhere musically.

When Santana was just a schoolboy, he began playing guitar himself at the local cantinas, translating American pop and blues into Spanish to entertain the ubiquitous tourists of this border town. His father had since moved to San Francisco and one day he brought Carlos back a hollowbody Gibson guitar.

Santana learned to love music and his guitar quickly. There were radio stations pumping an eclectic potpourri of different music into his ears; blues, gospel, and early rock 'n' roll left the deepest imprint. He especially loved playing the blues, and by the time he was 14, he began getting prime-time gigs in real nightclubs. He'd play from four in the afternoon right through till dawn the next day. Santana was essentially on his own during this time in his life. He made his own schedule, answering to no one but himself. This early independence expedited his maturity. Growing up on the mean streets of Tijuana demanded a significant amount of self-assurance.

Santana's early musical influences were generally in the blues/R&B field:

Jimmy Reed was the first thing I listened to, then B.B. King, Bobby "Blue" Bland, early Ray Charles, stuff like that, but it was mainly B.B. King who knocked me right out. As soon as I heard a guitar player like that, I thought, "Man, that's the stuff—this is the sort of music I want to do when I grow up." (Grundy, Stuart, and John Tobler, *The Guitar Greats*. London: BBC Books, 1983, n.p.)

* * *

But the Santanas didn't want their six kids to consider Tijuana home, so they uprooted in 1961 and headed north to San Francisco. Only Carlos resisted the move. He'd grown comfortable living and playing music there. His mother and older brother had to physically remove him from his low-life haunt in Tijuana. And so it was under these difficult circumstances that Carlos Santana experienced a change of scenery.

In San Francisco, young Santana's musical education escalated. He delved into the blues, specifically Chess recording artists like Muddy Waters and Howlin' Wolf. He also plunged into other guitar talents. "Names like T-Bone Walker, Lonnie Johnson, Django Reinhardt, Charlie Christian—they're the ones that invented the shoe; we created a style with it, but they invented the shoe!" (Gill, 1999).

Besides the blues, Santana was influenced by the music of the city's Mission District, where the Santanas lived. Populated by Spanish people—Mexicans, Nicaraguans, Salvadorans, Costa Ricans, Panamanians, Brazilians—the district featured the talents of many artists, muralists, and musicians of all kinds. The creative and cultural explosion that surrounded him affected Santana, and he deepened his appreciation of all the arts.

Fired up with ambition, primed with blues and Latin music, it wouldn't be long before he would be adding his own panache. With the financial backing provided by a dishwashing job, he convened his first American group, and called it the Santana Blues Band.

MUSIC

San Francisco in the mid-1960s was the epicenter of America's cultural expansion. It spearheaded the move toward a deeper consciousness, with celebrations of the arts, of people, of greater understanding. The city itself heaved with change. In 1965, psychedelia, free love, hippiedom, and an accompanying drug culture became predominant ethos, and the burgeoning counterculture found a healthy reception in both New York and San Francisco.

It was during these culturally transitive times that Santana formed his first band. The Santana Blues Band featured keyboard player and singer Gregg Rolie, bassist David Brown, percussionists Mike Carabello and Marcus Malone, and drummer Doc Livingston. The group was given its name due to a musician's union requirement that a single person be named a band's leader, and it did not at first indicate that the young Carlos Santana, only 20 at the time, was in charge. In fact, rather soft-spoken and unassuming, he felt uncomfortable designating himself as "bandleader."

Back in 1966, the fledgling blues act celebrated the dawning of this "new consciousness" by embarking on a two-month tour of college and university campuses: Fresno, Berkeley, San Diego, Los Angeles. The gigs were successful; the wide-open genre-mixing concert bills of the time played directly into Santana's style-fusing strengths. Right from the start, Santana and the band took electric blues traditions and incorporated them with rich, pulsating Afro-Cuban rhythms. These Afro-Cuban and Latin rhythms did not stem from Santana's Tijuana childhood. Rather they came directly from San Francisco, in the parks of the city, where congas resonated in every street- corner band. He also picked up some Latin flair from a local guitarist Gabor Szabo, who produced his best work, the conga-ridden *Spellbinder* in 1966. At the center of the band's sound was Santana's guitar: lyrical, sweet, flowing, even at this early age.

The band acquired a reputation for brilliant musicianship, and, as they made a name for itself in the Bay Area music community, their gigs grew in attendance. A stellar blues guitarist named Mike Bloomfield, one of the leading lights in American blues guitar of the 1960s, befriended Santana and invited him to play at one of his studio recording sessions, Santana' first. Bloomfield introduced him to concert promoter Bill Graham. Impressed with Santana's talent, Graham took the band under his wing and began booking them as support to the many big-name acts that played at his venue, the Fillmore West

Courtesy of Photofest

auditorium. This turn of events displayed some degree of irony. Santana as a young teen often sneaked into shows there to hear his favorite bands.

Eventually, Graham expanded his role and became Santana's manager. Based on this affiliation and the band's ability to win over audiences, Graham secured a slot at Woodstock for the band. Until that time, the band Santana—they had shortened their name by now—had a record contract but no album to show for it; it was still some weeks away from release. Woodstock ultimately served to whet the appetite of hundreds of thousands of fans.

Some accounts of Woodstock paint a dismal picture of that legendary Love and Peace jam, that it was a disorganized nightmare of drugs and discord. Santana disagreed:

> It all depends on who you talk to, man .... You're always gonna get people who sour beautiful things. I saw a lot of beauty. I saw a lot of potential. I saw an ocean of flesh and eyes and teeth and arms. And this ocean represented an opposition to the official corporate America. And I saw that these people who smoked hashish, or whatever they did, this was the equivalent of the French Resistance, the Bohemians. Woodstock was our thing. (Snowden, Don, "Cooling into the Norm," *Musician,* March 1985, n.p.)

They brought down the house and were one of the surprises of the festival. They received $1,500 for their appearance and another $750 for film rights to their set. The rights fee seemed a pittance, and several bands scoffed at it. But the exposure of their 11-minute instrumental "Soul Sacrifice," aired in the *Woodstock* film and on the soundtrack album, substantially increased Santana's popularity. Santana emerged as an international musical force, embracing various Latin music traditions, Santana's soaring guitar, and the exhilarating foundation provided by multiple percussionists.

When they debuted with *Santana* in late August 1969, the record stormed the charts, reaching the Top Five. A single from that album, a song Bill Graham recommended they cover called "Evil Ways," climbed into the Top 10 on the *Billboard Hot 100.* Santana received a huge boost that same fall when the *Woodstock* film was released and their "Soul Sacrifice" performance dominated the film. The double album based on the *Woodstock* festival came out in 1970.

In December of that year, the band also appeared on the bill at Altamont, the disastrous and violent concert organized by the Rolling Stones in California, that resulted in a man being beaten to death by a group of Hell's Angels, recruited to "police" the show. Santana described Altamont as a nightmare and has spoken little of it since.

The band's second album, *Abraxas,* was released in September 1970 and was even more successful than *Santana.* It hit #1, stayed on the charts nearly two years, and sold over four million copies. Top Five hit "Black Magic Woman" and Top 10 tune "Oye Como Va" were on everyone's lips and Santana dominated the rock scene.

Released in September 1971, *Santana III* also reached #1, eventually selling over two million copies while spawning the Top 10 hit "Everybody's Everything" and the Top 20 hit "No One to Depend On." The recording boasted the presence of a young whiz-kid guitar player named Neal Schon. Joining just in time to appear on *III,* Schon had opted to join Santana after also being given the invitation to join Eric Clapton's Derek and the Dominos act.

It was at this time that Carlos Santana, deluged by publicity and the rigors of being in the spotlight, not to mention nonstop touring, turned to religion. His speedy ascendance from obscurity to international stardom jarred him. "I got slapped by reality," he recalls, grimacing at the memory. "All of us in the first band were fried. Platinum albums in my house, drugs, food, flesh and all those kinds of things, but I felt such an emptiness. Everything felt dead because I was not aware. I was not taking time to acknowledge my inner body" (Goldberg, Michael, "Carlos Santana's Journey Toward Perfection," *Rolling Stone,* February 1980, n.p.).

Santana's search for spirituality led him to Sri Chimnoy, a Hindu guru (see sidebar), in 1971. John McLaughlin, a guitar player for the jazz fusion group the Mahavishnu Orchestra, one of Santana's favorite performers, introduced him to Chimnoy.

Just as Santana pursued spirituality, he and the band also looked to drugs for an escape. Mind-expanding narcotics swept through the Santana lineup like a swarm of angry bees, and relations within the group began to suffer.

> It was important in the sense that at least people were experimenting. The thing about drugs is that there's a difference between self-expansion and self-deception, and that goes for booze, power, ego-tripping . . . Two year old children, as soon as they start to walk, go round and round in circles until they get dizzy and start giggling 'cos they get a buzz. (Goldberg, 1980)

But drugs began to erode the camaraderie and the performance of the band, and Santana decided to regroup. Following the lengthy tour to support *III,* he retained the rights to the band's name and started again, which he did in early 1972. For their fourth album, *Caravanserai,* the new lineup brought about an intensely different sound and marked a strong change in musical direction, closer to jazz fusion than the Latin flavored rock of their first three albums.

The album was released in September 1972; it peaked in the Top Five and was eventually certified platinum. It was nominated for a Grammy Award for Best Pop Instrumental Performance, but it essentially marked the end of the band's initial commercial dominance as a Top 40 rock act. The influx of new players and the change in the band's sonic direction compelled Gregg Rolie and Neal Schon to leave. They eventually went on to form the successful radio rock act Journey.

Santana and McLaughlin recorded an album together, *Love, Devotion, Surrender* with members of Santana and the Mahavishnu Orchestra, along with percussionist Don Alias and organist Larry Young, both of whom made appearances on *Bitches Brew,* Miles Davis'

A RELIGIOUS EXPERIENCE

In an attempt to escape his drug indulgences and the heartbreak of seeing his young rock brethren—Jimi Hendrix, Janis Joplin, and Jim Morrison—die tragically early, Santana turned to spirituality.

He was first turned on to the spiritual teachings of Sri Chimnoy in 1972 by his friend, guitarist John McLaughlin of the Mahavishnu Orchestra. Santana respected and idolized McLaughlin as a person and as a musician, and at the time, he'd been searching for a spiritual grounding to offset his stratospheric rise on the rock scene.

Sri Chimnoy was a Hindu Guru who preached of "love, devotion, and surrender" to God. Under Sri Chinmoy, Santana adopted the name "Devadip," which roughly translated means, "The light of the lamp of the Supreme." Like other devotees, Santana adhered to a strict regimen of self-denial, deprivation, and asceticism.

"You don't drink, you don't smoke, you abstain from sex," said Santana in *Rolling Stone.* "There were a lot of regulations that I abided by for about nine or 10 years. But then I realized that it's just like West Point for the Marines. It's a discipline. But once you know discipline, you can move on" (Goldberg, 1980).

The belief system altered Santana's musical output. He and McLaughlin undertook an album project, called appropriately *Love, Devotion, and Surrender.*

Santana ultimately dropped the teachings of Sri Chimnoy in 1980. He discovered that his guru appeared to possess a lust for immortality. Santana began to suspect that the motives behind his teachings were not entirely selfless.

After a while you realize that he's just like anybody else, and gurus become very paranoid when their students transcend their philosophy. So I don't follow popes, swamis, gurus or anything like that any more. I don't have middle men between the Lord and myself. It's a personal relationship and I can hear the Lord telling me, There's a red light—stop. There's a green light—go. Yellow—slow down. (Gill, 1999)

1969 landmark. Santana continued moving further from his rock and blues roots, infuriating his record company and losing a few fans. He believed hardily in his art and didn't pay nearly as much attention to his commercial viability as his record company would have liked.

"I can claim inspiration and dynamism from just about anybody as long as they're sticking their neck out," he said. "I'm not into selling as much as I am expressing because I don't hear the cash register. A lot of people don't listen to music. All they can listen to is the cash register so I'm glad I'm on the other side" (Snowden, 1985).

Santana recruited jazz vocalist Leon Thomas for a tour of Japan, which was recorded for the live, high-energy *Lotus* album. But CBS records would not allow its release unless Santana condensed the material into a single album, down from its sprawling, three-record state. He did not agree to those terms and the album was available in the United States only as an expensive imported set. The group didn't flinch, despite CBS's lack of cooperation; they entered the studio to record *Welcome*, a work further demonstrating the artist's obsession with fusion and the spirituality of Sri Chinmoy.

Santana dug deeper into the avant-garde, dabbling in Eastern Indian and classical as well. He collaborated with Alice Coltrane, John Coltrane's widow, as well as jazz players Jack DeJohnette and Dave Holland, alums of Miles Davis. These recordings were well received by the various avant-garde critics, and he was widely respected for following his muse. But Santana's sales plummeted and Bill Graham, now in charge of his affairs, focused on returning his charge to the street-wise blues and Latin rock that made them stars.

Santana actually did get back on track, enough to stay viable through the 1980s. He experienced relative success, no easy feat considering the changing musical landscape of the period. One of the compromises Santana settled on with his record company was that he'd record traditional, Santana-styled band projects, while given the chance to make solo records outside the Santana purview. *The Swing of Delight,* for example, released in 1980, featured some of his musical heroes, including Herbie Hancock, Wayne Shorter, Ron Carter, and Tony Williams, all jazz greats.

During the 1980s, Santana insisted on shaking things up. He recorded *Havana Moon,* an album of songs inspired by his time in Tijuana and 1950s rock 'n' roll. It would become his best-selling work outside of his band to date. He undertook his first film score, composing the soundtrack to *La Bamba,* a biopic on the life of Ritchie Valens. Another solo album, *Blues for Salvador,* did not sell particularly well, but the title track won Carlos Santana his first Grammy Award for Best Rock Instrumental Performance. He left Columbia in 1990 after 22 years. His new label home, Polygram, gave him his own label to tinker with.

And tinker he did, retreating from recording for five years or so, after releasing *Milagro* in the spring of 1992. He returned in 1999 with *Supernatural,* which, unexpectedly, became the biggest hit of Santana's entire career. Featuring tracks co-written by guest stars like Rob Thomas of Matchbox 20, Eric Clapton, Lauryn Hill, and others, the album eventually sold over 10 million copies and earned eight Grammy Awards.

A follow-up, *Shaman,* utilized the same formula—Carlos Santana collaborating with several hot recording artists—but it didn't fare quite so well. Still, it landed in the Top 10 on the album charts and produced a couple of Top 40 hits, in "The Game of Love" featuring Michelle Branch, and "Why Don't You and I" with Nickelback's Chad Kroeger.

Santana recorded *Possibilities* with Herbie Hancock and Angelique Kidjo in 2005 and another Santana album *All That I Am* later the same year. The latter album featured further collaborations, including songs with Aerosmith's Steve Tyler, Joss Stone, Sean Paul, and Michelle Branch. Despite its repeated success, the formula had run its course.

"I'm proof that a musician can coexist with everyone from Wayne Shorter and Kirk Hammett to Placido Domingo and P.O.D.," exclaimed Carlos Santana as he reclined in his San Rafael, California, headquarters. "I'll even play with Kenny G., Billy Joel, or Elton John if the song is right" (Fox, Darrin, "Carlos Santana Spreads the Gospel of Tone," *Guitar Player,* May 2005, n.p.).

TECHNIQUE/STYLE

"Playing guitar is both a physical and a metaphysical experience," Santana has said. "It's a beautiful way to touch yourself and to touch other people. My goal is to always play the guitar from the heart" (Shapiro, Marc, *Carlos Santana: Back on Top,* New York: St. Martin, 2000, p. 2).

While Santana is as unique a stylist as anyone in rock music, he would rather express his work in abstract, almost New Age, terms rather than in concrete terms that might actually aid the study and practice of young players.

The component elements are well documented: the clear, piercing tone with roots in blues masters like B.B. King, the immaculate phrasing copped from a variety of soul singers, and a sense of economy that never wavered even when many of his contemporaries stepped up the gymnastic potential of their fretboards.

Combining rock, blues, fusion, and Latin music forms into a single dynamic blend, Santana holds the esteemed position of being the father of Latin Rock. Throughout his career he has distinguished himself as a master of tone, with an ability to shift seamlessly between scales, from minor pentatonic, natural minor, and Dorian sounds.

His formative years may help to explain the mélange of musical styles. His father, an accomplished mariachi violinist, taught Carlos the basics of music theory and instilled in him an understanding of composition and the value of a note. Latin music and its percussive rhythms, part of that education, formed the bedrock of all that he would play as a professional guitarist.

> What I'm learning more and more is that there are a lot of tones within myself that I can form simply by looking inward. Sure, Dumbles are incredible amps. But Alexander Dumble himself would tell you that Larry Carlton, Robben Ford, Eric Johnson, and myself have our own fingerprints with or without a Dumble amplifier. I can tell you every little piece of gear I've ever used, and you're still not going to sound like me. Your sound as an individual comes from sitting and playing for one, two, or three hours nonstop. It's where you get into this zone, and something takes over where the music truly plays you, and your mind is free of insecurities. The muscle memory and mechanics will handle themselves at a certain point, and you can get down to the matter of true expression that goes straight to the instrument from your heart. You have to reach inside yourself. There's absolutely no substitute for locking yourself away and not coming out until you have your own sound. (Fox, 2005)

Carlos Santana is far more comfortable talking about music in abstract or metaphorical terms than engaging in nuts and bolts analysis. One question about the amount of rhythmic experimentation when the band hammers its material into shape yielded a reply which boiled down to "The rhythm is like shoes. You can wear any style as long as it's the same color."

> I was reading this interview with Cecil Taylor and they were asking him what does he practice today with harmony, theory or scales or chords. He says he just practices one note until that note plugs into the universe. Some people call it the Spaloosh feeling. We call it helium and it's those moments when everything is intertwined. You can play almost any key and almost any beat you want and it's just happening. That's the something that consciously or unconsciously we're trying to create as much as possible. (Fox, 2005)

EQUIPMENT/GEAR

Carlos Santana hasn't altered his basic setup much since the 1960s. His main guitar is a custom Paul Reed Smith or a Yamaha SG-175B used for ballads. He plays a Santana II model guitar using PRS Santana III pickups with nickel covers and a tremolo, with .009–.042 gauge D'Addario strings.

Santana's guitar necks and fretboards are constructed out of a single solid piece of Brazilian Rosewood instead of the more traditional mahogany neck/Indian rosewood fretboard combination found in stock Santana models and other PRS guitars. The Brazilian Rosewood helps create the smooth, singing, glass-like tone for which he is famous. He also occasionally uses a classical guitar, the Alvarez Yairi CY127CE with Alvarez tension nylon strings.

In the 1970s, he was endorsed by Gibson. He played an SG Special with P-90 pickups at Woodstock.

Historically, Santana has run his guitars through a small Mesa/Boogie Mark I combo amp. But he has more recently turned to Dumble amplifiers. Specifically, Santana combines a Mesa/Boogie Mark I head running through a Mesa/Boogie cabinet with Altec 417-8H (or recently JBL E120s) speakers, and a Dumble Overdrive Reverb and/or a Dumble Overdrive Special running through a Marshall 4x12 cabinet with Celestion G12M "Greenback" speakers, depending on the desired sound. Dumble is a boutique concern known for its clean-sounding tone; it features Tone Tubby Alnico hemp-coned speakers and those speakers provide a durability as well as a mellower tone.

For rhythm guitar, he switches to Marshall amplifiers for distorted rhythm and Fender Twins for a cleaner sounding rhythm. Additionally, a Fender Cyber-Twin Amp is mostly used at home.

Given his preference for clean-sounding guitars, Santana does not utilize many effects in his playing. His PRS is connected to a Mu-Tron or Dunlop 535Q wah-wah pedal and a T-Rex Replica delay pedal then through a customized Jim Dunlop amp switcher that determines which amps or cabinets are used. He has also used an Ibanez Tube Screamer and a Heil talk box as well for an occasional solo.

Santana records with nearly the exact same setup, with the only difference that instead of a delay pedal he uses an old 1/4″ Studer tape machine or a Lexicon PCM-80 for about 350 ms of delay. He tracks everything in the control room, and he typically uses Royer ribbon mics on the 4x12s, and a Neumann microphone on the Mesa/Boogie 1x12.

ESSENTIAL READING

Fox, Darrin. "Carlos Santana Spreads the Gospel of Tone." *Guitar Player,* May 2005, n.p.
Gill, Chris. "Carlos Santana." *MOJO,* September 1999, n.p.
Goldberg, Michael. "Carlos Santana's Journey Toward Perfection." *Rolling Stone,* February 1980, n.p.
Grundy, Stuart, and John Tobler. *The Guitar Greats.* London: BBC Books, 1983, n.p.
Leng, Simon. *Soul Sacrifice: The Santana Story.* Firefly, 2000.
Shapiro, Mark. *Back on Top.* St. Martin's, 2000.
Snowden, Don. "Cooling into the Norm." *Musician,* March 1985, n.p.

ESSENTIAL WORK

"Black Magic Woman/Gypsy Queen" (1970)
"Jungle Strut" (1971)
"She's Not There" (1977)
"Song of the Wind" (1972)
"Soul Sacrifice" (1969)

ESSENTIAL LISTENING

Abraxas (Columbia/Legacy, 1970)
Blues for Salvador (Columbia, 1987)
Caravanserai (Columbia, 1972)
Lotus (Columbia, 1974)
Santana (Columbia/Legacy, 1969)
Santana III (Columbia/Legacy, 1971)

Slash

Before the tastes and whims of America's youth veered toward alternative music styles, Guns N' Roses were the last great rock 'n' roll band. When the Los Angeles quintet exploded onto the scene in the mid-1980s, their style, presence, and potent image ushered in a new era of no-nonsense hard rock and metal. With the slightly silly glam metal holding forth as the reigning style of guitar rock, Guns N' Roses came in like a bandit and robbed the scene of all its glitz, in the process offering up grittier, more traditional slabs of rock music, inspired more by the pre-punk rock 1970s than the flashier shred of the 1980s. Axl Rose has on record stated that the band was heavily inspired by bands like Aerosmith, the Rolling Stones, and AC/DC and that the sound of their landmark debut recording *Appetite for Destruction* was based on the influence of those bands. Like most brilliant acts, Guns N' Roses enjoyed worldwide success for a very brief time, from 1987 through 1993. Clashing personalities, along with alcohol and drug abuse expedited the band's self-destruction.

Admittedly, they were not nice boys, which is why their presence on the rock 'n' roll scene was so refreshing. They reintroduced risk and danger to the art form. They were ugly, political, misogynist, and violent; but they were also funny, vulnerable, and occasionally sensitive, as their breakthrough hit, "Sweet Child O' Mine," demonstrated. While guitarists Slash and Izzy Stradlin spewed hard and venomous riffs, Rose screeched out his tales of sex, drugs, and sleaze in the big city.

Bassist Duff McKagan and drummer Steven Adler served up agile and powerful tempos and rhythms, but also kept the music appropriately loose. There hadn't been a hard rock band this raw or talented in years, and they were given added weight by Rose's primal rage and Slash's searing licks. As the 1980s turned into the 1990s, the quintet ruled the rock world like dictatorial kings, stomping around and leaving nothing but tire tracks in its wake.

But their existence had been precarious to begin with. Band personalities were mercurial and, later, irascible. Thrust into the spotlight, they had difficulty coping with the rigors of fame, and they all at one time or another turned to hard drugs and alcohol. Their moods shifted, and they turned on each other. Egotism, especially Axl's, made them all very difficult to handle.

But it was an amazing journey while it lasted. For six or so years, nobody could out-rock Guns N' Roses. *Appetite for Destruction* is widely hailed as the greatest debut album of all time and one of the best albums of the rock era, selling 27 million copies worldwide. The band's second recordings, 1991's *Use Your Illusion I* and *Use Your Illusion II* debuted on the two highest spots on the *Billboard 200* and have sold a combined 14 million copies.

In January 2007, Slash was honored with a star on the Rock Walk of Fame, his name being placed side by side with friends and legends Jimmy Page and Eddie Van Halen. "Welcome to the Jungle" is considered to be one of the greatest hard rock anthems of all time, ranked #2 on VH1's 40 Greatest Metal Songs; "Paradise City" is ranked #21 on the same list. "Sweet Child O' Mine" placed #37 on *Guitar World*'s list of the "100 Greatest Guitar Solos." In March 2005, *Q* magazine placed it at #6 in its list of the "100 Greatest Guitar Tracks." The introduction's famous D-flat riff was also voted #1 riff of all time by the readers of *Total Guitar* magazine and was also named as one of *Rolling Stone*'s "40 Greatest Songs that Changed the World."

EARLY YEARS

Saul Hudson was born in Hampstead, England on July 23, 1965 and raised in Stoke-on-Trent, Staffordshire, England. Both his parents worked in the entertainment business. His mother, a black American, was a clothing designer. His father, a white Englishman, functioned as an art director for a record company. When Hudson was 11 he moved with his mother to Los Angeles, leaving his father behind in England to rejoin them in Los Angeles years later.

Hudson had a rough transition to life in the United States. He was an outcast at school and had trouble making friends. His unorthodox appearance and long hair set him apart uncomfortably from his classmates. And southern California conservatism rubbed him the wrong way even as a kid. Surrounded by the eccentric friends of his parents, he lived a bohemian life at home and grew accustomed to the craziness of the music world. He would later admit that this sort of lifestyle prepared him for coping with the stress of the music industry and its straddling of art and commerce.

In the mid-1970s, his parents separated and Hudson moved in with his grandmother. It was at the time that Slash found a passion: BMX riding. Slash plunged into this hobby, found camaraderie in the pursuit of the sport, and was quite good at it. In fact, as a semiprofessional rider he won several awards, including cash prizes, in regional BMX competitions.

When he was 15, in middle school, he added another passion to his life: the guitar. His grandmother gave him his first guitar, an acoustic with, for some reason, just a single string. The quality of the guitar, though, didn't matter. He played it all day. His devotion to the instrument distracted him from school, and he'd often skip classes all together and play guitar all day. And when he didn't play guitar he was out on the streets stealing motorcycles and minibikes.

He took lessons briefly, but he had little patience for the deliberate approach to learning. After a few weeks of "Mary Had a Little Lamb" he abandoned the traditional lessons and simply had his instructor show up and guide him. Hudson would learn at his own pace, which was rapid indeed, and his instructor would give him playing suggestions. The technique worked, and Slash maintained an intense interest in the instrument.

Music also helped Hudson build confidence. When his classmates discovered he had talent and they heard him play, they accepted his odd appearance and idiosyncrasies more willingly. He no longer concerned himself with being an outcast.

Enamored with the guitar, he quit school, listened to music and played his instrument all day, often for 12 hours a day. His immersion in music led him to meet a variety of personalities and a vast network of musicians. One day at a playground, with Hudson doing BMX tricks on a half-pipe, he met a kid on a skateboard. Actually, he had fallen hard off of his skateboard and Hudson went to see if he needed any help. The fallen boy happened to be Steven Adler, a music enthusiast himself. The two hit it off, and they listened to Kiss records together. Eventually, they formed a band called Road Crew.

> I started from the get go. As soon as I could play a bar chord, I started playing in bands. I don't remember a space in time when I was learning to play and not playing with somebody else. I was so focused, even in junior high, knowing that this was the only thing I ever wanted to do that I went through a lot of people because they were not willing to give up everything— school, home—just to jam. Steve is the only guy I stuck with, because he was as into it as I was. (Unattributed, "Low Life In The Fast Line," *Kerrang*, September 1996)

MUSIC

Guns N' Roses formed in June 1985. Initially, the band consisted of singer Axl Rose, guitarists Tracii Guns and Izzy Stradlin, bassist Duff McKagan, and drummer Rob Gardner. The name was derived from the last names of Guns and Rose and makes reference to its members' previous bands, Hollywood Rose and LA Guns.

Axl Rose, born William Bruce Rose Jr., was raised in a tough, working-class Indiana family. Abused by his stepfather, he dropped out of high school and devoted himself early on to a life of crime, compiling a long rap sheet by age 20. His misdemeanors included public intoxication, criminal trespass, and contributing to the delinquency of a minor. To separate himself from a sordid future, and a life of crime, he moved to Los Angeles in 1982. He established himself in Los Angeles as a competent front man and began assembling bands.

An ELO and Queen fan, the singer became friends with Izzy Stradlin, and the two joined forces with guitarist Guns and McKagan.

Slash entered the picture when Guns left to reform his former band, L.A. Guns. The lineup—Rose, Hudson, Stradlin, McKagan, and Gardner—was set for now. Slash recalls the time he first met Axl.

> When we first hooked up, it was pretty uneventful, the first time we met actually I answered an ad that Izzy and Axl had in the paper looking for a guitar player. I went down there to where they were staying, which were some little guest room off of a house above Sunset. It was real dark, it was one room, they had like a bed that took up 75 percent of it, a TV that took up another 10 percent, and there was like 15 percent walking space. (Broadley, Erin, "Slash and Marc Canter of *Reckless Road*," *suicidegirls.com*, February 2008)

That first time lasted only a short while. Hudson, now calling himself "Slash," tired of Rose's demeanor and decided he could only take so much. One night he got into a fight with a fan in the crowd at a Troubadour gig. Another night Rose nearly killed himself when he threw himself out of Hudson's car. Hudson grew tedious with the unexpected behavior and left.

A few months later, Rose found Slash working at a Hollywood video store and asked him if he'd like to play with Stradlin and McKagan. Hudson liked playing with Stradlin, a rhythm guitar player, especially, and so, despite his reservations and a small dose of animosity toward Rose, he consented. Guns N' Roses was formed.

"As much as I was really unsure about dealing with Axl again, I really liked Izzy and I liked Duff, obviously, so it seemed like maybe it'd be a cool idea. I went and jammed with

Izzy one night and he had the song called 'Don't Cry' and we put the guitars together and that's really what started it" (Broadley, 2008).

* * *

Based on the reputation of its players—Rose, McKagan, and Slash had all been thieves of some sort—the band quickly developed a bad boy image. This suited the band just fine. They were more than willing to add the thrill of danger to their stage show. McKagan, who had northwest roots, plotted a Pacific Coast tour to Seattle. When Gardner chickened out on the tour, the band replaced him with Slash's boyhood friend, Steven Adler.

The band embarked only to break down 100 miles north of Los Angeles. They hitchhiked the rest of the way. "That's really what cemented the band. The chemistry just on a human level between the five of us . . . just as guys who stick to their guns with what it is they want to do. That trip really had a lot to do with it" (Broadley, 2008).

The road trip also toughened the boys up. When they returned they were essentially a street gang more than a band, ready for anything. They attacked the Los Angeles music scene with a vengeance. The songs they

Courtesy of Neil Zlozower

wrote and the gigs they played grew more explosive every day, so dynamic was the band's chemistry.

The climate in the city at the time agreed perfectly with what Slash and the boys were doing. They were the perfect antidote to the excessive glam metal—hair spray and spandex—acts that saturated Hollywood. Bands like Motley Crue, Ratt, Warrant, and all the post-Van Halen offshoots dominated Sunset Boulevard.

"We were sort of like the ugly ducklings of that whole thing. We didn't fit in with any of it. We were the black sheep and we enjoyed that; we loved the fact that we were the scary band out of the bunch. We hated the rest of them and we provided a kind of entertainment that was very seedy" (Broadley, 2008).

As a group, they were driven and inspired. They had focus and passion. They were together all the time. They experienced life as a band in a seedy one-room apartment, motivated only by the prospect of becoming superstars.

It didn't take long.

Guns N' Roses released their first EP in 1986, a self-produced, demo-styled project entitled *Live ?!*@ Like a Suicide*. While it didn't sell, it did lead to a contract with Geffen Records. The following year, 1987, the band released their debut, and what an album it was. *Appetite for Destruction* is a masterpiece and the best-selling debut in history. Oddly enough, the album didn't start selling until a year after its release, when music television put the song "Sweet Child O' Mine" into heavy rotation. The song, and the album, shot straight to #1, and Guns N' Roses became one of the biggest rock bands in the world.

Part of the album's appeal lied in its timing. To that point in 1980s rock, hair metal had dominated. "Hair metal" represented rock as nothing more than girls and guitars. Hair metal bands crooned about parties and good times. Guns N' Roses, the outsiders they were, turned all that inside out. They made nasty, dangerous, street-tough music, and it helped to offset the preponderance of all that good-timey stuff.

On the surface, Guns N' Roses may appear to celebrate the same things as their peers— namely, sex, liquor, drugs, and rock and roll—but there is a nasty edge to their songs, since Axl Rose doesn't see much fun in the urban sprawl of L.A. and its parade of heavy metal thugs, cheap women, booze, and crime. The music is as nasty as the lyrics, wallowing in a bluesy, metallic hard rock borrowed from Aerosmith, AC/DC, and countless faceless hard rock bands of the early '80s. It's a primal, sleazy sound that adds grit to already grim tales. (Erlewine, Stephen Thomas, allmusic.com)

After "Sweet Child O' Mine" played incessantly across the national airwaves, the band reissued their debut single "Welcome to the Jungle," and it screamed into the Top 10. The same went for "Paradise City."

The acknowledgment of Slash's effectiveness as a composer took a while to surface. But his work on *Appetite* was astonishing. As a lead guitarist, he recognized the value of a great rhythm player like Izzy Stradlin. The solid and tuneful texture of Stradlin's rhythm work on *Appetite* and the way it naturally interwove with Slash's lead playing made for complex, guitar-driven music.

By the end of 1988, they released *G N' R Lies*, which paired four acoustic songs, including the Top Five hit "Patience," with their first EP.

"It was a collaborative effort, every single song. Then we became very successful at that time but we were this vagabond bunch of drunken gypsies that sort of stuck together. But we were still pretty naïve really in a lot of ways" (Broadley, 2008).

After multiple world tours, the band commenced production on the follow-up to *Appetite*. Expectations were high. Tensions in the band were as well. During the debauchery following the release and triumph of the album, band members also began indulging in drugs. In October of 1990, the band fired Adler, claiming that his drug dependency caused his playing to deteriorate. He was replaced by Matt Sorum, drummer for another LA-based band called the Cult.

During recording, the band added Dizzy Reed on keyboards. By the time the sessions were finished, the new album had become two new albums, adding a significant delay to the process. A year after its intended release date, the albums *Use Your Illusion I* and *Use Your Illusion II* were released in September 1991.

The pair of recordings showed that Guns N' Roses wanted to become more than just a full-throttle guitar band. There were attempts at balladry, acoustic blues, and soulfulness, and Axl's lyrics were unexpectedly introspective.

At least they proved, momentarily, that they were ready to work hard and issue recordings more regularly. There was one additional and quite unexpected obstacle though. Nirvana's juggernaut album *Nevermind* hit the top of the charts in 1992. And while that doesn't seem like it should have had a deleterious effect on a solid rock band like Guns N' Roses, the fact was that the emergence of Nirvana precipitated change in the overall climate of rock music. Dozens and dozens of popular rock bands—with all their pretensions and rock star indulgences—suddenly came across as tired and dated. Nirvana signaled the arrival of alternative rock, a massive musical revolution that essentially steamrolled everything in its path.

* * *

Axl Rose handled the change by becoming more demanding. He grew egotistical and unreasonable and threw tantrums onstage. When Izzy Stradlin left the band by the end of 1991, Guns N' Roses lost a valuable ingredient. Gilby Clarke replaced him.

Guns N' Roses released an album of punk covers *The Spaghetti Incident?* in 1993. It enjoyed a warm reception, but it didn't tide their fans over like a fresh new studio album would have. By the middle of 1994, there were rumors flying that the band was about to break up, since Rose wanted to pursue a new, more industrial direction and Slash wanted to stick with their blues-inflected hard rock. The volatility of the experience destroyed the pleasure of making music within the band.

> I don't think volatility fuels anything. I don't agree with people who think you need that controversy to make music. It's not really conducive to writing songs. If you have chemistry, you don't need all that other shit [laughs]. Anyhow, but it started off cool and I liked Axl . . . he came and stayed at my house but then the yin and yang of Axl's personality started to present itself. One minute he was really, really cool and somebody that I liked a lot. You could spend almost two days with him like that. Then the smallest little thing would turn around and change his personality completely. I'm pretty even keeled; nothing really fazes me. I'm probably like that to the extent that some people don't understand how I can be so fuckin' blasé about things [laughs]. So we had a real contrast going on, but the music was cool. When we had a good time, we had a great f*cking time. But when it was bad, I couldn't understand the origins of some of these issues and why they would be blown out of proportion to the extent that they were. To him, it meant everything. But to me, I could just never understand it. (Broadley, 2008)

* * *

The band remained in limbo for several more years to the point that it had become something of a joke. To avoid the ridicule, Slash resurfaced in 1994 with a side project called Slash's Snakepit.

As the story goes, Slash started jamming out some material with drummer Matt Sorum in his "Snakepit," his studio, named after his fondness for snakes. He and Sorum had intended for the material to be presented as new Guns N' Roses songs. Gilby Clarke contributed some rhythm guitar, and McKagan some bass. But when the crew brought their new stuff to Axl, he flat out rejected it. Disappointed and frustrated, Slash decided he'd use it for his own purposes. They recruited singer Eric Dover to lay down vocals and the lineup was set.

The band released *It's Five O'Clock Somewhere* in February of 1995. It eventually surpassed platinum status worldwide and satisfied temporarily the fans fed up with Axl's shenanigans. As far as Guns N' Roses fans were concerned any material was good material, and Slash's Snakepit benefited from the work of a handful of Guns N' Roses denizens. It also enjoyed production services from Guns N' Roses engineer Mike Clink and A&R man Tom Zutaut, making it a Guns N' Roses recording without the "Rose."

"What sets Slash apart from most guitar heroes is that he seems genuinely uninterested in showing off how fast he can play or how long he can jam. Instead he lavishes his creative energy on the rhythm riffs and instrumental arrangements, working and reworking them until each line seems to snake out and coil back as though it had a life of its own" (Considine, J. D., *Rolling Stone,* February 23, 1995).

Because Rose prevented any new material from being released by the Guns N' Roses camp indefinitely, Slash opted to leave the band in 1996. This left Rose as its only original member. He retreated into seclusion.

*   *   *

In 2002, Slash formed another important rock group, Velvet Revolver, with drummer Matt Sorum, bassist Duff McKagan, and singer Scott Weiland from the popular alt-rock band Stone Temple Pilots. With the discovery that the Guns N' Roses chemistry was still going strong, the trio began pushing around some new music for what became known as "the Project."

The band signed a deal with RCA and spent the rest of 2003 gigging and recording to get the act underway. RCA announced an April 2004 release for their debut, *Contraband,* but the date was then pushed to May, and finally to June. Velvet Revolver also released the single "Slither," an ambitious rocker spearheaded by Slash's signature guitar sound. The single climbed the rock charts, and the album came out to general appreciation.

Velvet Revolver's sophomore effort, *Libertad,* followed in 2007, distinguished from its predecessor in terms of coherence and the muscular production and big guitars of Brendan O'Brien, a colleague of Weiland's who'd worked with Stone Temple Pilots.

TECHNIQUE/STYLE

Entirely self-taught, Slash learned to play guitar by listening to records and trying to mimic what he heard. Playing as much as 12 hours a day, one of the first songs he learned was Deep Purple's "Smoke on the Water." Slash's techniques hail from the late 1970s. He uses a wide, fast vibrato and uses his left hand for speed. He also uses pull-offs and hammer-ons to sound notes. His right hand does muting, and you will see him during some rhythm and lead passages rest his hand on the bridge to make notes sound more percussive.

Despite his significant body of work, a study of Slash's work must begin with his masterwork. *Appetite for Destruction* still serves as Guns N' Roses' definitive album and the foundation of Slash's searing guitar style. The disc's trio of classics, "Welcome to the Jungle," "Sweet Child O' Mine," and "Paradise City," were all powered by his hell-bent Gibson axes.

At the soul of his very best work—and at the root of his style—is Slash's love for blues, specifically the British blues of players like Clapton and Jeff Beck. You can hear their influence resonate in Slash's heavy use of vibrato, which he adorns with pinched overtones, subtle moments of feedback, and the full-tilt application of major pentatonic and minor harmonic scales in his hot rod solos.

"Paradise City" remains the defining showcase for Slash's rhythmic vocabulary.

CHINESE DEMOCRACY

Fifteen years in the making, *Chinese Democracy* is, supposedly, the upcoming sixth studio album by Guns N' Roses. When released, it will be the band's first album since 1993 and their first album of original studio material since the simultaneous release of the pair of *Use Your Illusion* albums.

Unfortunately, the very concept of *Chinese Democracy* has become a monstrosity. Geffen Records has purportedly dumped more than $13 million into this train wreck, giving various commentators cause enough to dub it "The Most Expensive Album Never Made." *Blender* magazine called it one of the 20 "Biggest Record Company Screw-Ups of All Time."

Recording for *Chinese Democracy* began in 1994. But by that time, the band was so splintered that nothing really got started or completed. Slash eventually left the band in 1996, which hampered the effort considerably. In his autobiography, *Slash,* Slash writes that his departure from the band in 1996 was caused by "Axl wanting control to the point that the rest of us were strangled" (blabbermouth, November 9, 2007).

The whole mess started when Axl and the band's manager had the other members of the band sign a contract that gave Axl control of the group name if they ever broke up. Then on August 31, 1995, Axl dropped a bomb on Duff and Slash, the only remaining members at the time, when he sent them a letter saying he was leaving the band and taking the name with him under the terms of the contract.

Slash was replaced by Nine Inch Nails touring guitarist Robin Finck, Tommy Stinson replaced McKagan, and Josh Freese joined as the drummer. Many other guitarists were recruited to fill in for Slash, such as Brian May of Queen, Sebastian Bach (Skid Row), Buckethead, and Dave Navarro.

Axl has taken the show on the road and played a few new Guns N' Roses tunes. But the specter of a new album does not appear optimistic. Most recently it was promised *Chinese Democracy* would be released in 2006, but that didn't happen. Then a 2007 release date came and went and everything fell silent again. Incredibly, the album is now slated for release in late 2008, or early 2009.

His playing on the number is relentless, constantly shifting between power chords, low-string riffs, and arpeggios, creating the juggernaut momentum that propels the tale of the band's struggle for survival in L.A.'s rock and roll underbelly. Throughout the song, Slash also deploys multi-string bends to approximate the weeping steel guitars that are a hallmark of classic country music. Another flourish Slash nicked from country players is the simultaneous use of a flatpick and finger-picking, which allows him to vary the sound of his chords or blend power-strokes with plucked frills. (No attribution, "Get That Slash Tone and Style," www.Gibson.com)

Slash holds his pick between his index finger and thumb, and he sometimes plucks strings with his free fingers. He creates tonal variations within his songs, such as the ones in "Paradise City," by changing pickup selections as he plays. One of his preferred lead settings for lead is the neck pickup with the tone control rolled back. This is also known as "woman tone" and is a favorite of Eric Clapton, too. He also uses feedback to sustain notes on solos and intros.

EQUIPMENT/GEAR

Slash's first electric was a copy of a Gibson Explorer, but he certainly built an imposing collection following that one. Today, Slash owns several late 1950s Les Paul Standards. Once, a treasured Standard that originally belonged to Aerosmith's Joe Perry came into Slash's possession. Perry begged Slash to return it, but he didn't, not until Perry's fiftieth birthday.

He also owns a 1959 Les Paul copy, a 1956 Les Paul gold top, a 1969 Les Paul custom, and several new Les Pauls that he plays live. There are also a 1959 Gibson Flying V, a 1958 Gibson Explorer, two Ernie Ball/Music Man Silhouettes, a 1952 Telecastor, a 1965 Fender Stratocaster, both a 1963 and a 1965 Gibson Melody Maker, and a 1960s Gibson SG, all of which are used for recording.

Slash occasionally plays slide, and when he does he uses a Travis Bean electric. His acoustics include a Guild 12-string, a Gibson J-100, a Martin D-28 acoustic, a Ramirez classical, and a dobro. Gibson also made a Slash Signature Les Paul Classic model with the Snakepit insignia. Most of Slash's guitars are kept entirely stock.

Back in 1999, Slash started showing off his newest signature guitar, a sweet double neck Slash designed and Guild guitars manufactured. The Crossroads Double Neck changes from a wailing six-string to a mellow Guild 12-string with the flip of a mini-switch. The body is carved from a solid mahogany block with an acoustic chamber under the 12-string side. This chamber has a traditional rosewood bridge for a true acoustic 12-string sound. The body of the electric side is solid and sports Seymour Duncan pickups.

To get his full rich tone, Slash has always had a no-nonsense, stripped-down approach to his gear. Distortion pedals and a trusty wah-wah were part of his sonic arsenal early on, but even as Guns N' Roses were being courted by labels and tearing up clubs on Los Angeles's Sunset Strip, Slash was already relying exclusively on Marshall amps and cabinets to generate his monolithic sound. And he changed tones the good old-fashioned way: by flicking his Les Paul's pickup selector to different settings, often mid-solo (www.Gibson.com).

The core of Slash's lead sound comes from Clapton's searing work in Cream. Slash's leads in "Sweet Child O' Mine" possess a warm, high, wailing sound, achieved with a humbucker-equipped Les Paul or an SG—by moving the pickup switch straight up to the rhythm position, rolling the tone knob all the way down, and turning up a good high-gain amp like a Marshall.

Though not much of an effects user, Slash often employs a Jim Dunlop rack-mounted Crybaby wah controlled by a volume pedal, a noise reduction pedal, a compressor, a Yamaha SPX 900 multieffects unit, a Boss DD-5 digital delay, a 10-band graphic equalizer, a Boss GE-7 graphic e.q. for solos, and a Dunlop Heil talk box. The DBX compressor and Yamaha SPX 900 for clean sound processing. He favors the Nady 950-GT Wireless System. All signals go through the Bob Bradshaw Custom Splitter System.

Marshall produces a line of Slash amps—100-watt tube heads with two pull knobs for channel switching and extra gain. On stage he prefers a pig-pile of these, including a 50-watt head dedicated exclusively for the talk box. He also boasts four, straight-faced 4x12 cabinets, arranged in two stacks and equipped with 70-watt Celestion Vintage 30 speakers. The two top cabs are driven by two separate JCM SLASH signature amps dedicated to his clean sound. The bottoms are for grungier tones. The studio amps are Marshall 2555 with EL34 output tubes and the Marshall JCM 800 (modified) with 6550 output tubes.

The Slash Signature amp, the first Marshall signature amp for any artist, is based on the amp Slash has used since the beginning, the Jubilee 2555 head of 1987. Many great artists, including Hendrix, have sworn by Marshalls, but something unique about Slash's playing style led the company to recognize him above other guitarists.

As for strings, Slash uses Ernie Ball Slinky R.P.S. strings of gauge 11–48. He likes to play with the heaviest picks he can find and prefers purple Dunlop Tortex 1.14 mm picks. Most of his live guitars are equipped with Seymour Duncan Alnico II pro humbuckers.

ESSENTIAL READING

blabbermouth, November 9, 2007.
Bozza, Anthony, and Slash. *Slash.* New York: Harper Entertainment, 2007.
Broadley, Erin. "Slash and Marc Canter of *Reckless Road*." suicidegirls.com, February 2008.
Canter, Marc. *Reckless Road: Guns N' Roses and the Making of Appetite for Destruction.* Shoot Hip Press; 3rd edition, November 1, 2007.
Considine, J. D. *Rolling Stone,* February 23, 1995.
Erlewine, Stephen Thomas. allmusic.com.
No attribution. "Get That Slash Tone and Style." www.Gibson.com.
Unattributed. "Low Life in the Fast Line." *Kerrang,* September 1996.

ESSENTIAL WORK

"November Rain" (1991)
"Paradise City" (1987)
"Set Me Free" (Velvet Revolver, 2004)
"Slither" (Velvet Revolver, 2004)
"Sweet Child O' Mine" (1987)
"Welcome to the Jungle" (1987)

ESSENTIAL LISTENING

Appetite for Destruction (Geffen, 1987)
Contraband (Velvet Revolver, Geffen, 2004)
Use Your Illusion I (Geffen, 1991)
Use Your Illusion II (Geffen, 1991)

ESSENTIAL VIEWING

Guns N' Roses Welcome to the Videos (Geffen, 1998)

Pete Townshend

While Jimmy Page was exploring mysticism, Eric Clapton was delving into his blues roots, and Hendrix was off on his own rather psychedelic experience, Pete Townshend was busy communicating with regular people. He was rock's first angry guy, a musician and composer who could speak the language of social angst both through his lyrics and on his guitar. Just as Hendrix and Clapton were larger than life and Page was erecting a stairway to heaven, Townshend preferred to remain loud and live, and in his audience's face. More than any other successful rock player of the 1960s and beyond, Townshend related to and empathized with the people who bought his records.

In this way, he made guitar playing more accessible than the others. Again, while Hendrix's mind-boggling solos were dazzling and technically improbable, Townshend banged on his guitar like a violent delinquent, played brilliant rhythm chords, and wrapped up his shows by destroying his guitar altogether in a show of solidarity with his audience. Many say his guitar smashing—one of the first instances of guitar destruction onstage— impressed a young Jimi Hendrix in 1965 and led directly to Jimi burning his.

Certainly, Townshend offered much more than just an outlet for frustration. He was one of the greatest songwriters of the rock era, and one of rock's first superstars, with entertaining antics like his trademark windmill strums, washes of distortion, and leaping power chords. Townshend was also the first guitarist to "stack" his speaker cabinets onstage, creating the full stack of amps that are now synonymous with rock 'n' roll.

Also synonymous with rock 'n' roll is his band, the Who, one of the most turbulent and intense acts in the genre's history. Consisting of four very divergent and incompatible personalities, the Who single-handedly exploded rock conventions with a dynamic, reckless approach. "It is impossible to convey to anyone who never saw the Who on stage how such totally opposed, combative, feuding, contentious, brawling, individually brilliant young musicians could blend into such a perfect gestalt of mind and music whose power, rage, and compassion was both anguish and sheer, unadulterated delight" (Altham, Keith, "Who, me? The Who in Britain," liner notes, *The Who Thirty Years of Maximum R&B*, MCA, 1994).

As the primary songwriter for the group, Townshend deserves much of the credit for this reputation. Through 11 studio albums, Townshend wrote over 100 songs for the Who—not to mention 100 or more in addition for his solo albums and various miscellaneous work.

With the Who behind him, Townshend scorched a trail through the mid to late 1960s and the 1970s as a guitar player, composer, and later, singer and multi-instrumentalist. Along the way, he wrote some of rock's most memorable songs "I Can't Explain," "Pinball

Wizard," and "Baba O'Riley," and introduced more than one generation to the power of the electric guitar.

Thanks to their quality material and their unpredictable demeanor, both onstage and off, the Who became a must-see band. They gave disaffected youth rallying cry after rallying cry and fans of hard rock and pop a blast of fresh air. Early on, Townshend, the spokesperson for the band, if not the true front man, gave kids hope that the rock 'n' roll dream could be theirs also. At his best, he distilled the pent-up energy and chaos of rock 'n' roll into its purest form, while at the same time infusing their music with literate vision and insight.

"For years, Townshend mirrored the hopes and fears of the 'give it to me now not later' generation. He wrote a whole series of brilliant cameos of the times, captured the feelings of millions of young people" (Altham, liner notes, 1994).

Despite regular internal fighting, the group's longevity was assured thanks to Townshend's knack for producing great three-minute singles that reflected the mood and feelings experienced by his audience. In later years, he would say that his writing reflected what the band's early Shepherds Bush audience wanted him to write about. No subject escaped the scope of Townshend's literary prowess, although some had to be heavily disguised. Divorce, cross-dressing, and masturbation were just some of the subjects he turned into hits, and all before he was 22. Few of his contemporaries could match this ability to take such serious subject matter and turn it into acceptable pop.

His first major youth anthem, his first of many, was "My Generation," and the first song he brought to the Who in rehearsals was "I Can't Explain." With these aggressive songs, he emphasized the conflicting relationship between youth and authority. At the same time, thanks to this musical illustration of defiance and rebellion, the Who became the first entry in what would later become punk music. This happened before the term "punk" even existed.

From their Mod-era so-called "maximum R&B" to rock operas like "Tommy" and "Quadrophenia" and classic 1970s hard rock, the Who reigned supreme. In their prime, they were a unit whose individual personalities fused into a larger-than-life whole and into one of history's very best and most anarchic rock 'n' roll bands. They were invited into the Rock 'n' Roll Hall of Fame in 1990, in the fifth class of inductions.

Townshend was awarded the Ivor Novello Award by his songwriter peers in 1981 and was given the British Phonograph Industry Award in 1983 for service to the British music industry. He has been nominated for two Grammys and an Academy Award (for the *Tommy* film score). He was most recently honored with the 1993 Tony Award for Best Original Score for *Tommy* on Broadway.

EARLY YEARS

Townshend was born in Chiswick, London, in 1945 just days after the German surrender of World War II. Like fellow future Who bandmates John Entwistle and Roger Daltrey, Townshend grew up in the middle-class London suburb of Shepherd's Bush. He was born into a musical family. His father Cliff was a professional saxophonist in the Squadronaires Royal Air Force dance band, and his mother Betty was a singer with the Sidney Torch Orchestra. Not surprisingly, given the circumstances, Townshend exhibited a fascination with music at an early age, a situation augmented by the fact that Pete toured with his parents as a young child.

He also had significant exposure to American rock 'n' roll and watched the film *Rock Around the Clock*, with Bill Haley and the Comets, repeatedly with his friends. When he turned 11 his parents separated and sent their son to live with his maternal grandmother, a rather unstable woman that Pete didn't like all that much.

Still, she knew enough to buy him his first guitar, a "cheap Spanish thing," at the age of 12. Guitars weren't unusual to him or his family. His father played the guitar when he was young and so did his Uncle Jack, who worked for Kalamazoo, a subsidiary of Gibson. Pete's original intention was to take after his father, a man he admired, and play the saxophone. But he didn't take to that particular instrument and he dropped it, first in favor of the harmonica, then for the guitar.

Pete actually bristled when he saw the guitar his grandmother bought him. He'd been expecting a nice guitar from his dad for Christmas that same year, but it turned out his grandmother decided to make the purchase and do the presenting. Pete resented the guitar, and he had some difficult playing it. For a time he tried learning the banjo instead.

To make matters worse, he had a difficult time in school. As a sensitive kid, he became intensely aware of his large nose, often a subject of derision at school. It embarrassed him, and he often sought escape, which came in the form of music.

But instead of wallowing in self-pity he chose defiance. When he started performing he cursed the audience if it appeared they were laughing at him or his nose. Then he grew increasingly angry, and this hot streak began to run through his early days as a musician.

MUSIC

In 1961, Townshend enrolled at Ealing Art College and, a year later, he and John Entwistle, a friend from grammar school, assembled their first band. They called themselves the Confederates; Townshend, then 14, played banjo, Chris Sherwin the drums, and Entwistle the trumpet. Sherwin and Townshend didn't get along, and a rift at their school playground resulted in the band breaking up.

From there they moved into skiffle, a popular music influential to British youth in the late 1950s and early 1960s. Rock 'n' roll was also burgeoning in America and the United Kingdom, with acts like Chuck Berry, Cliff Richard, and Elvis Presley all surging in popularity. Townshend bought a reasonably good guitar, a little amplifier, and went electric.

One day when he and Entwistle were at home playing, Pete's grandmother told him to turn the noise down. Pete, still impatient when it came to his relationship with his caregiver, yelled back and told her to be quiet. He rose up, grabbed the amplifier, and heaved it at her, breaking it into pieces. He'd just bought it; worked three years to earn the money. In essence, it marked a sign of things to come.

At school in 1962, Pete attended lectures by jazz, classical, and experimental musicians. He painted during class and listened to musicians discuss their art. The experience inspired Townshend to create art and music of his own. During school, he met an American student named Tom Wright. A photography major, Wright heard Townshend playing his guitar and asked him over to his flat to teach him some licks. When Townshend arrived he found that Wright had an impressive collection of blues, R&B, and jazz recordings that were impossible to find in the United Kingdom. They hit it off, delving into Wright's equally impressive supply of marijuana, and Pete absorbed all the music Wright had to offer.

In terms of the blues and R&B, Townshend related more to the roughhewn solos of artists like John Lee Hooker and Chuck Berry over the more refined work of articulate masters like Buddy Guy and B.B. King. He also developed an appreciation for the work of Ray Charles, Jimmy Smith, and Mose Allison.

Following the breakup of the Confederates, Pete and John joined the Detours, a band led by a sheet metal welder named Roger Daltry who also played guitar. Daltry was a combative personality, prone to fights when he didn't get things his way. The Detours, who played around London, were nothing if not versatile; Entwistle doubled on the bass and trumpet, and Daltry played the trombone in addition to the guitar. They performed pop and skiffle as well as country music. They shuffled their lineup a few times and finally settled on Daltry singing and a crazy new 19-year-old drummer named Keith Moon, who'd been playing with a Shadows'-style instrumental/surf band called the Beachcombers, joining on to play the kit.

Together, the Detours became a prototype for the Who. In 1963, they opened for Johnny Kid and the Pirates at a gig in southwest London. The Pirates had a reputation for power and wild antics on stage, so the experience proved to be a big influence on the Detours. The guitarist for the Pirates, Mick Green, was one of Pete's first influences. "He was the first big note bender, particularly on the G. And you'd freak over him and wonder how he got that sound. I went backstage to see him and I asked him if I could play his guitar and he said, 'Sure, man.' I picked it up and he's got strings like bloody piano strings, they're huge!" (Wilkerson, Mark, *Amazing Journey: The Life of Pete Townshend*, Lulu.com, 2006, p. 18).

The volume and power of the Pirates led the Detours to pursue new equipment. Unfortunately, they were broke. Daltry actually made the initial guitars for the band, and the band made their speaker cabinets. About that time, music manufacturer Jim Marshall started making his amps. John managed to afford a speaker cabinet for his bass, and his volume doubled. The revelation changed the band, and soon Pete saved up enough to buy his own Marshall cabinet.

Not content with double the volume, Pete saved enough to buy a second cabinet, and he piled it on top of his first. Suddenly, he was playing his guitar through a Marshall "stack" and getting tremendous "feedback" from his guitar by banging it and holding it close to the amps. The turn of events enraged the Marshall company; they insisted on a cleaner sound with their new product. But the Marshall stack, complete with purposely manipulated feedback, in what is now *de rigeur* for loud rock players. About the same time, Jimmy Page and Jeff Beck, both premier guitarists on the London scene, also began experimenting with feedback.

> To tell the truth, Dave Davies, Jeff (Beck) and me have got a tacit agreement that we will all squabble 'til the day we die that we invented it. I think possibly the truth is that it was happening in a lot of places at once. As the level went up, as people started to use bigger amps, and we were all still using semi-acoustic instruments, it started to happen quite naturally. I think the development of it was the word was around the street and then Lennon used it at the beginning of that record "I Feel Fine" and then it became quite common and a lot of people started to use it. (Rosen, Steve, "Townshend Talking," *Sound International*, April 1980)

Combined with their high-powered repertoire, which included songs by Berry, the Beatles, Howlin' Wolf, and Muddy Waters, the amplified techniques made the Detours a hot ticket around London.

* * *

Under Townshend and Daltry's leadership and a manager-type named Pete Meaden, they changed their name from the Detours to the Who. Meaden, a man about London, knew the club scene well and possessed significant music industry connections. He also lived and breathed all things "Mod," a youthful segment of the British population with money rather high style, and some swagger. Townshend also connected with the Mods, and he appreciated the efforts Meaden made to reach out to them.

In a ploy designed to appeal to the Mods, the Who decided to change their name again, this time to the High Numbers. They also changed their dress and altered their sound slightly to gear to the Mods. The ploy worked, and they signed a recording contract. Their first official single release came in 1964. "Zoot Suit" emerged as their first single, and the band issued a handful of other tunes as the High Numbers as well.

"Zoot Suit" captured the attention of local creative entrepreneurs Chris Stamp and Kit Lambert. Under the aegis of Stamp and Lambert, the band changed its name back to Who, and they began to refine their potent blend, coined "maximum R&B."

Courtesy of Neil Zlozower

At this early point, Townshend and company solidified their reputation as irascible and brazen kids, bolstered by the copious press they received when Townshend inadvertently smashed his first guitar onstage. Here's how it happened.

The band was playing at a venue called the Railway Hotel in Harrow, which had a particularly low roof. During one of his guitar moves, Townshend thrust the guitar over his head and accidentally cracked the neck. He became so angry about it that he systematically destroyed the rest of his instrument, bringing the show to an abrupt end.

Townshend remembers it this way:

> I started to knock the guitar about a lot, hitting it on the amps to get banging noises and things like that and it had started to crack. It banged against the ceiling and smashed a hole in the plaster and the guitar head actually poked through the ceiling plaster. When I brought it out the top of the neck was left behind. I couldn't believe what had happened. There were a couple of people from art school I knew at the front of the stage and they were laughing their heads off. One of them was literally rolling about on the floor laughing and his girlfriend was

kind of looking at me smirking, you know. So I just got really angry and got what was left of the guitar and smashed it to smithereens. About a month earlier I'd managed to scrape together enough for a 12-string Rickenbacker, which I only used on two or three numbers. It was lying at the side of the stage so I just picked it up, plugged it in and gave them a sort of look and carried on playing, as if I'd meant to do it. (www.thewho.net/whotabs/rick.htm)

The onstage destruction of instruments soon became a regular part of the Who's performances, and the buzz began to build. Thanks to a four-month residency in London on Tuesday nights at the legendary Marquee Club, the Who cultivated its reputation at the best live band in rock. Everyone took notice, leaving the Marquee on Tuesday nights drenched in sweat.

Here's what journalist Keith Altham witnessed during his first Who show:

The long, lanky guitarist with the big hooter was doing a passing impression of a malfunctioning windmill, all the while extracting tortuous scream from his guitar which sounded as though several Siamese cats were being electrocuted inside his speaker cabinet. This, I was reliably informed was "feedback." Then the surly looking blond thug up front screaming "I'm a Man" threw his microphone at the drummer who retaliated by hurling sticks at his head and thrashing around his kit like a whirling dervish. The bass player's hair was dyed jet black (his tribute to Elvis) and in his black clothes on a very dark stage was almost invisible. He made up for this by turning his volume control up so high he could be heard in the next world. (Wilkerson, *Amazing Journey: The Life of Pete Townshend*, p. 37)

The Who began work with ubiquitous producer Shel Talmy. Blown away by their live show, Talmy signed the Who to his production company and, as he was enjoying significant success with the Kinks, got the Who a contract with Decca in America and with their subsidiary Brunswick in Britain. It was his task to produce recordings modeled on their live performance.

In 1965, he succeeded. The band released three U.K. top-10 hit singles, two written by Townshend: "I Can't Explain," "Anyway Anyhow Anywhere" (co-written with Daltrey), and "My Generation." From there the band's popularity soared. Few bands in the mid-1960s cranked out the rockin' R&B the way the Who did. Townshend enthralled audiences with his frustrated lyrics and aggressive guitar. "I felt uncomfortable most of the time. I was unhappy a lot of the time. I always felt like the people in the audience were a burden to me."

We were pretty intense about our playing, and about performing. We all adored show business for its own sake, too. We liked stunts, tricks, gimmicks, ideas and special effects. But, deep down I think a lot of our power may have come from frustrated anger—a sense of impotence. Other artists didn't seem to share this in quite the way we did. Our music was quite vengeful in a way. The uplifting subtext came from a mixture of humour and a genuine belief that music could set us all free. It seems trite—and I think we knew that if music could do anything at all it would do it only for a short period—but that is what we believed. So, we were truly passionate. (Kayceman, "12 Questions with Pete Townshend," www.jambase.com)

Talmy produced other notable singles for the Who before producing their first album, *My Generation,* aka *The Who Sings My Generation* in the United States, a collection of original songs and R&B covers. However, tensions arose between Talmy and one of the band's managers, Kit Lambert. Lambert fired Talmy. (Talmy eventually sued successfully for breach of contract.)

More friction ensued. On September 26, Roger and Keith got into a brawl over Keith's pill use after a show in Denmark. Roger was fired after the group's return to England, only to be allowed back in until a suitable replacement could be found. For the next year, the music press was filled with reports of the Who at each other's throats, reports that were often true as Roger remained on probation and Keith and John auditioned for other bands, desperate to find a way out of what could only be called a turbulent mess.

It was under this rather dark mood that they began making national TV appearances in the United Kingdom, particularly on the popular program "Top of the Pops." They also began playing bigger gigs, opening for the Yardbirds and the Moody Blues. As the band grew, so did their egos, however, and the tone of the band grew incredibly tense. Despite the upbeat tone of success surrounding the band, they failed to find a common ground upon which to relate to each other. Those surrounding the band felt the Who would never be around long enough to appreciate its success.

In 1967, when serious music came from the likes of the Beach Boys (*Pet Sounds*), the Beatles (*Sgt. Pepper's Lonely Hearts Club Band*), and Hendrix (*Are You Experienced?*, *Axis: Bold as Love*), the Who proved that you didn't have to be stone-faced and surly to make great rock. They issued their first great album, *The Who Sell Out*, at the end of 1967, and though it's overlooked in the face of these other masterworks, it's just as unified and impressive.

In the States, the Decca label made little happen for the Who in terms of record sales. They were revered mostly as a live band, and for good reason. In 1967, they started playing what was then called the "psychedelic ballroom circuit," places like the Boston Tea Party, the Grande in Detroit, and the Fillmores in New York and San Francisco. In June of 1967, they played the infamous Monterey International Pop Festival, along with Hendrix and Sly and the Family Stone, among many others. The live myth of the Who had successfully crossed the Atlantic.

"The Who played [their] gigs like a rowdy family of boisterous, bickering but ultimately unified brothers. They could slam out half a dozen hits in twenty minutes, or dip into an exotic blues for fifteen minutes, harangue the crowd about its lack of discernment or each other about personal, musical, or theatrical inadequacies" (Marsh, Dave, "The Who In America," *The Who: Thirty Years of Maximum R&B*, liner notes, 1994, n.p.).

* * *

Still, the Who's records sold scantily in the United States partly because they were very English. Some English bands couldn't communicate with American audiences simply because they lacked the ability to identify with the American experience. This changed for the Who in 1969, when they released *Tommy*, an ambitious rock opera written entirely by Townshend, who was quickly becoming the leader of the band. Then again, the Who consisted of four leaders, which became a root of the group's problems.

Tommy, a perfect crystallization of the Who's arty yin and blues rock yang, seized the imagination of the American public like no previous Who album or single had. In writing it, Townshend searched for a spiritual meaning in rock. He was obsessed with the relationship between rock musicians and their fans, and he constantly grappled with how to effectively communicate this struggle to his audience.

That struggle was epitomized at Woodstock. Townshend viewed the event rather tragically as "the triumph of star culture over the hippie rock scene and their egalitarian dreams" (Marsh, liner notes, 1994). In response to Woodstock, he went on to write two other storylines: *Quadrophenia* and the aborted *Lifehouse,* both about disaffected youth and poignant ruminations on the disconnect Townshend felt between his music, his life, and the people for which he composed.

Following *Tommy,* the Who began selling records, and selling out venues in America. As the guitarist began penning new material, the band released *Live at Leeds* in 1970, considered to be one of the great concert recordings of all time. It yielded the hit singles "Summertime Blues" and "The Seeker," and its success bought Townshend writing time. He spent it hammering out another opera/conceptual album called *Lifehouse,* which featured electronic instruments and boundary-pushing subject matter. Unfortunately, the rest of the band didn't go much for the material and Townshend shelved it. (It would come out in 2000.) His bandmates' reluctance and the frustration he underwent finishing *Lifehouse,* led to Pete suffering a nervous breakdown.

Once he recovered, the group picked up the pieces of the now-abandoned project and recorded *Who's Next* with producer Glyn Johns. The album boasted harder rock and many hits, including "Baba O'Riley," "Bargain," "Behind Blue Eyes," and "Won't Get Fooled Again." The album became a staple of FM radio, and the Who reigned as superstars. *Quadrophenia* ultimately came out in 1973, *Odds and Sods,* a rarities collection, in 1974, and *Who by Numbers* in 1975. Following that, the Who took an extended hiatus.

In 1978, Townshend teamed up with Small Faces bassist Ronnie Lane to make a fine, highly acclaimed album *Rough Mix.*

But the late 1970s found the band aging. Townshend revealed, after years in front of his Marshall stack, he had permanently damaged his hearing. Keith Moon collapsed onstage in 1976 a few minutes into a show at the Boston Garden. He never stopped partying in his time with the Who, and his presence—comical, ludicrous, and often violent— kept Daltry and Townshend from focusing too much on the animosity they felt for each other. But it wasn't to last. In 1978, three weeks after they released *Who Are You,* Moon died of a drug overdose.

Another tragedy befell the band in 1979. A tour stop in Cincinnati turned deadly when fans eager to get the best seats in a general admission show triggered a stampede. Eleven people were killed in the rush.

SOLO WORK

After Keith Moon died, the Who gradually disintegrated. The Cincinnati show stole the band's renewed momentum, and Townshend turned heavily to drugs. He almost overdosed in 1981. At the same time, Daltrey and Entwistle both pursued ill-fated solo careers. But it was Townshend who dried out and became the Who's most successful solo artist.

As his solo career matured, 1980's New Wave kicked in and Townshend essentially jumped the shark. Like many artists of the era, Pete stepped into a booby trap of synthesizers, studio polish, and eye shadow, all of which helped to produce his least appealing work. *Empty Glass,* with "Rough Boys" and "I Am An Animal," is passable. But from this point, Townshend, emboldened and sober, began to overreach. *All the Best Cowboys Have Chinese Eyes, Deep End Live,* and *White City: A Novel* are embarrassing and overwrought. *The Iron Man,* another of Pete's stabs at a conceptual recording, this time for kids, is

MEHER BABA

In the beginning of the Who's career, Townshend showed no predilection for religious belief, and few fans would have mistaken him, his aggressive attitude, and often violent performance style for spiritual. But beginning around 1968, when the Small Faces' Ronnie Lane introduced him to the writings of the Indian "perfect master" Meher Baba, Townshend was intrigued, and then obsessed. In his writings, Baba blended elements of Vedantic, Sufi, and mystic schools, and this spiritual thinking intoxicated Townshend and provided him with an escape from his often turbulent musical career.

In January 1968, the Who recorded his song "Faith in Something Bigger," which came out on the band's *Odds and Sods* album. It was at this time that Townshend, who had been searching the past two years for a basis for a rock opera, created a story inspired by the teachings of Baba and other Indian spiritualists that would ultimately become *Tommy*.

But what usually gets left out of the well-documented history between Townshend and Baba are three albums Townshend participated in at the beginning of the 1970s. The LPs were published privately in limited editions by the Meher Baba Association, although some copies did show up at least briefly in some record stores. On *Happy Birthday,* issued in 1970 in celebration of Meher Baba's birthday (as apparently were all three albums), Townshend contributed six of eleven tracks. For the second album, *I Am* (1971), Townshend contributed five tracks, one of which is the original version of "Baba O'Riley," a nearly 10-minute version of the classic that would later appear on *Who's Next.*

On the third effort for Meher Baba, Townshend had a smaller presence. *With Love,* released in 1972, finds the guitarist appearing on only four of the album's dozen tracks.

Collectors note: Who fans aren't aware of this special trio of recordings. They are extremely rare yet well worth seeking out, especially for Who and Townshend completists.

perhaps his most misguided effort, despite the bizarre presence of John Lee Hooker and Nina Simone.

Even through 1993s *Psychoderelict* Pete was plagued by a glut of ambition; time and again he tried ramming a huge square peg of conceptualism into a small round hole of rock 'n' roll. And worse, his subject matter had become excessively egocentric. "I became the central character in my own dark (but amusing) rock opera," he admits in the liner notes to *Scoop 3.* Which is why we should all thank the gods for the *Scoop* remasters! These two-disc collections are the perfect antidote for Townshend's errant ambitions and a great way to reconnect with his raw writing abilities. The first *Scoop* is a set of stripped-down demos, alternative versions, and outtakes that have, since its 1983 release, pleased Who fans with fresh, alternate renditions of familiar tunes like "Squeezebox," "Magic Bus," "Behind Blue Eyes," and a positively giant "Love Reign O'er Me." *Another Scoop,* originally released in 1987, nearly surpasses the first with consistently good outtakes of classics: "Happy Jack," "Substitute," "Pinball Wizard," and "The Kids Are Alright," among others, 27 in all. The final *Scoop* release, *Scoop 3*, doesn't succeed the way its predecessors do. Most of the worthwhile vintage demos had already seen release, and so Townshend didn't have much in the well from which to draw. Still, it provides an intimate look at his private inner creative sanctum, even though its focus on later period, synth-based work might not thrill folks. None of these *Scoop* sets features additional tracks, just stellar remastering by longtime band associate Jon Astley. As this batch of reissues illustrates, Townshend's solo work begins strongly, but then tapers off.

TECHNIQUE/STYLE

One thing that distinguished the Who was the manner in which the band established its rhythmic structure. The band often built off Townshend's rhythm guitar, enabling drummer Moon and bassist Entwistle to wind their way around that rhythm in almost a lead-like way.

This is not a standard procedure for rock bands, but it did make Townshend one of the best rhythm guitar players in the history of rock music. Moon and Entwistle were both faster and more virtuosic than Townshend, and so the band inverted the formula to emphasize their strengths, with Pete's guitar just propping up the more lead instruments of the bass and drums.

Because he excelled in powerful rhythms, with chugging chords, Townshend is often credited with the invention of the power chord, something he developed prior to the Who's emergence in 1965. He was also the first important guitarist to be a significant composer as well. His ability to combine salient lyrical work with blistering guitar playing had, up to the time he showed up on the London scene, been nonexistent. He was by turns, ferocious and literate, controlled and uncontrollable. His guitar playing was simply an extension of who he was, a mortal, a common kid, who got angry and frustrated at times and who was able to look at the world the way it really was and echo that reality with his guitar.

He opted out of finely crafted leads, the kind played by many of his London comrades. Instead, he chose to prove that armed with just a handful of passionately played chords, anyone could write great music. In doing so, he brought rock 'n' roll closer to the audience, bridging the gap between band and fan.

His defiance of the predominant style of the times led him to discover his own strength.

And Clapton was around and various other people who could really play and I was very frustrated because I couldn't do all that flash stuff. So I just started getting into feedback and expressed myself physically. And it just led to when, one day, I was banging my guitar around making noises and I banged it on this ceiling in this club and the neck broke off, because Rickenbackers are made out of cardboard. And everybody started to laugh and they went, "Hah, that'll teach you to be flash." So I thought what I was going to do, and I had no other recourse but to make it look like I had meant to do it. So I smashed this guitar and jumped all over the bits and then picked up the 12-string and carried on as though nothing had happened. And the next day the place was packed. It turned into another form of expression for me: it was a gimmick of course. It is a very physical thing to be a stand up guitar player—and the way you feel and the way you move and the way you move your body is a big part of it; the fact that to sometimes pull a string up by the right amount you have to give it some momentum, so that you can't play sitting down in the way you can play standing up. And so for me all that macho stuff became an expression. (Rosen)

Like Hendrix, Townshend began to experiment with the electronic aspects of his instrument. He flicked the toggle switch thing to make the guitar sound like a machine gun when it was feeding back. And when he bought his first Rickenbacker, he packed it with paper and found it could actually produce feedback on select harmonics, something he could reproduce live as well. It was a stunning example of how the Who was able to reproduce difficult studio recordings live.

On Pete's Rickenbacker, the strings are closely spaced on a narrow neck and the fingerboard is lightweight but well balanced. This suited Pete's chordal style, and he invented several new chord shapes using that neck that have since become standard rock shapes. The lightweight neck allowed Townshend to produce vibrato techniques by moving the neck backwards and forwards. This became another characteristic of his style. So, while the Rickenbacker was not the quality guitar that the Fenders or Gibsons were, Pete turned its weak points into strengths.

EQUIPMENT/GEAR

Townshend is brutally honest when it comes to his instrument. "I've never had any respect really for the guitar. I've respected guitar players of course and I understand their need for a good instrument but for years and years I didn't care what the guitar was like" (Rosen, 1980).

Throughout his solo career and his career with The Who, Townshend has played (and destroyed) a large variety of guitars. In the early days with The Who, Townshend played an Emile Grimshaw SS De Luxe along with 6-string and 12-string Rickenbacker semihollow electric guitars. But as his habit of instrument-smashing became increasingly integrated into the Who's concert sets, he switched to cheaper guitars for destroying.

In the late 1960s, most notably at the Woodstock and Isle of Wight shows in 1969 and 1970, Townshend began playing Gibson SG Specials. By 1972, Gibson changed the design of the SG Special but Townshend didn't like the alterations, so he used Gibson Les Paul Deluxes, some with only two mini-humbucker pickups and others modified with a third pickup through the 1970s. He used several of these guitars in the documentary "The Kids Are Alright."

During the 1980s, Townshend mainly returned to Rickenbackers and Telecaster-style models built for him by Schecter and others. Beginning in the late 1980s, Townshend used the Fender Eric Clapton Signature Stratocaster, with Lace-Sensor pickups, both in the studio and on tour.

Along the way, he has supplemented these main instruments with a number of other guitars, including various Gretsch, Gibsons, Guild, Takamine, and Gibson J-200 acoustic models. Currently, there are Gibson Pete Townshend signature guitars, including the Pete Townshend SG, the Pete Townshend J-200, and three different Pete Townshend Les Paul Deluxes. There has also been a Pete Townshend signature Rickenbacker limited edition guitar.

Over the years, Pete Townshend has used many types of amplifiers, from Vox and Fender to Marshall and Hiwatt. For the bulk of the 1960s, he used Fender amps, a Fender Pro and a Fender Bassman, and they drove two Marshall 4x12 speaker cabinets. From there, he briefly used the Vox AC-30 amp. But since he discovered the Hiwatt just prior to making *Tommy*, he has stuck with the company ever since. In a classic bit of reverse psychology, Townshend admitted that he tended to choose a guitar that fit his amplifier rather than the other way around.

Townshend figured prominently in the development of what is widely known in rock circles as the Marshall "stack." Townshend became a user of Marshall cabinets very early on in Jim Marshall's business cycle. He ordered several speaker cabinets that contained eight speakers in a housing standing nearly six feet high with the top half of the cabinet slanted slightly upward. These were heavy and difficult to gig with. On Townshend's suggestion, Marshall then cut the massive speaker housings into two separate cabinets, with each one containing four 12-inch speakers. One of the cabinets had half of the speaker baffle slanted upwards and Marshall made these two cabinets stackable. Townshend used these as well as Hiwatt stacks, though Hiwatt amps have been his main preference for the better part of four decades.

In 2006, Townshend had a pedal board designed by gear guru Pete Cornish. The board is comprised of a compressor, a Boss OD-1 overdrive pedal, and a T Rex Replica delay pedal.

ESSENTIAL READING

Altham, Keith. "Who, me? The Who in Britain," liner notes, *The Who Thirty Years of Maximum R&B*. MCA, 1994.

Barnes, Richard. *The Who: Maximum R&B*. New York: Plexus Publishing, 2004.

Guiliano, Geoffrey. *Behind Blue Eyes: The Life of Pete Townshend*. New York: Cooper Square Press, 2002.

Kayceman. "12 Questions with Pete Townshend." www.jambase.com.

Marsh, Dave. *Before I Get Old: The Story of the Who*. New York:Plexus Publishing, 2003.

———. "The Who In America." *The Who: Thirty Years of Maximum R&B*, liner notes, 1994, n.p.

Rosen, Steve. "Townshend Talking." *Sound International*, April 1980.

Wilkerson, Mark. *Amazing Journey: The Life of Pete Townshend*. Lulu.com, 2006.

ESSENTIAL WORK

"Baba O'Riley" (1971)
"Happy Jack" (1966)
"Pinball Wizard" (1969)
"Won't Get Fooled Again" (1971)
"Young Man Blues" (1970)

ESSENTIAL LISTENING

Live at Leeds (MCA, 1970)
Rough Mix (with Ronnie Lane) (Atco, 1977)
Tommy (MCA, 1969)
The Who by Numbers (MCA, 1975)
The Who Sell Out (MCA, 1967)
The Who Sings My Generation (MCA, 1965)
Who's Next (MCA, 1971)

Eddie Van Halen

In the long lineage of guitarists in the rock generation, few rank higher than Eddie Van Halen. Ten years after Jimi Hendrix turned the world of rock guitar upside down in the late 1960s, Van Halen, a young Dutch boy in Los Angeles, did it again in the mid-1970s. The legend began in 1976, quite unassumingly, during small Van Halen gigs. As the story goes, Eddie Van Halen would play remarkable solos, only instead of showboating as many guitars with his kind of ability would, he played with his back to the audience. He did this not because he was shy, but he was reluctant to reveal his secret techniques. No one in rock 'n' roll had conjured up the kinds of sounds the young Van Halen was making, and no one could figure out just how he was making them. That noise heralded a brave new talent, one that would eventually get enough attention that he'd have to disclose his mysterious method. It went something like this:

He used his picking hand to tap notes directly onto the fretboard, utilizing a technique called, predictably: "tapping." While tapping may be Eddie Van Halen's one major stylistic contribution to rock guitar, his innovation certainly didn't end there. His legacy runs much deeper.

He is also credited with advancements such as natural and artificial harmonics vibrato, and tremolo picking, combined with his rhythmic sensibility and melodic approach. As a total package, he has influenced the guitar playing standards and techniques of an entire generation. Like Hendrix, he redefined what a electric guitar sounded like.

Van Halen developed a blindingly fast technique from a variety of self-taught tricks. In addition to two-handed tapping, he favored concepts like hammer-ons and pull-offs, unusual ploys that evoked surreal sounds. With the added entertainment of David Lee Roth's acrobatics and lascivious antics, Van Halen became the most popular American rock 'n' roll band for over six years, beginning in the late 1970s and running to the mid-1980s.

Their impact rippled through rock 'n' roll for a decade after, through the bands that took both their guitar styles and entertainment qualities seriously. The movement spawned from Van Halen's antics, coined "hair metal," lasted right up to the 1990s, dominating rock music during that time frame until the advent of alternative music and grunge.

From their eponymous 1978 debut through their 1984 album, Van Halen sold over 75 million albums worldwide. At the same time, few rocked—or partied—harder than David, Alex, Eddie, and Michael. And it just so happened that in the process of all that celebrating, the quartet established an important new blueprint for hard rock, with Eddie Van Halen serving as the core of the band and the heart of its music.

EARLY YEARS

Born on January 26, 1955 in the Netherlands, Eddie Van Halen was a son of Dutch saxophonist and bandleader named Jan Van Halen and an Indonesian mother. The elder Van Halen moved his family to Pasadena in 1962 in order to make a living as a musician. Both Eddie and his older brother Alex learned to play the piano as kids, and both demonstrated an affinity for music at an early age. Eddie even won some early piano contests. But he also became profoundly bored with sitting at the piano and he soon started playing the drums, paying for a kit by maintaining a paper route. Meanwhile, his brother beat him to the guitar; his Mom signed brother Alex up for flamenco guitar lessons.

Guitar beckoned, though, and one day, after he heard that his brother could play the *drums* better than he could, he put down the sticks and picked up Alex's guitar.

He sat in his room for hours practicing. He walked around his house with the guitar strapped around his neck, strumming. The first songs he learned how to play were classic surf instrumentals like "Pipeline" and "Wipe Out." He and his brother also learned to play some British Invasion pop rock as well, like the Kinks and the Dave Clark Five. The Kinks' "You Really Got Me" would go on to become a favorite cover in early Van Halen sets, and one of the songs that would help the band define its primal rock sound. By age 14, he had memorized all of Eric Clapton's licks in his band Cream. The year was 1969, and Cream was the hottest hard rock band on the planet. During elementary and middle school, Eddie and Alex formed several different bands at different times, with names like "The Trojan Rubber Company," "The Broken Combs," and "The Space Brothers." They finally agreed on "Mammoth," and they began gigging in the area. Eddie Van Halen began as the guitarist and singer, but soon tired of doing double duty. They had no PA of their own, and rented one from a guy named David Lee Roth, front man of a band called Redball Jet. Roth admired the Van Halen brothers' work and Mammoth carefully considered the fact that if they invited Roth to join the band, Eddie wouldn't have to sing and the band wouldn't have to spend money renting Roth's PA. A deal was struck. Michael Anthony, a bass player in a local band called Snake, joined Mammoth, replacing original bassist Mark Stone, and the lineup was complete. They discovered that the rights to their band name though had already been taken, and so they decided to call themselves Van Halen.

MUSIC

In 1977, Kiss bassist Gene Simmons saw Van Halen play a Hollywood venue and was impressed enough by them to finance their first demo. He flew the band to New York City to record "House of Pain" and "Runnin' with the Devil." Rumor had it that Eddie Van Halen disliked his playing on the demo, largely because he wasn't using gear of his own. He'd overdub his parts later.

Later in 1977, Van Halen secured a deal with Warner Brothers, based on a 25-song demo that the label executives Ted Templeman and Mo Ostin had heard. They released their inaugural record early in 1978, comprised of nine songs from that demo. Their first single was "You Really Got Me," a cover of the Kinks song. Produced by Templeman, the album only took three months to go gold and six months to hit platinum, eventually selling over six million copies. Radio embraced it wholeheartedly thanks to album rock staples like "Jamie's Cryin'" and "Runnin' with the Devil."

Much touring and hard work ensued. Van Halen's second record was released in March 1979. In January, barely 48 hours after the end of their first tour, the boys went back into Sunset Sound in Hollywood to work on *Van Halen II*. Produced again by Ted Templeman, the recording took only 10 days to finish. Templeman had worked wonders on Van Halen's first record, and he got the most out of the band, using instrumental overdubs on just three songs. Except for one number written in the studio, Van Halen had performed the rest of the album on stage, some since the band's club days. *Van Halen II* sold over five million copies and charted as high as #6 in the States and #23 in the United Kingdom. Eddie Van Halen also garnered his second *Guitar Player* magazine accolade as "Best Rock Guitarist of the Year."

One of the highlights on *II* was "Somebody Get Me a Doctor," a tune written about the same time as "Runnin' with the Devil" and performed frequently during the band's club days. Listen closely and hear the applause at the end of Van Halen's guitar solo. Apparently, when the band was recording live in the studio, which they often did, his solo performance tore everybody there apart, giving way to applause. For this version, he also changed the song's intro from the early club version, reversing chords. The solo section of "Doctor" was extended during gigs and often turned into a jam session. Another highlight was the "Spanish Fly," the unaccompanied guitar solo that exhibited his work on acoustic. He recorded it on a nylon-string Ovation guitar, and its success led him to incorporate many parts of this song into his live guitar solos.

Van Halen's third album came out in March 1980. *Women and Children First,* produced by Templeman again, marked the first all-original album the band recorded. Recorded in just over two weeks, the band recorded most of the songs live with very few overdubs. While it didn't yield a hit single, the album charted high, at #6 and became the band's third multiplatinum release in three tries.

The band followed the album with an extensive tour, called the "Invasion Tour" in 1980, which turned out to be more successful than their previous two tours. Eddie Van Halen also received his third straight "Best Rock Guitarist of the Year" award from the readers of *Guitar Player* magazine. *Fair Warning* was the album where Van Halen, appearing to have given up hopes of stardom, settled for mere greatness. The critical response was overwhelming. Critic Greil Marcus wrote that *Fair Warning* was "where Van Halen stared down these bleak '80s and barely won. Brutally vicious hard rock mixed with funk and fervor" (Marcus, Greil, *Creem*, February 1984, n.p.).

* * *

But it was the album *1984,* released on New Year's Day of the same year, that broke the band internationally. Shifting from an instrumental origination to a song-oriented emphasis—with hooks, melodies, and irresistible sing-alongs—*1984* was the best set of songs that Van Halen had made to date, and generally considered the finest album of their career. The anthemic tunes "Panama" and "Hot for Teacher" grab center stage with sizzling signature performances, but virtually all the songs are noteworthy, including "Top Jimmy," "Drop Dead Legs," and the dense yet funky closer, "House of Pain." It's the best showcase of Van Halen's instrumental prowess and also a perfect setting for Roth's unmatched routine.

Despite the band's creative apex, all was not well. Rising tensions between Roth and the other band members were increasingly evident; on their 1984 world tour the band didn't even play on the same stage, but rather performed on four separate platforms, symbolic of the escalating rift among its members. Finally, in 1985, after taking time off to record a successful solo album (and delaying work on the follow-up to *1984*), Roth walked away from Van Halen.

REVOLVING SINGERS

Replacing the inimitable Roth was a daunting task. Finding a successor actually came about rather serendipitously. Eddie Van Halen's auto mechanic also happened to be the mechanic of a guy named Sammy Hagar, a singer formerly of a successful album rock band called Montrose. At the time they met, Hagar had come off a successful year as a solo artist (his 1984 album *VOA* yielded the hit "I Can't Drive 55"). When Van Halen approached Hagar with the offer to be front man, Hagar agreed and he also consented to play rhythm guitar onstage. The first Hagar album, 1986's *5150*, became the band's first #1 album on the *Billboard* charts, driven by the keyboard-dominated singles "Why Can't This Be Love," "Dreams," and "Love Walks In."

Hagar's style, more conventional than Roth's both musically and lyrically, spread the Van Halen sound to a wider audience. Many die-hard VH fans, though, remained attached to the David Lee Roth–era line up and proved difficult to convert. From Van Halen's point of view, he'd never been happier. Hagar was more predictable, more reliable, and much easier to work with.

All four studio albums produced during Hagar's time with the band—*5150*, *For Unlawful Carnal Knowledge*, *OU812*, and *Balance*—reached #1 on the charts. A total of 17 singles also made the top 12 of the mainstream rock tracks chart. In addition, Van Halen was nominated for two Grammy Awards with Hagar, winning the 1991 Best Hard Rock Performance with Vocal award for *For Unlawful Carnal Knowledge*.

Hagar did, however, confront problems with one VH project, a compilation album slated for release in 1996. Hagar felt like a hits collection was not a logical step in the band's career and he pressured management to cancel the plans. He felt that a compilation including songs by both him and David Lee Roth would leave fans having to choose between the Roth material and the Hagar material; an issue Hagar wanted to put behind him and the band.

The debate never subsided and Hagar left the band. Actually, he claimed he was fired. The band claimed he quit, so even *that* debate continues. In any event, the extensive media coverage of the melodrama facilitated Hagar's own subsequent solo career.

* * *

Of course, it also put Van Halen in the unenviable position of finding another singer, not to mention the fact that it gave them the reputation of being particularly difficult to work with. They grabbed a recruit named Mitch Malloy, with whom they recorded a few demos and impromptu jams. He had been friends with Eddie Van Halen and knew the band socially. About the same time, Roth reconnected with the guitarist to discuss what tracks he wanted to include on the upcoming hits collection. The "reunion" felt good to both parties and Van Halen invited him to his home studio. Shortly thereafter, Roth and the band entered the studio with producer Glenn Ballard to record a couple of songs for the hits project.

Soon after that, Roth and the original lineup were invited to an MTV awards show in 1996. It would be their first public appearance together in nearly a dozen years. The appearance and the publicity it generated boosted the compilation to the top of the album chart. At the time, though, Roth didn't know that the band was still auditioning singers for his spot. Still, Malloy saw the writing on the wall and decided the band could not be successful with a new vocalist. The timing certainly wasn't right. He called bassist Michael Anthony and submitted his resignation. Roth too had been put off by the hullabaloo surrounding a prospective reunion, and so he left the picture as well. The events led to another search for a front man. This time they turned up Gary Cherone, formerly of hugely popular Boston band Extreme. The result was *Van Halen III* in 1998. Many songs on the album were longer and more ethereal, a reflection of the way Cherone and Van Halen worked together. It was less rocking and more thought-provoking. The result disappointed fans and became the poorest-selling Van Halen album ever, the only release that did not sell at least double platinum. It ended up achieving only gold status, moving less than one million units. Embarrassed, the Cherone-led version of Van Halen entered into the studio with tail between its legs in early 1999. They started work on a new album, rumored to be called *Love Again*. Working titles of songs included "Left for Dead," "River Wide," "Say Uncle," "You Wear it Well," "More Than Yesterday," "I Don't Miss You Much," "Love Divine," and "From Here Where Do We Go?"

Courtesy of Neil Zlozower

But the new album was left unfinished when Cherone, citing musical differences, left amicably in November 1999.

* * *

Years passed, and little word emerged from the Van Halen camp. Eddie Van Halen struggled with cancer and drug addiction. He had been in and out of rehab, the latest bout in the spring of 2008. In December 2006, Eddie Van Halen announced that David Lee Roth had been invited to rejoin the band. Roth, though, said that he had not spoken with Van Halen in years, and that no reunion was being discussed.

In the spring of 2007, Van Halen was elected into the Rock 'n' Roll Hall of Fame, with Velvet Revolver serving as the inductors. At the same time, the band announced plans for a reunion tour. The tour got underway in the fall of 2007 and ran until the spring of 2008, before the guitarist entered into rehab. After three weeks drying out, he rejoined the tour and saw it through to its conclusion in June 2008.

TECHNIQUE/STYLE

His principal stylistic innovation, two-handed tapping, took the rock world by storm. He admitted to having been introduced to it by a former instructor, who picked it up from someone else; the list of former "tappers" is pretty lengthy, and includes Queen's Brian May, Harvey Mandel, Frank Zappa, Ritchie Blackmore (Deep Purple), and Ace Frehley of Kiss, among others.

Yet it is still something the young Van Halen single-handedly introduced to a vast new rock audience. He recalls seeing Jimmy Page of Led Zeppelin tap out part of his solo in "Heartbreaker," and thinking, "I can play like that, and you wouldn't know if I was using this finger [points to left hand] or this one" [points to right hand]. But you just kind of move it around, and it's like, "You got one big hand there, buddy. That's a hell of a spread!" (Hiatt, Brian, rollingstone.com, June 12, 2008).

The one song that introduced Van Halen's tapping to the world, "Eruption," began as a torrid instrumental *without* tapping. Early versions of "Eruption," then untitled, started a few years previous and featured the guitarist going for it without tapping. On the rendition found on the band's 1978 debut, *Van Halen,* he is indeed tapping away, so sometime between 1974 and 1976 he perfected the art, and grew confident enough to record himself doing it.

"We recorded our first record on Sunset Sound in Hollywood, and we were warming up for a weekend gig at the Whisky. And I was just rehearsing, and [engineer] Donn Landee happened to record it. It was never intended to be on the record. So the take on the record was a total freak thing. It was just an accident. He happened to be rolling tape" (Hiatt, rollingstone.com).

Van Halen, who captured the solo on the first take, also used an MXR Phase 90 when recording the "Eruption" solo as well as a Univox EC-80 echo box. Says Van Halen: "I didn't even play it right. There's a mistake at the top end of it. To this day, whenever I hear it I always think, 'Man, I could've played it better' " (Hiatt, rollingstone.com).

*   *   *

Like virtually every other rock player in the 1970s, Van Halen was playing blues-based licks with heavy overdrive to create the classic, arena-rock sound. He had a variety of influences growing up, notably Clapton, whom he calls his main influence, Queen's Brian May, Allan Holdsworth, and Ronnie Montrose, a cadre of stylists who all contributed style cues to his own.

But Eddie Van Halen managed to make them heavier and more idiosyncratic. His ability to use quintuplet rhythms has helped define his phrasing, his use of simple 1-2-4 finger pattern across all six strings—a pattern he invented—came to be called unofficially, the "EVH scale."

"I was so used to doing old blues licks with the first three fingers. When I started using my pinky and finding more spread things, that's when I started getting my own style" (Stix, John, *Guitar Classics XI: Guitar Presents #27,* 1995).

Van Halen's playing is also natural, sans effects. "That's the beauty of music to me. Everybody is an individual. It's your personal way of expressing yourself, and it starts here, with your fingers. Nobody sounds like anybody else" (Schroedl, Jeff, "The Man Who Would Be King," *Guitar One,* October 1998).

Van Halen also excels as a rhythm player, a fact that goes unnoticed by nonplayers, most of whom worship him as a lead player and gymnastic soloist. While his soloing is indeed innovative and hailing from the proper place, his rhythm playing keeps the band's material moving; especially live, as the only guitar player, his responsibility is immense. Just starting out, Eddie and Alex never had a bass player, so he served as the young band's rhythm section. This helped him fill out the sound and develop a critical sense of rhythm guitar playing.

Van Halen always believed that his band's music should hold up without any vocals at all. "Listen to Beethoven, you know. There's no singing on it" (Hiatt, rollingstone.com).

EQUIPMENT/GEAR

Van Halen plugged his "Frankenstrat" with a slanted vintage Gibson humbucker (sealed in surfboard wax) into a Marshall plexi head, then ran it through a Variac, a

FRANKENSTRAT: THE MONSTER GUITAR

Eddie Van Halen admittedly didn't have much electronic wherewithal when he built his guitar, which is why he installed just a single pickup and a single volume knob. He searched but ultimately didn't have the patience to put together a decent bridge and neck pickup combination. Upon installing the humbucking pickup, he didn't know how to wire it into the circuit, so he rigged up the simplest working circuit to get it to function.

Eddie Van Halen also built the rest of his first guitar by hand in 1975, using an imperfect body and a used neck he picked up at Wayne Charvel's guitar shop. He bought the ash body for $50 and the neck for $80. The neck sported Gibson jumbo frets that Van Halen admits he crazy-glued on. His goal was to construct a guitar that gave him a Gibson sound and a Fender feel. Originally, the body came with single-coil bridge, neck, and middle pickup positions pre-routed. Van Halen, with a chisel, instead carved out a hole for a humbucker in the bridge position. In the hole, he placed a P.A.F. from a 1961 Gibson ES-335. The pickup was, as Van Halen noted, "ruined," but sounded good so he left it. The single-coil neck pickup was completely disengaged. The tuning heads were Schallers.

He sprayed the instrument with black then white acrylic lacquer bike paint and mounted a black Strat-style pick guard, which he also made and which barely covered the two front routings. This "Frankenstrat" first appeared as the black and white guitar pictured on the band's debut album, *Van Halen*.

He eventually repainted the guitar with red, black, and white stripes, and added orange truck reflectors to the back. The nut was brass and the tailpiece unit was from a 1961 Fender Stratocaster. This guitar was Eddie Van Halen's main instrument for the first several albums and tours. During the band's second world tour, he replaced the original tremolo with a prototype Floyd Rose. A coin was attached just under the top-back side of the Floyd Rose to keep it from rising up.

That first Charvel shop neck was broken by the guitarist's rigorous stage antics and replaced with whatever was handy (including a Danelectro at one point). "There's really no secret. The reason I use what I use is through trial and error" (www .classicvanhalen.com).

voltage regulator to fully drive the tubes without the earsplitting volume and out through Marshall 4x12 cabs. Insiders referred to it as the "Brown Sound," and it set a new high-water mark in rock guitar tone.

The "Brown Sound" came about rather accidentally. At an early audition a talent scout told Van Halen his amp was up too loud, so he turned the amp around instead of turning it down, then he put a cover on it. But those fixes didn't seem right. He wanted to find a way to leave his Marshall all the way up to keep the gain but not remove the tone. One day he accidentally plugged his Bassman amp into the external "out" and into the Marshall cabinet. It was quieter, but it still had great, dynamic tone. The mistake gave him an idea. He took a cheap plastic light switch with a dimmer from his home, along with two wires, and he connected it to the amp. Now, he had the same great tone he was looking for, without the insane volume, and it was controllable. "I wasn't spanking the tubes as hard at the lower volume level. I lowered the voltage that went to the amp. It wasn't 110 volts; I was plugging into 80 volts. So I've never used a fuzz box in my life. I've never owned any distortion or overdrive unit in my life. I don't like to have stuff in between" (Schroedl, 1998).

While on the subject of tone and amplifiers, the Marshall in question ran on standard EL34 Sylvania tubes, at least during the early years. When Van Halen's Marshall started to fail him in the early 1990s, he switched to Soldano SLO100. Van Halen has settled in on his Peavey 5150 and 5150 II signature series amps. Although he has had his vintage Marshall restored, he relies on the 120-watt 5150 series amplifiers for most studio and tour applications.

* * *

Van Halen uses a nonfloating Floyd Rose tremolo system that preserves the bridge to guitar-body contact giving a more stop tail piece level of sustain and tone. "I don't know anybody that uses the damn tone control on a guitar, at least I don't. For me, it's all the way up, period"—EVH. "I like thin frets, that way it's more precise, the bigger, the fatter the fret is the worse the intonation is" (www.classicvanhalen.com). He used the Frankenstrat guitar in his most fruitful period, through 1984.

Van Halen's later guitars include various Kramer models from his endorsement phase with the company. This phase featured his Kramer 5150 model, when Gibson owned the company back in the early 1980s. Although a Kramer EVH signature model was never officially created, the Kramer "Baretta" was modeled after Van Halen's Frankenstrat. Other axes include the Ernie Ball/Music Man Edward Van Halen model (now the Ernie Ball Axis), the Peavey EVH Wolfgang (now the HP Special), and the Charvel EVH Art Series on which Van Halen does the striping before they're painted at the factory.

Beginning with the *5150* album in 1986, Van Halen began working with Steinberger guitars, a so-called Trans Trem–equipped guitar. The trans-trem tremolo can be heard on the songs "Summer Nights" and "Me Wise Magic" to name a few.

Add in his outrageous use of the MXR Phase 90 flanger, the MXR 10-band EQ pedal, and his innovative Floyd Rose whammy technique and you've got Van Halen's secret recipe. EVH guitars are strung with Peavey extra-light strings, gauges .009 to .042. He sets his action as low as possible for the easiest playability with the least amount of resistance. "I lower the strings to the point of buzz and then back it off just a hair. Why make it hard?" (www.classicvanhalen.com).

Essential Reading

Hiatt, Brian. rollingstone.com, June 12, 2008.
Marcus, Greil. *Creem,* February 1984, n.p.
Sanchez, Abel. *Van Halen 101.* Author House, 2005.
Schroedl, Jeff. "The Man Who Would Be King." *Guitar One,* October 1998.
Stix, John. *Guitar Classics XI: Guitar Presents #27,* 1995.

Essential Work

"Dance the Night Away" (1979)
"Eruption" (1978)
"Hot for Teacher" (1984)
"Jamie's Cryin' " (1978)
"Romeo Delight" (1980)
"Runnin' with the Devil" (1978)

Essential Listening

1984 (Warner Bros., 1984)
Van Halen (Warner Bros., 1978)
Van Halen II (Warner Bros., 1979)
Women and Children First (Warner Bros., 1980)

Stevie Ray Vaughan

In the mid to late 1970s, after longtime blues icons Buddy Guy, Albert King, and Muddy Waters receded from view, it seemed like the blues would simply trot off into the sunset. Then along came a Texas Tornado named Stevie Ray Vaughan, with a tone and technique as big as the Longhorn State itself. With his weathered Strat and large, muscular hands, Vaughan single-handedly revived the blues and in the process earned a reputation as the greatest electric blues guitarist in history.

Like most blues guitarists in the post–World War II era, SRV combined the styles of his forbears, generally speaking, players like Waters, King (B.B. and Albert), and Robert Johnson. But no one had ever taken the blues and made it sound like Stevie Ray could. Like one of his heroes, Jimi Hendrix, he *owned* whatever he played. He attacked his songs with attitude and aggressiveness, and his approach put him in a class by himself. SRV played every note in every solo with passion and credibility.

Throughout his career Stevie Ray paid homage to all sorts of blues, from Texas to Chicago and the Delta. His very presence reignited interest in blues and blues rock. In the late 1960s, the first wave of blues rock and British blues powered through the States, but had long ago run its course. Stevie Ray rekindled that genre by channeling Hendrix, playing loud, and charging his guitar solos with rock 'n' roll fury. Just as the blues had been on the brink of extinction, Stevie Ray came to the rescue.

When Eric Clapton himself first heard Stevie play, he said that no one he had ever heard commanded more respect: "Whoever this is, I've got to find out. Whoever this is is going to shake the world. It's going to be a long time before anyone that brilliant will come along again" (Forte, Dan, liner notes, "Stevie Ray Vaughan's Greatest Hits," *Epic/Legacy,* 1995).

Clapton was fascinated by the fact that Stevie Ray never seemed to be lost in any way. "It was as though he never took a breather, or took a pause to think where he was gonna go next, it just flowed out of him . . . I didn't get to see or hear Stevie play near often enough, but every time I did I got chills and knew I was in the presence of greatness. He seemed to be an open channel and music just flowed through him. It never seemed to dry up."

When Vaughan emerged onto the rock scene in the early 1980s, the music industry was suffering through a creative slump in the wake of punk's decline and disco's rise. America enjoyed peace and prosperity, yet an underlying anxiety proved that all was not well. President Reagan was popular enough to be assured of reelection, but there was also a polarizing force that left many uneasy about the future. Stevie Ray's blues was the perfect antidote for such an anxious undercurrent.

As the 1980s progressed and the gap between rich and poor materialized and grew wider every year, Stevie Ray surged to the forefront of blues and rock. He achieved true heroic status, the first player since Hendrix who truly shook the world of blues guitar.

Vaughan worshiped at the altar of Hendrix, brazenly inviting comparisons with him and even recording one of his songs, "Voodoo Chile." Like Hendrix, Vaughan could play rhythm and lead simultaneously. He played fast and loud manipulating feedback like a snake charmer mesmerizing a cobra. "He played a song the way Jackson Pollock painted a painting—with one fluid, masculine gesture, never pausing to think about what he would do next" (Weisel, Al, "A Bluesman's Lingering Notes: Six Years After His Death, Stevie Ray Vaughan Is Hotter Than Ever," *Washington Post*, September 7, 1996).

The Hendrix parallels continued. Hendrix, a black man, played rock, a "white" musical style. Vaughan, a white man, played blues, a "black" musical style. They both managed to bring two worlds together, making audiences judge talent by content rather than color.

For most of his career, Vaughan shared something *else* with Hendrix: a taste for the fast life. His career was nearly destroyed by Crown Royal and cocaine. Yet while Hendrix succumbed to his addictions in 1970, Vaughan actually survived his. After going through rehab, he spent the last three years of his life clean and sober.

"The master of 12-bar blues became a 12-step success story. Today, as drugs and alcohol fell one musician after another, Vaughan's story offers a ray of hope" (Weisel, 1996).

Sadly, also like Jimi, Stevie Ray's total career output during his lifetime was astonishingly small. He recorded only four studio albums and a live set under his own name while alive and he spent roughly six years in the limelight, from 1983 to 1989. One can only speculate what might have been had Stevie Ray Vaughan survived his plane crash to make more music. He had beaten back the demons of drug abuse and seemed poised to rejuvenate his own career the way he jump-started the blues a half dozen years earlier.

At the time of his death, he'd been reaching for that next note. "I'm ready to really pour it on," he told his longtime drummer Chris Layton.

When *Rolling Stone* compiled its list of rock's greatest guitar players, Vaughan figured in at #7. In 1983, *Texas Flood* was voted Best Guitar Album in the *Guitar Player*'s magazine Reader's Poll. Also, Stevie won the Best Electric Blues Player category (beating out Eric Clapton)—an honor he enjoyed four years in a row, and Best New Talent. In 1984, Stevie was named Entertainer of the Year and Blues Instrumentalist of the Year at the Fifth Annual W. C. Handy Awards (Blues Foundation), the first time in the history of the event that a white person had won either category. So, in addition to making a vast and triumphant contribution to the electric guitar, to the blues, and to his generation, SRV also, perhaps unwittingly, broke down cultural and social barriers, bringing people together with the kind of spirited blues and rock that the whole world, regardless of color, could really enjoy.

EARLY YEARS

Born on October 3, 1954, Stevie Ray Vaughan, the son of Jim and Martha Vaughan, grew up in the Oak Cliff section of Dallas. Jim grew up on a cotton farm in Rockwall County east of Dallas. Martha was a clerical worker in Dallas.

Jim played some piano as a youngster and had an excellent ear, but he didn't focus much on his music. Instead, he spent time in the Navy and bringing up his boys, Stevie Ray and Jimmie.

Jimmie was the early pride of the family. He'd shown the ability to hear a tune and pick it up quickly on guitar. Martha and father Jim didn't pay all that much attention to Stevie, though Stevie was paying close attention to what Jimmie was doing. When the Vaughans tucked their boys in at night, though, they did see that both were sleeping with their guitars.

The boys also listened ceaselessly to their cheap transistor radio at night, when the signal was clearest. The transistor served as the next small step in the Vaughans' learning process. At the time, in the early 1960s, the Beatles were all over the States. But the Vaughans listened to the blues and rhythm and blues; those tunes made the Beatles sound tame.

At such an early age—Steve was only 10 or so—Jimmie did most of the learning and Steve did most of the watching. "He taught me how to teach myself," remembered Stevie. "And that's the right way" (Patoski, Joe Nick, and Bill Crawford, *Caught in the Crossfire.* Boston: Little Brown, 1993, p. 14).

Bands in Dallas like the Nightcaps started blazing some trails in R&B, even though they were white. Jimmie learned all the parts to their songs as Steve watched closely.

In time, Jimmie formed his own band, the Chessman. While Stevie was putting his band together, Jimi Hendrix was turning the world on its ear with his playing. The revolution in sound inspired Steve, and he began experimenting on his guitar. Jimmie brought "Purple Haze" home in 1967, which to him sounded like Muddy Waters on acid. He went out and bought the album and began learning whatever he could from it. So, not coincidentally, did his little brother.

Hendrix came to Dallas that year, and Jimmie's band the Chessman were tapped to open the show. Jimmie Vaughan's showmanship and dexterity impressed Jimi Hendrix; enough so that after the show Hendrix gave Vaughan $40 and his wah-wah pedal in exchange for Jimmie's Vox wah wah.

The next year, when Stevie entered an Oak Cliff high school, he had already had some legitimate blues and R&B credentials. His band names changed almost weekly. His first bands were called the Chantones, the Epileptic Marshmallows, and the Brooklyn Underground, among others. About this time, the hippie movement had drifted south from San Francisco to Dallas—at least a petite version of it—and Steve and his band would play an open space in Dallas called Lee Park, which was populated by free, Ripple-drinking spirits.

While Jimmie and the Chessman owned Dallas, playing Top 40 covers, Stevie struggled trying to find the right combination for his own band. He watched as his brother's band partied nightly, smoked marijuana, popped pills, and swapped needles to shoot speed. One of Jimmie's bandmates, Doyle Bramhall, contracted a serious illness, and the band fell apart.

When Doyle recovered, he and Jimmie formed Texas Storm, a Texas R&B act. Unfortunately, the gig didn't pay as well as a cover band, and so they struggled even as they ruled musically. One night, their bass player couldn't make a gig, on account of being tossed in jail. Jimmie turned to his kid brother and asked him if he wanted the gig. He nodded quickly, downtuned his brother's Barney Kessel guitar to sound like a bass, and started gigging with his brother for the very first time.

Stevie played Dallas and Austin haunts, and the band made big impressions in both cities, though little brother had a hard time keeping up with the band's extreme indulgences.

Back home, Stevie didn't care much for school. He'd often hang at the back of the class and sleep; his late hours playing music seriously affected his ability to absorb academics. The only class he truly enjoyed attending was art, and he actually had a few of his illustrations published in the school newspaper.

Word of his underachievement reached home, where his parents were waiting for him. His father, angry that Stevie was trying to do what Jimmie had already done much more successfully, grew frustrated with Stevie and started beating him. His dad, a short-tempered racist, also had a drinking problem. Stevie would normally escape his wrath by leaving the house quickly, but occasionally he wasn't quick enough, and he'd be seen at school all bandaged up.

He escaped the pain by doing drugs, including aything and everything he could find, from alcohol to glue and nose spray to pills.

> I started off my drinking and using career, oh, I guess . . . early '60's, when I was somewhere around seven or eight years old. I grew up in an alcoholic family. My father was an alcoholic and even though I saw the problems that alcohol caused in our family, I still found it attractive for some reason. I don't know what that was, I thought I was missing something. I was always a kid who was afraid I was gonna miss something.
>
> I would see someone, who I really cared about and know that they . . . this is a pattern that's gone on most of my life and I still don't understand why it's attractive to me, or has been. I would see someone who I really cared for and loved and that they couldn't do anything unless they were shooting something, and I would see that it would be literally killing them . . . and that would be a good reason for me to try it. I don't know . . . I don't understand that. That's the pattern that I've developed. I saw it with my father, I saw it with very close friends and I've seen it with people who are no longer alive, you know. (Stevie Ray Vaughan's Alcoholic's Anonymous speech, 1/3/90)

∗　∗　∗

For Stevie, the short-term solution of his father's violent nature appeared imminent. Like his brother Jimmie and his father before him, he'd quit school and leave home. He finished his junior year and cut all ties with his formal education.

In Austin in 1969, Jimmie and Stevie watched in awe as Johnny Winter opened for Muddy Waters at a prominent hippie venue called the Vulcan Gas Company. Muddy slayed them; he was the real deal, and so both Jimmie and Stevie Ray tabled their quest for stardom and repositioned themselves as genuine blues articles.

Stevie formed Blackbird with a friend from Dallas, Christian Plicque, a black soul singer. But Plicque couldn't project his voice over Stevie's guitar and that band split. Krackerjack came next, and it would be the first band to make a lasting impact on Stevie Ray's future: it had Tommy Shannon on bass and Uncle John Turner on drums, otherwise known as the rhythm section of Johnny Winter's band. Stevie actually joined the band to replace guitar slinger Jesse Taylor, a Lubbock native and a pretty good six-stringer in his own right.

Krackerjack cut a wide swath through the southwest playing the blues circuit. But drugs destroyed the band quickly, despite considerable promise. Authorities arrested Shannon, and one of the conditions of his probation was to cease employment with Krackerjack. Case closed. Stevie didn't get arrested, but he did delve deeply into drugs from that point on.

In 1973, Marc Benno invited Stevie to record in his band called the Nightcrawlers, which featured Doyle Bramhall. The Nightcrawlers were almost successful until their record label A&M decided not to release the record. On his way back home from Los Angeles, Stevie purchased a battered 1959 Stratocaster in Ray's Music Exchange in Austin. He named it "Number One" or "First Wife," and this became his favorite guitar for the rest of his life.

Stevie left the Nightcrawlers one year later, disappointed. He joined the Cobras next, one of Austin's most popular bands. It was here that Stevie Ray got his first crack at singing. For the next two and a half years, he played with the Cobras on the Austin Club Circuit. They eventually won "Band of the Year" in the 1977 Austin music poll with a lineup that included W. C. Clark (bass), Lou Ann Barton (vocals), Freddie "Pharoah" Walden (drums), and Mike Kindred (keyboards).

The following year, Clark, the band's bassist, resigned and was replaced by Jackie Newhouse. Freddie Walden later quit the band and was replaced by Chris "Whipper" Layton. Following the departure of Freddie Walden, the band renamed itself Triple Threat. In 1980, Lou Ann Barton left Triple Threat to join Roomful of Blues. Stevie Ray renamed what remained of the group "Double Trouble."

Their big break came in 1980, when they performed at the Steamboat 1874 club in Austin on April 1. This performance was recorded for radio and later released as the 1992 album, *In the Beginning.* At the outset of 1981, Tommy Shannon stepped in for Jackie Newhouse on bass. The band recorded another performance, this one at an Austin music festival, and it ended up in the hands of the Rolling Stones' Mick Jagger. Impressed, Jagger invited Double Trouble to play a semiprivate party for the Rolling Stones at New York's Danceteria on April 22.

AP photo

Now their reputation had begun to expand almost uncontrollably. Without a label deal or an official recording in stores, the band performed at the Montreux International Jazz Festival in Switzerland that same spring. They were the first unsigned and unrecorded band to do so.

The album, *Live in Montreux,* features the crowd booing as well as applauding. Their song didn't match the genteel aesthetics of the event, and so the audience, when faced with the band's brash, propulsive blues, let Double Trouble and festival organizers know how they felt.

* * *

Backstage after the set the band was devastated. But they did end up meeting two musicians that would take the edge off that disappointment: David Bowie and Jackson Browne. Bowie offered Stevie the lead guitar spot on his upcoming *Let's Dance* album, and Jackson

TEXAS BLUES

The Texas Blues style developed as a more refined form of music. Although just as deliberate and direct, it was not as raw and rudimentary as the Delta style. In Texas blues, the guitar played a vital role, providing the text with sophisticated variations from verse to verse. Texas blues differs from Chicago blues in its instrumentation, especially the heavy emphasis on guitar. Stevie Ray Vaughan contributed to the style by incorporating slide, swing, and jazz licks, ala another Texas blues icon, T-Bone Walker. Texas blues also relies on using licks as bridges during its songs.

Texas blues began in the early 1900s when African Americans, recruited to work in the oil fields, brought the Delta style to Texas. Blind Lemon Jefferson became one of the first innovators of Texas blues. He employed jazzy improvisation and single-string accompaniment in his early work. Lightnin' Hopkins, an acoustic player, also popularized the Texas brand, while Walker brought the hollow-body electric into play. During the Depression, many of the blues musicians moved to Texas urban centers, and labels, such as the Duke and Peacock labels, popped up in those centers to accommodate all the talent. From there, popular performers emerged and the Texas blues style, now unified by these performers, emerged.

With Blind Lemon Jefferson on the early side and Stevie Ray Vaughan on the later side— the Texas blues bookends—many volumes of style and substance came in between, including Blind Willie Johnson, Walker, Hopkins, and Big Mama Thornton in the first few decades and ZZ Top, Jimmie Vaughan, the Fabulous Thunderbirds, and Chris Duarte more recently.

Browne offered Double Trouble free use of his studio. The demo they recorded there became their debut album, *Texas Flood*.

Another legend, A&R man John Hammond, finally signed Stevie Ray Vaughan and Double Trouble to Epic Records, and they released *Texas Flood* in June of 1983. The repercussions were enormous. It was nominated for two Grammy awards, one as Best Traditional Blues Recording, and another for Best Rock Instrumental Performance for the song "Rude Mood." Stevie won three categories in Guitar Player's Readers Poll: "Best New Talent," "Best Blues Album," and "Best Electric Blues Guitarist," beating out Eric Clapton and becoming only the second guitarist in history to win three Guitar Player awards in one year (the first is Jeff Beck).

The next spring, Stevie and the band released *Couldn't Stand the Weather*. From the album, a live version of "Texas Flood" won a Grammy for Best Traditional Blues Recording, and a cover of Hendrix's "Voodoo Chile" (Slight Return) earned a nomination for Best Rock Instrumental Performance.

In 1985, keyboard player Reese Wynans joins Double Trouble and Epic releases *Soul to Soul*, which would become their third gold album in a row. More Grammy nominations ensued. SRV was also contracted to produce Lonnie Mack's comeback album *Strike Like Lightning,* and he played on several of Mack's tunes. On April 10, Stevie echoed another Hendrix antic when he played "The Star Spangled Banner" for opening day of the National League baseball season at the Houston Astrodome where, unlike Hendrix, he was booed by the crowd. It was a minor setback that Vaughan took seriously.

No longer the underdog, success came to Stevie Ray and Double Trouble with a price. The consumption of drugs and alcohol took its toll. In fact, Stevie had never really let up since his earliest days in Austin. He looked horrible and his energy ebbed; a problem because he and the band toured constantly around the world.

I would wake up and guzzle something, just to get rid of the pain I was feeling. Whiskey, beer, vodka, whatever was handy. It got to the point where if I'd try to say "hi" to somebody, I would just fall apart, crying and everything. It was like . . . solid doom. There really was nowhere to go but up. I'd been trying to pull myself up by my bootstraps, so to speak, but they were broken, you know? (Milkowski, Bill, "Resurrection," *Guitar World,* September 1988)

He supplemented his activities and expedited his decline with some creative recreational pursuits, like pouring cocaine into his drinks to prolong the buzz. "I tore up my stomach real bad by doing that. I didn't realize that the cocaine would crystallize in my stomach and make cuts inside there. Finally, I had a breakdown. I mean, everything fell apart. I surrendered to the fact that I didn't know how to go without the stuff. I had envisioned myself just staying high for the rest of my life, you know? But I had to give up to win, 'cause I was in a losing battle" (Milkowski, 1988).

By the time the band recorded and released the ironically titled *Live Alive,* Stevie Ray was about to crack. In Ludwigshafen, Germany, during a full-blown 1986 tour in Europe, he began vomiting blood in his hotel room. Later in the tour, at the Hammersmith Palais, he fell off a gangplank when leaving the stage, prompting the cancellation of the rest of the tour. Stevie entered a drug rehabilitation clinic in London under the care and supervision of Dr. Victor Bloom. He then moved to a treatment facility in Marietta, Georgia. Tommy Shannon also checked into rehab.

* * *

He left the hospital sober and committed to the Twelve Step Program of Alcoholics Anonymous. He addressed a chapter of AA soon after.

I realized I am still alive now and, that's an amazing thing to me. When I was 17, I thought I wouldn't make it to 21. When I made it to 21, I thought something was . . . something's up, you know? [laughs] You know, "What's going on here?" [laughs] When I passed 30, I thought something's wrong. [laughs] I'm just glad to be alive today. I don't know, I don't have a whole lot to say about anything, other than knowing that if I let this program and if I let God do what He's gonna do in my life, through you, or through whatever . . . that it's a whole lot better than I ever could have done it myself before I came to this program. (www.srvrocks.com/aa.htm)

* * *

Following his recovery, Double Trouble released his fifth album, *In Step,* in 1989. It won the band a second Grammy, this time for Best Contemporary Blues Recording, and many consider it his best studio recordings. Not surprisingly, it's the first album he and the band made without the aid of narcotics. "Crossfire," the lead single off the album, became his first #1 radio hit. Double Trouble toured North America with Jeff Beck and appeared on *Austin City Limits,* a popular public television show, for the second time.

DEATH

When performers played at Alpine Valley in East Troy, Wisconsin, a difficult-to-reach venue, they often stayed in Chicago and flew in for the show. Stevie Ray did just that. He had just done two nights sharing the bill at Alpine Valley with Eric Clapton. The gigs ended with a big blues jam, featuring Clapton with Vaughan, his brother Jimmie, Buddy Guy, and Robert Cray all on stage. After the second show, he boarded a helicopter on a densely foggy night. The craft slammed into the side of a man-made ski mountain and everybody aboard—Stevie Ray, the pilot, and three members of Clapton's entourage—was killed instantly. He was 35.

Over 1,500 people, including Jackson Browne, Dr. John, Ringo Starr, Buddy Guy, Bonnie Raitt, and Stevie Wonder, attended his memorial service in Dallas. Three thousand more waited outside the chapel. He was buried on August 31 at Laurel Land Memorial Park in South Dallas. The city of Austin erected a memorial statue of Stevie Ray Vaughan on November 21, 1993. It is located on Town Lake, near the site of his last Austin concert.

* * *

Prior to his death in 1990, Vaughan collaborated with his brother Jimmie, a founding member of the successful Fabulous Thunderbirds, on *Family Style,* a duets album.

Family Style appeared in October and entered the charts at #7. It went platinum three months after its release and won a Grammy. It also commenced a string of popular, posthumous releases, including *The Sky Is Crying,* a collection of studio outtakes compiled by his brother that was released in October of 1991; it entered the charts at #10 and went platinum three months after its release.

At the 1990 Austin Music Awards, the local music community recognized Vaughan's immense contribution to the city. Among other accolades, they named *Texas Flood* album of the decade and Vaughan himself *Musician of the Decade.*

In some ways, Vaughan is as popular now as he was before his death. Robert Rodriguez, a film director, is planning to make a movie of his life. Tribute bands from Finland to California try to cop his licks, and every hotshot guitarist has been slapped with the label of "the next Stevie Ray Vaughan." Indeed, he has influenced every blues guitarist of the current generation with his work.

TECHNIQUE/STYLE

He played the whole instrument, it wasn't just notes anymore. And he didn't necessarily stick to making your guitar have anything to do with a guitar, with the way he played it. In a very, in a very melodic way, and musical way, he seemed to ignore frets and things like that, you know (laughs) and uh, it turned, I don't know, he just turned it into something else (Sebastian, John, "Rock Stars Radio Program," March 12–25, 1990 air dates).

Technically, Stevie Ray derived his style from his many blues influences, including Albert Collins, Magic Sam, Albert King, B.B. King, Buddy Guy, Hubert Sumlin, Muddy Waters, Guitar Slim, Johnny Copeland, and many others. Then there were rockers like Hendrix, Clapton, and Beck—the three massive Stratocaster innovators on the rock side.

> The Beatles, early rock, I loved everybody that was pullin' from rhythm & blues, blues, rock 'n' roll, old style rock 'n' roll, rockabilly. And then I owe a lot to my brother, because not only did he familiarize me with all this music, and all these people that play this music as well, but he was able to emulate a lot of their styles. But then, he was already developing his own. I've still never heard anybody play quite like Jimmie. So, as a result, I have to say Jimmie Vaughan is probably my biggest influence. (www.srvrocks.com)

Signatures of Stevie Ray's style include hyper, multistep bends, jazzy chordal tendencies, and the chord melody influence of Hendrix. In addition to setting a new high-water mark for electric blues players, he also set a standard for tone as well. His sound derived in part from heavy gauge strings (ordinarily .013s), tuned down a half step to E-flat. The principal ingredient to this overdriven tone was a pair of Ibanez TS-808 Tube Screamers, run through earsplitting Fender Vibro-Verbs and Super Reverbs.

Vaughan's use of the low-pitch tuning was Hendrix inspired.

"It gives you different overtones," says Stevie Ray. "It's an interesting sound, and I find it a lot easier to sing to." He's also acquired the wah pedal used by Hendrix to record "Up from the Sky." He speaks without any self-consciousness about Hendrix, with whom he has often been compared. In May, Vaughan played a solo version of "The Star Spangled Banner" at the Houston Astros' home opener at the Astrodome. "Immediately, people recalled the world-weary, apocalyptic version played by Hendrix at Woodstock in 1969. And the performance triggered yet a new round of comparisons between Hendrix and Stevie" (Nixon, Bruce, "It's Star Time!" *Guitar World*, September 1985).

One of the most crucial elements of Vaughan's sound is the way he uses his fingers. "Sometimes I slide 'em, rubbing the sides of the strings," he explains. "To get a big, fat sound that punches out I pop the strings with either my second or third finger. Usually I'll hold the pick but ignore it, and get my second or third finger under the string, pull it and let go. Basically, it's what modem bass players do—it gives me a real bright, peppier tone. But now I can get that same tone with my thumb, just by laying into the string a little harder." Here Vaughan pauses to laugh at himself. "But like my brother Jimmie says, I play like I'm breaking out of jail anyway" (Joseph, Frank, "Before the Flood," *Guitar World*, September 1983).

EQUIPMENT/GEAR

In the 1960s as a boy, Stevie went through a number of guitars. Many were handed down by his brother Jimmie, including a Gibson Messenger, 1952 Fender Broadcaster, 1954 Gibson Les Paul TV, 1952 Gibson Les Paul Gold-top, a Gibson Barney Kessel from 1972, and a 1959 Gibson dot-neck 335. He mainly used these guitars until he obtained the now-famous Number One.

Stevie acquired Number One in 1973 from an Austin guitar shop. It had a tobacco-sunburst finish and thick rosewood neck that accommodated Stevie's large hands. He replaced the white pickguard with a black one and added his initials. The original right-handed tremolo unit was replaced with a gold left-handed unit in 1977. A couple of Stevie's heroes, Hendrix and Otis Rush, were left-handed and played right-handed guitars turned upside down. He also replaced the frets, adding jumbo style bass frets to add sustain and facilitate string bending. Stevie used extremely thick strings, (.013s) which was hard on his fingers. He eventually switched to smaller strings to save wear and tear on his hands.

Number One took a beating. Stevie's heavy strumming stripped the surface of the guitar almost entirely and stripped its finish. By 1989, Stevie had thought about hanging the guitar up, retiring it, and moving on. The neck had been fixed and refixed so many times that it would not hold new frets even when he tried glueing them on. In 1990, some stage scenery fell on a rack of Stevie's guitars and Number One's neck broke again. He ordered a replacement neck from Fender, and the company sent him a replica of the original 1963 neck.

All of Vaughan's guitars have stock pickups.

Stevie's distinctive sounds stemmed partly from his seasoned guitars, but also from his peculiar amplifier and effects setup. Vaughan was constantly tinkering with his equipment to find the sound he wanted; that tinkering also occurred because he wore down his equipment rather quickly, especially his guitar necks, which constantly needed replacing. Stevie did use a Fuzz Face on some songs, especially later in his career, and mostly in concert rather than on an album. Stevie used the Fuzz Face specifically for distortion, while he used the Tube Screamer mostly for added gain (make it louder). You can hear the Fuzz Face on "Leave My Girl Alone" on *In Step*. Stevie turns the Fuzz Face on as he begins his solo. You can hear how his tone becomes much more distorted at that time. You can set your distortion box to this type of fuzz, too. It may not be as "smooth" as a Fuzz Face, but it'll produce the extra distortion.

"I use the Tube Screamer because of the tone knob," he says. "That way you can vary the distortion and tonal range. You can turn it on slightly to get a Guitar Slim tone, which is how I use it, or wide open so your guitar sounds like it should jump up and bite you" (Joseph, 1983).

Tube amps naturally introduce some compression, but mainly when you drive them hard. A small amount of pedal compression will help sustain and smooth out the pops and thumps when you play hard, like Stevie's attack. This will help a lot when you play at lower volumes. His playing style had a lot of string pulls, finger plucks, and rakes, which means the "volume" of the sound when you use these playing techniques will greatly vary. The compressor will smooth these out. To the best of our knowledge, Stevie never used a chorus unit, or a Rotovibe. Unless you can afford a vintage Vibratone (the Leslie-style speaker cabinet), either of these effects can approximate the shimmering sound found on songs like "Cold Shot" and "Couldn't Stand the Weather." Set the depth to shallow and the speed to medium-fast, about six or seven beats per second. You want just a hint of an organ tone, not a full-out, phased and echoed goth-rock effect (www.guitarglen .freeuk.com/srv.htm).

ESSENTIAL READING

Forte, Dan. Liner notes, Stevie Ray Vaughan's Greatest Hits, *Epic/Legacy*, 1995.
Joseph, Frank. "Before the Flood." *Guitar World*, September 1983.
Milkowski, Bill. "Resurrection." *Guitar World*, September 1988.
Nixon, Bruce. "It's Star Time!" *Guitar World*, September 1985.
Patoski, Joe Nick, and Bill Crawford. *Caught in the Crossfire*. Boston: Little Brown, 1993.
Sebastian, John. "Rock Stars Radio Program," March 12–25, 1990 air dates.
Stevie Ray Vaughan's Alcoholic's Anonymous speech, 1/3/90.
Weisel, Al. "A Bluesman's Lingering Notes: Six Years after His Death, Stevie Ray Vaughan Is Hotter Than Ever." *Washington Post*, September 7, 1996.

ESSENTIAL WORK

"Cold Shot" (1984)
"Couldn't Stand the Weather" (1984)
"Pride and Joy" (1983)

ESSENTIAL LISTENING

Albert King with Stevie Ray Vaughan *In Session* (Stax, 1999)
Couldn't Stand the Weather (Epic/Legacy, 1984)

In Step (Epic/Legacy, 1989)
Live at Carnegie Hall (Epic, 1997)
SRV (Epic/Legacy, 2000)
Texas Flood (Epic/Legacy, 1983)

ESSENTIAL VIEWING

Stevie Ray Vaughan *Live at Montreaux* 1982 & 1985 (Sony, 2004)

Neil Young

From his late 1960s roots through four decades to the present day, Neil Young has always followed his own impulses. His reputation for waywardness and defiance comes through loud and clear throughout his performances and recorded work. This restlessness has also prevented his fans from taking the artist for granted; he rebels against the notion of the aging rock star resting on laurels and playing the vacuous, yet financially rewarding oldies circuit. "I never want to get to the point where I'm just going through the motions," he says (Pareles, Jon, "A Believer in the Magic of Glitches," *The New York Times,* August 8, 1997).

And he never has. For 40 years, from his critically important years with Buffalo Springfield and his brief alliance with Crosby, Stills, and Nash, through a solo career that has included hits (like "Heart of Gold" in 1972), raw uncommercial masterpieces (like the harrowing album "Tonight's the Night" in 1975), and misfires, Young has never rested on anything. He's made classic albums, disastrous albums, commercial records, and blatantly noncommercial ones.

Although Young has experimented widely with differing music styles, including swing, jazz, rockabilly, blues, and electronica throughout a varied career, his most accessible and best-known work generally falls in two styles: acoustic country-tinged folk rock and crunchy electric rock, as in songs like "Cinnamon Girl," "Rockin' in the Free World," and "Hey Hey, My My (Into the Black)."

That restlessness also carries over to his performing. On the road he's been at his finest with his longtime scruffy noisemakers Crazy Horse, a band he's led on and off since 1969. But he's also toured with Stax soul legends Booker T. and the MGs as his backup band. On another, he brought the Seattle rock band Pearl Jam with him for accompaniment. Still another, he decided to go it alone with an acoustic guitar.

Although he has occasionally tried elaborate productions, most of Young's music possesses a bedrock of simplicity. In his work with Crazy Horse, his songs are primal, energetic stomps, his vocals surrounded by a maelstrom of feedback and distortion. In more placid settings, he approaches his material the way an old-time mountain balladeer would. It is the yin and yang, the bookends, of Neil Young's evocative approach.

Throughout his career, he has been considered one of rock 'n' roll's most influential artists. The brawny rock he plies with Crazy Horse is a direct ancestor of the grunge and alternative rock of the 1990s—complete with flannel shirts and torn jeans. His rootsy acoustic sounds found on classic albums like *After the Gold Rush* and *Harvest* presaged the alternative country music that flourished in the late 1980s and 1990s.

Often, like many true artists, his modus operandi seems contradictory. On the one hand, he pursues perfection with relentlessness. On the other, he is obsessed with letting the flaws in his performance shine through. "Perfection for perfection's sake is terrible," Young says. "But seeking perfection in the name of spiritual expression is an impossibility that you should constantly be striving for: to try to get to this place you can never get to" (Pareles, 1997). In other words, he is a perfectionist who embraces imperfection.

Musically, Young conjures mysteries from basic structures and plain language. His songs are limited, utilizing only a handful of chords, with melodies suggesting old-time folk music. His lyrics are also often blunt and plain. Occasionally, they are blatantly political and outspoken, as in "Ohio," one of rock's great protest songs; that is when they're not poetic or mysterious, in which case they convey a very different feeling.

These ironies underscore the tremendous impact Young has had on generations of rock, country, acoustic, and roots music fans. He has served as a touchstone for bands in the aforementioned grunge scene like Pearl Jam and Nirvana. He also helped jump-start the Jam Band scene, with his profound effect on bands like .moe and Phish. And, with his avant-garde work, he's fueled the creativity of essential fringe acts like Sonic Youth and late-period Radiohead.

Young also became an outspoken advocate for environmental issues and farming. He cofounded the massive benefit concert Farm Aid and, with his wife Pegi, helped establish the Bridge School for disabled children and annual fund-raising shows.

His accolades spread out across the decades, but have really been rolling in lately. In a "100 Greatest Guitarists of All Time" list in the June 1996 issue of *Mojo* magazine, Young was ranked #9. *Rolling Stone* slotted him in at #35 on their list of "The 100 Greatest Artists of All Time." More recently, *Paste* magazine put him at #2, right behind Bob Dylan, in its list of our "Greatest Living Songwriters."

He has been inducted into the Rock 'n' Roll Hall of Fame twice, once as part of his band the Buffalo Springfield (1997) and once as a solo artist (1995). He was also inducted into the Canadian Music Hall of Fame way back in 1982.

EARLY YEARS

Neil Young was born in Toronto, Ontario, Canada in 1945 to Scott Young, a sportswriter and novelist and "Rassy" Ragland. Young's father moved frequently to accommodate his growing career as a journalist. While he worked in Toronto, the family lived in a small country burg known as Omemee, northeast of the city.

Young was sickly as a kid. He was diagnosed with diabetes as a child and he suffered a case of polio at age six that left him with a weakened left side and a slight limp. In the mid-1950s, when rock 'n' roll blossomed, Young was listening to hobo, cowboy, prairie, and railroad music by Frankie Laine and others. "Rawhide" and the like were big in Canada at the time and Young recalled walking down the railroad tracks every day on his way to school.

Musically speaking, neither of his parents had a propensity for the art. They'd listen to the old big bands at home like Glen Miller and Tommy Dorsey, singers like Cab Calloway, Lena Horne, and Della Reese. His parents divorced when he was 12 though and he moved back to Winnipeg, his mother's home, to live with her in the working class suburb of Fort Rouge. There he attended first Earl Grey Junior High School and then Kelvin High.

He received his first guitar at age 14, as well as a plastic Arthur Godfrey ukulele, then a banjo, both of which he learned to play like a guitar. He worked at it and slowly learned his chords and began writing songs. It didn't take him long to get a band together. Young played electric lead guitar in an all-instrumental band called the Jades.

Young didn't bother with lyrics initially. At the time, his idol was Hank Marvin, Cliff Richard's guitar player in the Shadows. He was the hero of many of the guitar players around Winnipeg at the time, including Randy Bachman, later of the Guess and Bachman Turner Overdrive.

He started rocking out in a community center teenage band. They initially called themselves the Esquires, then the Stardusters, and finally the Squires. The Squires enjoyed a local hit called ''The Sultan.'' Through his touring, he began connecting with other big Canadian stars, including Joni Mitchell, Randy Bachman, and Rick James.

In 1964, Young briefly joined a band called the Mynah Birds, an R&B group based in Toronto. The Mynah Birds were significant, not because they made any notable recordings, but because its lineup teamed Young with soon-to-be funk superstars James and Bruce Palmer, with whom Young would go on to form Buffalo Springfield.

Earlier incarnation of the Mynah Birds, incidentally, included Goldie McJohn and Nick St. Nicholas, both of whom would later join Steppenwolf. Another Canadian star, Bruce Cockburn, also spent some of his early years in the regionally popular group as well. The Mynah Birds signed a seven-year deal with the Motown label in 1966 and recorded a number of tracks for the Detroit company. Their debut album was in the works, with Neil Young in the lineup, but Rick James, the band's leader was arrested for deserting the Navy. Unwilling to deal with James and the group, Motown shelved the band's recordings.

MUSIC

After the Mynah Birds' near miss, Young and bassist Bruce Palmer relocated to Los Angeles. While there, Young hooked up with Stephen Stills, a guy he'd met at a Thuner Bay Ontario folk club. That encounter—both were playing with bands of their own—prompted the pair to begin work together.

One of Stills's bandmates, Richie Furay, was also around. One day, Stills and Furay spotted Young and Palmer stuck in traffic on Hollywood's Sunset Boulevard. Young was driving an instantly recognizable car, a tricked out 1953 Pontiac hearse. They formed a band with drummer Dewey Martin, calling themselves the Buffalo Springfield, after a name they saw on the side of a steamroller owned by the Buffalo-Springfield Roller Company.

The new band lasted only two years, but they made a powerful impact on rock 'n' roll. They recorded and released just three albums, but wrote a bevy of material all tolled, including the classic ''For What It's Worth.'' Unfortunately, despite their potent creativity, the personnel never really gelled. Palmer was deported a couple of times for drug possession, a problem that also affected Young's enthusiasm with the band. Producers deemed Young's vocal contributions too strange, so they tapped Furay to sing most of the songs, even Young's own work, a problem that also deflated the Canadian.

Additionally, the band grew disappointed with their recorded output, which is why most of their songs remained unreleased. Critics point to *Buffalo Springfield Again* as their most complete effort and the group's finest record. It includes tracks such as ''Mr. Soul,'' ''Rock & Roll Woman,'' ''Bluebird,'' ''Sad Memory,'' and ''Broken Arrow.'' Although the Buffalo Springfield was never a major commercial success, the group's reputation grew stronger after its breakup. Young had fond memories of the band when speaking in 1975. ''That was a great group, man. There'll never be another Buffalo

Springfield. Never" (Crowe, Cameron, "The Rolling Stone Interview: Neil Young," August 1975).

Immediately following the effort, he recorded his first solo album with the assistance of Jack Nitzsche, a composer/arranger who'd helmed some of the Buffalo Springfield efforts. He followed that debut up just four months later with his first official album with Crazy Horse, *Everybody Knows This Is Nowhere*. The songs on this classic were deliberately underwritten, their lyrics more suggestive than complete. But this incompleteness made them perfect for extended improvisations, especially on songs like "Down by the River," "Cinnamon Girl," and "Cowgirl in the Sand," three of Young's best rock compositions.

* * *

Following the dissolution of Buffalo Springfield, Stephen Stills formed a band with David Crosby of the Byrds and Graham Nash of the Hollies in 1968. Young embarked on his solo career, but interrupted that with a brief interlude with Stills's new band, creating Crosby, Stills, Nash & Young (CSN&Y). Richie Furay and Jim Messina founded the country rock band Poco. Messina went on to form Loggins & Messina with friend Kenny Loggins, and Furay became one-third of Souther, Hillman, and Furay.

Young, fully committed to his solo career, was approached by Atlantic Record's head Ahmet Ertegun who suggested that Crosby, Stills, and Nash, looking for a fourth member, speak with Neil Young. At first, Stills and Nash had apprehensions, mostly due to the problematic history of Young and Stills in their previous band. But after a few meetings, the two parties hammered out an agreement, one that allowed Young full freedom to maintain a parallel side project with his new band, Crazy Horse.

* * *

CSN&Y played their second gig at Woodstock and a subsequent show at Altamont, the ill-fated festival headlined by the Stones. They also released *Déjà Vu* in the spring of 1970, which included songs like Young's legendary "Ohio" and their version of Joni Mitchell's "Woodstock." The next year they released *Four Way Street*, a double album, but cracks were already beginning to weaken the band's foundation. In the next year or so, all four members produced solo albums. Young's entry was *After the Gold Rush*.

With no plans for the upcoming year, Young recorded *Harvest* in 1972, an album that yielded the #1 single "Heart of Gold." In the summer of 1972, the four members convened to begin the construction of a new album, tentatively called *Human Highway*. But the bickering that characterized the initial phase of the band returned, sinking plans for a new album or a future at all. In his 1975 interview with *Rolling Stone*, it was clear that Young was really confused about his experience:

> I just couldn't handle it toward the end. My nerves couldn't handle the trip. It wasn't me scheming on a solo career, it wasn't anything but my nerves. Everything started to go too . . . fast, I can tell that now. I was going crazy, you know, joining and quitting and joining again. I began to feel like I didn't have to answer or obey anyone. I needed more space. That was a big problem in my head. So I'd quit, then I'd come back 'cause it sounded so good. It was a constant problem. I just wasn't mature enough to deal with it. (Crowe, 1975)

Stills and Young stayed together to record *Long May You Run*, despite an occasionally strained relationship. They toured for a while, then Young pulled out abruptly.

* * *

During a phase with Crazy Horse in 1972 after the successful release of *Harvest,* Young was planning a nationwide tour. But his guitarist Danny Whitten frustrated him. A drug abuser and addict, Whitten could barely function within the framework of the band. At tour rehearsals, he proved incapable of retaining any information. It got so bad that Young, acting as bandleader, had to let him go. A week or so after his termination from the band, Whitten turned up dead of a drug overdose. The event devastated Young. "The night the coroner called me from L.A. and told me he'd ODed. That blew my mind...I loved Danny. I felt responsible. And from there, I had to go right out on this huge tour of huge arenas. I was very nervous and insecure" (Crowe, 1975).

Time Fades Away, a live album of the Crazy Horse tour, didn't capture the commercial audience that *Harvest* had. It was a dark nervous album full of angst and emotional intensity. He came under fire for not releasing a more pleasing album.

Courtesy of Photofest

I imagine I could have come up with the perfect follow-up album. A real winner. But it would have been something that everybody was expecting. And when it got there they would have thought that they understood what I was all about and that would have been it for me. I would have painted myself in the corner. The fact is I'm not that lone, laid-back figure with a guitar. I'm just not that way anymore. I don't want to feel like people expect me to be a certain way. Nobody expected *Time Fades Away* and I'm not sorry I put it out. I didn't need the money, I didn't need the fame. You gotta keep changing. Shirts, old ladies, whatever, I'd rather keep changing and lose a lot of people along the way. If that's the price, I'll pay it. I don't give a shit if my audience is a hundred or a hundred million. It doesn't make any difference to me. I'm convinced that what sells and what I do are two completely different things. If they meet, it's coincidence. (Crowe, 1975)

* * *

The recording period spanning the years between 1973 and 1976 was indeed dark for Young. His band family had just lost Whitten and Bruce Berry to heroin and his frustrations were beginning to show. *On the Beach* (1974) is harrowing. *Tonight's the Night* (1975) is the darkest, most dreadful recording of Young's career. Young called it an OD letter. *Zuma* found Young's demons exorcised with a more commercial effort. The album's standout track (apparently the only holdover from an early intention to present songs with historical subjects) was the seven-and-a-half-minute epic "Cortez the Killer," a commentary on the Spanish conqueror of Latin America that served as a platform for Young's most extensive guitar soloing to date.

Young released *Decade* in 1977, a three-record set documenting his first 10 years of making music. This is the material Young's established his reputation with, including the blockbusters "Like a Hurricane" and "Cortez the Killer" but also mixing in more unreleased recordings as the set draws to a close. It's accessible and designed to be a primer of sorts for Young's new fans.

The next important recording Young released was in 1979. *Rust Never Sleeps* features two sides, an electric portion and an acoustic portion, some of them recorded on his 1978 concert tour. The metaphor is particularly apt, outlining Young's quest to avoid creative deterioration. He demonstrates quite clearly that his chief tools to battle "rust" were his imagination and his ability to continue creating archetypal music in many styles and colors. A live album illustrating the tour that followed *Rust Never Sleeps* didn't receive the same praise.

* * *

The 1980s were Young's most controversial decade. The critics turned their noses up at his work and so did fans. He scored films, made a synthesizer record (*Trans* 1982), laid down a rockabilly album (*Everybody's Rockin'* 1983), and he wrote and codirected a comedy *Human Highway*. His work ended up being so uncharacteristic that David Geffen, his record label's president, sued Young for releasing such unrepresentative music. In 1987, he reformed Crazy Horse and recorded *Life*. The album fulfilled his contract with Geffen's label, after which Young made a move to the Warner Brothers' Reprise imprint.

But the change didn't deter Young from continuing his explorations. He recorded *This Note's for You* in 1988 with a full brass section and a swingin' R&B beat. The title track became his first hit single of the decade, thanks to a clever video that satirized the music industry, corporate rock, and the pretensions of advertising. MTV banned the song initially, before an uproar reinstated it, on its way to being awarded the MTV Video Music Award for Best Video of the Year in 1989.

After an unusual decade in which he skipped from genre to genre rather spastically, Young settled down right around the turn of the 1990s. He returned to his folk and country roots on albums like *Freedom,* which included some of his more strident lyrics. Next came *Ragged Glory,* an acclaimed Crazy Horse album, essentially a springboard for extended guitar travel. He continued that work on the avant-garde *Arc* and the live guitar celebration with Crazy Horse *Weld*. *Harvest Moon* took it down a notch with some acoustic strumming. But not for long, as *Sleeps with Angels* and *Mirror Ball* revved things up again. The former is a Crazy Horse album while the latter features the backing of Pearl Jam, an offshoot of Young's tour of the same year, 1995.

The 1990s were a varied and productive decade for Young, with no less than 12 albums, both live and studio, coming from one or the other of his creative outlets. That productivity continued into the 2000s, with the hyper-ambitious *Greendale,* an album and film of the same name that emerged in 2003. *Greendale* received more attention than any Neil Young album in years, but it wasn't positive. Young trotted out his concept album/song cycle, about an extended family in a small town called Greendale, torn apart by a murder. The record pleased many but irked some, a reaction that possibly pleased Young. He released the bucolic, lithesome *Prairie Wind* in 2005, and since then has focused on releasing material from his generous collection of archived songs (see sidebar).

FOREVER YOUNG

Since the 1980s, Neil Young fans have been promised the release of an exhaustive archive of music, photos, video, and other material from his four-decade career. In fact, the promises have been so great and so sincere the project has achieved legendary status. But so far, fans have only received two recordings: *Live at Massey Hall* acoustic performance and a fiery Crazy Horse gig, *Live at the Fillmore*. Both are, as promised, excellent performances with nonpareil audio. But the two albums have so far fallen short of expectations at least in terms of sheer volume. Where is everything?

The persnickety Young has attributed the serial delays to technical shortcomings and sound-quality problems in media ranging from CD-ROMs to DVDs. Larry Johnson, the project's producer, says the first installment is expected to include well over 100 songs, 18 of them never before released. There are to be 200 photographs, 160 lyrics manuscripts and more. Neil Young talked about it as a mammoth box set, or perhaps a series of box sets each chronicling a different era in his career, comprised entirely of unreleased recordings, some live, some studio. It was an eagerly anticipated set, because everybody knew that he had scores of unreleased recordings in his vaults.

The prolific Young customarily scrapped not just songs, but full albums at the last minute for a variety of reasons. Young regularly tested out new songs on tour, sometimes rewriting them later, sometimes never releasing them on album. Some of his colleagues, like Bob Dylan and the Beatles, had similar archival aspirations. Both of those artists have since released their rare material in highly acclaimed collections. Dylan released his *Bootleg Series.* The Beatles released their *Anthology* material. Not so for Young, whose camp insists that there are eight discs ready to be rolled out, including the aforementioned two. He was just waiting for the right audio format. Yet with audio formats changing almost monthly, waiting for the right one is risky business.

TECHNIQUE/STYLE

Neil Young's electric guitar sound is 100 percent primal and unequivocally based on feel rather than technique. Young used an apt phrase for his playing as the title to his 1990 album: *Ragged Glory.*

Bill Graham, the man behind San Francisco's Fillmore Auditorium and a rock 'n' roll magnate, once called Crazy Horse "the third Best Garage Band in the World." While we're not entirely sure who Graham slotted above Crazy Horse (The Stones? The Faces?), we do know that he got it right in mentioning Crazy Horse on the list. The San Francisco–based group came together with Young in 1968 after trying their hand at doo wop and folk-rock. When Young joined on after leaving the Buffalo Springfield, he ushered them into an entirely different aesthetic, more country and garage, more noise and growling emotion. Over the years, as Young's star ascended, Crazy Horse became referred to, against Young's wishes, as the artist's backing band.

Much of that noise came in the form of Young's expressive solos. In one of his most famous excursions, he pounds out an endlessly one-note, two-string solo in "Cinnamon Girl," with the help of his wang bar, or tremolo bridge. "It sounds like it's all different in that one place. As you're going in farther, you're hearing all the differences, but if you get back, it's all one . . . '' The Bigsby adds quite a bit to Young's tone, giving his lead lines anything from a jagged, angular irregularity to a bouncing, wobbly vibe. The Bigsby also serves as a trigger into feedback and is used to bend decaying notes to nail down the howl zone.

And speaking of feedback, Young's guitar, "Old Black" features a custom Gibson Firebird mini-humbucker designed to impact his guitar tone significantly (see Equipment/Gear). The pickup also eases Young's entry into feedback-laden passages, a tool he utilizes much more than most. (Listen to Young's noisy *Arc*, a montage of feedback segments, for a good example of that.)

> You can tell I don't care about bad notes. I listen for the whole band on my solos. You can call it a solo because that's a good way to describe it, but really it's an instrumental. It's the whole band that's playing. Billy Talbot is a massive bass player who only plays two or three notes. People are still trying to figure out whether it's because he only knows two or three notes or whether those are the only notes he wants to play. But when he hits a note, that note speaks for itself. It's a big motherf**kin' note. Even the soft one is big. (Obrecht, Jas, "In the Eye of the Hurricane," *Guitar Player*, March 1992)

With his stellar acoustic sound accompanying a brash electric vibe, Neil Young's guitar playing touches on all points of the sonic spectrum. On electric, Young made his greatest impact and biggest impression with his work in Crazy Horse along with Danny Whitten and Frank "Pancho" Sampedro. Young and Crazy Horse have collaborated on 13 albums, many of which, including *Everybody Knows This Is Nowhere* (1969) and the archival release *Live at the Fillmore East* (1970/2006), serve as some of the best work of Young's career.

Nowhere, especially, forms the bedrock of Young's guitar playing, with songs like the aforementioned "Cinnamon Girl" and "Down by the River," a dark song that gets an extended jam workout on the Fillmore live album.

> The sound is so deep, the groove is so deep—even when they're off, it still sounds great, because they feel it so much. I don't usually go for that approach. I like Sly and the Family Stone, Miles Davis and Mingus. I like consummate steady musicianship. I grew up on jazz. I didn't listen to rock music until I played in my first rock band when I was in high school. I went from progressive to Hendrix to funk to full-on L.A. punk. That's when I had the realization that emotion and content, no matter how simple, were valuable. A great one-chord punk song became as important to me as a Coltrane solo, and I've had the same feeling about Neil Young. He changed the way I thought about rock music. As a bass player, I used to be into very boisterous, syncopated and rhythmically complex songs. After hearing Neil, I appreciated simplicity, the poignancy of "less is more." (Flea, "The Immortals," *Rolling Stone*, March 2004)

In more recent years, Young has adopted elements from newer styles of music, like industrial and grunge. As an acoustic player, the story, and the technique, are different. Although he accompanies himself on several different instruments, including piano and harmonica, his style of hammer-on acoustic guitar is a lynchpin of his evocative acoustic ambience. Young's spare, elegant acoustic, known as "Hank," and harmonica work conjure a starkly atmospheric vibe that allows complex emotions to seep through.

In the end there lies a rare contradiction to Young's music. As a songwriter, he labors over his chord work, his melodies, and his lyrics. But at the same time, when he performs these songs, especially the electric pieces, he destroys them. Like Rodin, who'd finish a sculpture only to chop its arms off, Young polishes his songs to a shine then vandalizes them with noise, distortion, and feedback. Instruments splinter off and veer wildly out of tune and end up on a live record for all the world to hear. And he doesn't care. He wants to retain the essence, or heart, of his songs. Rather than rely on a formula, he would rather represent where he is at the time, mentally, physically, and socially. That's what's so remarkable about tracing the arc of Neil Young's career. It represents utter truth, and that truth is not always perfect.

EQUIPMENT/GEAR

Young collects both acoustic and electric guitars, but when he's performing he limits his choices to just a few reliable instruments. On electric, that means "Old Black," his 1953 Gibson Les Paul Goldtop. It is his primary electric guitar and the one featured on his best-known rock albums. Old Black, originally gold, got its name from a paint job the original owner had petitioned before Young acquired it in the late 1960s. In 1972, Young replaced the P-90 standard pickup with a mini-humbucker pickup from an old Gibson Firebird, and the alteration affected Young's sound dramatically. Larry Cragg, Young's guitar tech, explains how this happens: "The Firebird pickup is constructed with two alnico bar magnets, positioned one each within the two coils, in a dual-blade-styled design. Using magnetic material within the coil helps to increase a pickup's definition and treble response; the Firebird pickup is, therefore, a little weaker than the standard PAF-style humbucker or mini-humbucker, and also a lot brighter than either" (McDonough, Jimmy, *Shakey: A Neil Young Biography*. Anchor, 2003).

Young also installed a Bigsby vibrato tailpiece in 1969, an effect Young used frequently, especially on "Cowgirl in the Sand."

His principal acoustic guitar is a Martin D-45, on which he wrote "Old Man," and many of his other 1970s acoustic gems. He also owns a Martin D-28, nicknamed "Hank" after a previous owner, country legend Hank Williams. The guitar was purchased by Young from Tut Taylor in the early 1970s, and Young has toured with it for over 30 years.

Young's effective use of feedback is enabled by the right amp and the right amp settings. He uses a late 1950s tweed Fender Deluxe. With just two volume controls and a single, shared tone control, and it puts out a mere 15 watts, and carries just a single 12″ speaker, but has powered Neil Young's rock sound in stadiums and arenas around the world since he acquired it in 1967. (The sound is, of course, fed through other amps.)

The small amp breaks up early, with a lot of tube-induced compression at most volume levels. The Deluxe's hot gain produced the other important element of the guitar player's lead and feedback tone. In order to access the Deluxe's varying degrees of overdrive, Young uses a custom-made amp-control switching device known simply as "the Whizzer." The Whizzer allows Young to stomp a footswitch on the floor to command the unit to twist the Deluxe's volume and tone controls to preset positions. This allows Young to use no booster, overdrive, nor distortion pedals to get his insane tone: just a 50-year-old Tweed amp and the Whizzer.

Young does use a range of pedals and devices to create effects. He stomps on a vintage Fender tube reverb unit, which is set up with a separate spring pan mounted to the top of a microphone stand that is anchored on the floor below the stage. He also uses analog and digital delays, an octave divider, and a flanger.

ESSENTIAL READING

Crowe, Cameron. "The Rolling Stone Interview: Neil Young," August 1975.
Downing, David. *A Dreamer of Pictures: Neil Young, the Man and His Music.* Cambridge, MA: Da Capo Press, 1995.
Flea. *Rolling Stone.* "The Immortals," March 2004.
McDonough, Jimmy. *Shakey Neil Young's Biography.* New York: Anchor 2003.
Obrecht, Jas. "In the Eye of the Hurricane." *Guitar Player,* March 1992.
Pareles, Jon. "A Believer in the Magic of Glitches." *The New York Times,* August 8, 1997.
Rolling Stone, eds., *The Neil Young Files: The Ultimate Compendium of Interviews, Articles, Facts and Opinions.* New York: Hyperion Books, 1994.
Young, Neil. *The Guitar Styles of Neil Young* (Paperback). Alfred, 1999.

ESSENTIAL WORK

Acoustic

"After the Gold Rush" (1970)
"Comes a Time" (1978)
"Expecting to Fly" (1967)
"Harvest Moon" (1992)
"Heart of Gold" (1972)
"The Needle and the Damage Done" (1972)
"Old Man" (1972)

Electric

"Cinnamon Girl" (1969)
"Cowgirl in the Sand" (1969)
"Down by the River" (1969)
"For What It's Worth" (1967)
"Hey Hey, My My (Into the Black)" (1979)
"Like a Hurricane" (1977)
"Mr. Soul" (1967)
"Ohio"

ESSENTIAL LISTENING

After the Gold Rush (Reprise, 1970)
Buffalo Springfield Again (Atco, 1967)
Déjà Vu (Crosby, Stills, Nash & Young, Atlantic, 1970)
Everybody Knows This Is Nowhere (with Crazy Horse, Reprise, 1969)
Live at the Fillmore (Reprise, 1970/2006)
Live at Massey Hall (Reprise, 1971/2007)
Rust Never Sleeps (Reprise, 1979)

Essential Viewing

Greendale (2003)
Human Highway (1982), Neil Young, director
Rust Never Sleeps (1979), Neil Young, director
Year of the Horse (1997), Jim Jarmusch, director

Frank Zappa

Frank Zappa played many roles during his life. He was a notable, often outrageous personality, one of rock's first iconoclasts, a thinker and quasi-intellectual whose innovations in popular music made him an unsung legend.

He was also a humorist. His sardonic and satirical attitude played central roles in the development of a rock 'n' roll that was often too serious for its own good. He possessed a wickedness, scorn, that often lapsed into bad taste. But in projecting that absurdity, he attracted legions of fans that viewed the world in the same scathing way.

Frank Zappa was also an immense, larger-than-life musical talent and an extraordinary composer. Early on, he developed an understanding and appreciation of abstract classical composers like Stockhausen and Varese. But he also developed a profound appreciation for popular music, doo wop, R&B, early rock, and pop vocal music. He worked in both electronic and orchestral idioms, conducting vast projects with dozens of musicians, and alone, with a guitar. These two diametric extremes comprised the core of his early production and his affinity for classical composition surfaced throughout his career until his death in 1993.

In the same way, he produced an abundance of material throughout his life. In fact, he may have been the most prolific composer of his time, churning out record after record with little pause, in various genres, from classical to garage rock, jazz and instrumental to pop. The numbers are astonishing. Zappa has more than 60 albums to his credit, as composer, arranger, guitarist, and bandleader.

Pigeonholing Zappa as a rock artist is a bit like labeling Johann Sebastian Bach a church organist—it only tells a small part of the story. With his daredevil approaches to meter, harmony, and composition, and his ambitious orchestral pieces, the electric-guitar iconoclast arguably had more in common with classical innovator Igor Stravinsky than he did Eric Clapton. And the only thing more cutting than Zappa's tone was his razor-like wit and keen sense of satire. (Workman, Josh, "Guitar Heroes A–Z," *Guitar Player*, October 2007, n.p.)

* * *

Zappa was the de facto spokesperson for a dying breed of rock and roller. He testified famously in front of Congress against censorship and made a name for himself as an outspoken critic at a significant time in the life of popular music. Musically speaking, he was known for challenging the conventional wisdom, of pop, rock, jazz, and blues, as well as musical concepts like improvisation.

"When people would ask Frank how he wanted to be remembered," says [his son] Dweezil Zappa, sitting in the studio control room tucked inside the rustic confines of Zappa Family Headquarters, "he would say, 'I don't. It's not important.' Well, to me it is important. I want my kids, and my kid's kids to feel as strongly as I do about my dad's music, because it's so unique. Especially living in a world where so much music sounds the same, there isn't anything that sounds like Frank" (Fox, Darrin, "All in the Family," *Guitar Player*, July 2006, n.p.).

Zappa was posthumously inducted into the Rock 'n' Roll Hall of Fame in 1995, and he received a Grammy Lifetime Achievement Award in 1997. In 2005, his 1968 album with the Mothers of Invention, *We're Only in It for the Money*, was inducted into the U.S. National Recording Preservation Board's National Recording Registry. The same year, *Rolling Stone* magazine ranked him #71 on their list of "The 100 Greatest Artists of All Time."

EARLY YEARS

Frank Vincent Zappa was born in Baltimore in 1940, the oldest of four children. His father, a Sicilian Immigrant who became a government scientist/mathematician, played guitar on the side. His mom was also from Sicily but had French blood as well.

The Zappas moved often during Frank's childhood, depending on where the Department of Defense sent his father. As a child, Zappa suffered from various illnesses, including asthma and earaches. At least one family move was made to provide him with better air quality and improve his asthmatic symptoms. Because of this nomadic existence, Zappa attended no less than five high schools during his childhood.

As a young teen, Zappa spent his early years being mischievous and a little wacky. He'd occupy his time experimenting with things around the house, blowing stuff up, and playing with fire, literally. Zappa and his family moved to California, where he developed an interest in doo wop, R&B, and early rock 'n' roll. He played various instruments in the orchestra as well as the drums at home, and he also began listening to the French avant-garde composer Edgard Varese.

He formed his first band, the Ramblers, in the mid-1950s at a high school in San Diego. They were a short-lived group that dissolved when Zappa moved away. In the desert town of Lancaster, California, his next home, he formed a biracial band called the Black-Outs, a band that included Euclid James "Motorhead" Sherwood, a musician who would factor into Zappa's Mothers of Invention later on.

Because of the racism of the age, the Black-Outs were forbidden to play at their own school, so they were compelled to organize events independently. From the beginning young Frank was a rebel and trailblazer.

During this time in his life, he began listening to everything and anything he could, from modern jazz to sea shanties, from folk to avant-garde and classical. By many counts, Zappa was often bored in school. He'd distract the class with juvenile pranks in order to liven up the days. He participated in his high school marching band and studied 12-tone music, as well as conducting and composing for ensembles. It was during these years that Frank realized he wanted to inject change into the music industry.

By the end of high school, he had given up playing the drums and made the switch to guitar to suit his desire to compose. He had received his first guitar in 1957.

> I began when I was 18. I didn't hear any guitarists until I was about 15 or so, because in those days the saxophone was the instrument that was happening on record. When you heard a guitar player it was always a treat, so I went out collecting R&B guitar records. The solos were never long enough, they only gave them one chorus, and I figured the only way I was going

to get to hear enough of what I wanted to hear was to get an instrument and play it myself. Then I started figuring out chords and finally got a Mickey Baker book and learned a bunch of chords off that. (Rosen, Steve, *Guitar Player*, January 1977, n.p.)

Zappa made his first informal recordings while attending Antelope Valley Junior College, with his brother Bob and his friend Don Van Vliet, a man later known to many as Captain Beefheart. He only matriculated at the junior college for one semester. All through his schooling, Zappa maintained a bad attitude about formal education and his experience at the junior college proved no exception. (He even took his own kids out of school at 15, and refused to pay for college.) Still, in the liner notes of *Freak Out!* he acknowledged two of his music teachers.

He moved out on his own shortly thereafter, in 1959, in search of a career as a musician.

MUSIC

After moving out, Zappa gigged steadily and received commission to compose a couple of low-budget film soundtracks. He also began writing and producing cuts for local artists. One such track, "Memories of El Monte," was recorded by famed doo wop group, the Penguins.

Around that time Zappa took a job working for Paul Buff, an innovative recording engineer who had built his own five-track recording studio in Cucamonga, unusual at the time given most studios were one or two track. For a year, the pair attempted to churn out hit records for various labels, unsuccessfully, before Zappa assumed ownership of the studio with his own money. He changed the name to "Studio Z" and immersed himself in multitracking as a full-time gig.

Strangely, he lost that studio when the San Bernardino police arrested him for creating a pornographic audiotape, one that he made as a joke with a friend. He served 10 days of a six-month sentence and lost his studio in the process.

Shortly, Zappa bumped into Ray Collins, an artist he met while working with Buff. Collins invited him to play guitar in the Soul Giants, a cover band founded by drummer Jimmy Carl Black and bassist Roy Estrada. When he joined, it didn't take long for Zappa to convince the others that in order to get anywhere in the music business, they should start performing his originals. After a brief time as Captain Glasspack and his Magic Mufflers, the band changed its name to the Mothers, on Mother's Day in 1965.

* * *

Early on the Mothers struggled. But a chance encounter with promoter Herb Cohen turned things around. Cohen, a booking and management specialist, offered to manage the band and in short time the Mothers were rolling. By October 1965, they had snared legitimate, multinight gigs at Los Angeles clubs the Action and the Whiskey A-Go-Go; Cohen also arranged for MGM producer Tom Wilson to witness a Mothers performance, and by March 1966, Zappa had secured his first big-time record deal. For its part, MGM forced Zappa and the band to change their name to the Mothers of Invention, so as not to sound profane.

Several months after getting signed, *Freak Out!* emerged, the world's first rock 'n' roll double LP. It would be the beginning of Zappa's streak of trailblazing recordings that would continue until he died. *Freak Out!* combined all of Zappa's musical interests, from doo wop and R&B to modern classical and avant-garde, while the lyric content ranged

Courtesy of Neil Zlozower

between social commentary, (somewhat tongue-in-cheek) tales of heartbreak, and Dadaistic absurdity.

" 'Who Are the Brain Police' is one of the scariest songs ever to emerge from a rock psyche, a Kafka-esque vision of contemporary America where personal identity and individuality are erased" (no author listed, *The Mojo Collection: The Greatest Albums of All Time*, edited by Jim Irvin. Mojo Books, Edinburgh, 2000, p. 86).

In November of 1966, the Mothers recorded their second album, *Absolutely Free,* further expanding on the methods and themes established with *Freak Out!* By the time of its release, Zappa had relocated to New York, where Cohen had arranged a residency for the band at the Garrick Theater. He stepped up his outrageousness in New York City—with silly props, audience participation, and other antics—and the crowd responded. Inspired by the response, he stepped it up in the studio as well. The next two albums, both in 1968, showcased his crazed approach to making records. The first was the acidic social critique *We're Only In It For The Money,* with the second being the elaborate sonic collage *Lumpy Gravy.* The latter intertwined orchestral themes (many that would appear again in other forms on later albums), spoken word bits, and electronic noises through radical and painstaking tape editing.

Other offbeat projects followed. First, Zappa and the Mothers played at London's Royal Albert Hall in front of the London Philharmonic. Then they formed an alter ego, parody band called Cruising with Ruben and the Jets, a tribute to his doo wop roots. *Uncle Meat,* an album and a film, consumed Zappa in the late 1960s even though the film wasn't released until 1987.

When the MGM contract expired, Zappa formed his own label, Bizarre Records, with manager Cohen. Zappa not only released Mothers albums on the label, but he signed and produced acts like Alice Cooper and comedian Lenny Bruce. One of the more memorable projects coming from the imprint was *Trout Mask Replica,* the third effort by Don Van Vliet's music cult Captain Beefheart and the Magic Band, arguably one of the most outlandish blues albums in history.

Following a tour in the summer of 1969, and despite their soaring popularity, Zappa disbanded the Mothers. Many believe that Zappa's reluctance to consume recreational drugs along with the rest of the band created an adversarial relationship between him and the others.

JAZZ, ETC.

In an effort to diversify, Zappa pulled together a group of expert musicians, including some from the Mothers (Ian Underwood, Roy Estrada), to create instrumental music along the lines of jazz. He also began composing another soundtrack, to the film *200 Motels.* Another album released during this phase was the jazz-flavored offering *Hot Rats.*

In the mid-1970s, Zappa began working with a variety of players and releasing a vast spectrum of music. In 1973, he brought the Mothers back together on *Over-Nite Sensation.* This album found the artist simplifying his sound and focusing his lyrics on scatological subject matter. "Don't Eat the Yellow Snow" was a hit off the record, Zappa's biggest to date, and his album sales picked up. The equally commercial *Apostrophe (')* the next year featured more of the same and sales continued briskly. In 1975, he reunited with Beefheart on *Bongo Fury.* The two had suffered a falling out after Beefheart resented Zappa's marketing of his product for Beefheart's Bizarre recordings.

Zoot Allures (1976) brought another shift in his recording approach. His social satires featured a heavier rock sound and his instrumental pieces alternated between complex ensemble slants and settings for his scorching guitar.

The scatology and controversy persisted through the 1970s. In 1978, a song called "Jewish Princess" resulted in a formal complaint with the FCC filed by the B'nai B'rith Anti-Defamation League. A few months later, he enjoyed his first big hit single, the ironic "Dancin' Fool," a funny gem that nearly broke the Top 40 in 1979.

In 1980, Zappa released a single entitled "I Don't Wanna Get Drafted," which his label at the time, Mercury, refused to release. Zappa left the label and eventually established his own imprint, Barking Pumpkin. In 1981 he released notable music for guitar players, the all-instrumental, three-volume set of instrumentals known as *Shut Up 'n Play Yer Guitar.* The set included the aforementioned first installment, then *Shut Up 'n Play Yer Guitar Some More,* and *The Return of the Son of Shut Up 'n Play Yer Guitar.* They were initially sold via mail order by Zappa himself, but were later released commercially. The albums focused exclusively on Zappa as a guitar soloist, and the tracks, predominantly live recordings from 1979 and 1980, highlight his improvisational gifts. The albums were subsequently released as a three-album box set, and were followed in 1988 by *Guitar,* another focused instrumental album. A third guitar project, *Trance-Fusion,* completed shortly before his death, included Zappa's work throughout the 1980s and came out in 2006.

"Valley Girl," another hit single, entered the Top 40 in 1983. The recording provided him with enough cash to finance many of his much less lucrative orchestral projects.

By this time Zappa had become one of modern music's most demanding bandleaders. The players he recruited during this period included mainly unfamiliar names. But given the nature of even a short tenure in Zappa's band, musicians gained immediate credibility as pros. Several alums from Zappa's 1980s lineups emerged to launch their own careers, including drummer Terry Bozzio and guitarists Steve Vai, Mike Keneally, and Adrian Belew.

Zappa also grew contentious with his record companies. In 1976, he won a lawsuit against MGM that gave him control of his own music, and he did the same a year later with his new label Warner Brothers. Warner had expected four albums from Zappa. When he delivered them, all at once, to fulfill his obligations, Warner refused to cooperate with the strategy. Zappa won that suit also.

The 1980s also found Zappa consolidating his business affairs. He established Barking Pumpkin, a video company called Honker Home Video, a merch company, and a live production company. He also became more active in politics. As a longtime free speech advocate, he testified in front of a Senate Subcommittee in 1985 against the Parental Music Resource Center on the subject of censorship.

He had his work performed by the Berkeley Symphony, had his classical compositions performed and recorded by Pierre Boulez, and toured the world in 1988. That same year he also earned a Grammy for Best Rock Instrumental for *Jazz from Hell*, a synthesizer work. In 1989 he published his autobiography, *The Real Frank Zappa*.

He was diagnosed with prostate cancer in 1991. He worked constantly even after the diagnosis, releasing several more albums until death stopped him from making any more music. He died at his home in Los Angeles in 1993. He was 52 and had been planning a run for the U.S. Presidency.

TECHNIQUE/STYLE

"Once I get out onstage and turn my guitar on, it's a special thing to me. I love doing it. But I approach it more as a composer who happens to be able to operate an instrument called a guitar, rather than 'Frank Zappa, Rock and Roll Guitar Hero'" (www.zentao.com).

If Frank Zappa sounds rather contrarian about the way he plays guitar, he is. But he was also resolute in the fact that he was playing something totally unique.

There are a lot of good guitar players out there. But I'll guarantee you that I am the only person doing what I am doing. I don't approach it as a guitar star. I go out there to play compositions. I want to take a chord change or a harmonic climate and build a composition on the spur of the moment that makes sense, that takes some chances. That goes some place nobody else wanted to go, that says things that nobody else wanted to say, that represents my musical personality. That has some emotional content and speaks to the people who want to hear it. And the ones who don't want to hear it, who don't like guitar stuff, can forget it; it will be over in a minute and I'll be back to another part of the song. That's what it's all about. (Unattributed, *Guitar World*, March 1982, home.online.no/~corneliu/gw82.htm)

Frank Zappa was, among many other things, a truly gifted guitar player. But his reputation as a player took a back seat to his additional roles as composer, aesthete, bandleader, and outspoken political personality. Still, for guitar players, few could compete with his dexterity. As a solo guitarist, he played in irregular shapes, moving in conversational fits and starts. With his daredevil approaches to meter, harmony, and composition, and his ambitious orchestral pieces, the electric-guitar iconoclast had more in common with classical innovator Igor Stravinsky than he did Eric Clapton. And the only thing more cutting than Zappa's tone was his razor-like wit and keen sense of satire. There was only one catch:

The hardest thing for me to do is play straight up and down, absolutely the hardest to do. Stuff that everybody else does naturally just seems as impossible as shit to me. I don't think in little groups of twos and fours and stuff—they just don't come out that way. I can sit around and play fives and sevens all day long with no sweat. But the minute I've got to go "do-do-do-do, do-do-do-do" it feels weird, it's like wearing tight shoes. So I'm going to keep practicing. It's like learning how to speak English if you've been speaking something else all the time. It's like trying to develop a convincing English accent. (Ouellette, Dan, *Pulse!*, August 1993, n.p., http://home.online.no/~corne-liu/pulse.htm)

Zappa was grounded in the blues. His influences, bluesmen like "Guitar Slim" Jones, Johnny "Guitar" Watson, and Clarence "Gatemouth" Brown reflect a very personal style, one that had its definition from the very beginning of his recording career. It's evident in the distorted riff underscoring "Trouble Comin' Every Day," from 1966. Moving forward, "Nine Types of Industrial Pollution," a six-minute track on *Uncle Meat* (1969), offers the first example of what would become Zappa's signature solo-guitar style: complex, detailed, and vividly melodic monologues communicated over a modal vamp.

While Zappa's guitar work originally reflected the blues and its linear expression, he eventually came to prefer modified reggae. Zappa's most significant influence had to have been Jimi Hendrix. He extracted Jimi's blues influence wholesale and fused it to his playing. But one can also pick up more subtle aspects of his style in

ZAPPA PLAYS FRANK

Many say that Dweezil Zappa, Frank's son, inherited all the best musical qualities from his father. Most importantly, Dweezil, like his father, is an absolute shredder, a talented composer, and a vibrant personality, built with enough potential to assume complete control of his father's unwavering mantle. "My father once said, 'Progress is not possible without deviation from the norm.' He spent his life and musical career absurdly corroborating that statement."

And so, in a strange way, has Dweezil, his son, who in 2008 released *Zappa Plays Zappa,* as a tribute to his father. "Make no mistake about it. It's a labor of love for me and my family and its sole purpose is to officially celebrate Frank's music" (Zappa, Dweezil, liner notes, *Zappa Plays Zappa.* Razor & Tie, 2008).

After enjoying a solid early career beginning in the late 1980s, Dweezil fell out of the public eye. While in seclusion, he rededicated himself to learning guitar, changing his style a bit and adopting many of his father's picking techniques. In 2005, he assembled a crack band of younger players and recruited FZ alum like Steve Vai and Terry Bozzio for the critically acclaimed Zappa Plays Zappa tour, which hit the road in the summer of 2006. They performed an entire program of Frank Zappa compositions with Vai and Bozzio appearing as guests and Dweezil himself as lead guitarist/bandleader. The recording, *Zappa Plays Zappa,* is both a CD and DVD, and it pays serious tribute to Dweezil's father, one of America's greatest composers in the modern age.

genres like electric folk, jazz, and psychedelia, elements he may have heard in the playing of Carlos Santana and Jerry Garcia. These players likely influenced Zappa because they had strong rhythmic and narrative techniques.

Zappa used his guitar solos as launching pads for new songs. Starting in the late 1970s, specifically for *Sheik Yerbouti* and *Joe's Garage*, Zappa began stealing from himself, taking solos from his live performances and utilizing them in new studio compositions. In this way, he took improvised passages and turned them into static song elements.

In fact, laying down solos—one of his signature strengths—was a sensitive exercise for Zappa. He would often lay down 20 bars or so, and stop the tape, back it up, mark a spot and pick up where he left off until he hit something sour. He demanded much from his recordings, bordering on megalomaniacal perfection. He thought that a record was fixed, unchangeable, and that once it was done it ceased to be actual music. Rather it was an object.

"If you're going to leave your guitar solo on, you're stuck with that for the life of the record. I'm fairly fussy about it, but I'm sure I let a few go out on record that I could probably do better now. But I hope that's the way it's always going to be" (*Guitar World*, March 1982).

Zappa's stop-start, intermittent play is against the grain of traditional rock 'n' roll, which is probably why he had a hard time winning a mainstream audience. He was always seeking the unlikely approach, the unlikely rhythms, the *surprises*. He also loved to throw a wrench into the mix during improvisations, a ploy that kept the audience and his band off-balance.

The way he grasped his plectrum is also unusual. He would hold the pick flush against the meat of both his thumb and his forefinger as though he were picking out whiskers—pluck, pluck, pluck. "It's a something like a circular picking style, and it makes the sound pop. It's an aggressive, very masculine sound, for want of a better term. Frank often anchored his hand by placing his ring finger and pinky on the pickguard just under the neck, so a lot of his picking took place between the end of the neck and the bridge pickup. When he had his hand anchored there he'd create a slight harmonic when he chugged the low notes, which you don't get with the traditional technique where your right hand is muting at the bridge. Zappa dug into the strings, using upstrokes and downstrokes in odd combinations, and frequently scraping the pick across the strings to create gurgling clusters of notes" (Rotondi, James, *Guitar Player*, October 1995, n.p.).

He'd move his right hand up the fretboard toward the lowest strings and fret notes at the same time. He'd pick one note with his right hand, and play five with his left. The scraping technique was one way of picking out a bunch of notes in rapid succession. He leaves a big reservoir of notes, and you're just grabbing a handful of them and throwing them out. It wasn't sweep-picking precisely, but there was a sweeping motion involved.

Every note has power and distinction, and it was Zappa's goal to be the most distinctive.

"You've already heard all the good licks that all the good guitar players play. You've already heard ALL the unlikely melodies and modes. You've HEARD ALL THE pentatonic scale there ever WERE. You have heard all the chromatic scales that ever were. You've heard the Aeolian mode played with a muted palm of the hand. You have heard all of the nice bent notes. You have heard clean playing, accurate playing. You have heard it all" (Rosen, Steve, "One Size Fits All," *Guitar Player*, January 1977, http://home.online.no/~corneliu/gp77interview.htm).

So, while Zappa attempted valiantly to play uniquely, he preferred to do it by coming at the instrument with a fresh perspective. That is, he didn't like to practice.

Every time a tour ends and I put my guitar away, I don't touch it until the next season's rehearsals. And every time I pick it up it's like learning to play all over again. I don't have any calluses, it hurts, I can't bend the string, the guitar feels too heavy when I put it on. I just had a nine-month layoff where I lost all my technique. Then, suddenly, one night I didn't have a problem. I just went out there on stage and started blasting away. I think I've actually exceeded my goals on a couple of nights. (*Guitar World,* March 1982)

EQUIPMENT/GEAR

Frank Zappa got his first guitar at 18 for $150 at an auction, a generic archtop, with an f-hole and a cracked base. He didn't get his first real electric until he was 21, when he rented a Telecaster from a music store. Then he picked up a Jazzmaster, which he used to play lounge jobs early on. With the money from his first soundtrack job he bought a Gibson ES-S Switchmaster, which he used for about five years and he recorded the first three Mothers of Invention albums with that guitar.

Zappa bought a Gibson SG copy, modified to include an additional fret so it went up to an E, and it had an ebony fingerboard, humbucking pickups, and some inlay, and some real nice woodwork on it. He began collecting both Fenders and Gibsons, depending on the need. He liked to choose guitars based on the things they were good for. He had nearly 30 guitars in all. Another one of his Stratocasters is the one Jimi Hendrix burned at the Miami Pop Festival; it was given to Zappa by a former Hendrix roadie. Zappa frequently used a Vox cabinet with four JBLs in it (12″ each) and another Marshall cabinet with JBLs (www.zentao.com).

Zappa was also one of the first people to use the wah-wah pedal. He'd insisted he'd never heard of Jimi Hendrix at the time he bought the pedal in 1967. He had used wah-wah frequently on *We're Only in It for the Money,* utilizing it on the clavinet, guitar, and saxophone that year. Zappa also had a parametric EQ installed in his Strat guitar, which enabled him to boost frequencies to obtain feedback. He used hte other following Zappa pedals: Dan Armstrong Green Ringer, Mu-Tron Phase, MXR Digital Delays, Roland GP-8 Processor, 12 Button Stereo Relay Switcher, Mu-Tron III Envelope Filter, MicMix Dyna-flangers, Electro-Harmonix Big Muff, Rat Distortion Pedal, Hush II B Noise Reduction Unit, and the Electro Wagnerian Emancipator.

He used Fender Heavy picks, and a different set of Ernie Ball strings for each guitar.

ESSENTIAL READING

Fox, Darrin. "All in the Family." *Guitar Player,* July 2006, n.p.
Irvin, Jim, ed. *The Mojo Collection: The Greatest Albums of All Time.* Edinburgh: Mojo Books, 2000, 86.
Miles, Barry. *Zappa: A Biography.* Grove/Atlantic, 2004.
Occhiogrosso, Peter. *The Real Frank Zappa Book.* Fireside Books, 1990.
Ouellette, Dan. *Pulse!* August 1993, n.p. http://home.online.no/~corneliu/pulse.htm.
Rosen, Steve. *Guitar Player,* January 1977, n.p.
———. "One Size Fits All." *Guitar Player,* January 1977. http://home.online.no/~corneliu/gp77 interview.htm.
Rotondi, James. *Guitar Player,* October 1995, n.p.
Unattributed, *Guitar World,* March 1982. home.online.no/~corneliu/gw82.htm.
Workman, Josh. "Guitar Heroes A–Z." *Guitar Player,* October 2007, n.p.
Zappa, Dweezil. Liner notes, *Zappa Plays Zappa.* Razor & Tie, 2008.

ESSENTIAL WORK

"Cozmik Debris" (1974)
"Deathless Horsie" (1981)
"The Grand Wazoo" (1973)
"Joe's Garage" (1979)
"Peaches En Regalia" (1969)
"Willie the Pimp" (1969)

ESSENTIAL LISTENING

Absolutely Free (Rykodisc, 1967)
Apostrophe (') (Rykodisc, 1974)
Cruisin' with Ruben & the Jets (Rykodisc, 1968)
Freak Out! (Rykodisc, 1966)
Hot Rats (Rykodisc, 1969)
Lather (Rykodisc, 1996)
Over-Nite Sensation (Rykodisc, 1973)
200 Motels (Rykodisc, 1971)
Uncle Meat (Rykodisc, 1969)
We're Only in It for the Money (Rykodisc, 1968)

ESSENTIAL VIEWING

200 Motels (United Artists, 1971)

Bibliography

PRINTED MATTER

Abbott, Darrell, and Zac Crain. *Black Tooth Grin: The High Life, Good Times, and Tragic End of "Dimebag" Darrell Abbott.* New York: Da Capo Press, 2009.

Appleford, Steve. *The Rolling Stones: Rip This Joint: The Story Behind Every Song.* New York: Thunder's Mouth, 2000.

Armold, Chris. *A Vulgar Display of Power: Courage and Carnage at the Alrosa Villa.* New York: MJS Music Publications, 2007.

Babiuk, Andy. *Beatles Gear.* San Francisco, CA: Backbeat Books, 2002.

Barnes, Richard. *The Who: Maximum R&B.* New York: Plexus Publishing, 2004.

Bene, David. *Randy Rhoads: A Life.* Self-published, 2008.

Berry, Chuck. *Chuck Berry: The Autobiography.* New York: Random House, 1989.

Blake, Mark. *Comfortably Numb.* New York: Da Capo, 2007.

Bockris, Victor. *Keith Richards: The Biography.* New York: Simon & Schuster, 1993.

Bono, The Edge, Adam Clayton, Larry Mullen, Jr. *U2 by U2.* New York: HarperCollins, 2006.

Bozza, Anthony, and Slash. *Slash.* New York: Harper Entertainment, 2007.

Bushell, Gary, Mick Wall, and Stephen Rea. *Ozzy Osbourne: Diary of a Madman.* London: Omnibus Press, 1990

Canter, Marc. *Reckless Road: Guns N' Roses and the Making of Appetite for Destruction.* 3rd edition, Seattle, WA: Shoot Hip Press, 2007.

Carson, Annette. *Jeff Beck: Crazy Fingers.* San Francisco: Backbeat Books, 2001.

Case, George. *Jimmy Page: Magus, Musician, Man: An Unauthorized Biography.* Milwaukee, WI: Hal Leonard Publishing, 2007.

Christe, Ian. *Sound of the Beast: The Complete Headbanging History of Heavy Metal.* New York: HarperCollins, 2004.

Christgau, Robert. *Christgau's Consumer Guide: Albums of the '90s.* New York: St. Martin's Griffin, 2000.

Clapton, Eric. *Clapton, the Autobiography.* New York: Broadway, 2007.

Dalton, David. *The Rolling Stones: The First Twenty Years.* New York: Alfred A. Knopf, 1981.

Davis, Stephen. *Hammer of the Gods.* New York: Harper Paperback, 2008.

DeRogatis, Jim. *Milk It!: Collected Musings on the Alternative Music Explosion of the '90s.* New York: Da Capo Press, 2003.

Downing, David. *A Dreamer of Pictures: Neil Young, the Man and His Music.* Cambridge, MA: Da Capo Press, 1995.

Erlewine, Michael, Vladimir Bogdanov, Chris Woodstra, Stephen Thomas Erlewine, and Richie Unterberger, eds. *All Music Guide to Rock.* San Francisco: Miller Freeman, 1997.

Fitch, Vernon. *The Pink Floyd Encyclopedia.* New York: Collector's Guide Publishing, Inc., 2005.

Flanagan, Bill. *U2 at the End of the World*. New York: Delta, 1996.

Gardner, Elysa, ed. *U2: The Rolling Stone Files*. London: Sidgwick & Jackson, 1994.

Gibbons, Billy F., and Randy Poe. *Skydog: The Duane Allman Story*. San Francisco: Backbeat Books, 2006.

Graff, Gary, and Daniel Durchholz, eds. *MusicHound Rock: The Essential Album Guide*. Detroit: Visible Ink, 1999.

Guiliano, Geoffrey. *Behind Blue Eyes: The Life of Pete Townshend*. New York: Cooper Square Press, 2002.

Hammett, Kirk. *The Art of Kirk Hammett*. New York: Cherry Lane Music, 1997.

Leng, Simon. *George Harrison: While My Guitar Gently Weeps*. London: SAF Publishing, 2002.

———. *Soul Sacrifice: The Santana Story*. London: Firefly, 2000.

MacDonald, Ian. *Revolution in the Head: The Beatle's Music and the Sixties*. New York: Pimlico, 1995.

Marsh, Dave. *Before I Get Old: The Story of the Who*. New York: Plexus Publishing, 2003.

Mason, Nick. *Inside Out*. London: Phoenix, 2005.

Metallica, with Steffan Chirazi. *So What! The Good, the Mad, and the Ugly*. New York: Broadway Books, 2004.

McDermott, John. *Jimi Hendrix: Sessions: The Complete Studio Recording Sessions, 1963–1970*. Boston: Little, Brown, 1996.

McDonough, Jimmy. *Shakey Neil Young's Biography*. San Francisco, CA: Anchor, 2003.

McIver, Joel. *Justice for All: The Truth about Metallica*. New York: Omnibus Press, 2004.

Miles, Barry. *Zappa: A Biography*. New York: Grove/Atlantic, 2004.

Murray, Charles Shaar. *Crosstown Traffic: Jimi Hendrix & the Post-War Rock 'N' Roll Revolution*. New York: St. Martin's Griffin, 1991.

Pegg, Bruce. *Brown Eyed Handsome Man: The Life and Hard Times of Chuck Berry*. London: Routledge, 2002.

Occhiogrosso, Peter. *The Real Frank Zappa Book*. New York: Simon & Schuster, 1989.

Osbourne, Ozzy, Randy Rhoads, and Aaron Rosenbaum. *Ozzy Osbourne: The Randy Rhoads Years (Guitar Legendary Licks)*. New York: Cherry Lane Music, 2002.

Patoski, Joe Nick, and Bill Crawford. *Caught in the Crossfire*. Boston: Little, Brown, 1993.

Perkins, Willie. *No Saints, No Saviors: My Years with the Allman Brothers Band*. Macon, GA: Mercer University Press, 2005.

Putterford, Mark. *Metallica: In Their Own Words*. New York: Omnibus, 2000

Reynolds, Simon. *Generation Ecstasy*. New York: Routledge, 1999.

Robb, John. *The Nineties: What the F**k Was That All About?* London: Ebury Press, 1999.

Robbins, Ira, ed. *The Trouser Press Guide to '90s Rock*. New York: Fireside, 1997.

Rolling Stone editors, *The Neil Young Files: The Ultimate Compendium of Interviews, Articles, Facts and Opinions*. New York: Hyperion Books, 1994.

Sarzo, Rudy. *Off the Rails*. New York: Booksurge, 2006.

Schaffner, Nicholas. *Saucerful of Secrets: The Pink Floyd Odyssey*. London: Delta, 1992.

Scoppa, Bud. *Chuck Berry: The Definitive Collection*. Liner notes, New York: Chess Records, 2006.

Shadwick, Keith. *Led Zeppelin: 1968–1980*. San Francisco: Backbeat, 2005.

Shapiro, Harry. *Electric Gypsy*. New York: St. Martin's Griffin, 1995.

———. *Eric Clapton: Lost in the Blues*. New York: Da Capo, 1992.

Shapiro, Mark. *Back on Top*. New York: St. Martin's, 2000.

Sloman, Larry, and Anthony Kiedis. *Scar Tissue*. New York: Hyperion, 2005.

Strong, Martin C. *The Great Rock Discography*. London: Times Books, 1998.

True, Everett. *Live Through This: American Rock Music in the '90s*. London: Virgin, 2001.

Wilkerson, Mark. *Amazing Journey: The Life of Pete Townshend*. Lulu.com, 2006.

Young, Neil. *The Guitar Styles of Neil Young* (Paperback). New York: Alfred A. Knopf, 1999.

RECOMMENDED LISTENING

Darrell Abbott/Pantera

Cowboys from Hell (Atlantic, 1990)
Reinventing the Steel (East West, 2000)
Vulgar Display of Power (East West, 1992)

Duane Allman/The Allman Brothers Band

The Allman Brothers Band (Polydor, 1969)
At the Fillmore East (Polydor, 1971)
The Fillmore Concerts (Polydor, 1971/1992)
Idlewild South (Polydor, 1970)

Jeff Beck

Beck-Ola (Epic, 1969)
Blow by Blow (Epic, 1975)
Jeff (Epic, 2003)
Truth (Epic, 1968)
Wired (Epic, 1976)

Chuck Berry

The Chess Box (Chess/MCA, 1988)
Chuck Berry: Johnny B. Goode: His Complete '50s Chess Recordings (Chess/MCA, 2008)
The Great Twenty-Eight (Chess, 1984)

Eric Clapton/Cream/Derek and the Dominos

Bluesbreakers with Eric Clapton (Deram, 1966)
Disraeli Gears (Polydor, 1967)
461 Ocean Boulevard (Polydor, 1974)
Layla and Other Assorted Love Songs (Polydor, 1970)
Slowhand (Polydor, 1977)
Unplugged (Reprise, 1992)

Kurt Cobain/Nirvana

Bleach (Sub Pop, 1989)
From the Muddy Banks of the Wishkah (DGC, 1996)
In Utero (DGC, 1993)
Nevermind (DGC, 1991)

The Edge/U2

Achtung Baby (Island, 1991)
All That You Can't Leave Behind (Interscope, 2000)
Boy (Island, 1980)
The Joshua Tree (Island, 1987)
War (Island, 1983)

John Frusciante/Red Hot Chili Peppers

Blood Sugar Sex Magik (Warner Bros., 1991)
By the Way (WEA, 2002)
Californication (Warner Bros., 1999)
Curtains (Record Collection, 2004)
Live in Hyde Park (WEA, 2004)
Mother's Milk (EMI, 1989)
Shadows Collide with People (Warner Bros., 2004)
Smile from the Streets That You Hold (Birdman, 1997)
What Hits?! (EMI, 1992)

Jerry Garcia/Grateful Dead

Almost Acoustic (Warner Bros., 1988)
Anthem of the Sun (Warner Bros., 1969)
Europe '72 (Warner Bros., 1972)
Fillmore East: April 1971 (Grateful Dead, 2000)
Hundred Year Hall 4–26–72 (Grateful Dead, 1995)
Live at the Cow Palace: New Year's Eve 1976 (Rhino, 2007)
Live/Dead (Warner Bros., 1969/2003)
Rockin' the Rhein with the Grateful Dead, 1972 (Rhino, 2004)
Steppin Out with the Grateful Dead: England 1972 (GDM/Arista, 2002)
The Very Best of Jerry Garcia (Rhino, 2006)

David Gilmour/Pink Floyd

Dark Side of the Moon (Capitol, 1973)
David Gilmour (Capitol, 1978)
The Wall (Capitol, 1979)
Wish You Were Here (Capitol, 1975)

Kirk Hammett and James Hetfield/Metallica

. . . And Justice for All (Elektra, 1988)
Death Magnetic (Warner Bros., 2008)
Master of Puppets (Elektra, 1986)
Metallica (Elektra, 1991)
Ride the Lightning (Elektra, 1984)

George Harrison/The Beatles

Abbey Road (Capitol, 1969)
All Things Must Pass (Capitol, 1970/2001)
A Hard Day's Night (Capitol, 1964)
The Best of George Harrison (Capitol, 1976/1990)
Help! (Capitol, 1965)
Revolver (Capitol, 1966)
Rubber Soul (Capitol, 1965)
Sgt. Pepper's Lonely Hearts Club Band (Capitol, 1967)
Traveling Wilburys, Volume 1 (Wilbury, 1988)

Jimi Hendrix

Are You Experienced? (MCA, 1967)
Axis: Bold as Love (MCA, 1967)
Band of Gypsys (MCA, 1970)
Electric Ladyland (MCA, 1968)
Live at Woodstock (MCA, 1999)

Tony Iommi/Black Sabbath

Black Sabbath (Warner Bros., 1970)
Master of Reality (Warner Bros., 1971)
Paranoid (Warner Bros., 1971)
Sabbath Bloody Sabbath (Warner Bros., 1973)
Sabotage (Warner Bros., 1975)
Vol. IV (Warner Bros., 1972)

Yngwie Malmsteen

Concerto Suite for Electric Guitar and Orchestra in E Flat Minor Op. 1 (Pony Canyon, 1998)
Concerto Suite Live with Japan Philharmonic (Pony Canyon, 2002)
Marching Out (Polydor, 1985)
Rising Force (Polydor, 1984)
Trilogy (Polydor, 1986)

Jimmy Page/Led Zeppelin

Houses of the Holy (Atlantic, 1973)
How the West Was Won (Atlantic, 2003)
Led Zeppelin (Atlantic, 1969)
Led Zeppelin II (Atlantic, 1969)
Led Zeppelin III (Atlantic, 1970)
Led Zeppelin IV (Atlantic, 1971)
Physical Graffiti (Swan Song, 1975)

Randy Rhoads/Quiet Riot

Blizzard of Ozz (Jet, 1980)
Diary of a Madman (Jet, 1981)
Quiet Riot (CBS, 1977)
Tribute (Epic, 1987)

Keith Richards/Rolling Stones

Beggars Banquet (ABKCO, 1968)
Exile on Main Street (Rolling Stone, 1972)
Let It Bleed (ABKCO, 1969)
Some Girls (Virgin, 1978)
Sticky Fingers (Virgin, 1971)
Tattoo You (Virgin, 1981)

Carlos Santana/Santana

Abraxas (Columbia/Legacy, 1970)
Blues for Salvador (Columbia, 1987)

Caravanserai (Columbia, 1972)
Lotus (Columbia, 1974)
Santana (Columbia/Legacy, 1969)
Santana III (Columbia/Legacy, 1971)

Slash/Guns N' Roses

Appetite for Destruction (Geffen, 1987)
Contraband (Velvet Revolver, Geffen, 2000)
Use Your Illusion I (Geffen, 1991)
Use Your Illusion II (Geffen, 1991)

Pete Townshend/The Who

Live at Leeds (MCA, 1970)
Rough Mix (with Ronnie Lane) (Atco, 1977)
Tommy (MCA, 1969)
The Who by Numbers (MCA, 1975)
The Who Sell Out (MCA, 1967)
The Who Sings My Generation (MCA, 1965)
Who's Next (MCA, 1971)

Eddie Van Halen

1984 (Warner Bros., 1984)
Van Halen (Warner Bros., 1978)
Van Halen II (Warner Bros., 1979)
Women and Children First (Warner Bros., 1980)

Stevie Ray Vaughan

Albert King with Stevie Ray Vaughan in Session (Stax, 1999)
Couldn't Stand the Weather (Epic/Legacy, 1984)
In Step (Epic/Legacy, 1989)
Live at Carnegie Hall (Epic/Legacy, 1997)
SRV (Epic/Legacy, 2000)
Texas Flood (Epic/Legacy, 1983)

Neil Young

After the Gold Rush (Reprise, 1970)
Buffalo Springfield Again (Atco, 1967)
Déjà Vu (Crosby, Stills, Nash & Young, Atlantic, 1970)
Everybody Knows This Is Nowhere (with Crazy Horse, Reprise, 1969)
Live at Massey Hall (Reprise, 1971/2007)
Live at the Fillmore (Reprise, 1970/2006)
Rust Never Sleeps (Reprise, 1979)

Frank Zappa

Absolutely Free (Rykodisc, 1967)
Apostrophe (') (Rykodisc, 1974)
Cruisin' with Ruben & the Jets (Rykodisc, 1968)
Freak Out! (Rykodisc, 1966)

Hot Rats (Rykodisc, 1969)
Lather (Rykodisc, 1996)
Over-Nite Sensation (Rykodisc, 1973)
200 Motels (Rykodisc, 1971)
Uncle Meat (Rykodisc, 1969)
We're Only in It for the Money (Rykodisc, 1968)

WEB SITES

About
http://guitar.about.com
Impressive list of contributions relating to guitar players and their output.

Acoustic Guitar
http://www.acousticguitar.com
Good insight into more acoustic oriented players like Neil Young and George Harrison.

All Music Guide
http://www.allmusic.com
Authoritative site with discographies and biographies of popular artists.

Amnesta.net
http://www.amnesta.net
A peculiarly comprehensive study of the Edge's playing technique.

Billboard
http://www.billboard.com
Artist and recording news from the music industry bible.

Black Sabbath online
http://www.black-sabbath.com
Interviews and reviews on the work of Tony Iommi of Black Sabbath.

Chuck Berry
http://departments.colgate.edu/diw/pegg/chuck.html
Extensive research on Chuck Berry.

Digital Dreamdoor
http://digitaldreamdoor.nutsie.com
Technical and creative slants on guitarists and guitar playing.

The Douglas J Noble Guitar Archive
http://www.djnoble.demon.co.uk
Douglas J Noble is a music journalist, guitar instructor, and musician based in Edinburgh, Scotland.

Fender Players Club
http://www.fenderplayersclub.com
The instrument maker's artist-based Web site.

Gibson Guitars
http://www.gibson.com
The instrument maker's lifestyle Web site.

Guitar Player
http://www.guitarplayer.com
The online edition of the venerable instrument magazine.

Guitar Site
http://www.GuitarSite.com
Portal to an extended webbring on guitars and guitarists.

Guitar World
http://www.guitarworld.com
Comprehensive coverage of players and their techniques.

Harmony Central
http://www.harmony-central.comDecent coverage of guitar players and instruments.

The History of Rock
http://www.history-of-rock.com
An exhaustive editorial look at the rock era's significant styles and acts.

Invisible Movement
http://www.invisible-movement.net
A site dedicated to the life and work of Red Hot Chili Pepper guitarist John Frusciante.

The Jerry Site
http://www.thejerrysite.com
Everything you need to know about the Grateful Dead's Jerry Garcia.

Metallica Band
http://www.metallicaband.net
Impressive rundown of all things Metallica.

MSNBC
http://www.msnbc.msn.com/
News and information site with entertainment features.

Modern Guitars
http://www.modernguitars.com
Noteworthy site with vintage reviews and interviews of history's best players.

Pink Floyd
http://www.pink-floyd.org
Insight into the playing of David Gilmour, Pink Floyd's guitarist.

Pop Matters
http://www.popmatters.com
Pop music site with a plethora of content, including reviews and analysis.

Rhino Records
http://www.rhino.com
Premiere archival reissue specialists.

Rock 'n' Roll Hall of Fame
http://www.rockhall.com/hof
A guide to the inductees of the Rock Hall.

Rock's Back Pages
http://www.rocksbackpages.com
An extensive archive of vintage and contemporary music journalism.

Rock Critics
http://rockcritics.com
In which a community of rock critics agree and disagree with each other.

Rolling Stone
http://www.rollingstone.com

Thrasher's Wheat
http://www.thrasherswheat.org
A Neil Young archive.

Ultimate Guitar
http://www.ultimate-guitar.com
Kitchen sink coverage of players with news, reviews, and interviews.

Where's Eric
http://www.whereseric.com
A portal into the Web sites and coverage of Eric Clapton.

Wikipedia
http://www.wikipedia.com
Occasionally meaningful Web site featuring community-contributed entries.

Yngwie Malmsteen
http://www.yngwie.org
Artist's personal Web site.

Youtube
http://www.youtube.com
Visual evidence of players often in obscure vintage videos.

Index

Abbott, Darrell: birth of, 2; collaborations with, 7; death of, 2, 7–8; early years, 2–4; and Eddie Van Halen, 3; equipment/gear, 8–9; influences, 2–3, 8; music of, 4–5; side projects, 6–7; technique/style, 8; and Tony Iommi, 8
Aldridge, Tommy, 166
Alias, Don, 185
"All My Loving," 117
All That I Am, 187
All That You Can't Leave Behind, 63, 64
All the Best Cowboys Have Chinese Eyes, 208–9
All Things Must Pass, 111, 115
"All Together Now," 114
Allman Brothers, 11, 15–16
The Allman Brothers Band, 16
Allman, Duane: and the Allman Brothers, 16; and the Allman Joys, 14; birth of, 12; death of, 16–17; and Derek and the Dominos, 13; early years, 12; equipment/gear, 18–19; and Eric Clapton, 13; as guest player, 12; and the Hour Glass, 15; influences, 11; music of, 12–16; as slide guitar player, 11, 17–18; technique/style, 17–18
Allman, Gregg, 11, 12, 14, 16, 17
Allman, Howard Duane. *See* Allman, Duane
Allman Joys, 12, 14
alternative rock, 49–50
Altham, Keith, 206
"Ambitious," 25
American Beauty, 83
And Justice for All, 104
amps. *See* equipment/gear
Anderson, Ian, 134–35
"Angel," 122

Anger, Kenneth, 156
Animals, 89, 93–94
Another Scoop, 209–10
Anselmo, Phil, 2, 4, 5, 7–8, 139
Anthems of the Sun, 82
Anthony, Michael, 214
Aoxomoxoa, 82
Apostrophe ('), 251
Appetite for Destruction, 191, 195, 197
Appice, Carmine, 24
Arc, 240
Are You Experienced?, 121, 125, 130
"As Tears Go By," 153
Ataxia, 73
Atco Records, 4
Atlantic Records, 15
Atom Heart Mother (album), 92
"Atom Heart Mother" (song), 89
Attack, 146
Austin City Limits, 229
Averill, Steve, 59
Axis: Bold as Love, 121, 125–26, 130

"Baba O'Riley," 201–2, 208
"Bad," 61, 64
Baggy's Studios, 127
Baker, Ginger, 42–43
Balance, 216
Ballard, Glenn, 216
Balzary, Michael. *See* Flea (Michael Balzary)
Band of Gypsys, 121–22, 126–29
Band of Gypsys (album), 126
"Bargain," 208
Barking Pumpkin Records, 251, 252
Barrett, 91

About the Author

BOB GULLA is a professional writer and co-author of *The Greenwood Encyclopedia of Rock History* (2005) and *Icons of R&B and Soul* (2007).